Progressives, Leftists, and Black America

Progressives, Leftists, and Black America

How the Leftists Progressive Policies and Causes Have been Bad for Black America

By Brian Oglesby

Liberty Hill Publishing

Liberty Hill Publishing
555 Winderley Pl, Suite 225
Maitland, FL 32751
407.339.4217
www.libertyhillpublishing.com

© 2024 by Brian Oglesby

All rights reserved solely by the author. The author guarantees all contents are original and do not infringe upon the legal rights of any other person or work. No part of this book may be reproduced in any form without the permission of the author.

Due to the changing nature of the Internet, if there are any web addresses, links, or URLs included in this manuscript, these may have been altered and may no longer be accessible. The views and opinions shared in this book belong solely to the author and do not necessarily reflect those of the publisher. The publisher therefore disclaims responsibility for the views or opinions expressed within the work.

Paperback ISBN-13: 978-1-66289-915-7
Ebook ISBN-13: 978-1-66289-916-4

Table of Contents

	Introduction vii
1.	Liberalism and Leftism Are Different.............. 1
2.	The Feminist Movement 17
3.	Why the Black Community for Socialists?........ 59
4.	Public Housing................................ 68
5.	Rethinking Integration......................... 76
6.	The Prison Industrial Complex 125
7.	Is DEI the new Affirmative Action? 139
8.	The Educational System........................ 150
9.	The Black Power Movement 167
10.	Mass and Unchecked Illegal Migration 175
11.	Is Equity Really Fair? 183
12.	The Mainstream Media 191
13.	Legal Immigrants and Other Non-White Groups 220
14.	Black Organizations and Black Leadership....... 247
15.	Bad Neighborhoods and Really Bad Neighborhoods 265
16.	Black Wealth Has Taken a Hit 278
17.	The Republican Party versus the Democratic Party 290
18.	The Klan's Days Are Numbered................. 300
19.	Racial Biases on Both Sides and Does It Matter?......................... 304

20.	How Conservatives Have Changed 311
21.	Marxists, Social Justice Warriors, and the Black Lives Matter Movement. 323
22.	My Thoughts on Dr. Martin Luther King Jr. 337
23.	Loss of America's Moral Vision? 354
24.	My Thoughts on President Obama 360
25.	Sex, Drugs, Rock and Roll, and the LGBTQIA Agenda 366
26.	Think about This for a While 376
27.	The Right versus the Left for Blacks 396
28.	What if Black America Were a Nation? 401
29.	Is This Progress or Is It Progressive? 412
30.	Rethinking Reparations from Slavery 417
31.	Conclusion 428

Introduction

DISCLAIMER: *This book is not intended to condemn or offend anyone, whether they are a Liberal or a Conservative or whether they support the Left or the Right. It is not intended to make a contrast and a comparison of the two in a way that denigrates your beliefs or core values. After reading this book, feel free to keep those. After completing this book, if you do not agree with the points expressed in it, your own opinion is respected. If error was brought up in any of the facts presented to prove the points of this book and even the interpretation of them, then feel free to insert what you think is factual where it needs to be inserted. I can only write based on trends in society that I have seen happen over a period of years from observation, the testimonies of others, and my own research. The book was not written by a go-to person or authority on this subject.*

Since there is other data on these subjects that was not incorporated into the research for this book for even some of the subjects that have been presented to prove several points, reeducation on some of the points and interpretation of them, if need be, are possible. Some of the facts and research presented here will almost certainly change in the future, making the outlook different, but it is all relative and subject to change, so look at everything in this book with perspective like a big-picture thinker or as someone who can see things outside of the box and from a different angle. Again, the context was not intended to offend anyone; neither was it intended to slander or to be judgmental. The purpose for this book is more for comparison and contrast.

I've done this out of respect and consideration for your right to believe the way you want to believe; you can trust me. I never intend to start any movements. I am only doing this to make a point, so I would kindly suggest that you not refer to me as being a militant or an activist. I am not an activist, and I don't ever intend to get out and organize people and events to make changes. I am just trying to prove some points. Here is my version of it.

When America declared its independence from England in 1776, the declaration later included a constitution that stated, "We hold these truths to be self-evident, that all men are created equal, that they are endowed by their Creator with certain unalienable Rights, and among these are Life, Liberty and the pursuit of Happiness."[1] It also included a Bill of Rights, which guaranteed all Americans the privileges of the first 10 articles of the Constitution.[2] From then to the end of the Civil War none of these privileges really applied to blacks. Soon afterward the 13th, 14th, and 15th Amendments of the Constitution were passed, which were intended to give blacks the same constitutional rights granted by these amendments as their white counterparts.[3,4,5] For the next 100 years laws were passed and enforced by whites from all over America that placed restrictions on blacks, and with the cultural and social norms and some of the

---

[1] "Declaration of Independence: A Transcription, America's Founding Documents," National Archives, retrieved August 3, 2022, https://www.archives.gov/founding-docs/declaration-transcript.

[2] "The Bill of Rights," National Constitution Center, retrieved August 4, 2022, https://constitutioncenter.org/learn/educational-resources/historical-documents/bill-of-rights?

[3] National Archives Milestone documents retrieved March 19, 2022 https://www.archives.gov/milestone-documents/13th-amendment

[4] Ibid

[5] Ibid

Introduction

beliefs[6] of the day about blacks allowed for at times some horrific acts of violence to ensure that they did not enjoy the same rights and privileges as their white counterparts by some traditional conservatives and probably even some classical Liberals including sundown town laws, Jim Crow laws, and vagrancy laws (which got you arrested and put in work brigades in near-slave conditions for anything whether guilty of a crime or not, and this is not a complete list) while at the same time Progressives seemed to be friendlier or maybe more well-meaning to blacks at least on the outside. But was this really the case? After the Civil Rights Movement and all of the previous restricting laws have been amended in essence by a series of civil rights acts, blacks are still behind whites in many ways, so the Progressive Left is now telling the black community the reason why they are in the condition they are in is because America is systemically racist and hateful to you, Conservatives who are privileged Right wing Republican white supremacists oppressors are doing everything possible to make sure you stay an inferior oppressed class in society, but we have your back with fairness, justice, equality, and equity. However, if you look at things from another angle you will see a different picture.

There are other reasons why the black community is in the condition it is in, whether it be from slavery or other unfair policies or events that happened in the past, that are too complex and extensive to really try and explain in this article.

Several Leftist policies and causes will be pointed out and explained how they have been detrimental to the black community. Some future consequences of these causes and why the black community will be dealing with them are also discussed. Before

---

[6] Jim Crow Museum of Racist Imagery (witness understand heal), retrieved May 16, 2023, https://jimcrowmuseum.ferris.edu/.

getting into this book, keep in mind that most Liberals are not biased against black people but neither are most Conservatives.

Liberalism is not wrong; it is radical Leftism that is bad, and the Left has gone too far in America. Conservatives, who are usually on the right, do not necessarily have the answer to everything either, but they make a lot of good points too, so you need a healthy balance of both in society. Balance is important, and I will be bringing it up later in this book. Often societies that are too conservative have problems too. Some regimes that have been patterned by conservative motivation can be horrible, too, but that is a whole other story. In this book, I am talking about how destructive the current Leftist movement is, which is led mostly by Progressive Liberals. This is not intended to divide along the lines of Liberal vs. Conservative.

Ever since the civil rights movement (around 1955 or 1960), all the way back to the British colonial period in America (maybe late 1500s), white people and the Caucasian race were considered the gold standard of what societal norms, culture, reasoning, logic, morals, and physical appearance were based on. Black people, to a greater or lesser extent, were considered to be backward, uneducated, ignorant, inferior, and almost savage until this point in America.[7] More so at the beginning of this period than at the end. They had been scorned, rejected, the brunt of jokes, and excluded for the most part by the greater white or "right" society up until then.[8] This was the general consensus among enough traditional conservative whites and classical Liberals and probably some progressives all with more traditional beliefs about race before the civil rights movement about Blacks but especially before the Civil War. After the Civil War the general population of whites slowly started

---

[7] Ibid.

[8] Ibid.

Introduction

to change their beliefs about blacks. However, some changes have come about during this period. A group of whites who called themselves Progressives expressed interest in the black community in a way that has never been expressed before. With this different kind of attention from any segment of white society, it gave the impression to blacks that they could be a part of something that the greater white society was a part of, which meant acceptance at last. The color of one's skin didn't matter, only the content of one's character was the determining factor. This was very exciting to the black community that they were getting attention like this from whites, which were the "right" group of people. Up until this point, to the psyche of blacks, anything that whites thought or did as a group had to be great whether it was good or bad, so both the Progressives and the Leftists were great.

Blacks were affected by post-traumatic slavery syndrome[9] and Willie Lynch Letter advice.[10] The Willie Lynch letter was just advice in a letter from a Caribbean slave owner in 1712 to the slave owners of Virginia on how to keep slaves divided so they could be controlled by their slave masters, with a guarantee that it would last for the next 300 years or maybe even 1,000 years, but that is a whole other book. Since black people had these mentalities, they were at some disadvantage to any group of whites, and the Left knew this, so they had the battle half won.

This mentality actually worked to the advantage of white Leftists and to a disadvantage for blacks. The military has units referred to

---

[9] Monica Hinton June 19, 2023 Understanding Post Traumatic Slave Syndrome Sharp Health News retrieved August 16, 2023 https://www.sharp.com/health-news/understanding-post-traumatic-slave-syndrome

[10] Charles Johnson, "Middle Passage: The Willie Lynch Letter and the Making of a Slave," https://www.saberesafricanos.net/phocadownloadpap/libros/Lets_Make_A_Slave_The_Making_Of_A_Slave.pdf.

as PSY OPS, or psychological operations, which use information to influence the emotions, motives, and objective reasoning processes of groups of people and individuals to induce or reinforce certain types of behavior on a group of people for the objectives of the US military,[11] but in the case of the black community up until this point, the conditioning had already been done for some favored outcomes of the Progressive Left.

In this book, the terms *Liberal* or *Progressive* and *Conservative* will be used often, but it is more about Right versus Left, so when Progressive or Progressives is used, it is really referring to the Left; when Conservative is used, it is really referring to the Right, so keep that in mind throughout the entirety of this book.

This book discusses some trends that happened to the black community for the worse since the Left has had such considerable influence in the black community, and it will discuss some ways the black community may have been better off if it had supported more conservative causes—or if Conservatives had had more influence at least over the past 40 or 50 years.

The black community was approached by Progressives and Leftists in this manner for a number of reasons. Before the civil rights movement, Jim Crow laws[12] in the South and the zoning codes[13] or Black Codes[14] everywhere else in America, whether in

---

[11]

[12] History.com Editors, Updated Aug. 19, 2020, Original: Feb 28, 2018, "Jim Crow Laws," retrieved September 7, 2020, https://www.history.com/topics/early-20th-century-us/jim-crow-laws.

[13] Michael H. Wilson, May 21, 2019, Foundation for Economic Education, "The Racist History of Zoning Laws," retrieved September 7, 2020, Page 2, https://fee.org/articles/the-racist-history-of-zoning-laws/.

[14] PBS, "Slavery by another name Black Codes and Pig Laws," retrieved September 7, 2020, https://www.pbs.org/tpt/slavery-by-another-name/themes/black-codes/.

its big cities and smaller towns or everywhere else in the country, ensured whites stayed in areas with better facilities and more resources. This restricted movement of Blacks[15] ensured that whites remained a privileged class.[16] The movement also forced changes to be made in the way the justice system treated blacks unfairly, as far as the law was concerned, which made it easy to disenfranchise the black population. After the Civil Rights Movement, Jim Crow laws in the South and the zoning codes[17] in the North and everywhere else in the country, which ensured blacks stayed in certain impoverished neighborhoods were made illegal, and areas blacks lived in had to be improved and any other restrictions that specifically applied to blacks that were not removed had less validity. At that point, blacks could not be legally disenfranchised as much as a result of the Civil Rights Acts that were passed. Now whites are no longer a privileged class anymore.

Blacks were now for the first time in a position where they could sue in a court of law more fairly and obtain justice. The many previous unfair restrictions on blacks made it impossible to become first-class citizens. However, with this new setup, this time, there would essentially be no difference in class in society between blacks and whites, and it would be next to impossible to keep whites a privileged class. This goes for wealth and educational attainment, as well, and many other areas. So a new approach with new strategies and a new look had to be implemented to legally maintain as many of

---

[15] VCU Libraires, "Social Welfare History Project Jim Crow Laws and Racial Segregation," retrieved May 2, 2020, https://socialwelfare.library.vcu.edu/eras/civil-war-reconstruction/jim-crow-laws-andracial-segregation/.

[16] Ibid, page 1.

[17] Christopher Silver, "The Racial Origins of Zoning in American Cities," retrieved September 4, 2020, https://www.asu.edu/courses/aph294/total-readings/silver%20—%20racialoriginsofzoning.pdf.

the previous class and race divisions and unfair inequalities as possible to ensure blacks would remain second-class citizens or at least as minimalized as possible. Thus, a more progressive approach was implemented, and it seems to have worked pretty well. Not only that, both saw the black community as a tool or a strategy with strategic moves that they could use to accomplish more of their goals for different agendas. One of them was to increase government control over everyone's lives and eventually have it the most powerful institution in the country, which you will see by the end of this presentation.[18] Another goal for Progressives was to fundamentally change America into something different from what it was ever intended to be or stand for.[19]

Whites are now no longer a privileged class over blacks. They haven't been since before the civil rights movement, but they do still, as a group but not as individuals, have some advantages over blacks as a group. For example, higher education and income levels both give an individual advantages regardless of race or ethnicity. Some other factors do as well, but both of these two are big ones. In America, whites generally still have higher education and higher incomes than blacks, but there are millions of black people who have higher education and/or income levels or some other factor that gives them an advantage that millions of whites don't have, so to say that whites all have advantages over all blacks due to white privilege and systemic racism has very little validity. I say this

---

[18] Dennis Prager, *The National Review*, "Differences Between Left and Right: It's All about Big Government Politics & Policy," July 7, 2015, retrieved September 20, 2019, https://www.nationalreview.com/2015/07/differences-liberal-conservative-big-government-greece.

[19] Ruy Teixeira, March 2009, "New Progressive America Twenty Years of Demographic, Geographic, and Attitudinal Changes Across the Country Herald a New Progressive Majority Center for American Progress," p. 46, PDF retrieved December 15, 2020, https://cdn.americanprogress.org/wp-content/uploads/issues/2009/03/pdf/progressive_america.pdf?_ga=2.104124169.822538617.1608044348-961247580.1607829922.

Introduction

because there are too many exceptions to the rule of black individuals having advantages over white individuals in reference to the above categories.

Whites still do have some advantages over blacks (and most of that is in the hands of a small minority of whites) for two reasons. One is because for years, when they were a privileged group and as individuals were able to take advantage of some things that black people mostly were not able to take advantage of, they have had positions, possessions, and power that black people as a group don't have. Another reason is because black people just don't practice group economics[20,21] like other groups do. In other words, one reason is because that is just the way things were set up in America years ago, and it was to no fault of most whites, and the other reason is because blacks should have been doing some different things as a group for the past 50 years or so, such as practicing group economics and not voting a straight Democratic ticket, which puts all Democrats in power in the community and some other things. Voting for the person instead of the party would have resulted in some better outcomes. So, most of the Leftist's claims about white privilege in today's America are shallow and have limited rationale. How can you blame today's young whites for the deeds of their grandparents and great-grandparents, who are now mostly all dead?

The black community and people with Leftist leanings were just tools that the Progressive Liberals used to achieve their agenda.

This book discusses some unique effects or changes that have happened to the black community as a result of the Left's intent

---

[20] Koereyelle DuBose, November 23, 2016, "Rolling out Black dollars equal Black power: How to use group economics," Nov. 23, 2016, retrieved October 17, 2020, https://rollingout.com/2016/11/23/group-economics/.

[21]

and new intents that Progressives have made as a result of influences from the Left.

In 1901 Republican president Teddy Rosevelt a Progressive era reformer[22] who was wealthy and white invited Booker T Washington a former slave and a prolific leader in the black community to the White House to discuss a path to success and equality for blacks through the ideals of American Liberty and hard work.[23] He stated "The only wise and honorable and Christian thing to do is to treat each black man and each white man strictly on his merits as a man, giving him no more and no less than he shows himself worthy to have,"[24] Keep in mind that he also believed white men of European descent were innately superior to all other races,[25] and that he supported and endorsed eugenics sterilization of darker skinned races.[26] Up until the end of Roosevelt presidency Progressive politics and the progressive movement were actually good for blacks or at least better than politics as usual. The Progressive movement changes for blacks with the presidency of Woodrow Wilson a progressive era politician[27] from 1913 through 1921[28]. During his presidency

---

[22] Kirstin Swinth The Gilder Lehrman Institute of American History The Square Deal: Theodore Roosevelt and the Theme of Progressive Reform retrieved December 18, 2023 https://www.gilderlehrman.org/history-resources/essays/square-deal-theodore-roosevelt-and-themes-progressive-reform

[23] Ibid

[24] Christopher Klein Updated: August 24, 2023 | Original: August 11, 2020 How Teddy Roosevelt's Belief in a Racial Hierarchy Shaped His Policies retrieved History December 19, 2023 https://www.history.com/news/teddy-roosevelt-race-imperialism-national-parks

[25] Ibid

[26] Ibid

[27]

[28] Woodrow Wilson The 28th President of The United States The White House retrieved December 18, 2023 https://www.whitehouse.gov/about-the-white-house/presidents/woodrow-wilson/

Introduction

he makes some radical changes that I think changed progressive politics and maybe even the progressive movement and he was very racist[29] and so were some of his changes,[30] like segregation of the federal government[31], the new requirements of quotas on immigrants of color to include Hispanics, Asians, southern, and eastern Europeans from immigrating to America[32]. He required the viewing of Birth of A Nation to White House staff [33], where he accuses African Americans of being aggressors during the reconstruction error[34] and praises the Klan for their deserved aggression against Negroes.[35] Black voters supported the Republican Party, at the time decided to support Wilson, a Democrat,[36] so he gained the support of many black voters to include W.E.B. Dubois and Booker T. Washington,[37] since his campaign promise of equal treatment.[38] His racial segregation order "came swiftly and suddenly which came as a shock to the black community[39]. The Progressive movement had its pros and cons for the black community from the beginning of Wilsons term until the end of the Civil Rights Movement. After the

---

[29] President Wilson House Wilson and Race retrieved December 18, 2023 https://woodrowwilsonhouse.org/wilson-topics/wilson-and-race/

[30] Ibid

[31] Ibid

[32] Ibid

[33] Ibid

[34] Ibid

[35] Ibid

[36] Morgan Foy October 27, 2020 How Woodrow Wilson's racist policies eroded the Black civil service retrieved December 18, 2023 https://newsroom.haas.berkeley.edu/research/how-woodrow-wilsons-racist-segregation-order-eroded-the-black-civil-service/

[37] Ibid

[38] Ibid

[39] Ibid

Civil Rights Movement until today it has been largely a failure to the black community, almost disastrous in some respects.

1.
Liberalism and Leftism Are Different

In an article by Dennis Praeger of Praeger University, he described the difference between the Left and Liberals. First let's discuss the difference between Liberals, Conservatives, the Left, and the Right. According to Craig Biddle, online Liberals are open to new behavior or opinions and willing to discard traditional values.[40] Conservatives are more likely to hold to traditional attitudes and values and are cautious about change or innovation, typically in relation to politics or religion.[41]

A 1913 dictionary defines "Progressive" as "Favoring improvement, change, progress, or reform, especially in a political context; - used of people. Contrasted with conservative. Disposed toward adopting new methods in government or education, holding tolerant and liberal ideas, and generally favoring improvement in civic life; - of towns and communities." The same dictionary defines "Conservative" as "One who, or that which, preserves from ruin, injury, innovation, or radical change; a preserver; a conserver. Jeremy Taylor said, 'The Holy Spirit is the great conservative of the new life.'

---

[40] Craig Biddle, June 26, 2012, The Objective Standard, Fall 2012. "Political 'Left' and 'Right' Properly Defined." Ayn Rand & objectivism politics & rights, The Political Spectrum Essentialized, retrieved April 24, 2020, https://www.theobjectivestandard.com/2012/06/political-left-and-right-properly-defined/.

[41] Ibid.

One who desires to maintain existing institutions and customs; also, one who holds moderate opinions in politics; - opposed to revolutionary or radical." The Free Dictionary online and Merrian Webster online defines a conservative as one favoring traditional views and values. The same dictionary defines a progressive as "(Government, Politics & Diplomacy) (often capital) favoring or promoting political or social reform through government action, or even revolution, to improve the lot of the majority: a progressive policy."

By conservative here I mean as a general rule those whites who were more traditional in their attitudes and beliefs historically about race because many classical liberals were the same as many conservative whites, and all conservative whites at the time were not the same about race, so I am using this term very generally with of course plenty of exception to the rule. Keep that in mind while reading this book.

These values were not traditionally good ones, but it does not mean that the direction that political and social reforms that seem revolutionary that the Progressive Left has pushed, especially in the past 50 years, give or take a few, have been good for America since race relations have changes since integration. I will discuss race relations in more detail as this came with some negatives for the black community. The good ones of the free market with capitalism and the constitutional republic with relatively small government and low taxes are the ones that conservatives are more likely to stand for. These ones have served America well since it has existed and have made it a refuge for the world.

The Homestead Act of 1860 and Louisiana Purchase 1804 and Spanish land grants and the Civil War and the passing of the 13th, 14th, and 15th Amendments and signing of the Alaska Treaty in 1867 were all a result of big government and they were all good things for America and now to include black Americans vs sundown towns, Jim Crow Laws and Black Code Laws which were all enforced on local municipal and state levels so even big government has not always been bad for America but it is the direction and the plan that the progressive left has to use big government for America in the future that is bad.

People on the Right who are called Right-wing or far right also tend to agree more with this belief. Since the Left's bottom line was to change society, the best group of people in that society to work with were people who are open to new opinions and willing to discard traditional beliefs.[42] It appears as if though the Left has worked with Liberals in the greater society instead of Conservatives. The Left and the Right are mostly political viewpoints,[43] whereas liberalism and conservatism are beliefs that the greater society lives by and puts into practice in daily life that affect society,[44] generally having nothing to do with a political process or causes. The Left seems to be more concerned with equality and conformity, and the Right seems to believe more in hierarchies, based on natural law or tradition.[45] They seem to use these two very different core standards as the impetus and direction in which to maintain or change society for two different reasons and two different causes.

Leftists are more often Liberals, and they believe that it is better if government takes a bigger role in providing for society.[46] Rightists or Right-wingers are more often Conservatives, and they believe it

---

[42] Ibid.

[43] Ibid.

[44] Ibid.

[45] Ibid.

[46] DIffen, "Left Wing vs. Right Wing," retrieved December 12, 2019, https://www.diffen.com/difference/Left_Wing_vs_Right_Wing.

is better if government is smaller and rights, opinions, and expressions of the individual are more important.[47]

Many of the abolitionists who fought to end slavery and to give civil rights to blacks afterward for some time were Liberals,[48] which was good for blacks, meaning Liberalism is not wrong. It is wrong when both schools of thought with Conservatism are unfairly balanced. At the same time in history, many more traditional Conservatives and classical Liberals were fine with slavery and keeping their slaves and all of the injustices for blacks that come with it. That does not mean, however, that all Conservatives or classical Liberals approved of slavery. Now both Liberals and Conservatives have changed agendas from the ones they believed in during the more classical liberal periods.

Most of the rest of the Conservatives who called themselves Christians did not care if slavery continued and if black people continued being treated unfairly as second-class citizens.[49] Neither did most Liberals care about the lot of black people during that time in America because plenty of them were racists, and plenty of them didn't have a problem with slavery.[50] Actually many of them at this time in history had slaves themselves. In fact, most traditional conservatives at the time were probably very racist, but many of America's

---

[47] Ibid.

[48] Damon Root, February 19, 2015, "Libertarian History and Philosophy Libertarianism, the Anti-Slavery Movement, and Black History Month," retrieved May 2, 2020, https://reason.com/2015/02/19/libertarianism-the-anti-slavery-movement/.

[49] Dan Arel, Salon, April 23, 2014, "The insane lie about slavery that Christian conservatives are spreading," retrieved April 11, 2020, https://www.salon.com/2014/04/23/the_insane_lie_about_slavery_that_christian_conservatives_are_spreading_partner/.

[50] Walter Johnson, Boston Review: A Political and Literary Form, "To Remake the World: Slavery, Racial Capitalism, and Justice," retrieved April 11, 2020, http://bostonreview.net/forum/remake-world-slavery-racial-capitalism-and-justice/andrew-zimmerman-when-liberalism-defended.

Founding Fathers during the period of classical Liberalism didn't have a problem with slavery, and actually, many of them had slaves themselves.[51] Even years after slavery, many Liberals probably didn't have a problem with blacks being inferior and/or the lower class of society.

For quite some time in American history, during and after slavery, certain Liberals, often Progressives for their time, probably did more to make life better for black people[52] than Conservatives. In many cases, a lot more of them were on the frontlines of change than Conservatives[53] and actually lead the charge. Throughout slavery and up until about 1955 when Rosa Parks was jailed for refusing to give up her seat on a bus in Birmingham to a white man, it would have been better for the sakes of black causes if Liberals had had more influence over American society, even though many of them could be very racist as well. After Martin Luther King Jr., which is about 1968, until the present, I think it would have been better for blacks if conservative republicans and more right-wing thinkers had had more influence in America. More on this throughout the book.

It is often hard to tell if someone is a Liberal or a Conservative because you could be a conservative liberal or a more liberal conservative, and there may not be much of a difference between the two, but according to one source, Republican President Abraham Lincoln was probably a Liberal.[54] I am going to go out on a limb here and say

---

[51] Ibid.

[52] Richard M. Ebeling, Foundation for Economic Education, "The 5 Great Crusades of Classical Liberalism," July 17, 2018, "The Liberal Crusade Against Slavery," retrieved March 26, 2020, https://fee.org/articles/the-5-great-crusades-of-classical-liberalism/.

[53] Ibid.

[54] Lochlainn Seabrook, "Abraham Lincoln Was a Liberal, Jefferson Davis Was a Conservative: The Missing Key to Understanding the American Civil War Paperback," March 7, 2017 (Book Overview), Sea Raven Press, retrieved March 11, 2022, https://www.amazon.com/Abraham-Lincoln-Liberal-Jefferson-Conservative/dp/1943737444.

he may have even been a Progressive Liberal for his time. But even he believed some things that were typical of the regular population about the position and status of black people in American society back then.

Now we can talk about Progressive Liberals and how the Left had been working with them to change them in favor of their cause, the end result of which being a changed society. First, let's start with the history of liberals. Liberals at one time in the not-so-distant past believed that capitalism[55] was great because it has lifted a lot of people out of poverty. The Progressive Liberals of today are demanding socialism[56] and the redistribution of wealth because it is unfair that some people are very wealthy, and some are very poor. They believe something needs to be done about it. This is what the Left has always believed, and they have convinced Progressive Liberals to follow suit.

Even though capitalism has its flaws, and it can be wasteful from overproduction—no system is perfect—it has also proven to be a great way to pull great numbers of people up out of poverty, too, and even its flaws outweigh its negatives, by more than the flaws of socialism. Capitalism is superior in productivity and morally.[57]

To sum up why I am putting more emphasis in Socialism rather than Communism is because according to an article from the History Channel, Marxists often refer to socialism as the first,

---

[55] Dennis Prager, September 12, 2017, retrieved September 21, 2019, "Here Are the Differences," https://www.dailysignal.com/2017/09/12/leftism-not-liberalism-differences/ Leftism Is Not Liberalism.

[56] Ibid.

[57] Matt Michel, Contracting Business, Sep. 25, 2015, "Presidential HVAC. Ten Reasons Why Capitalism Is Morally Superior," retrieved February 2, 2020, https://www.contractingbusiness.com/residential-hvac/article/20868486/ten-reasons-why-capitalism-is-morally-superior.

necessary phase on the way from capitalism to communism.[58] so I am addressing where we may already be first rather than where we are headed, even though I really think that we are headed toward a full blown communist takeover. Even its founders did not clearly differentiate between the two to ensure confusion between the meaning[59] and intent of the two. They both lead to something bad, and the black community was used to accomplish that in America.

Liberals during the classical liberal period at one time were all for national sovereignty and the protection of US borders.[60] Now many of today's Progressive Left–leaning Liberals believe it is wrong to have ICE agents on the border with Mexico that stop people and detain them for not having a visa or for entering the country without having a reason for political asylum due to adversity in their country of origin.[61] Liberals have always approved of freedom of speech of any kind,[62] but now the Progressive ones are not protesting free speech spaces on college campuses,[63] which confine speech to only certain areas on campus and its content.[64] Now they approve of it,

---

[58] Sarah Pruitt, updated: November 4, 2020, original: October 22, 2019, "History: How Are Socialism and Communism Different?" Retrieved June 4, 2023, https://www.history.com/news/socialism-communism-differences.

[59] Ibid.

[60] Dennis Prager, "Here Are the Differences," September 12, 2017, retrieved September 21, 2019, https://www.dailysignal.com/2017/09/12/leftism-not-liberalism-differences/Leftism Is Not Liberalism.

[61] Tom Homan, *Fox News*, "ICE detention facilities—The left is working hard to keep critical information from you," retrieved June 12, 2020, https://www.foxnews.com/opinion/tom-homan-ice-detention-facilities-democrats-nazi-concentration-camps-illegal-immigrants.

[62] Ibid.

[63] Jonathan S. Tobin, July 3, 2018, *National Review*, Politics & Policy, "Liberals Sour on the First Amendment," retrieved April 22, 2023, https://www.nationalreview.com/2018/07/free-speech-liberals-turn-against/.

[64] Ibid.

and the Left has convinced them that some types of speech should not be spoken if it is what they deem to be offensive.[65]

Classical Liberals traditionally have favored Western civilization and the ideas that it stands for and its Judeo-Christian heritage,[66] but the Left has been convincing modern liberals that western civilization is racist, sexist, homophobic, Islamophobic, and some other bad things—and some of them believe it and now want to see America changed for the causes of the Left.[67] Now liberals and, in particular, Progressives are more likely to be atheists than they were in the classical Liberal era.[68]

According to the Center for American Progress series on American Progressivism, the Founding Fathers of America were involved in Progressivism in America, which would put its start at the late 1700s,[69] so you can argue that this school of thought of American Progressivism started that long ago.[70] The site also defines it as an intellectual movement that happened officially between 1890 and 1920.[71]

---

[65] Ibid.

[66] Dennis Prager, "Here Are the Differences," September 12, 2017, retrieved September 21, 2019, https://www.dailysignal.com/2017/09/12/leftism-not-liberalism-differences/ Leftism Is Not Liberalism.

[67] Ibid.

[68] Paul Bedard, October 9, 2012, "Opinion: Washington Secrets Washington Examiner Majority of atheists are liberal," retrieved February 1, 2020, https://www.washingtonexaminer.com/majority-of-atheists-are-liberal

[69] Center For American Progress, "The Progressivism of America's Founding Part Five of the Progressive Tradition Series," retrieved June 16, 2023, https://www.americanprogress.org/article/the-progressivism-of-americas-founding/.

[70] Ron Rivers, Nov 6, 2018, "The Founding Fathers were Progressives," retrieved June 17, 2023, https://medium.com/@ronrivers/the-founding-fathers-were-progressives-e17a2b51ec94.

[71] Center for American Progress, June 16, 2023, "The Progressive Intellectual Tradition in America, Part One of the Progressive Tradition Series," https://www.americanprogress.org/article/the-progressive-intellectual-tradition-in-america/.

The original Progressive era is known primarily for two major developments, political and economic reforms.[72] In terms of its political values, Progressivism throughout the years stressed a range of ideals, which remain important today, of freedom, the common good, pragmatism, equality, social justice, democracy, cooperation, and interdependence.[73] The Progressives that were around before the civil rights era were what I will refer to as Old Progressives, the ones that emerged during the civil rights movement but mostly after are who I will refer to as the New Progressives. Since beliefs, cultural and social norms, and laws in society that governed the affairs of blacks with restrictions and sometimes exclusion from some sectors of society altogether despite all of the progress that happened for Blacks then, you could argue with confidence also that maybe the Old Progressive movement had some better intentions for blacks than today's New Progressives if you look at the condition of the black community today vs. what its condition could have been. Today's new Progressive movement, which is almost totally composed of Democrats, stresses equity rather than equality, political correctness, LGBTQ+ rights, radical feminism, identity politics, BLM and its social justice warriors, critical race theory, pro Hamas sentiment and Anti-Israel protests and socialism (which often leads to communism). You can even argue that the black community went backward in a lot of areas in relation to all other ethnic groups and that they are worse off in some of these areas and even as a whole than they were during the old Progressive movement, as well as that compared to the circumstances the black community was under in during the old progressive movement, they actually made progress, unlike the new one.

---

[72] Ibid.

[73] Ibid.

Dictionary.com's definition for "counterculture" is a way of life and set of attitudes opposed to or at variance with the prevailing social norm. Its definition for "progressive" is a person advocating or implementing social reform or new, liberal ideas. Slave abolitionists did advocate for change in society that did not happen all at once, that went against a social acceptance for the lot of blacks. It was a small group of liberal whites who were the progressives of their time and who led the charge in radically changing society during slavery.

It was the revolutionary actions of the abolitionists, which went against the grain of what was accepted in society at the time by so many whites, that led to the end of the slave trade and the emancipation and later freedom of black slaves. This would also be the beginning of the change in cultural and social norms and beliefs about blacks, which although lasted for quite some time afterward, slowly began to fade. This revolutionary action against slavery changed society for blacks in a good way that forced slow but progressive acceptance of them into society but the 1960s countercultural Liberals changed American society for the bad by forcing Americans to accept bad cultural influences like radical feminism, common core no child left behind educational system which has dumbed down the American populace and now equity, diversity and inclusion rather than acceptance by merit. During the same period the same counterculture changed a lot for women in what was referred to as the first wave of the feminist movement, or the Women's liberation movement, which went counter to some of the acceptable cultural and social norms for women up until that point, and this change again was gradual and progressive. In the 1960s revolutionary countercultural changes were not good for blacks, although maybe some were good for women.

During slavery and afterward all the way until the end of the civil rights movement, this counterculture was a good thing for African

Americans. Since this really went against many of the social and cultural norms and traditional beliefs about blacks in society, this group would probably be the equivalent to the Progressive- or far-left–leaning Liberals in American society for the past 50 or maybe 60 years, who led the countercultural revolution that was going on back then and that still, in reality, has been for quite some time. So Progressives can give themselves a pat on the back for this, and the black community can thank them for it.

In fact, after slavery and up until the end of the civil rights movement in America, including the period of slavery, this counterculture was good for blacks, and during this time, as a group, conservatives and even some classical liberals and their school of thought at least as it related to race was bad for blacks. Thanks to counterculture, the stage was set for the acceptance of the civil rights movement and the eventual acceptance of the Civil Rights Acts of 1964 and 1967. All the way up until this point, progressive counterculture, often led probably mostly by ultra-liberal thinkers, was good for black people, so the more progressive thinkers of this era in American history can be proud of the changes they made for the good of African Americans. It was good up until a certain point in history. Throughout the civil rights movement, it was the more progressive Liberal whites again who championed the civil rights of blacks more so than conservative whites. This small constituent of liberals did this at a time when most of the roadblocks and barriers including laws and cultural and social norms and beliefs that prevented this progress for blacks was placed in society by conservative whites, most of whom had no or very little interest in black people's progress or rights.

In fact, this band of conservative whites was often hostile to such ideas with radical opposition, and they had no interest in changing society in favor of blacks.[74,75] Most Klansmen and their sympathizers were conservatives as well.[76] Keep in mind that not all Liberal whites supported these changes and not all conservative whites opposed all of them, either. While researching the subject, there was not really a lot of anything out there on what traditional conservatives did as a group or any one group of them did to end slavery in America, so I am just going to assume that practically all of them did not really care to end slavery in America, and afterward, most of them did not really care for black civil rights after slavery. With this said, most are probably wondering why I am telling you that conservatives new stand for things that the black community needs now to prosper. That doesn't make sense. You will see what I mean by the end of this book.

There are still liberals today who are classical liberals or at least they consider themselves as such.[77] Throughout the rest of this book, just remember that all of the liberal beliefs that they have fallen for come from the Left's agenda. Progressive Liberals support leftist causes more passionately than most other liberals, not the more conservative or maybe even some of the more moderate liberals and certainly not classical liberals. Now some liberals are not really even liberals anymore; they are really Leftists. It is really not even fair to call them liberals.

---

[74] "After Slavery: Race, Labor, and Politics in the Post-Emancipation Carolinas, Unit Five: Conservatives Respond to Emancipation," retrieved April 24, 2020, https://ldhi.library.cofc.edu/exhibits/show/after_slavery/unit_five_as.

[75] David Neiwert, March 8, 2016, "No, the Ku Klux Klan Has Never, Ever Been a 'Leftist' Organization," retrieved May 12, 2020, https://www.splcenter.org/hatewatch/2016/03/08/no-ku-klux-klan-has-never-ever-been-leftist-organization.

[76] Ibid.

[77] Derek Robertson, June 16, 2018, Politico Magazine, "Political Science: Why the 'Classical Liberal' Is Making a Comeback," https://www.politico.com/magazine/story/2018/06/16/why-the-classical-liberal-is-making-a-comeback-218667.

Liberalism and Leftism Are Different

Consider the following analogy. Of the four basic temperaments that people can have, between phlegmatic, melancholic, sanguine, and choleric,[78] most bullies tend to be of the choleric temperament, but few cholerics are bullies.[79] Bullies are probably generally a very small group of people in society. Most who are on the Left are Liberals, but most Liberals are not on the Left, since true Leftists are a growing but still a small group in society. Sometimes there is considerable overlap between liberal and conservative beliefs.[80] At times, it can become so pronounced that the two can become indistinguishable.[81] Remember this analogy throughout the book.

A lot of Liberals are more conservative than other liberals and a lot of conservatives are more liberal than many other conservatives, and it is really hard to tell the two apart; they can both agree to a great extent sometimes.[82] When this is the case, the two seem more like moderates and not really liberal or conservative.[83] Even moderate Liberals and moderate Conservatives can agree on a number of things,[84] and a little more often, they can tolerate one another.[85] Some Liberals can even lean right.[86]

---

[78] "The Four Temperaments," Tobias Cornwall © 2012–2020, retrieved October 11, 2021, https://temperaments.fighunter.com/?page=choleric.

[79] Ibid.

[80] Stephanie Pappas, December 12, 2012, Live Science Publication, "Liberals & Conservatives More alike than You Think," retrieved September 12, 2020, https://www.livescience.com/25491-liberals-conservatives-not-that-different.html.

[81] Ibid.

[82] Ibid.

[83] Ibid.

[84] Ibid.

[85] Ibid.

[86] Ibid.

Years ago, years before *Roe v. Wade*, most Liberals would never have had a partial birth abortion done on an unborn baby, the thought would never have crossed their mind, but just ten or twenty years after its passing, some Liberals didn't have a problem with it, and now a lot more of them feel that way. Years ago, liberal teaching of evolution versus the creation and transgenderism and homosexuality as a normal way of life would never have been an issue under most or nearly all circumstances, but now the Left has[87] been influencing Liberals to think differently. Gender rearrangement surgery and puberty blockers would never have been an issue for progressives years ago but now it's being advocated in some circles as acceptable, even necessary. Some more Progressive Liberals don't have a problem with these changes to society. Most Conservatives, those who identify with the Right, are opposed to these changes.

As society has changed over the years, what is considered liberal has changed and evolved a lot,[88] and every time society is changed due to leftist thoughts and ideologies, Conservatives have been forced to adjust and, in a sense, given ground to more liberal schools of thought.[89] Thus, what is conservative has evolved and changed over the years too.[90] During the classical liberal period in America, many Conservatives were Loyalists to the British colonial

---

[87] Richard M. Ebeling, July 17, 2018, Foundation for Economic Education, "The 5 Great Crusades of Classical Liberalism: The Liberal Crusade Against Slavery," retrieved March 26, 2020, https://fee.org/articles/the-5-great-crusades-of-classical-liberalism/.

[88] Patrick Wood, June 4, 2018, Citizens for Free Speech, A Nation of Defenders Founding Fathers, "What is a Classic Liberal?" retrieved May 19, 2020, https://www.citizensforfreespeech.org/what_is_classic_liberal.

[89] Ibid.

[90] Marc Chase , Kelly Mullaney, May 16, 2017, "Today's conservatives are yesterday's liberals," retrieved May 19, 2020, https://www.nwitimes.com/opinion/letters/today-s-conservatives-are-yesterday-s-liberals/article_537a88f4-30b8-55b8-8829-bc2712ce22f1.html.

authorities, which may not have been a good thing either.[91] If these Conservatives had gotten their way, America may have ended up under British rule for a lot longer, like Canada which did not get its independence until 1960[92] and Australia until 1986.[93] The two are still very impressive nations on the world stage but not as impressive or as influential as America has been. Those counterculture liberals who opposed British colonial rule against the Loyalists would have been the equivalent to today's countercultural Progressive liberals who demanded something different from what was the norm in society for that time, so liberal schools of thought have been good for America too, maybe even progressive ones as well.

For example, when America was more conservative as a rule, promiscuous behavior that resulted in things like out-of-wedlock sex and teenage pregnancies did not happen as often as a rule and in some places in society it did not happen at all. If a woman or a teenage girl got pregnant out of wedlock years ago, which did happen sometimes in a more conservative America, it was frowned upon, and to make amends, it was almost a given that she would marry the young man responsible, and he would take care of her and the baby. Some things that were considered liberal years ago are now considered almost conservative. If today Conservatives voice their opinions too harshly on out-of-wedlock birth to keep from being considered cruel and mean, they don't say anything. This is the new Conservative. The old 1950s Conservatives would probably have

---

[91] Patrick Woodon, June 4, 2018, Citizens for Free Speech, A Nation of Defenders Founding Fathers, "What is a Classic Liberal?" retrieved May 19, 2020, https://www.citizensforfreespeech.org/what_is_classic_liberal.

[92] History May 19, 2020 Canadian Independence Day https://www.history.com/this-day-in-history/canadian-independence-day.

[93] KidsZone.ws Independence, retrieved May 19, 2020, https://www.kidzone.ws/history/australia/independence.htm.

looked down on this woman or outright ostracized her from the church or maybe even society in some cases. The examples that were used above would not have been tolerated under most circumstances during the classical liberal period by Liberals or Conservatives, but thanks to the Left, some of them are now tolerated by both.

This leftist movement has changed America's bearings, or its compass, to a different setting, as it refers to what is socially, morally, and ethically acceptable. These changes over time will destroy a culture and a society, which is what the Left seems intent on doing.

Feminism, socialism, integration (for a certain effect in society on progressives' terms), mass and unchecked immigration, the dumbing down of the American education, political correctness, wokeness, LGBTQIA rights, and some more issues were all created, orchestrated, and implemented by the Left, not Liberals. A minority of more progressive Liberals are just following suit; they have just chosen to get with the leftist program, and as a result, they have some of the same causes from the changes in society as Progressives do, but they are not to blame. The left's cultural, moral, social, and political changes that have taken place in America over the past fifty to maybe eighty or ninety years have had some unique effects on the black community that no other community has experienced.

I think progressive leftism probably stemmed from liberal out-of-the-box thought, which can be good, but in this case it morphed into something that was not tolerant of other schools of thought, which is not liberal.

2.

The Feminist Movement

The women's rights movement in America, which started with the women's suffrage movement in 1848[94] up until just before the civil rights movement, including the time of the women suffragettes like Susan B. Anthony[95] was only about women's rights and equality for women, until they got the right to vote with the Nineteenth Amendment to the Constitution.[96] This was the first wave of feminism. The first wave according to another source started in the late 1830s or maybe early 1840s and ended roughly sometime after World War I but before World War II.[97] The women's rights activists of the first wave did not generally accept black women as counterparts[98] in their sisterhood of more progressive-minded white

---

[94] Nancy Hayward, Ed., 2018, National Women's History Museum, "Susan B. Anthony 1820–1906," retrieved March 4, 2022, https://www.womenshistory.org/education-resources/biographies/susan-b-anthony.

[95] Ibid.

[96] Ibid.

[97] Constance Grady, Updated Jul 20, 2018, "The waves of feminism, and why people keep fighting over them, explained" VOX, retrieved December 24, 2021, https://www.vox.com/2018/3/20/16955588/feminism-waves-explained-first-second-third-fourth.

[98] Quinn Angelou-Lysaker, March 25, 2021, "Ida B. Wells: Lessons from an Early Black Freedom Activist Socialist Alternative," retrieved March 16, 2022, https://www.socialistalternative.org/2021/03/25/the-90th-anniversary-of-ida-b-wells-death-lessons-from-an-early-black-freedom-activist.

women. Early during the first wave, however, were some very strong and fierce abolitionists. Before this movement, woman's rights (even to the point of being her husband's property), a woman's independence and even identity was controlled by her husband.[99] Actually Susan B. Anthony's family were abolitionists, which made it even better for blacks.[100] This is an example of how progressive counterculture, often led by the Left, was good for blacks. The second wave began in the late 1960s, and the third wave didn't begin until the 1990s. It was not until the second wave that black women were accepted by the feminists. When the feminist movement really kicked off in the late 1960s until the present, you have had second and third wave feminism and now the MeToo movement, which has had maybe a lot of negative repercussions for the black community.

At the beginning of the movement and for quite some time later,[101] one of the biggest women suffrage organizations the National American Women's Suffrage Association (NAWSA) even though they had interest in black feminists[102] since they wanted to

---

[99] Caroline Zielinski, April 15, 2015, *The Daily Telegraph*, "First comes love, then comes marriage. Not for me, thanks," retrieved September 13, 2020, https://www.dailytelegraph.com.au/rendezview/first-comes-love-then-comes-marriage-not-for-me-thanks/news-story/d53ae485a9015c0562b3f054427796f4.

[100] History.Com Editors, "Susan B. Anthony" Updated: Nov. 20, 2019, Original: Mar. 9, 2010, "Susan B. Anthony: Early Life and Abolitionist Movement," retrieved August 11, 2020, https://www.history.com/topics/womens-history/susan-b-anthony.

[101] Quinn Angelou-Lysaker, "Ida B. Wells: Lessons from an Early Black Freedom Activist Build a Working Class Fight Back," retrieved April 15, 2023, https://www.socialistalternative.org/2021/03/25/the-90th-anniversary-of-ida-b-wells-death-lessons-from-an-early-black-freedom-activist/.

[102] Ibid.

attract more followers who were indifferent about race[103], chose not to work with them due to the racism and prejudice of the day[104].

At the beginning of the 1960s the feminists (who were a branch of the leftist movement) had a goal of dismantling the family, and this cause has added to the destruction of the black family.[105,106] Meaning the traditional 1950s families, like the setting of the 1950s sitcom *Leave it to Beaver*, where Hugh Beaumont as Ward Clever was the father and Barbara Billingsley as June Clever was the mother, and maybe even the *Little House on the Prairie* family, where the husband and wife had distinct roles. In the *Leave it to Beaver* setting, Barbara was basically a wife and mother who did the cooking and the cleaning, she did the shopping for the kids to make sure they had clothes for school, and she did the grocery shopping. She made sure Hugh's shirts were ironed for the office in the morning and that his breakfast was ready in the morning before work. Some women had careers back then, but they were usually more traditional ones such as schoolteachers (usually grades K-12), nurses, or medical assistants. Hugh, the father and her husband, had some different responsibilities. His was to provide the house they live in with most or all of his salary, provide cars for her and the family, provide medical, dental, and life insurance for his family, and basically be the head of the family. It was also his responsibility to provide much of the money Barbara needed for shopping for the household. The children were to do as their mother and father told them to, and Hugh

---

[103] Ibid.

[104] Ibid.

[105] Nikita Coulombe, Jan. 15, 2017, "Why Feminism Wants to Dismantle the Family," retrieved May 30, 2019, https://medium.com/@NikitaCcoulombe/why-feminism-wants-to-dismantle-the-family-long-4695d45bcf88.

[106] Mona Charen, July 7, 2018, "Feminism has destabilized the American family," retrieved May 8, 2019, https://nypost.com/2018/07/07/feminism-has-destabilized-the-american-family/.

was essentially designated as the head of the household. This is an example of a more stable family unit, and according to researchers, this stability resulted in better outcomes for society.[107]

This family structure, a lot less common now, and a rarity in the black community in many cases, is an example of how society has become destabilized. Some other results of destabilization in the black community are bad neighborhoods, excessively high amounts of single-mother households, the fact that the prison industrial complex has a disproportionately high number of African Americans, and all of the bad statistics that result from children being raised in single-mother households are just some of the other signs of destabilization. Conditions during slavery mandated that lots of the heads of black households be the mother,[108] but is it any better now than it was during slavery?[109] When this happens, the code of conduct in society suffers, society is less orderly, and things become more chaotic. This does not mean it could not happen if society were more traditional, but the setup that has happened isn't helping matters any if you can put it that way. I will discuss some more reasons why it can happen later on.

While listening to an issue of a program on YouTube by philosopher Stefan Molyneux, the guest on the show brought out a good point. In this issue, his guest on the show was a black woman whose parents immigrated to the United States from the Caribbean

---

[107] Jeff Johnston, The Daily Citizen Social Issues, "Kids Need a Mom and a Dad—That's What the Research Shows," retrieved April 27, 2019, https://dailycitizen.focusonthefamily.com/kids-need-a-mom-and-a-dad-thats-what-the-research-shows.

[108] Erol Ricketts, "The origin of black female-headed families," retrieved September 16, 2020, https://www.irp.wisc.edu/publications/focus/pdfs/foc121e.pdf.

[109] Heather Andrea Williams, University of North Carolina at Chapel Hill National Humanities Center Fellow Freedoms Story, "How Slavery Affected African American Families," retrieved September 16, 2020, http://nationalhumanitiescenter.org/tserve/freedom/1609–1865/essays/aafamilies.htm.

nation of Grenada, who said after living in a Brooklyn, New York, neighborhood but later moving to a more suburban neighborhood because of gang violence over time, with drugs and drive-by shootings among some other things, she didn't really have a lot in common with African American culture and did not see very many marriage prospects to African American men, so she is now dating a white man from the eastern European country of Ukraine. She said the black community in America is marked with low expectations, underachievement, and low motivation. She said her old Brooklyn neighborhood was filled with women of various ages and lots of children but no men; there was an absence of men, so there were essentially no male role models around for the children when they were growing up. The women go to church every Sunday and bring their children with them and just about the entire congregation consists of women and children but no men. In church, people have this mentality that you just look up to God for everything without using the intellect, talent, ability, and resources that He has given to you to help yourself, so there are no networks for job prospects, for businesses, or anything else because of this almost helpless sense of dependence and no effort on the part of the individual. She said the African American community, at least in this small pocket where she was raised, was totally dependent on the state and the government to provide for them and on each other, since so many owed each other money, things, and favors for ones rendered but never paid for. So you have a community with low expectations where people discourage one another and do all sorts of destructive things to one another without taking responsibility for what they have done, and no one dares to condemn anyone else for their irresponsible and destructive choices, and where nothing is being created.

To explain in more depth what happens in a society when there is an absence of men, she used an example from a group of women marooned on a desert island with no men in an episode of the TV series *Survivor*, and she said they were just completely worthless; they were just chillin' and getting sunburned. They did this to exhibit a form of girl power to give women the chance to prove they could hang with the men. The men, on the other hand, who were marooned on another island by themselves, were finding sources of water to drink, pieces of sticks and rocks to build structures to live in or to make a fire to cook on, putting together maybe palm limbs to make a net to caught fish or to trap something to eat. The women just did not have this ability, and she admitted that she was guilty of the same thing. So eventually they had to combine men and women together, or the women would have died by themselves. Though not nearly to this extent, this is an example of what is happening to the black community, especially in certain little pockets of the community, but this is the current state some sections of the black community are in, and feminism is partially the problem, since so many black children have been raised by single moms and because there are just less men. I will discuss why this is later on.

Before this era of strong leftist ideologies, which have sprung up in America, not so many black people in many small pockets of black America had some of the mentalities and dysfunctionalities as a group that they have today, and the testimony from the young lady from Grenada is proof. In my opinion, this is why especially in these little pockets in the black community you have less structure, vision, purpose, and this unique ability that men have to create—unlike other communities of all the other various ethnic backgrounds that have a more realistic male presence—is not there. Therefore, I would agree with just about everything she said here. The Heritage Foundation's website has a section on the negative effects of welfare on children. It is too extensive for me to go over in this book, but it is good reading to enlighten you on the subject.

In a society, men, not women, are basically the creators and the designers of society. They are and have been, traditionally and historically, the architects of societies theology, mathematics, science, business and commerce, the arts, education, technology, aviation, engineering, philosophy, agriculture, entertainment, and so many more endeavors a society gets its cultural meaning and its framework and backbone, and its support from for existence. If you remove the men and their role in society, it results in chaos and the collapse of that society, which is what is happening in some small pockets of the African American community.

That does not mean that women have not played roles on society because they have. An example is the American Red Cross (ARC) created by Clara Barton.[110] It has now become a multibillion-dollar institution of compassion and caring that has provided care and comfort for millions around the world in times of need, and the ARC is an example of how women have contributed to these institutions, and many more have also. She is not the only female visionary; there are plenty of other women like her, but women have not created institutions like the ones men have. If you take men out of their traditional roles in society, starting with the family, this stops, and society becomes more destabilized. Once a society is completely destabilized it will depend on other sources for its needs, which is one reason why I think the black community, especially in certain little, small pockets, is much more dependent on the government and other outside sources for its mere existence than most other ethnic backgrounds. Institutions such as those listed are just not being created and/or maintained in the black community (in certain pockets of the community) like they are in other ethnic

---

[110] The American Red Cross Home Page, https://www.redcross.org/about-us/who-we-are/history/clara-barton.html.

communities in America, which is another one of the results of destabilization. The destabilization in black America may be one of the worse examples the world has ever seen anywhere and especially when you consider how much America has and how much it has to offer its citizens and how successful immigrants can become in this country, there is no reason for the black community in these little pockets to be like it is.

Since a disproportionately high percentage of black people are on government assistance programs compared with other ethnic backgrounds, and the black people who aren't on assistance are disproportionately more likely to work for the government,[111] that means blacks are more dependent on the government for their mere survival than most other ethnic backgrounds. Since a disproportionately high number of blacks, compared with other societies, have been raised in single-mother homes by a matriarchy, with no patriarchs, for the past two generations, they have become acclimatized to find provision by some other source.[112] The male role as provider is more absent in the American black community especially in these little pockets in society than in any other in the country. Now we have a community where a lot of its members just want its security, and it doesn't care where it gets it, even if it is from the government.

---

[111] Corey Dade, May 9, 2012, "Government Job Cuts Threaten Black Middle-Class," St. Louis Public Radio, Economy, retrieved August 8, 2020, https://www.npr.org/2012/05/09/152297370/government-job-cuts-threaten-black-middle-class.

[112] The Annie E. Casey Foundation, Kids Count Data Center, "Children in single-parent families by race in the United States," retrieved November 27, 2019,
https://datacenter.kidscount.org/data/tables/107-children-in-single-parent-families-by-race#-detailed/1/any/false/871,870,573,869,36,868,867,133,38,35/10,11,9,12,1,185,13/432,431.

But what you must understand is that the government with over $30 trillion of debt[113] doesn't have black people's best interest at heart anymore. However, the leftist movement, largely through feminism, has driven the patriarchs, who have been traditional providers, away from the families and with that, the vision that men have to create on a grander scale.

A disproportionately high number of African American women in comparison with other races and ethnic backgrounds in America are single, and a lot of these women have children to raise without a father or a husband, whether it be from no-fault divorce for child support (which is a bad leftist policy)[114] or just for the government (welfare) benefits. Those government benefits that they were promised would sustain them are not raising most of these black families above the poverty line, and if they are above it, they are not very far above it. Eighty percent of high school dropouts,[115] 70 percent of children in juvenile detention,[116] 63 percent of those who commit suicide,[117] and 61 percent of all prison inmates and rapists[118] were raised in single-mother households.[119] Many black children and adults are now dealing with all of the bad statistics that are

---

[113] Truth in Accounting, "Our National Debt Clock," retrieved February 15, 2021, https://www.truthinaccounting.org/about/our_national_debt?gclid=Cj0KCQiA1KiBBhCcARIsAPWqoS-rgVYAMv8q-ldyrvutR13UeZ3kWJe4PTmC8IckSBnGYp0FI_QVU-F8aAhLzEALw_wcB.

[114] Ryan C. MacPherson, The Natural Family, "Whose Fault Was No-Fault Divorce? The Story behind America's Most Enduring Oxymoron," retrieved February 15, 2021, http://familyinamerica.org/journals/winter-2015/whose-fault-was-no-fault-divorce/#.YCs1cTKSk2w.

[115] The Fatherless Generation, "Statistics," retrieved May 29, 2020, https://thefatherlessgeneration.wordpress.com/statistics/.

[116] Ibid.

[117] Ibid.

[118] Ibid.

[119] Ibid.

characteristic of children who grow up without a father .The aftermath of it will affect them and large segments of the black community for the rest of their lives. No-fault divorce and extensive spending for these programs have fostered a breakdown of the black family, and with it goes a breakdown in black society. Had it been up to Conservatives, it would probably not have come to this, or if so, it would not be as bad as it is now for the black community.

According to an article from Focus on the Family, and this has been confirmed by more than just this source,[120] fathers and the way they parent have huge benefits for a child's development.[121] The article did a comparison and contrast of several different areas that determine outcomes for life that can have negative consequences for a child if they do not get the proper balance of parenting styles from both a mother and a father.[122] They range from linguistic, academic success, violent behavior, self-discipline, and several others with the lack of the father resulting in their own unique outcomes.[123] This does not mean that some single mothers have not done an excellent job at raising children because some have, or that some children who were raised by a mother and a father have not turned out to be monsters because that certainly has been the case, too, but generally the outcomes are just so much better for children who are raised by a loving mother and father.

---

[120] Glenn T. Stanton, January 1, 2004, Focus on the Family, "The Involved Father," retrieved May 2, 2019, https://www.focusonthefamily.com/parenting/the-involved-father.

[121] Ibid.

[122] Ibid.

[123] Ibid.

According to a study, money was the second highest reason for divorces,[124] and since the typical black household is now poorer than 90 percent of white households,[125] and African Americans, as a group, compared with whites, have lower credit scores[126] with lower incomes, it makes sense that the divorce rate would be high among blacks.[127] If men don't make enough money, they are often not as attractive for marriage[128] and/or they won't feel as comfortable in a marriage, so they will have dates with women but make no proposals for marriage. Black men are more likely to be in this predicament, which is not good for black marriages or if black women want black husbands. Maybe money is a factor why marriages are not happening in the black community as often as they do in other communities to begin with. To make matters worse, African Americans have the highest divorce rate of any ethnicity in America.[129]

---

[124] Dave Ramsey Media, "Relations Money Ruining Marriages In America: A Ramsey Solutions Study," retrieved June 27, 2020, https://www.daveramsey.com/pr/money-ruining-marriages-in-america.

[125] Kriston McIntosh, Emily Moss, Ryan Nunn, and Jay Shambaugh, February 27, 2020, The Brookings Institute, "Examining the Black White Wealth Gap Up Front."

[126] Ibid.

[127] Ibid.

[128] Jeff Haden, Contributing Editor, Inc. "New Research Claims Fewer 'Economically Attractive' Men Causes Fewer Couples Than Ever to Get Married. But 1 Thing Might Matter a Lot More," retrieved September 7, 2020, https://www.inc.com/jeff-haden/new-research-claims-few-economically-attractive-men-means-less-people-than-ever-are-getting-married-but-1-thing-matters-a-lot-more.html.

[129] Ralph Richard Banks, the Jackson Eli Reynolds Professor of Law at Stanford Law School, January 20, 2012, "A Definite Shortage of Marriageable Black Men," The New York Times, retrieved November 17, 2021, https://www.nytimes.com/roomfordebate/2011/12/20/black-men-for-black-women/a-definite-shortage-of-marriageable-black-men.

Since 1960, the rise in single fatherhood has increased significantly for all ethnic groups across the board.[130] Black children are also disproportionately more likely to be with their fathers in a single-parent household.[131] Single fathers tend to be less educated with lower incomes than married fathers, according to the same source.[132] This goes counter to the more traditional 1950s dad in the sitcom *Leave it to Beaver*, who was a strong, smart, dominant provider and wise advisor or leader of the family, the destruction of which was one of the objectives of the feminist movement that was behind marginalizing the patriarchy and fatherhood.

It is still harder for single dads to get the entirety of benefits the welfare system offers.[133] Since incarceration rates are higher in the black community than any other community,[134] it would make sense that men who are currently incarcerated or who were at some time in life would find it a lot more difficult to acquire welfare benefits for their families and children.[135] The Brookings Institute article I got this information from was from 2006. If things haven't changed a lot since then, why wouldn't it be similar today? In any

---

[130] Gretchen Livingston, July 2, 2013, "The Rise of Single Fathers: A Ninefold Increase Since 1960," Pew Research Center, retrieved August 7, 2020, https://www.pewsocialtrends.org/2013/07/02/the-rise-of-single-fathers.

[131] Ibid.

[132] Ibid.

[133] Ron Haskins, August 19, 2006, Brookings Institute, "Welfare Revisited: Young Men Need Incentives," retrieved August 26, 2020 https://www.brookings.edu/articles/welfare-revisited-young-men-need-incentives/#:~:text=Men%20generally%20do%20not%20qualify,and%2C%20for%20many%2C%20incarceration.

[134] Ibid.

[135] Ibid.

of the above scenarios, the mother is the next in line to have to raise the children.[136]

According to The Good Men Project, there are five fears that men have most. The second and third most common fears men have are the fear of failure[137] and the fear of not being able to be a good provider, respectively.[138] If a man cannot be a good provider because of financial issues, he sees himself as a failure,[139] and society still does see him as that in a way, even though throughout the second and third wave of the feminist movement lots of men have been eliminated from various high-paying positions and they have been replaced by women.[140] Men still have it in their nature to want to, or need to, be providers of resources and leaders and when they can't, they feel like failures. This discourages them from committing to a marriage if they may be one day forced to face a fear. A lot of men just aren't making marriage proposals, and the African American community, even though all other community's men are dealing with the same thing, has a lot more men that are dealing with this, so this gives black men more incentive not to commit.

For the black family, it has been disproportionately worse than for any other group in America. According to the Moynihan Report written in 1965, the demise of the Negro family has caused

---

[136] Ibid.

[137] Jason Rogers, June 26, 2016, "5 Fears Men Try to Hide From the World,". retrieved June 26, 2020, https://goodmenproject.com/featured-content/5-fears-men-try-hide-world-dg/.

[138] Ibid.

[139] Ibid.

[140] Hanna Rosin, 2010, "The End of Men," Atlantic Magazine July/August Issue 2010, retrieved March 18, 2022, https://www.theatlantic.com/magazine/archive/2010/07/the-end-of-men/308135/.

an unforeseen expansion in welfare dependency.[141] The welfare state that was constructed after World War II was largely constructed by Progressive Liberals,[142] who have now become agents for the Left. That is even more so the case nearly 50 years later. Throughout the 1980s, the inner city and the black family continued to disintegrate.[143] Child poverty hit a high of 22.7 percent in 1993.[144] Government assistance dependency went from two million to five million in just 25 years from 1970 to 1995.[145] During the end of that same period, 65 percent of all black babies were being born to single mothers.[146]

When referring to the amount of government assistance low-income families can get, many are financially better off if they choose not to marry.[147] That's why it is understandable that poor parents might remain unmarried when the income from the second parent is not enough to offset a loss in government benefits. This demographic of black women who are on government assistance are all

---

[141] Daniel Patrick Moynihan, The Moynehan Report 1965, "The Negro Family A Case for National Action," retrieved May 1, 2019, http://www.blackpast.org/primary/moynihan-report-1965.

[142] Roger E. Backhouse, Bradley W. Bateman, Tamotsu Nishizawa, and Dieter Plehwe, July 2017, "Liberalism and the Welfare State: Economists and Arguments for the Welfare State," Oxford Scholarship Online: July 2017, retrieved May 5, 2019, http://www.oxfordscholarship.com/view/10.1093/acprof:oso/9780190676681.001.0001/acprof-9780190676681.

[143] Kay S. Hymowitz, 2005, "The Black Family: 40 Years of Lies Rejecting the Moynihan report caused untold, needless misery," Summer 2005, retrieved May 9, 2019, https://www.city-journal.org/html/black-family-40-years-lies-12872.html.

[144] Ibid.

[145] Ibid.

[146] Ibid.

[147] Angela Rachidi, July 27, 2016, "Do welfare programs discourage marriage?" AEIdeas Economics, Poverty Studies, Society and Culture, retrieved May 15, 2019, https://www.aei.org/publication/do-welfare-programs-discourage-marriage.

single, and just about all of them have children. This is not most black women, but it is a pretty good-sized minority of them. In some cases, welfare pays more than a minimum wage job.[148] This doesn't give incentive for many who are on welfare to get off it.

At the time the Moynihan Report was written, then-President Johnson was warned that the poverty rate was growing in the black community,[149] and the growing matriarchy[150] and the disappearing patriarchy were factors.[151] That was in 1965.[152] One fourth of black families were headed by a women then.[153] This has been a plus for the feminists, who must be pleased that the patriarchy has been replaced by so many single-female household heads in the black community. This cause seems to have worked better in the black community than any other in America. The patriarchy has been dismantled worse in the black community than in any other demographic in America, thanks in part to leftist Democrats who sponsored so many of the Section 8 Housing and WIC benefits that were only designed for women and their children, provided they had no husband or father in residence with the children, along with no-fault divorce, so a father or

---

[148] Michael D. Tanner, August 19, 2013, CATO Institute, "Commentary: When Welfare Pays Better than Work," retrieved August 28, 2020, https://www.cato.org/commentary/when-welfare-pays-better-work.

[149] Daniel Patrick Moynihan, The Moynehan Report 1965, "The Negro Family: A Case for National Action," retrieved May 1, 2019, http://www.blackpast.org/primary/moynihan-report-1965.

[150] Ibid.

[151] Ibid.

[152] Ibid.

[153] Ibid.

husband was no longer needed.[154] No-fault divorce is another reason why so many African American women are single if they have not remarried, and most of them have children.

Since money is more of a problem for the black community and black people have and/or make less of it than Whites and Asians, it affects negatively a man's ability to provide, and this is probably another reason why so many African American women are single[155] and why so many black men are not proposing. This may be an incentive for African American women to divorce their husbands more than for women from other ethnic backgrounds. This one is in relation to no-fault divorce. At all ages, black Americans have lower marriage rates than do other racial and ethnic groups, and marital instability is more common for blacks than just about all other ethnic backgrounds.[156] Remember the standard for what is acceptable to be middle income is the same for blacks as it is for whites, even in dollar amounts. In 2008, only 32 percent of Blacks were married compared to 61 percent in 1960. Blacks also get divorced more often and remarry less frequently than whites.[157] This did not really start to happen for Blacks until the feminist movement.

---

[154] Paul Winfree, August 1, 2015, "How Welfare Spending Hurts the People It's Supposed to Help," retrieved May 6, 2019, https://www.dailysignal.com/2015/08/01/how-welfare-spending-hurts-the-people-its-supposed-to-help.

[155] Jason Rogers June 26, 2016, "The Good Men Project: 5 Fears Men Try to Hide From the World 11, Comments," retrieved May 2, 2019, https://goodmenproject.com/featured-content/5-fears-men-try-hide-world-dg/.

[156] R. Kelly Raley, Megan M. Sweeney, and Danielle Wondra, , "The Growing Racial and Ethnic Divide in U.S. Marriage Patterns HHS, Author Manuscripts PMC4850739," HHS Public Assess US National Library of Medicine, National Institutes of Health, retrieved November 14, 2019, https://www.ncbi.nlm.nih.gov/pmc/articles/PMC4850739/.

[157] Dawne Mouzon, Rutgers University, October 26, 2013 "Why Has Marriage Declined among Black Americans? Race Ethnicity Children and Families," retrieved November 14, 2019, https://scholars.org/brief/why-has-marriage-declined-among-black-americans.

Jon Birger, author of *Date-o-nomics: How Dating Became a Lopsided Numbers Game*, did some interesting research on dating and marriage patterns in America. He discovered that according to the US Census Bureau for young men and women aged 22 to 29, there are 5.5 million college-educated women for every 4.1 million college-educated men.[158] He did research in Silicon Valley, Santa Clara County, California, where the tech industry attracts a surplus of men.[159] He discovered that the oversupply of men has changed the demographics of dating and marriage. According to his research, divorce rates are lower and marriages are generally more stable with the ratio skewed in favor of men,[160] and there are fewer divorces. When women are scarcer, men have to make greater commitments.[161] It seems from this that women can afford to be choosier about the men they date and marry, and men are forced to work harder to attract a mate with more competition.[162] Birger claims according to the book "Too Many Women," in societies with a surplus of women they were more likely to be raped and the crime was punished less severely.[163] He also claims criminologists and sociologists have studied criminology and FBI data and they have come to

---

[158] Jon Birger, Nov 11, 2015 "The Economics of Dating: How Game Theory and Demographics Explain Dating in D.C. The Cato Institute, retrieved November 27, 2019, https://www.youtube.com/watch?v=IBDUOi9IhfE (3 mins and 55 secs).

[159] Ibid. (14 min and 50 secs).

[160] Ibid. (15 min and 55 secs).

[161] Ibid. (20 min and 25 secs).

[162] Simon Denyer and Annie Gowen, Illustrations by Jasu Hu, April 18, 2018, "Too Many Men," *The Washington Post*, retrieved November 30, 2019, https://www.washingtonpost.com/graphics/2018/world/too-many-men/.

[163] Jon Birger, "The Economics of Dating–How Game Theory and Demographics Explain Dating in DC," the Cato Institute, https://www.youtube.com/watch?v=IBDUOi9IhfE, (29min and 50 sec).

the same conclusion.[164] Also in the words of University of Arizona sociologist Robert O'Brian sexual assaults also seem to be more common in countries that have an excess of women.

O'Brian also mentioned that in the working class who are not as likely to have college degrees the men who marry make the highest incomes,[165] but black people are more likely to be unemployed or make lower wages.

Birger compared Santa Clara with other cities in the country, such as Washington, DC, Chicago, and Boston, with a more typical ratio of men to women like the rest of America.[166] In these cities, women tended to be more numerous than men among its college educated.[167] From his research, he found where women were more numerous, the dating culture became more sexualized, and the single men were in no rush to settle down and commit, so marriage rates declined, and divorce rates went up.[168]

This demographic is more characteristic of the black community in America than in any other ethnic background and especially in certain pockets in the black community, since the black community has so many more women than men due to incarceration, homicide, and various other reasons that seem to plague the black community more.[169] This is another explanation why marriage is at an all-time low in the African American community, and that

---

[164] Ibid (29 min and 55sec).

[165] Ibid.

[166] Ibid (19 min 42 sec).

[167] Ibid (19 min 55 sec).

[168] Ibid. (19 min 58 sec).

[169] Justin Wolfers, David Leonhardt, and Kevin Quealy, April 20, 2015, "1.5 Million Missing Black Men," The Upshot, retrieved April 12, 2019, https://www.nytimes.com/interactive/2015/04/20/upshot/missing-black-men.html.

goes for the college educated and the non-college educated both male and female, as well. It does not help that the African American men have one of the highest school[170] and college dropout[171] rates in the nation, so the numbers game is even more lopsided for college-educated black women. It is actually more lopsided for all black women in general. If it is, in fact, this lopsided, you have to ask yourself if this is why the black community has pockets where you have men with children from multiple baby mommas and women with children from multiple baby daddies. A black woman with an undergraduate degree, aged between 35 and 45, is 15 percent less likely to be married than a white woman without a undergraduate degree.[172] So the sexualization of relationships and dating have taken on some different dynamics in the black community than in other communities in America, especially in some small pockets of the black community. It was not like this for the black community until the feminist movement took off and went into second- and third-wave feminism. It would not surprise me if Birger's stats were actually worse for the black community than for whites since stats like this always seem to be worse for blacks and Latinos, so the picture may not be quite this bad for whites but even worse for blacks.

---

[170] Nation Centers For Education Statistics Facts Sheet Dropout Rates, retrieved November 27, 2019, https://nces.ed.gov/fastfacts/display.asp?id=16.

[171] Emily Tate, April 26, 2017, "Inside Higher Education: Graduation Rates and Race," retrieved November 27, 2019, College completion rates vary by race and ethnicity, report finds (insidehighered.com).

[172] Richard V Reeves and Katherine Guyot, December 4, 2017, "Black Women Are Earning More College Degrees, but That Alone Won't Close the Racial Gap," The Brookings Institute, Social Mobility Memos, retrieved November 24, 2019, https://www.brookings.edu/blog/social-mobility-memos/2017/12/04/black-women-are-earning-more-college-degrees-but-that-alone-wont-close-race-gaps/.

According to a new survey, dating has become too expensive for 30 percent of millennials due to student debt and rising living costs.[173] This does not bode well for marriages and families in the future for the black community since the blacks are more likely to be poorer. This is a good recipe for more babies being born out of wedlock, and if out-of-wedlock sex continues, we will continue to have single moms for some time to come, who will be raising a lot of the black children on their own.

Married men are happier, more successful, and make more money than single men.[174] That is probably true, but they generally have more money and resources and things to impress a mate than single men do to begin with.[175] One of those things is a steady income and the ability to provide a house, college for the kids, two cars, and so forth. Men who are in this position with resources like these are the ones who are more likely to do the marriage proposals to begin with.[176] In the black community, men are not as likely to be in this position as they are in other communities, so they are more likely to either postpone marriage or not pursue it as an option at all.[177] Going into a marriage without these things doesn't guarantee that you will acquire them or acquire a better ability to acquire them during the course of the marriage. There are plenty of single, never-married blacks who are in their 30s, 40s, 50s, and even 60s who have never married, and it is surprising how many have no children

---

[173] "Study: 30% of millennials can't afford to date," *USA Today National*, July 30, 2019, Updated July 30, retrieved May 18 2019, https://www.wflx.com/2019/07/31/study-millennials-cant-afford-date/.

[174] Nicholas H. Wolfinger, May 28, 2019, "Are Married People Still Happier?" Institute for Family Studies, retrieved January 23, 2020, https://ifstudies.org/blog/are-married-people-still-happier.

[175] Ibid.

[176] Ibid

[177] Ibid.

either. When marriages, families, and children are not happening the traditional way in a community, and nearly half of the babies have been aborted before birth, and a lot more of people have been killed from homicide than any other group of people; that is an existence-ender for the group.

Forensic psychiatrist Dr. Helen Smith, author of *Men on Strike*, was interviewed on *Fox News*, and when asked by Journalist Carlson Tucker, stated that men were getting away with not marrying the women that they are having children by. Dr. Smith stated that 40 percent of the lower socioeconomic-level women who are breadwinners and are making around $17,000 to $23,000 a year, who use the government to pay for their needs, don't want a man.[178] Black people are more likely to be in lower-income brackets like this, with more dependency on the government for a lot more things. Financial troubles can be categorized as one of the biggest causes for divorce, following infidelity, which is the number one reason.[179]

Abortion on demand was another leftist policy that has proven to be devastating to the black community. As of January of 2020, just over 61 million abortions[180] have happened in America. As of year's end 2019, according to another source, over 62 million abortions have happened[181] and on average one million occur each year, so if you add another two million for 2020 and 2021 you get a total

---

[178] "Words of the Wise: Dr. Helen Smith Stands up for Men across America," retrieved May 3, 2019, https://www.youtube.com/watch?v=CxalGnK2DxA (8 mins 12 secs).

[179] Shellie Warren, "10 Most Common Reasons for Divorce Life. Expert Verified Expert," retrieved May 18, 2019, https://www.marriage.com/advice/divorce/10-most-common-reasons-for-divorce.

[180] "Texas Right to Life Abortion News. Texas Right to Life," January 21, 2020, retrieved February 19, 2020. https://www.texasrighttolife.com/category/news/issues/abortion/.

[181] American Life League Home. Learn. "Abortion: Abortion Statistics," retrieved March 21, 2022, https://www.all.org/learn/policy-politicians/.

of 64 million,[182] and when you consider that 35 percent of them typically have been black,[183] that's just over 21 million. Since *Roe v. Wade* of 1973 was 50 years ago, if all of the babies that were aborted before 2002 had lived, by now they would have their own children, and with just zero population growth, there would be another 21 million black people in America for a total addition of 42 million. If all of the black babies who were aborted from 1973 through 1980 had not been aborted, by now they would have had grandchildren for a total of a few more million. All totaled, if it had not been for just this one thing, abortion, there may have been maybe 45 million more African Americans. When you add the total, or 36 million, currently you get another estimated total of around 80 million.

Abortion is the leading cause of death for African Americans, more than all other causes combined, including AIDS, violent crimes, homicides, accidents, cancer, and heart disease.[184,185] This has been nothing less than genocide on the black community. Every black community has easy access to Planned Parenthood clinics, where abortions are performed. Planned Parenthood was the brainchild of racist, liberal, feminist Margaret Sanger. She attended a number of Klan meetings, although these were not white sheet,

---

[182] First Choice Pregnancy Center, "Abortion facts," retrieved March 21, 2022, https://firstchoiceprc.com/pro-life-movement?gclid=CjwKCAjwxOCRBhA8EiwA0X8hi73l_NoiH3GAgNfxeF6ws5xqVIAD7HmqXhMaD8lxiQqdni5MH-EA_xoC810QAvD_BwE.

[183] Dr. Mark Hodges, Dec 5, 2016, "CDC: 35% of aborted babies are black," https://www.lifesitenews.com/news/cdc-statistics-indicate-abortion-rate-continues-to-be-higher-among-minoriti.

[184] "Pro-lifer says abortion is leading cause of death in black community," January 19, 2012, Catholic Review, retrieved May 18, 2019, https://www.archbalt.org/pro-lifer-says-abortion-is-leading-cause-of-death-in-black-community.

[185] Paul Stark, Aug. 2, 2018, "Researchers Find Abortion is the Leading Cause of Death, Surpassing Heart Disease and Cancer," National, Washington, DC, retrieved May 6, 2019, https://www.lifenews.com/2018/08/02/researchers-find-abortion-is-the-leading-cause-of-death-surpassing-heart-disease-and-cancer.

The Feminist Movement

white-hooded, cross-burning meetings that were notorious to the Klan. One such meeting was a women's auxiliary branch of the Ku Klux Klan.[186] At one of those meetings, the topic of discussion was "The Negro Problem" and how to ethnically cleanse America of so many Negros.[187] After this meeting, Sanger went to Germany to meet with Adolf Hitler's former minister for racial hygiene in Nazi Germany to find out how he exterminated so many Jews during the Holocaust.[188] She praised his programs and was very excited about implementing them in America on African Americans.[189] Planned Parenthood, which she founded, was just another clever tool used to exterminate the America's black population. You may think otherwise, but shortly after Planned Parenthood clinics opened their doors in 1982, the population in America has been increasing. Up until this point, the black population has been increasing at a much slower rate than it has been for Asians and Hispanics;[190] however, some of this increase was due to immigration and not live births.[191]

Sanger had a plan to use people within the black community to appeal to Blacks. That was a good strategy because if you give something a face that you are more comfortable dealing with, it makes it more appealing, even if was intended to deliver a fatal blow.

---

[186] National Catholic Register, "Margaret Sanger Wasn't Just a Racist—She Also Targeted Disabled People," retrieved September 13, 2020, https://www.ncregister.com/blog/margaret-sanger-wasn-t-just-a-racist-she-also-targeted-disabled-people.

[187] Mary Anne Dion, April 10, 2019, "Hitler, The Ku Klux Klan, and Margaret Sanger," The Currier-Herold, retrieved September 13, 2020, https://www.courierherald.com/letters/hitler-the-ku-klux-klan-and-margaret-sanger/.

[188] Ibid.

[189] Ibid.

[190] Mark Mather, Associate Vice President of US Forms, retrieved June 26, 2020, https://www.prb.org/us-population-growth-decline/.

[191] Ibid.

With this kind of appeal, people will be more honest about their ignorance, superstitions, and doubts. It is interesting to note that that is the same strategy that predatory lenders used just before the foreclosure crisis in America to appeal to a disproportionately high number of Blacks and Hispanics. More details will be discussed on this subject later on.

It seems that Sanger had some stereotypical beliefs about the black community that you could appeal to them with a religious appeal, through a pastor's speeches and thoughts, which would have to almost certainly be influenced by Sanger herself. She wanted it kept very quiet or completely unspoken that she didn't want it known that her plot was to exterminate the Negro.[192] She sounded like she had a plot to get rid of African Americans. This liberal feminist appears to be racist to me. From this, people are going to say she is just one bad feminist, and you can't make that judgment from one bad apple. That's true, but it is not the individual feminist; it is the fact that the idea comes out of their cause, and it is endorsed by the feminist movement including Sanger. Both feminism and abortion (not eugenics that was Sanger's plan for the black community) were two very radical leftist causes that many Progressive Liberals and leftists were on board with.[193,194]

---

[192] Cassy Fiano, June 8, 2017, "That Awkward Moment When Planned Parenthood Tries to Cover Up Their Racist Past Pro-Life," Save The Storks Pregnancy Centers, retrieved May 11, 2019, https://savethestorks.com/2017/06/awkward-moment-planned-parenthood-tries-cover-racist-past/.

[193] Dr. Michael Brown, "Hamilton Strategies Evil Agenda of Radical and Militant Pro-Abortion Feminists Is the Wicked Spirit of Jezebel at Work," retrieved June 26, 2020, https://hamilton-strategies.com/evil-agenda-of-radical-and-militant-pro-abortion-feminists-is-the-wicked-spirit-of-jezebel-at-work-says-author-dr-michael-brown/.

[194] Mary Meehan, September 1980, "Abortion: The Left has betrayed the sanctity of life," The Progressive, retrieved June 26, 2020, http://groups.csail.mit.edu/mac/users/rauch/nvp/consistent/meehan_progressive.html.

Planned Parenthood had a policy in seven states where you could earmark your funding for an abortion specifically for a baby of a particular race or ethnic background.[195] It was called their women-in-need fund. African American babies were commonly targeted for this funding.[196,197] In one of these dialogues, the Planned Parenthood employee chuckled in agreement when the donor stated, "There are way too many black people out there for my kids to have to compete with."[198] People who approve of abortion like this are more likely to be Liberals,[199,200] keeping in mind that although a small minority of them are Liberals, they can be very racist too. I am not saying that she is a racist, but some Liberals and sadly fewer but still some Conservatives still have a flip it attitude like this about the murder of innocent little black babies. This cause of abortion, however, is more of a progressive left leaning one than a liberal one, and it is certainly not a purpose behind the Conservative movement in America.

A commentary on a Christian radio station stated that India had performed millions of sex-selective abortions over the past 30 years

---

[195] "Planned Parenthood and Racism," Students for Life of America: Planned Parenthood Racism Investigation, retrieved February 4, 2020, https://studentsforlife.org/high-school/planned-parenthood-and-racism/.

[196] Ibid.

[197] Zach Behrens, February 29, 2008, "News: Race in LA Planned Parenthood Accepted Racially Motived Donations According to a UCLA Magazine," retrieved September 7, 2020, https://laist.com/2008/02/29/planned_parenth.php.

[198] Ibid.

[199] StudentNewsDaily.com, Compiled by the Editors. Copyright 2005 (revised 2010), "Conservative vs. Liberal Beliefs," retrieved February 4, 2020, https://www.studentnewsdaily.com/conservative-vs-liberal-beliefs/.

[200] Wheen M., 1987, "Abortion: the extreme liberal position," *J Med Philos*. 1987 Aug;12(3):241–65, doi:10.1093/jmp/12.3.241, PubMed, retrieved February 4, 2020, https://www.ncbi.nlm.nih.gov/pubmed/3668400.

or so;[201] now they have millions of young men who will never have a wife[202] because so many of India's baby girls were aborted over that period.[203] The same has happened in China with nearly 35 million sex-selective abortions (all girls) from 1980 until they discontinued their one-child policy in 2015.[204] Now they also have lots of young men who will probably never be married. Between China and India, the two of them will have approximately 70 million fewer women[205] to have children, and that will have negative consequences for both countries such as sex trafficking, prostitution, and so forth. For all of the little baby girls who were aborted in India and China, there will be a price to pay.

America has had millions of abortions, with Planned Parenthood—and with the vision of its brainchild, Margaret Sanger, lots of them have been race selective. The vision of Planned Parenthood was to ethnically cleanse as many black people from America as possible. The resulting consequence was a victory for white supremacy, and the black community is paying the price for it with a lot fewer black people as a result. America will pay because there will be fewer tax-paying citizens for all of its retirees in the future with fewer working people. You can have immigrants with

---

[201] Simon Denyer and Annie Gowen, Illustrations by Jasu Hu, April 18, 2018, "Too Many Men," *The Washington Post*, retrieved November 30, 2019, https://www.washingtonpost.com/graphics/2018/world/too-many-men.

[202] Ibid.

[203] Ibid.

[204] History.com editors, July 22, 2019, "China announces the end of its controversial one-child policy," The History Channel, retrieved January 4, 2020, https://www.history.com/this-day-in-history/china-ends-one-child-policy.

[205] Simon Denyer and Annie Gowen, Illustrations by Jasu Hu, April 18, 2018, "Too Many Men," *The Washington Post*, retrieved November 30, 2019, https://www.washingtonpost.com/graphics/2018/world/too-many-men.

different beliefs to come over as a workforce like some of the illegal ones who are streaming across the border to pay into social security, but if too many of them have different cultural values than traditional American ones, they will change America into something different than it is now. If so many babies had not been aborted and raised to be proud loyal Americans (a third of them being black) that would not be a threat now, but the left is educating children to hate America.

Since this is the case when feminism, along with integration on progressive terms, have been enforced in the black community too, it had some uniquely negative consequences for the black community. I will discuss why I think integration had its snares for the black community later on. Since the feminists who started the movement were white, it put them in a position to exploit the black community in a way that helped them accomplish their goals without doing any real good for the black community, and under some circumstances, making things worse. Some of this exploitation had racist motives to it, such as Margaret Sanger's sinister Planned Parenthood agenda.

One and a half million black men are missing from American society,[206] which is another way that is visible that the patriarchy has been taken down in the black community—and for various other reasons that will be explained to you later on in this book. Some are missing due to homicide,[207] some to incarceration[208] and some to other reasons,[209] but this is another reason why so many African American women are single: there just aren't enough men for them

---

[206] Justin Wolfers, David Leonhardt, and Kevin Quealy, April 20, 2015, "1.5 Million Missing Black Men," The Upshot, retrieved April 12, 2019, https://www.nytimes.com/interactive/2015/04/20/upshot/missing-black-men.html.

[207] Ibid.

[208] Ibid.

[209] Ibid.

in their community. In many of these families, the matriarch is in charge, and they have ruled in some cases for several generations. This is one the feminists can celebrate about. It must make them feel great to see what has been created in the black community. Conservatives, on the other hand, were more traditional in their approach about a lot of things, like keeping the family intact and not destroying the patriarchy, whereas the feminist movement and all of those government handouts, mostly endorsed by Democrats for women and children, was not one of their priorities. If it were up to Conservatives, we would still have a lot more men in the picture as fathers and husbands in the black family and in black society, period.

While watching a PBS special about East Lake Meadows, which was a housing project in Atlanta, one of its former tenants explained how trash pickup was sporadic, the grass was often not cut for long periods of time, and raw sewage would sometimes back up in the units.[210] You would have to call someone for quite some time to get it fixed, and it took extended time periods to get any services. Another one of the tenants interviewed stated that even though there was not a total absence of men, the mothers and grandmothers ruled,[211] but democratic socialists think we need more public housing because it is affordable.[212] When mothers and grandmothers rule, you have a matriarchy, not a patriarchy, and why wouldn't that be the case in all of the other housing projects across America?

---

[210] Kevin Burns, "East Lake Meadows: A Public Housing Story," a film by Sarah Burns and David McMahan, retrieved March 28, 2020, https://www.pbs.org/kenburns/east-lake-meadows/.

[211] Ibid.

[212] Jimmy Tobias, August 10, 2018, "These Democratic Socialists Aren't Just Targeting Incumbent Politicians," The Nation, retrieved March 28, 2020, https://www.thenation.com/article/archive/democratic-socialist-campaigns-target-isnt-incumbent.

The International Socialist Review did an interesting article on black feminism and intersectionality.[213] It explained essentially that it was difficult to place black women into the narrative and exposed the real purpose behind the feminist movement since black women were affected negatively by the black experience in America and to a lesser extent because they were women.[214] Race is usually used to refer to the male persona of a group, with the female persona attached indirectly.[215] The article claimed, "This framework frequently renders black women legally 'invisible' and without legal recourse."[216] In other words, when you consider that the feminist movement was designed out of the injustices that white women have experienced being white women only, it was never really intended to address the unique issues of black women.[217] It was intended to address the issues in society that white women were having, and a lot of those were issues black women could not relate to.[218] On the other hand, black women were having challenges in society as black women that white women could not relate to as black people, or the unique problems only black women could relate to as black and women. Most likely a purpose or a narrative had to be created for black women in the movement to make them seem more like victims as women, rather than as black people. This was probably

---

[213] Sharon Smith, "Gender and Sexuality Theory: Black feminism and intersectionality," *The International Socialist Review*, retrieved May 14, 2019, https://isreview.org/issue/91/black-feminism-and-intersectionality.

[214] Ibid.

[215] Ibid.

[216] Ibid.

[217] Ibid.

[218] Betty Freidan, 1963, *The Feminine Mystique*, W W Norton Company Inc. New York, Library of Congress Catalog Card Number 62—10097, retrieved January 22, 2020, file:///C:/Users/Owner/Desktop/How%20Liberal%20Policies%20and%20Causes/FeminineMystique.pdf.

not most often the case and especially during and before the civil rights movement, but sometimes this may have been true under some circumstances.

From the welfare system, it appears as if men only really apply for food stamps, despite the fact that they are still responsible for child support and are more likely to be incarcerated for not paying.[219] Mothers, on the other hand, qualify for other benefits that are worth a lot more than fathers are eligible for.[220] With so many more benefits offered to single mothers by the system,[221,222] it provides a safety net for single women with children. Under these circumstances, the mother and children are more likely to end up in poverty.

So unless she gets addicted to crack cocaine, heroin, meth, or some other illegal drug, which is a worst-case scenario, which government benefits don't pay for, and she has to support her habit by some other means and maybe someone else's habit, too, she and her children are stuck basically at a life just above or below the poverty line. This has been going on now in some cases for going on the third generation in some black settings, but no one seems to have a solution for this. Ever since the feminist movement has taken off in America, the epidemic of out-of-wedlock births has exploded in the black community from less than 20 percent in 1960 to 72 percent

---

[219] Ron Haskins, August 19, 2006, "Welfare Revisited: Young Men Need Incentives," The Brookings Institute, retrieved May 14, 2019, https://www.brookings.edu/articles/welfare-revisited-young-men-need-incentives/.

[220] Ibid.

[221] Elizabeth Stuart, Feb. 25, 2014. "How Anti-Poverty Programs Marginalize Fathers," The Atlantic, Politics Section, retrieved May 14, 2019, https://www.theatlantic.com/politics/archive/2014/02/how-anti-poverty-programs-marginalize-fathers/283984.

[222] "Single Parent House Holds Safe Harbor," US Govt. Publication. retrieved April 29, 2019. http://lib.post.ca.gov/Publications/Building%20a%20Career%20Pipeline%20Documents/Safe_Harbor.pdf.

in 2010.[223] According to Fatherless.com from July of 2012 statistics 57.6% of black children[224], 31.2% of Hispanic children[225], and 20.7% of white children[226] are living absent their biological fathers. That is still way too many black children in fatherless homes!!

If Conservatives had had a more dominant role in shaping American society over the past 50 years or so, they would not have approved of this feminist movement that resulted in more destabilization of the black community than in other communities, and a lot more black children would have a father in the home because the patriarchy would still be present in places in the black community where it currently is not anymore. A lot fewer black people would be on government assistance programs because Conservatives would not have allowed the welfare state to expand like it has, but the black community would probably not have completely integrated with whites and lost a lot of its businesses; instead, it would have grown a larger business community and become more independent economically, which will be explained later in more depth. If more had been up to Conservatives, and no-fault divorce in so many cases would not have been allowed, where the mother gets custody of the

---

[223] Emily Badger, Princeton's Sara McLanahan and Harvard's Christopher Jencks, Dec 18, 2014, "The Unbelievable Rise in Single Motherhood In America over the Past 50 Years," *The Washington Post*, retrived November 6, 2019, https://www.washingtonpost.com/news/wonk/wp/2014/12/18/the-unbelievable-rise-of-single-motherhood-in-america-over-the-last-50-years.

[224] Fatherless.com Encouragement Support and Guidance retrieved March 25,2024 https://fathers.com/the-extent fatherlessness/#:~:text=57.6%25%20of%20black%20children%2C%2031.2,living%20absent%20their%20biological%20fathers.

[225] Ibid

[226] Ibid

children 80 percent to 85[227] percent of the time, more black kids would have a father in the home.

Since it is more difficult for men to get government assistance benefits for housing,[228] when the boys from these family settings become adults, they must leave the house and get a job and make it on their own. If they don't, which is often the case, they go into a life of crime to survive, which means a life of burglary, theft, selling crack cocaine, heroin, and marijuana, and maybe some other illegal activities. Some are lucky enough to be allowed by the mother of their child to stay in the Section 8 housing with her, but she is really the authority figure and the head of the house because she is actually providing it and she can have him thrown out when she wants, and this happens sometimes. What this does is diminish the role and the purpose behind having a dominant and effective patriarchy. In the case of a divorce, if he is paying child support because she got custody of the children but he is not present, it still minimizes his need to be present as a father, thus minimizing the traditional patriarchal role of fathers. In a setup like this, the matriarchy rules, or it at least changes the significance of a matriarchy, and in some cases, there is no patriarchy, which is just what leftist and progressive liberal feminists like seeing. That is not always good for a society or a community either.

If you have been a convicted felon for certain offenses, you can be denied Section 8 housing, and it varies, depending on the

---

[227] Robert Hughes, Jr., Contributor, Professor of Human Development, University of Illinois at Urbana-Champaign, June 9, 2011, updated November 29, 2011, "Are Custody Decisions Biased in Favor of Mothers?" *The Huffington Post*.

[228] Judith Cummings, 1983, "Breakup of Black Family Imperils Gains of Decades," Archives 1983 Welfare, retrieved April 27, 2019, https://www.nytimes.com/1983/11/20/us/breakup-of-black-family-imperils-gains-of-decades.html.

federal or local and state laws where you live.[229] Additionally, since incarceration rates are so much higher in the black community[230] and men are a lot more likely to be incarcerated than women,[231] it is harder for them to get this assistance both while in prison and after being released. Consequently, under these circumstances, the children end up with their mothers. Certain felony offenses limit their public assistance choices for housing, either temporarily or permanently.[232] In those cases, mothers are still more likely to have custody of the children. WIC is another benefit that only applies to single mothers, so since mothers can get some extra benefits that fathers can't, it makes more sense to let the children stay with their mothers. This contributes disproportionately both to the destabilization of the traditional family structure and the marginalization of the patriarchy in the black community; it has had bad consequences for society,[233] which was one of the goals of the feminist movement.

Feminists expected to have their high-powered careers instead of being housewives; many of them are not wives, and some of them are neither wives nor mothers, and that was one of the consequences of second- and third-wave feminism because feminism on that level destroys the patriarchy, and that is traditionally where husbands

---

[229] Michelle Seidel, October 19, 2019, "What Types of Felonies Can Stop You From Getting Section 8 Housing?" Legal Beagle, retrieved August 14, 2020, https://legalbeagle.com/8610638-types-getting-section-8-housing.html.

[230] "The Sentencing Project: Racial Disparity," retrieved August 14, 2020, https://www.sentencingproject.org/issues/racial-disparity/.

[231] Ibid.

[232] "Section 8 Facts: State and County Guidelines for Felons Applying for Section 8," retrieved August 14, 2020, https://section8facts.com/can-a-convicted-felon-get-section-8.

[233] Mona Charen, July 7, 2018, "Feminism has destabilized the American family," *The New York Post*, retrieved August 14, 2020, https://nypost.com/2018/07/07/feminism-has-destabilized-the-american-family/.

have come from. In fact, feminism on that level has removed lots of men from positions of prominence, dominance, authority, and visibility in society, which would make them attractive patriarchs for marriage. Not only that, it has changed the rules of what is sometimes expected of a man, and it is not always good for building patriarchies or making good, solid men. When men are in a position like this, they are not likely going to make the commitment to a relationship, which results in marriage. Studies have shown that women still prefer to marry men who earn a higher salary than them.[234] That is from a women's natural desire to be want to be provided for and protected.

That is in spite of the fact that the popular culture and society is telling women to be the CEO of your corporation, get a PhD in a STEM field, be a man's equivalent in society, even take on dominant roles of leadership in society that have traditionally been his, even though nature is telling women to be something else like a less dominant mother and wife.

The message for men from the popular culture and society is confusing since they have been told to be sensitive and don't be so masculine because too much masculinity is toxic,[235] yet he must man up and take care of his wife and family with the same salary as hers. Do this in spite of the risks associated with divorce, paying child support, and alimony. The risks from all of these are higher for men to end up losers.

---

[234] The Editors Institute for Family Studies, November 7, 2016, "Better-Educated Women Still Prefer Higher-Earning Husbands," retrieved December 21, 2019, https://ifstudies.org/blog/better-educated-women-still-prefer-higher-earning-husbands.

[235] Amy Morin, Updated on November 25, 2020, Medically reviewed by Akeem Marsh, MD, "What Is Toxic Masculinity?" Very Well Mind EMOTIONS, retrieved March 25, 2022, https://www.verywellmind.com/what-is-toxic-masculinity-5075107.

Men are not as likely to make a marriage proposal under conditions like these, since to be good bets for marriage it is it is good if they earn a larger income than their female partner, and if they don't, they are not as likely to propose. Therefore, in lower-income communities such as the black community, the men just aren't making marriage proposals as much. This also comes from a man's nature and traditional role as a patriarch to be provider and a leader, and if he doesn't feel this way, marriage is an uncomfortable or awkward prospect for him,[236] especially since it is still unclear in American culture if he is expected to be the breadwinner or not. However, it seems like it is still really preferable under most circumstances if he is.[237, 238] In the black community, the high-earning men are not as numerous and sometimes not nearly as numerous as black women, so the marriage and dating scene has taken on some different dynamics in the African American community than in most other communities in America. This was not in the best interests of feminists, but it was for the Left, and it is what happens when a society has been destabilized.

---

[236] Ester Bloom, May 18 2017, "Make it Economists: Men now need more than just money to be 'marriageable,'" retrieved December 21, 2019, https://www.cnbc.com/2017/05/17/economists-men-now-need-more-than-just-money-to-be-marriageable.html.

[237] Casey Bond, July 12, 2018, "Marriages with Female Breadwinners Still Struggle. Here's How To Make It Work," Huffpost, retrieved December 27, 2019, https://www.huffpost.com/entry/female-breadwinners-marriage_n_5b3ef51fe4b09e4a8b2b780c.

[238] Kim Parker and Renee Stepler, "Americans see men as the financial providers, even as women's contributions grow,". Pew Research Center, "retrieved December 27, 2019, https://www.pewresearch.org/fact-tank/2017/09/20/americans-see-men-as-the-financial-providers-even-as-womens-contributions-grow/.

With black people being only 12 percent of the population, but with 65 percent of black children[239] being raised in single-parent households as compared to 30 percent for white children[240] and 35 percent of all abortions,[241] it shows a greater need to provide more funding for Planned Parenthood and more tax dollars for government assistance programs. This fueled the feminist cause more, and the black community provided more participants for the cause. In some cases, the single mothers of these families will allow the fathers of the children to live with or visit the children (which is really not legal) for a while without the authorities knowing about it, but when she decides he must go, she can have him put out, whether the cause is for reasonable or unreasonable purposes. Since these children were not raised by a patriarchy, it gives the single moms, who are basically being cared for by the government, a different position of authority in these homes, and that works as a dismissal or marginalization of male authority, presence, and responsibility—which is what was intended by the feminist movement. So from this last example, black men get a nasty dose of feminism from the black community, from policies enforced through the feminist movement in a way that black women can enforce them on them because they are black men, and they are subject to feminist policies from the greater American society because they are men. White men are off limits to enforcement of these policies by black women, for the most

---

[239] Kay S. Hymowitz, Summer 2005, "The Black Family: 40 Years of Lies Rejecting the Moynihan report caused untold, needless misery," retrieved May 9, 2019, https://www.city-journal.org/html/black-family-40-years-lies-12872.html.

[240] Alfred Lubrano, Updated November 12, 2018, "Rate of births to white single moms accelerates," *The Philadelphia Examiner*, retrieved August 3, 2020, https://www.inquirer.com/philly/news/unwed-white-mothers-babies-marriage-philadelphia-poverty-women-20181112.html.

[241] Walt Blackman, Guest Opinion, February 25, 2020, "Abortion: The overlooked tragedy for black Americans," *Arizona Capital Times*, retrieved August 3, 2020, https://azcapitoltimes.com/news/2020/02/25/abortion-the-overlooked-tragedy-for-black-americans/.

part, so they are only subject to what happens to men in the greater society of America. This has changed the fabric of black society, especially in certain places. So recruiting black women to work for the feminist movement was a plus for white feminists, but it was doubly bad for the black community.

Conservatives are not against women's rights; it's this radical feminist agenda that they have not really been pushing. It's this second and third wave of feminism that has gotten most of its power by the leftist movement that is hurting the black community as well. Now we have the MeToo movement that so many men have been victims of, such as Bill Cosby, which will be discussed later in this book. It is interesting to note that a black woman is the face of the #MeToo Movement,[242] which she herself founded in 2006.[243] A number of other men have been victims of the MeToo movement, but Bill Cosby had his case dragged out for a longer time than any other man's. More in-depth discussion will be brought up about it. Notice with Bill Cosby's case, he had accusers of all races and ethnicities, and a lot of his accusers were white women.

White women feminists can destroy both black men and white men like this. Black women who are feminists can destroy black men like this, but they can't really do this to white men because society and popular culture doesn't really allow it; if they do, they will have very strict limitations on what they can say about the man and maybe even how much they can say it. Therefore, accusing white men is off limits to black women. It appears that in this arena, black men, in particular, can potentially be more vulnerable since they can be exposed to attacks from two different fronts.

---

[242] Natalie Morin, June 12, 2018, "Faces of the #MeToo movement," retrieved January 23, 2021, https://stacker.com/stories/1153/faces-metoo-movement.

[243] Ibid.

According to ListVerse.com, there are 10 indications that Western society is collapsing, which is probably partially a result of destabilization caused by some of the effects of the feminist movement and for several other reasons. The 10 indicators that they listed on their website are: (1) Gender fluidity; (2) the collapse of the family; (3) the rising dominance of virtual worlds; (4) fusion with technology; (5) mass immigration from undeveloped countries; (6) inequality under the law; (7) erasure of history; (8) rising financial inequality; (9) drug abuse; and (10) nihilism.[244] At least five and maybe seven are affecting the black community worse than most of the rest of society. The five that are disproportionately more damaging to the existence of the black community are:

1. The collapse of the family;
2. Mass immigration from undeveloped countries;
3. Inequality under the law;
4. Erasure of history;
5. Rising financial inequality.

Also affecting the black community are the dominance of virtual worlds (since black youth tend to watch more TV featuring drama and scandal than most other ethnic backgrounds) and drug abuse (since more blacks are arrested and either jailed or imprisoned for it much more often than whites). These are signs that black society has destabilized more than the rest of America from so many of its policies and causes. Remember this was one of the reasons for

---

[244] Samuel Popejoy, Updated November 3, 2019, "Our World 10 Indications That Western Society Is Collapsing," retrieved April 12, 2020, https://listverse.com/2018/04/13/10-indications-that-western-society-is-collapsing/.

implementing the feminist movement to begin with.[245] The black community especially in some pockets in black America may be the only setting in history where more than half of its children have been raised by single moms for the past two generations, so how can you say that it is not a factor in the cause of its issues?

The Merriam-Webster dictionary online used the word "unstable" in a sentence rather like this: If you put a stack of books on an unstable desk or table, it will go crashing to the floor. So if something else is not there with more stability for the books to depend on, it will crash. In the black community, the dependency is dependence on jobs from government institutions and other non-black or white institutions for more of the black community's employment—more so than other communities do. It also is related to the inability to keep order in society in the really bad little pockets of the black community with really bad neighborhoods where most of the kids grew up without a father. When something is unstable, it will be more dependent on outside entities to hold it up or support it or maybe even to keep it viable. The black community is more dependent on government and other entities, such as white businesses and organizations, for its economic infrastructure than any other ethnic background in America. This was one of the effects that the feminist movement intended for society but look at the impact for the black community. I am not saying that this was all caused totally because of the feminist movement, because most definitely there were other factors involved for the black community.

According to psychotherapist Mary Jo Rapini on an interview with Houston's Fox News 26, a father's love is one of the great

---

[245] Mona Charen, July 7, 2018, "Feminism has destabilized the American family," retrieved May 8, 2019, https://nypost.com/2018/07/07/feminism-has-destabilized-the-american-family/.

impacts on a child's personal development.[246] The research was done on a group with and without dads over a period of time, who were followed from early childhood until adulthood.[247] The group who were raised with fathers were more considerate, more empathetic, and more able to control themselves.[248]

According to Chicago's chief of police superintendent, there are 117,000 gang members in Chicago,[249] and several hundred gang conflicts daily.[250] He said in 2020 as of July 22, in a press conference on Fox News, that 5,000 guns were recovered on Chicago's streets.[251] He didn't state how many of the gang members were black, white, Asian or Latino, but this is an example of what happens when young boys grow up without fathers, especially in really bad neighborhoods. The boys look for role models where there are just no male role models and no patriarchy. The mayor mentioned that a lot of the deaths from gun violence are from retaliation crimes.[252] She said too many of their young men were growing up without caring about the sanctity or the preciousness of life.[253] What is happening to Chicago is happening in pockets all over black America. This is what happens when kids grow without the empathy that is given to

---

[246] Mary Jo Rapini, June 13, 2016, "Father's influence in raising empathetic, considerate children," retrieved July 25, 2020, https://www.fox26houston.com/houstons-morning-show/fathers-influence-in-raising-empathetic-considerate-children.

[247] Ibid., 28 secs.

[248] Ibid., 40 secs.

[249] "Live: Chicago mayor speaks on rising violence, Trump's threat to send federal troops," FOX News https://www.youtube.com/watch?v=h4dKPTD1vBs, 28 mins and 10 secs.

[250] Ibid., 32 mins. and 55 secs.

[251] Ibid., 34 mins. and 45 secs.

[252] Ibid., 15 mins. and 54 secs.

[253] Ibid., 17 mins. and 38 secs.

a child who grows up with a father in the home.²⁵⁴ Children who grow up without a father in the house are not as likely to be able to exhibit self-control or act as responsibly.²⁵⁵ When fathers modeling sensitivity and compassion are involved in a child's life, the child is a lot more resilient with better well-being.²⁵⁶ Without that, it leads to a society with more chaos and violence.²⁵⁷ Another one of Chicago officials blame the drug cartels for all of Chicago's senseless violence, which has nothing to do with fatherless homes. That may also be a factor,²⁵⁸ but you cannot blame them on all of the retaliation crimes.

If right-leaning Conservatives had had more influence, this radical feminist cause of abortion, which has ethnically cleansed America of so many black people would not have come nearly to the extent that it has if it had happened at all, and America would have a lot more black people now. Since Conservatives are more likely to be Evangelical Christians, they are not as likely to be pro-abortion. Since they were not, if it had been up to Conservatives, we probably would not have so many Planned Parenthood clinics that are very accessible to the black community, which have been nothing more than another tool to legally exterminate the black community. Maybe if right-leaning Conservatives had had more influence they would probably have not allowed so many abortions by policies

---

²⁵⁴ Mary Jo Rapini, June 13, 2016, "Father's influence in raising empathetic, considerate children," retrieved July 25, 2020, https://www.fox26houston.com/houstons-morning-show/fathers-influence-in-raising-empathetic-considerate-children, 45 secs.

²⁵⁵ Mary Jo Rapini, June 15, 2016. "CHRON A dad's influence in raising empathetic and considerate children," retrieved march 14, 2020, https://www.chron.com/life/mom-houston/article/A-dad-s-influence-in-raising-empathetic-and-8196087.php.

²⁵⁶ Ibid., sec. 55.

²⁵⁷ Ibid.

²⁵⁸ "Live: Chicago mayor speaks on rising violence, Trump's threat to send federal troops," FOX News, https://www.youtube.com/watch?v=h4dKPTD1vBs.

like the overturning of Roe VS Wade and some other programs with ultrasounds and counseling which encourage enduring a pregnancy to full term, maybe they would have reached zero population growth because there would probably have not been so many abortions. If it had been up to Conservatives, second- and third-wave feminism and the #MeToo movement would never have happened. If Conservatives had had more influence, more black kids would have had both a mother and a father in the home, and there would be a patriarchy in a lot more black family settings. If Conservatives, who are more likely to be on the right, had had more influence, there would have been more marriages and in general a less destabilized black community, especially in certain pockets of the black community.

3.

Why the Black Community for Socialists?

Another reason why the socialists, who were a part of the far left, chose to use the black community as a strategic move is because black people were at some disadvantages in America up until this time in history from previous injustices until this point, and now from leftist policies and causes that were created later, so they were a weak spot in America. If you are an enemy, and you want to take an opponent out that is stronger than you, if you can attack him in a weak spot where he is most vulnerable, that is a smart approach to take. It is sensible to think at least sometimes from the looks of things that leftists and, to an extent now, Progressive Liberals are after America.

At the time when the socialists came on the scene like they did in the 1960s or maybe even the 1950s during the civil rights movement, blacks were the largest ethnic group that they could use to make changes. Native Americans, Hispanics, and Asians were other groups they also used. Native Americans were such a small group, too small to influence and really make the changes they wanted to see in society. Now that Hispanics are a larger demographic in America than blacks, they can use them to accomplish their goals, which will be discussed briefly later in the book.

During slavery which started at the beginning of the colonial period and continued until the end of the Civil War, which was about 200 to 250 years, most blacks either lived and worked on plantations as slaves or in some other form of servitude. Some northern blacks were free before the war. In a setting like that, the slave master, the mistress, and their family lived in what seemed like lavish wealth. To the slaves, their owners were treated like royalty, and the slaves themselves were just mere vassals or subjects whom they could treat however they wished. If owners' demands, whether reasonable or unreasonable, were not met by the slaves, they could be severely punished under this brutal, oppressive regime. To the slaves, it was obvious that one of the reasons for the slave owners' posh extravagant lifestyles and the misery that they lived in was because of their wealth and the slaves' lack of it, but a slave did not dare protest or question this fact. Socialists knew this. Wealth means power, so if the socialist could use black people's struggles and past hurts to redistribute some of it, why not do it, if it will help them get closer to one of their causes, which is enlarging their footprint in America. How negatively it affects blacks is not important, even if it means their destruction as a people.

Before the civil rights movement era, the parents and grandparents of blacks had witnessed lynchings, and even if they had not witnessed one, they had walked up on the dead bodies in the woods all hacked up and burned or they had been told about them. The brutal beatings and raping of innocent little black girls and women had already caused them to be intimidated and fearful of authority, as the Ku Klux Klan enforced the regime of white supremacy in the South. All the other pre civil rights era injustices like Jim Crow, Sundown Towns, Black Code Laws, etc. made it easier for them to convince blacks to trust them vs whites generally had a much better lot in society in many cases.

Why the Black Community for Socialists?

If socialists could not use mindsets imparted as a result of events like this to advance their cause, they could certainly use it to convince black people that there was something better than what they had been experiencing in America up until that time in history or that anything else was better for that matter. Thus was their argument to certain black influentials and intellectuals: Why not give socialism a try?

It was like this kind of brutality during slavery and for a time afterward for blacks, especially in the Deep South in places where peonage[259] was practiced because in these places, lynchings were commonplace if you did certain things. The practice of peonage, which was really slavery under another name, did not really end until the 1940s.[260] To many blacks, if they did certain things, it almost guaranteed someone was going to be lynched, even some of the innocent. Lynchings were as gruesome as public executions. So black people, at least the older ones, who were running things were raised by their parents and grandparents and had such a mindset.[261] Up until this point, this regime left so many scars and wounds in the minds of the black community that it affected its style to be functional in relationship with the rest of America[262] and the rest of society.[263] It even affected the individual's perception of him or

---

[259] Pete Daniel, "Slavery by Another Name. Slavery vs. Peonage," retrieved May 18, 2019, https://www.pbs.org/tpt/slavery-by-another-name/themes/peonage/.

[260] Ibid.

[261] Hicks, Shari Renee, "Dr. Joy Druy, A critical analysis of post traumatic slave syndrome: A multigenerational legacy of slavery," California Institute of Integral Studies, ProQuest Dissertations Publishing, 2015, 3712420, page 118.

[262] Ibid., page 136.

[263] Ibid., page 53.

herself in a negative way.[264] Maybe that is still the case today,[265] and the socialists realized this, so they intended to use it for their agenda.

The socialists were right about the grim realities and the horrible legacy of American slavery under its capitalistic system and all of the terrible injustices that followed afterward to blacks, also under its capitalistic system, and about how most of the indigenous people of the Americas were nearly exterminated and the remaining ones placed on reservations as a result of Western colonialism and how large portions of Texas and Oklahoma were stolen from Mexico through the Battle of the Alamo, but what they failed to admit is the horrible legacy of all of the world's largest socialist / communist regimes such as the former USSR,[266, 267] China,[268] Cambodia,[269] North Korea,[270] and many of Europe's Eastern Bloc nations[271] that held political prisoners in slave labor camps by the millions often for years[272] and sometimes for life.[273] Millions also died under these regimes.[274] This does not convince me that socialism or communism is any better than capitalism and a free-market economy in a

---

[264] Ibid., page 53.

[265] Ibid., page 53.

[266] YuriI N. Maltsev, "Mass Murder and Public Slavery, The Soviet Experience," retrieved July 5, 2020, https://www.independent.org/pdf/tir/tir_22_2_04_maltsev.pdf.

[267] R.J. Rummel, "How Many Did Communist Regimes Murder?" Retrieved Sept. 26, 2020, https://hawaii.edu/powerkills/COM.ART.HTM#*.

[268] Ibid.

[269] Ibid.

[270] Ibid.

[271] Ibid.

[272] Ibid.

[273] Ibid.

[274] Ibid.

Why the Black Community for Socialists?

constitutional republic with small government and lower taxes. Most of this happened before the civil rights movement, so the socialists knew about this. If this is the case, then why should they care about blacks in America becoming slaves again once they accomplish their agenda?

In fact, black people probably didn't even know that some of these people were socialists and that some were communists and what they were up to in the black community. The black community had a certain desperation to get out of the circumstances that they were in after being in them for so long, so just any old body who was willing to come to the rescue would do as long as they can get them out of it.

The NAACP is an organization that has been an icon of Civil Rights for the black community for years. According to an article from the University of Mississippi "eGrove" written and presented before the 55th Annual Convention of Peace Officers Weld in Atlanta GA in 1956[275], written by the Association of Citizens Council in Winona Mississippi[276] stated the idea of the NAACP originated in New York City as the brainchild of a Southern "ScallaWag" journalist and Russian-trained revolutionary, prominent socialist and descendent of a wealthy Kentucky slave owning family William E. Walling[277]. Also, according to the article that I got this information from: Its principal personalities during its early years were descendants of the rabble-rousing abolitionists who fomented the strife which precipitated the War Between the States[278], a conflict which

---

[275] Eugene Cook The Ugly Truth About the NAACP 1-1-1900 Pamphlets and Broadsides University of Mississippi eGrove retrieved January 7, 2024 https://egrove.olemiss.edu/cgi/viewcontent.cgi?article=1078&context=citizens_pamph

[276] Ibid

[277] Ibid

[278] Ibid

could have been avoided but for the activities of those abolitionists[279]. I think it would have been better if the war could have just been avoided resulting in the end of slavery by some more peaceful means like arrests, fines, jailtime, imprisonments of slaveowners, slave traders and any collaborators to the cause or maybe even boycotts of southern cotton products or through other legal means and laws but, I have no problem with them stirring up the conflict known as the American Civil War that eventually resulted in the 13th, 14th, and 15th Amendments of the constitution and the end of slavery, if it was necessary to accomplish slaveries end. The problem I have with this man and his backers is that they were all Russian Communists, and they had no interest in the betterment of the Negro race or America.[280]

I think their amie in starting the war was to destroy the country altogether. According to the same article the racial amies of the Communist Party of the United States and the NAACP are virtually identical.[281] Considering prior treatment of blacks in America especially before the NAACP's inception this should seem like a good thing for blacks. Since they along with the socialists have been brothers in arms or partners in crime depending on the circumstances in the fight to destroy America, you have to ask yourself do either have the best interest of the black community or America at heart? Because their racial amies for both races are the same doesn't mean they have black people's best interest at heart either but at the time I think it seemed like a better plan to black leadership to become a part of the greater American society than the plans of segregation and inferior places in society at any cost that a lot of other

---

[279] Ibid

[280] Ibid

[281] Ibid

Why the Black Community for Socialists?

traditionalists about race had. This I will have to credit progressives with. So why would the NAACP's bottom line for existing be in the best interest of the black community? The NAACP is not the only organization founded and probably funded by these white progressives that were not totally for the Negro with his interest at heart.

The Black Panther Party, founded by two pro-socialist college students in Oakland, California,[282] also had a goal to radically establish socialism through mass organizing and its community-based programs.[283] Malcom X of the Nation of Islam believed in some similar revolutionary strategies that the Black Panthers did.[284] Through these two organizations, they could really use Maoist, socialist, and even Marxist revolutionary tactics to accomplish an agenda[285] through the black community. But is this really in the best interest of black Americans or the leftists? In a free-market economy with capitalism, if you practice group economics and gain ownership and control of enough and you establish a code of conduct around like-minded people, you don't need mass organizing and community-based programs. I will explain group economics in more detail later on in the book.

The founders and propagators and some key officials throughout Marxism's existence, which has a very left-leaning agenda, were very racist,[286] but with political correctness and renaming things

---

[282] "The Black Panther Party National Archives," African American History, retrieved August 13, 2020, https://www.archives.gov/research/african-americans/black-power/black-panthers.

[283] "MIA: History: USA: The Black Panther Party Guerrilla War In the USA," retrieved August 13, 2020. https://www.marxists.org/history/usa/workers/black-panthers/.

[284] Ibid.

[285] Ibid.

[286] Marian L. Tupy, November 14, 2017, "FEE Stories. Anti-Racists Should Think Twice about Allying with Socialism Economics," retrieved December 21, 2021, https://fee.org/articles/anti-racists-should-think-twice-about-allying-with-socialism/.

differently, it is very difficult to detect. If it had been up to Conservatives, especially ultraconservative whites who are on the Right, this school of thought would never have happened.

Even in 1901 the socialist party had right-wing members that denounced social equality for black Americans and supported segregation,[287] while at the same time it had left-wing members who fought against black disenfranchisement and segregation.[288] This volatility disenchanted many, causing black socialists to leave and further contributing to the dissolution of the Socialist Party.[289] This was typical of the right wing, who tended to be Republican and the left-wing Democrats today, of who a great deal are probably socialist or communists. Today the socialist party almost certainly has no right-wing members. Today the right and the left stand for some different things.

Many of the black communities most effective organizers and grassroots theorists held to a political vision of what may be called socialism[290]. These grassroots organizers tremendously affected the political process of a lot of the black communities' politicians, and it has advanced to socialist cause a lot. This was the reason for Progressives being more tolerant with the black community.

---

[287] Sarah Pruitt Updated November 4, 2020, Original: October 22, 2019, "History: How Are Socialism and Communism Different?" Retrieved June 4, 2023, https://www.history.com/news/socialism-communism-differences.

[288] Ibid.

[289] Ibid.

[290] Rev. Andrew J. Wilkes, January 18, 2016, "Democrat socialist of America Democrat Left Socialism in Black America," retrieved June 20, 2023, https://www.dsausa.org/democratic-left/socialism_in_black_america_dl/.

Why the Black Community for Socialists?

Karl Marx and Che Guevara, who are both heroes of progressive leftist ideology, were both racist against blacks[291]. Marx, however, supported the Union during the Civil War because of its antislavery logic.[292] This was clearly because he and the Marxists (whose philosophies have both differences and similarities with the socialists) wanted something from blacks, not because they liked black people, so I question whether they do now.

What does the Socialist Party have in stake for black America is the question?

---

[291] Walter E. Williams, Syndicated Columnist, August 16, 2020, "Walter E. Williams: Did you know that Karl Marx was a racist and an anti-Semite?" *Panama City New Herald* Retrieved June 13, 2023, https://www.newsherald.com/story/opinion/2020/08/16/many-marxists-dont-realize-their-hero-racist-and-anti-semite/3369024001/.

[292] Charles R. Holm, University of Nebraska-Lincoln Department of History "Lincoln Black Radicals and Marxist Internationalism: From the IWMA to the Fourth International, 1864–1948."

4.

Public Housing

First before I get started on this topic, I wanted to make one thing clear most black Americans do not aspire to live in public housing. Unfortunately, they disproportionately have had no choice but to choose it due to the circumstances that they were in or maybe I will just say it was a better option for some. According to the US Department of Housing and Urban Development Office of Policy Development and Research, forty-eight percent of public housing households are black compared to only 19 percent of all renter households.[293] Taking income into account does not alter this conclusion, since only 30 percent of households with incomes low enough to qualify for public housing are black. Hispanic households are represented in public housing at a rate comparable to their share of renter households (10 percent versus 11 percent).[294] Non-Hispanic white households occupy 39 percent of public housing, considerably less than their share of the total renter population (66

---

[293] Public Housing Image VS Fact US Housing Market Conditions and Summary US Department of Housing and Urban Development Office of Policy Development and Research retrieved December 30, 2023 https://www.huduser.gov/periodicals/ushmc/spring95/spring95.html#:~:text=Forty%2Deight%20percent%20of%20public,percent%20of%20all%20renter%20households.&text=Taking%20income%20into%20account%20does,for%20public%20housing%20are%20black

[294] Ibid

percent).²⁹⁵ According to the same article Public housing tenants are very poor²⁹⁶ and in 1991 the average in come for its recipients was substantially less than the national poverty level for a family of three.²⁹⁷ The article was from 1995. From a 2012 article it remained largely unchanged with 45% of its residents being black, 32% being white and 20% being Hispanic.²⁹⁸ In 2022 African Americans still occupied 48% of public housing units despite being only 13% of the country's population²⁹⁹, virtually unchanged from 1995 and 2012. The author of the article claims subsidized housing planned by progressives includes policies that date back to the 1930's to present have been harmful to African Americans.³⁰⁰

After the black community had been destabilized more than any other ethnic enclave in America from the feminist movement and with no economic infrastructure as a result of integration (which I will explain in more detail later on), the socialists can just recruit a disproportionately higher number of people for all of their government-sponsored programs such as WIC, SSI, Section 8 housing, food stamps, and several other government programs, which have

---

[295] Ibid

[296] Ibid

[297] Ibid

[298] Housing Spotlight National Low Income Housing Commission Volume 2 Issues 2 of 2012 Who Lives In Federally Assisted Housing? Characteristics of Households Assisted by HUD programs retrieved December 30, 2023 https://nlihc.org/sites/default/files/HousingSpotlight2-2.pdf

[299] Howard Husock How Progressives' Grand Plans for Subsidized Housing Have Harmed African Americans FoxNews.com November 27, 2022 retrieved December 30, 2023 https://www.aei.org/op-eds/how-progressives-grand-plans-for-subsidized-housing-have-harmed-african-americans/#:~:text=Today%2C%20even%20as%20African%20Americans,of%20public%20and%20subsidized%20housing

[300] Ibid

done nothing but give control and influence of the black community over to the government.

YouTube did a special on public housing called *Crisis on Federal Street* about the high-rise government-sponsored housing in Chicago.[301] It was an example of what happens when government projects to end poverty grow more numerous and more generous but don't end poverty.[302] It fostered high school dropouts and teen pregnancies, and its job programs that supposedly were to foster employment seemed to create less of it.[303] The program was the story of one family of three generations that was typical of many others on government assistance.[304] It was described as a dangerous and frightening trap.[305] It was described as a lot of people living on top of one another with lots of chaos.[306] This is what happens when the government sponsors this type of housing that has some resemblance to the communist bloc housing of some Socialist countries. This is an example of a pocket in society where blacks are disproportionately more likely to be, but it expanded the government's footprint of dependency and a necessity to redistribute more wealth to programs like this. An official admitted it was an unofficial attempt by the city of Chicago to constrain the black

---

[301] Hadding Carter, 1982 "Crisis On Federal Street (1987)," PBS Documentary on the failed Chicago Housing Projects Cabrini Green, Columbia Pictures Television Unit of the Coca Cola Company Public Broadcasting System WTTW Chicago, viewed July 20, 2020, https://dailyblocks.tv/r/Documentaries/comments/e17j5x/crisis_on_federal_street_1987_pbs_documentary_on/.

[302] Ibid., 4 mins. and 54 secs

[303] Ibid., 5 mins. and 25 secs.

[304] Ibid., 5 mins. and 59 secs.

[305] Ibid., 8 mins. and 19 secs.

[306] Ibid., 11 mins. and 30 secs.

population in as small of a place as possible.[307] This program had over a billion dollars invested in it.[308] I could go on, but I will stop here. The Cabrini Green housing project, which was torn down between 1995 and 2011,[309]. Its last residents were moved out in 2010.[310] The CBS special was aired in 1987, but you have to ask yourself if things have changed much since then. Yes, some things have, but the same basic scenario or picture hasn't. All this was done at no interest to the black community. That does not mean that government is bad, because it is not; government is good for society and for communities but not when it tries to provide too much and mandate too much on society.

What I am about to explain does not apply to all black families, just some pockets in black America, and they are probably the worst places to be in the black community, but if you are black, you are more likely to be in one of these settings than people of other ethnic backgrounds. Remember, this was in 1986, so even statistics have changed since then, but some general things have not. An official on the documentary *Crisis in Black America: The Vanishing Black Family* stated the black family was destroying itself due to lack of motivation or role models from both parents in the home.[311] In this movie, a panel of young women raising children on their own

---

[307] Ibid., 14 mins. and 55 secs.

[308] Ibid., 13 mins. and 40 secs.

[309] Maya Dukmasova, November 16, 2015, "Documenting the Rise and Fall of Chicago's Cabrini-Green Public Housing Projects," retrieved September 4, 2020, https://inthesetimes.com/article/70-acres-cabrini-green-documentary-chicago-housing.

[310] Ibid.

[311] Ruth Streeter, Perry Wolf, edited by Bill Moyers, 1986 "The Vanishing Black Family Crisis in Black America: Special Report," retrieved September 6, 2020, https://www.youtube.com/watch?v=_vrw416MnJ8; and Walter J Brown Media Archives University of Georgia https://kaltura.uga.edu/media/t/1_ei7uc6rp (3 mins. and 25 secs.).

stated they did not need a man to help them raise their children, and male role models are not significant or necessary to them.[312] Then black teens had the highest pregnancy rate of the industrial world.[313] The setting of the show was in Newark, New Jersey.[314] One of the women admitted that welfare makes you lazy because you sit around and wait for a check.[315]

Police Officer Shahid Jackson of the Newark Police stated that some people needed welfare, and some take advantage of it.[316] He stated that since the government provides food stamps and medical care from Medicaid, a lot of the women were married to it,[317] so they don't need a husband, and the backbone of the family is coming from downtown or uptown offices,[318] so the man in the bed next to the women is just a physical thing.[319] It is obvious that it is providing them with cheap government houses since they get generous Section 8 vouchers to pay for most of the rent, and they only have to pay for some of it through money from a job. When asked by the reporter, "What do you think this cycle of dependency is doing to these kids' values?" he stated it makes them feel that someone owes them something[320] or that that someone will take care of them; it

---

[312] Ibid., (18 mins. 18 secs.) Part 1.

[313] Ibid., (16 mins. 22 secs.) Part 1.

[314] Ibid., (2 mins. 55 secs.) Part 1.

[315] Ibid., (25 mins. 40 secs.) Part 1.

[316] Ibid., (7 mins. 35 secs.) Part 2.

[317] Ibid., (8 mins. 5 secs.) Part 2.

[318] Ibid., (8 mins. 30 secs.) Part 2.

[319] Ibid., (8 mins. 35 secs.) part2.

[320] Ibid., (8 mins. 40 secs.) Part 2.

is a game that lowers self-esteem.[321] He said it is like being born into a dead end.[322]

When black Professor Dr. George Jackson, from Howard University, then a practicing psychiatrist, was interviewed about what happens with the breakdown of the family, he said he sees children raised by children, not being able to manage their feelings, so they want what they want when they want it.[323] He said a society was being bred that is destroying itself.[324] He said eventually if it affects one subpopulation in society, it will affect the whole society,[325] so you can run to the suburbs for a while, but you can't hide.[326] It will affect the black community first, but then it will affect the rest of America negatively.[327]

Caroline Wallis, another official that was interviewed earlier, who with her husband James Wallis founded the International Youth Organization, stated that a lot of black men were hanging out on corners doing nothing, and they had just given up.[328] She said there are no jobs for them, and society has made living without a man easy.[329] She stated that welfare provides these people with an income or something that you can just settle for.[330] When asked about teen pregnancies, she stated that to change that, you needed a change in morals,

---

[321] Ibid., (8 mins. 45 secs.) Part 2.

[322] Ibid., (9 mins. 6 secs.) Part 2.

[323] Ibid., (11 mins. 24 secs.).

[324] Ibid., (13 mins. 14 secs.).

[325] Ibid., (13 mins. 45 secs.).

[326] Ibid., (14 mins. 5 secs.).

[327] Ibid., (15 mins. 35 secs.).

[328] Ibid., (16 mins. 25 secs.).

[329] Ibid., (16 mins. 45 secs.).

[330] Ibid., (16 mins. 55 secs.).

and they come from God.[331] When asked about civil rights and Dr. King's movement, she said that some of the youth don't know what that means. The interviewer asked why can't the US government, the state government of New Jersey, and a white man like him and other whites talk about this,[332] and the interviewer, who was black, stated that someone needs to talk about it, so if we all talk about, it will become like a drumbeat.[333] A panel of black officials were questioned, and among then was Eleanor Homes Norton and Rev. Jesse Jackson, who talked about the terrible influences that mass media had on youth. Many of the other officials discussed problems, many of which were the same ones that were discussed by officials in the documentary, but they found no real solutions that worked. All this is a result of leftist progressive liberal policies over the past 50 years, and it is probably not much different now than it was in the 1980s, when these two documentaries were made.

The physical isolation of the buildings services to perpetuate both the psychological and behavioral problems, says Dr. Gail Crystal.[334] She said many did not really have the resources or the energy to venture outside of the community itself.[335] They don't realize there is something different out there, so this takes away from their ability to achieve goals and to dream.[336] So why wouldn't this and every other

---

[331] Ibid., (18 mins. 8 secs.).

[332] Ibid., (19 mins. 30 secs.).

[333] Ibid., (20 mins. 44 secs.).

[334] Hadding Carter, 1982, "Crisis On Federal Street (1987)," PBS Documentary on the failed Chicago Housing Projects Cabrini Green Columbia Pictures Television Unit of the Coca Cola Company Public Broadcasting System WTTW Chicago, viewed July 20, 2020, (17 mins. and 42 secs.), https://dailyblocks.tv/r/Documentaries/comments/e17j5x/crisis_on_federal_street_1987_pbs_documentary_on/.

[335] Ibid., (17 mins. and 52 secs.).

[336] Ibid., (18 mins. and 5 secs.).

scenario explained in the section of the article be the case in many other really bad neighborhoods across America today.

The story about the experience that the young lady from Grenada had with some of the residents of her old neighborhood in Brooklyn, New York, is another example of a mentality that has developed or fostered in an environment that is provided in these public housing setups. This does not mean that everyone living in public housing has an attitude about life like this.

Even though I could not find good strong links between the creation and flourishing of the welfare state with socialists or that it was started specifically by them, as you can see from the documentary and maybe even one or two examples from *Crisis on Federal Street* from the interviews with testimonies from people who have been raised in a society where lots of people are on it, and some of the more high profile officials with mentorships and programs to help people get out of the cycle of being on it, it does increase your dependency on a government-subsidized program—and expanding government and dependency on it is one of socialists' main goals. If it had been up to the right, who were more likely to be Conservative, public housing would not have happened, and if it had, it would not have ever been the monstrosity that it has become. Socialists were able to use the black community disproportionately more to accomplish this goal than with any other community since the black community was a weaker, more vulnerable one than most other communities in America. This is another place where government dependency and control could be expanded to the tune of billions of dollars by government contracts to build housing, for Section 8 vouchers, and so forth with the black community being used disproportionately for it.

5.

Rethinking Integration

I am not saying integration was wrong, I am just saying let's rethink it. I know some are going to disagree with me on some of what I am trying to say, some will agree with some of what I am trying to say, and some are going to miss my point altogether.

Integration was more of a cause than a policy that had both pros and cons for black America. One of the pros is some institutions that were created and owned and controlled by whites provided opportunities for blacks to participate in projects and endeavors and things and fulfill dreams that maybe a smaller community did not have the resources for or the need to provide, an example being an engineer, architect, electrician, carpenter, or bricklayer in the construction of one of the World Trade Centers or maybe a construction project like the Hoover Dam, the Willis Tower in Chicago or an interstate highway complete with bridges, underpasses, and tunnels and all other construction challenges involved in its construction that go from coast to coast, which was a big plus to integration. I will even go out on a limb and say that affirmative action programs even played a role in making this happen, but I will discuss affirmative action later on. Of course, there were other things that blacks benefited from as a result of both. Another pro was that whites and blacks were in a better position to talk with one another and discover our differences and similarities, our likes and dislikes, our interests, dreams, and so forth, and we discovered that we had a lot more in common with one another than we thought, and this I think changed some biases we may have had with one another or at least we can tolerate one another more. The cons of it were really bad, which I will be explaining to you in more detail in this section.

Integration on Progressives' terms was a terrible leftist cause for the black community in the context of what it was intended to achieve and some of its outcomes for blacks, not because it was a bad thing to do. Before this policy, there were some up-and-coming black communities that had enough small business and institutions to provide some employment, like the Greenwood District of Tulsa, Oklahoma, before it was burned to the ground by Klansmen and Klan sympathizers and several others like it across America, but these districts failed according to an article from the Atlanta Black Star for five reasons related to integration.[337] All five of the points they made I discussed in one way or another in this book.[338] In 1920, Oklahoma only had roughly 2,050,000 people,[339] so in today's percentages, if half were adult females and 24.7 percent children less than eighteen years of age,[340] that only leaves about 26 percent as adult males if you do the math. It was believed that the

---

[337] Atlanta Black Star, December 9, 2013, "5 Ways Integration Underdeveloped Black America," retrieved May 2, 2019, https://atlantaBlackstar.com/2013/12/09/5-ways-integration-underdeveloped-black-america.

[338] Ibid

[339] University of Tulsa McFarlin Library, "Composition and Characteristics of the Oklahoma Population, 1920 Census," retrieved May 3, 2019, http://www.lib.utulsa.edu/govdocs/census/1920/composition.htm.

[340] "Percentage of population under 18 years in the United States in 2017, sorted by state,". May 3, 2019, https://www.statista.com/statistics/306623/percentage-of-population-under-18-years-in-the-us-by-state-and.

Sooner State had over 100,000 Klansmen at the time[341] out of an adult male population of just over half a million; that's about one in five. If the Negro population was counted in the total, then less than a fourth were white males when you consider no Negros or women were Klansmen. By now, these communities would have had a lot more employment for the black community, and they would have just sprung up all over America. At the time, black money was exchanging hands in the black community in Tulsa between 36 and 100 times before leaving, which created an economic engine for jobs, wealth, and prosperity, but thanks to leftist policies and causes for integration and diversity, it may never happen again.

More than 95 percent of black businesses are sole proprietorships, which have no paid employees.[342] They only create one million jobs, which is enough to employ only 4 percent of the black workforce.[343] If their annual revenues were distributed equally throughout the black community to every working-age adult, they would not generate nearly enough to raise the black community above the poverty line.[344] Of all of the Black-owned businesses in 2012, only 2.2 percent more of them had paid employees from five years prior. These employees only employed 5.9 percent of the black population, and their payrolls only increased just under 16

---

[341] Scott Ellsworth, May 3, 2019, "Tulsa Race Riot: A Report by the Oklahoma Commission to Study the Tulsa Race Riot of 1921 Ku Klux Klan and related social organizations," Page 56, https://pages.uoregon.edu/kimball/1921-Tulsa.race.riot.htm#KuKlux.

[342] "The African American Population," retrieved April 23, 2019, https://blackdemographics.com/economics/black-owned-businesses.

[343] Ibid.

[344] Ibid.

percent.[345] According to another study from a CNBC news report, only 2.2 percent of Black-owned firms today have paid employees.[346]

A dollar spends considerably longer when circulating (exchanging hands) in the Asian community than any other community in America,[347] followed by the Jewish community, where money circulates in considerably less time,[348] followed by the rest of the white community where it circulates a couple of days less,[349] and finally is the Hispanic community, where it circulates for a considerably shorter time in days than the white community.[350] Last but not least, money only stays in the black community for a few hours before it is gone to the hands of someone else of another race or ethnic background. Very little money made by Blacks is spent in their own community.[351] Blacks have nearly $1 trillion gross national income, but only 2 percent is reinvested into black communities.[352]

That is partially because all of the other ethnic backgrounds did not make so much of an effort to completely integrate every element of their community with whites that they lost so much of their cultural and social identities, and they have not been destabilized so

---

[345] "The African American Population. From 2017 business data," retrieved April 23, 2019, https://blackdemographics.com/economics/black-owned-businesses.

[346] #CNBC, February 3, 2021, "Why Black-Owned Businesses Don't Survive," retrieved February 8, 2021, https://www.youtube.com/watch?v=MV4Nq1GaIAA (7 mins. 13 secs.).

[347] Randi Bryant, "Blackout: Why Don't Black People Support Black Businesses?" Retrieved May 3, 2019, http://whatsup.blackandsexy.tv/blackout-why-dont-black-people-support-black-businesses/.

[348] Ibid.

[349] Ibid.

[350] Ibid.

[351] Ibid.

[352] Greenwood, January 25, 2021, "How Dollars Circulate in Black Communities" retrieved June 18, 2023, https://gogreenwood.com/how-dollars-circulate-in-black-communities/.

much as a group by the feminist movement because of integration, which were both leftist progressive causes. If you spend billions of dollars like that in everyone else's community, sure they will be nice to you, but that does not help your community any; actually, it is a factor that will keep your community poor. A study found that a lot of jobs would be created if more successful Blacks spent 10 percent of the money with black businesses.[353] Another advantage that other ethnic backgrounds have over Blacks is that their money stays in their community for longer. A dollar according to a new source circulates one time in the African American community, six times in the Hispanic community, and nine times in the Asian community,[354] in comparison to it staying 20 days in a Jewish community and 30 days in an Asian community.[355] According to the same article, money circulates in white neighborhoods, an unlimited number of times[356] and about six times in Latino communities, but only once in black communities.[357]

The reason why integration or complete integration with whites was bad is because Blacks were under the impression that they could abandon the businesses in their community and spend billions of dollars annually at white-owned institutions, but whites did not spend billions of their dollars at Black-owned businesses. With 2.6

---

[353] Randi Bryant, "Blackout: Why Don't Black People Support Black Businesses?" Retrieved May 3, 2019, http://whatsup.blackandsexy.tv/blackout-why-dont-black-people-support-black-businesses/.

[354] Ibid.

[355] Greenwood, January 25, 2021, "How Dollars Circulate in Black Communities," retrieved June 18, 2023, https://gogreenwood.com/how-dollars-circulate-in-black-communities/.

[356] Ibid.

[357] Ibid.

million black businesses,[358] most whites don't spend a penny at any Black-owned businesses, even though they have plenty of choices of black institutions that they could patronize. The same with Asian and Arab and now maybe some Hispanic-owned businesses, and most of them don't spend a penny at Black-owned businesses. Some do, but not very many or not enough to make a big difference anyway. Instead, they keep their money in their own communities, and by doing so, they preserve the economic health of their communities. You can't really blame them because that is what all other ethnic backgrounds do. Since most of the customers for black businesses were from the black community, they lost all of their customer base, and the white businesses gained the customers from the black businesses—and it has been that way now for years. This resulted in black communities with very few if any Black-owned businesses that employ three or more people.

Therefore, black people are dependent on a small business or large corporation in the white community or the government for all of their employment unless they own their own sole proprietorship or partnership business. In other words, this resulted in an economic collapse of the previous segregation era up-and-coming economic infrastructure that was being created in the black community up to that point, and it has never been recovered. This was actually a benefit to other communities that have shops and stores in the black community as well as miles away from the black community where African Americans spend lots of their money. Whites, however, both Liberal and Conservative, preserved the economic health of their communities, but blacks didn't, thanks to this leftist cause. You cannot really blame whites for this because this is what

---

[358] "Black Demographics: The African American Population," retrieved September 26, 2020, https://blackdemographics.com/economics/black-owned-businesses/.

all other ethnic backgrounds do; they live, work, and spend a lot more of their money in places where the people are most like them, doing all of the above. Black people do some of the above but not all of the above.

As a result, unless you have a sole proprietorship or a partnership venture with someone, the black community is a totally dependent community on government benefits, government jobs, or jobs by people of another race or ethnic background for employment and/or their income. The black community really has nothing for you as far as employment is concerned. No other ethnic background in America is as dependent as the black community on resources outside of its community. No progressive policies are restoring economic stability of the black community.

I think mainstream white America's mentality on integration was why should we have to change or even make any adjustments in some cases for Blacks because we are mainstream America, and everyone integrating into America should be more like us at a minimum, if not a mirror image of us. The mentality among blacks with integration was, we need to change and become more like whites, but we could not really do that, and nothing has taken a natural course to make that happen because blacks come from such a different background from mainstream white America.

The reason why I say this is because when the first generations of whites immigrated to the United States mostly Irish, German, and Anglo-Saxon[359] and later Italian and eastern European and others first-generation immigrants who did not speak English or were not familiar with the need-to-know aspects of American culture tended to segregate themselves more often into separate communities or

---

[359] John R. Logan and Weiwei Zhang, "White Ethnic Residential Segregation in Historical Perspective: U.S. Cities in 1880," Pub Med Central retrieved May 16, 2023, https://www.ncbi.nlm.nih.gov/pmc/articles/PMC3813960/.

ethnic enclaves[360] with various stereotypes and bickering among different ethnicities with as much assimilation with the rest of America as possible[361]. This happened in large cities, in small towns, and in rural areas.[362] Their children the second generation who were born in America are culturally American, but they still have an affinity or maybe even an affection for the old neighborhoods that their parents came from and the culture that existed there even though they are a lot more and, in many cases, totally assimilated into American society[363]. Their grandchildren and great-grandchildren, who are now two or three generations and in some cases more removed from the country of origin of some of their grandparents, are totally American, and now the countries and customs of their countries are really foreign.[364] At this point all the descendants of the Europeans that immigrated to America are placed under one big umbrella identity as whites. Blacks have been placed under that same umbrella as Americans, but their racial classification in theory has still not gone away, but it still matters, and you can see that from what has been discussed in this book until this point and from what will be discussed throughout the entirety of it. Does it matter for whites? Yes, but for some different reasons than for Blacks, and now the progressive left can use these differences to their advantage to advance the causes by keeping everyone as divided as possible.

---

[360] Ibid.

[361] Ibid.

[362] Katherine Eriksson Zachary A. Ward, "The Ethnic Segregation of Immigrants in the United States from 1850 to 1940," NBER Working Paper Series, National Bureau of Economic Research, retrieved January 11, 2023, http://www.nber.org/papers/w24764.

[363] John R. Logan and Weiwei Zhang, "White Ethnic Residential Segregation in Historical Perspective: U.S. Cities in 1880," Pub Med Central, retrieved May 16, 2023, https://www.ncbi.nlm.nih.gov/pmc/articles/PMC3813960/.

[364] Ibid.

Progressives, Leftists, and Black America

The Progressive Liberals convinced the black community that everybody was one big happy family, and that race didn't matter, at least as much anymore, so you could just spend your money anywhere, and anyone would patronize you and your business regardless of race, but this is not what happened. Another thing that happened after integration was that unemployment for black men skyrocketed.[365] I will discuss unemployment later on.

African Americans were under the impression that as Americans, regardless of your race, ethnic background, or color, we were all a part of the big American melting pot, and it didn't matter where you lived, worked, or played. Maybe some things still did or do matter like where you spend your money. Or another question we might want to ask is: Are we really a melting pot? That is not to say that blacks should have completely separated themselves from American society and become a totally dependent but isolated community from the rest of America; that is actually unrealistic. I still think black Americans should be a part of America, and again I am fine with integration as long as all factors are set up to ensure the same success to blacks as whites. A black nationalist may think that blacks should separate from America, but America has a lot to offer the black community as it is. American first and black second is my preference.

In order for black people to be integrated with whites and to have a fair shot at competing with whites on every level of society, they would have to have ownership and control over enough of America's wealth, its commerce, its businesses. Without that, you could be competitive on some levels but not all. Having a fully

---

[365] ABS Contributor, December 9, 2013, "5 Ways Integration Underdeveloped Black America," *The Atlanta Black Star*, retrieved March 31, 2022, https://atlantablackstar.com/2013/12/09/5-ways-integration-underdeveloped-black-america/3/.

Rethinking Integration

integrated society does not necessarily guarantee this. This is why I think Booker T. Washington pushed for a strong black business community as a priority first before attempting to integrate into white society for Blacks. The socialists who are on the left that were fostering a lot of integration were about wealth redistribution, not ownership and control of wealth by the people; the control would be by the government. This expands governmental power, authority, and influence, not the people's; it actually takes it from the people, which is one of their major objectives. Not only that, it keeps blacks a weaker, more vulnerable, and dependent group on government so they can be used by socialists, Marxists and communists to shape America like they want it, when they don't really have black people's best interest at heart or the rest of America's either.

According to the website GreatSchools.org, a research study was conducted on student performance by ethnic background and how well they did in various schools across the country. The conclusion to the study indicated that in certain schools, black and Latino children performed very well, but they were very unlikely to attend those schools.[366] In comparison, white and Asian children were a lot more likely to attend schools where they do well and were not nearly as likely to attend schools where they do not do very well.[367] The study only identified 156 of these schools, and they were more likely to be in relatively high-poverty areas.[368, 369] My personal conclusion about this is if any of these schools were all black with black

---

[366] "Searching for Opportunity," Great Schools.org, retrieved November 27, 2019, https://www.greatschools.org/gk/searching-for-opportunity/.

[367] Ibid.

[368] Ibid.

[369] According to ED100 Lesson 2.2, "Poverty and Race How Do Students' Backgrounds Affect Their School Performance? Are poor students . . . poor students?" retrieved November 25, 2019, https://ed100.org/lessons/poverty.

faculty and staff, then why did black children have to integrate with whites for a better education, and why do you need a lot of money or to have it redistributed to provide a better education for students? Gaps in attaining educational success and rising income were narrowing in the '40s, '50s, and '60s, when everything was still very segregated.[370]

The Jim Crow South was often discouraging and hurtful to the black community because it cut them off from the American mainstream with societal restrictions. Out of this isolation and sometimes outright hostile rejection from the mainstream culture, the black community was forced to become entrepreneurial and produce goods and services if it was going to exist on a basic level. This was done by black businesses and entrepreneurs who had no choice but to do it with businesses. Part of this was also from white business's refusal to cater to black patrons.[371] Most black businesses were local, small scale, and family owned. Booker T. Washington, who established the National Businesses League in 1900,[372] did it so that black entrepreneurs could help themselves and their communities economically.[373] He believed the economic influence was the best way to challenge the racial prejudices that were a part of the fabric of the South's development and its creed.[374]

---

[370] Jason L. Riley, January 14, 2019, "Where Are You, Martin Luther King?" Prager U, retrieved October 5, 2020, https://www.manhattan-institute.org/video/prageru-jason-riley-martin-luther-king (1 min. and 25 secs.).

[371] "Black Entrepreneurs during the Jim Crow Era," February 21, 2018, retrieved May 8, 2019, https://www.thehenryford.org/explore/blog/black-entrepreneurs-during-the-jim-crow-era.

[372] Joseph Bernardo, "National Negro Business League (1900–)," BlackPast, retrieved June 20, 2020, https://www.blackpast.org/african-american-history/national-negro-business-league/.

[373] Ibid.

[374] Ibid.

As the civil rights movement gained momentum, Washington's ideas became less admired.[375] Nevertheless, more and more institutions in the black community but especially the Jim Crow South were named after him, proving his relevance to black entrepreneurs.[376] For Washington's plan to work, which I think is a better one than big government, you need to have a free-market economy and capitalism and a constitutional republic, which is where Conservatives and the right generally stand as opposed to Progressive Liberals and the left for big government. Booker T. Washington was born a slave on a plantation[377] in Virginia in 1856, and he had a different experience or a different reality about life than W.E.B. Du Bois, who was born a free man in Massachusetts.[378] Life was a different experience for these two men.

Washington was not a socialist as far as I know, unlike W.E.B. Du Bois, but Washington was willing to trade political power for economic development and staying segregated from whites[379] if they were not going to grant economic equality, justice, and educational opportunity,[380] an idea that W.E.B. Du Bois, a socialist, denounced where he laid out his plan to a group of more conservative whites[381]

---

[375] Ibid.

[376] "Black Entrepreneurs during the Jim Crow Era," February 21, 2018, retrieved May 8, 2019, https://www.thehenryford.org/explore/blog/black-entrepreneurs-during-the-jim-crow-era.

[377] History.com Editors, "Booker T. Washington," updated: Dec. 13, 2019, retrieved January 12, 2021, https://www.history.com/topics/black-history/booker-t-washington.

[378] History.com Editors, February 23, 1868 "W.E.B. Du Bois is born," History.com, retrieved January 12, 2021, https://www.history.com/this-day-in-history/w-e-b-dubois-is-born.

[379] History.com Editors, updated: Dec. 13, 2019, original: Oct. 29, 2009, "Booker T. Washington," retrieved October 11, 2020, https://www.history.com/topics/black-history/booker-t-washington.

[380] Ibid.

[381] Ibid.

called the Atlanta Compromise, insisting on political power and equality as a priority over economic influence.[382] I think there are advantages to having both, but economic power and influence is more important over political power and influence.

The Atlanta Compromise speech where socialist W.E.B. Du Bois wins a very critical debate before some key figures with former slave Booker T. Washington was a pivotal moment in the existence of black America. This one sent the ball rolling differently in some ways for blacks because it fostered the inception of the NAACP. I cannot confirm this, so don't quote me on it, but it wouldn't surprise me if the Atlanta Compromise debate between Washington and Du Bois was arranged by the very people who wanted Du Bois to win the debate with moderators and a panel of people who asked the questions to favor that very outcome. Two others were the signing into law the 13th,14th and 15th Amendments of the Constitution under a mostly Republican congress and a republican President, Abraham Lincoln, and the negotiation and signing into law the Civil Rights Bills of 1964, 1966, and 1967 by Dr. Martin Luther King.

Washington had a surprisingly large amount of support from both northern and southern whites.[383] The article did not make a distinction as to whether they were Liberal, Conservatives, Progressives, Democrats, or Republicans, so I am assuming that they were more or less from all of the groups and all walks of life. He had the support of southern blacks and some but less from northern blacks.[384]

---

[382] Ibid.

[383] "History of Black Education: Washington and DuBois," retrieved October 11, 2020, https://www2.kenyon.edu/Depts/Amerstud/blackhistoryatkenyon/Individual%20Pages/Washington%20and%20DuBois.htm.

[384] Ibid.

Tragically, he died in 1915.[385] Washington's Tuskegee Institute was founded to give the Negro industrial and vocational training to live on and off the farm,[386] which included some 30 trades by the time of his death in 1915.[387]

As an educator and founder of Tuskegee Institute he argued that African Americans must concentrate on educating themselves,[388] learning useful trades,[389] and investing in their own businesses.[390] He believed hard work, economic progress,[391] and merit, would prove to whites the value of blacks to the American economy.[392] To an all-white audience he said, "In all things social we can be as separate as the fingers, yet one as the hand in all things essential to mutual progress." [393]Washington went on to express his confidence that, "No race that has anything to contribute to the markets of the world is long in any degree ostracized."[394] White Americans viewed Washington's vision as the key to racial peace in

---

[385] History.com Editors, updated: Dec. 13, 2019, original: Oct. 29, 2009, "Booker T. Washington," retrieved October 11, 2020, https://www.history.com/topics/black-history/booker-t-washington.

[386] National Park Service ARTICLE Alabama: Tuskegee Institute National Historic Site retrieved https://www.nps.gov/articles/tuskinstitute.htm#:~:text=At%20Tuskegee%2C%20Washington%20used%20his,worked%20on%20farms%20to%20master

[387] Ibid

[388] Teach Democracy formally Constitutional Rights Foundation retrieved December 26, 2022 https://www.crf-usa.org/black-history-month/booker-t-washington#:~:text=Washington%20argued%20that%20African%20Americans,blacks%20to%20the%20American%20economy.

[389] Ibid

[390] Ibid

[391] Ibid

[392] Ibid

[393] Ibid

[394] Ibid

the nation.[395] I am assuming that means liberals and conservatives and whites from all walks of life. If he could have carried out his mission for a longer period of time, I think the black community would have been better off in many ways. His model fits the one of today's Conservative right movement versus the left's move toward socialism.

I don't, however, think everything about the Du Bois model was bad. For Washington's model to work, you needed a free-market economy and capitalism and small government with low taxation, but you have to practice group economics, which is where Conservatives and the right stand.

While surfing the web one day, I saw a simple picture of a Black man with a quote on it from a non-black businessman to him, and it said something simple, but it proves a good point. He basically said the black community was good for economic development because their money never stays in their own community. He was speaking about the transfer of money out of the black community into businesses of others. People of other ethnic backgrounds know this about the black community. They are fine with the status quo like this. It is good for all the Chinese, Korean, Arab, and East Indian shop owners in the black community and the white and Jewish businesses that black people drive miles away from their communities to patronize but bad for the black community because most of these people don't spend a penny of their money at Black-owned businesses. Instead the other communities keep their money in their communities, which generates wealth and prosperity for them.

Integration, which started with the public schools, was a socialist idea and ideology for their agenda. Ever since the black community has attempted to integrate with whites, black wealth

---

[395] Ibid

has left or has been leaving the black community because it has been redistributed to every other community. That is what happens with socialism; you have redistribution of wealth, but it is all redistributed to the government first, and next, they distribute it like they want it distributed. In the case of black wealth, it has been redistributed to the Arab community because they have so many cheap gas stations and grocery stores in black communities. It is being redistributed to the Chinese community because they have so many rice houses and cheap clothing stores in the black community that blacks spend billions of dollars at. It is redistributed to all of the Korean hair, nail, wig, and weave shops in the black community and to every other store and shop that black people shop at for everything else they need, which is usually owned by a white person or a Jew. This includes all of the white-owned chain stores and independently owned mom-and-pop stores. None of the ethnicities are redistributing billions of dollars of money from their communities back into the black business community. This is because in a free-market economy, where capitalism is the predominant economic system and people have the freedom to choose where they want to spend their money, they chose to spend and keep a lot more of it circulating in their own communities, unlike the black community. Not a lot of anyone else's dollars are being distributed back into the black communities' businesses.

You cannot blame this on the left or Progressives; this is what black Americans have chosen to do with so much of their money over so many years. A much higher percentage per capita of black income comes from government institutions than white's.

Capitalism with a free-market economy is not a utopian setup because it has its flaws, but it is a lot more efficient at creating wealth,[396] spreading new ideas, and providing goods and services[397] than one that is controlled by the government in a socialist society, and that is what black people should be trying to take advantage of through group economics. They don't need to leave America. They can still do that now before it is too late.

Black people are only 12 percent of the America population, but 18 percent of government employees are Black.[398] Only 2.1 percent of black small businesses have one or more employees, but 11.7 percent of their contracts are government contracts.[399] According to *BlackExcellist: Top 10 Richest Black Communities* (YouTube video), seven of the wealthiest black communities are in Maryland, which is close to Washington, DC, where a lot of people are dependent on the government for their incomes. So black people are disproportionately more dependent on the government for their income, which is where everybody's income comes from in a socialist state. This redistribution of wealth is because black people were convinced to integrate with everyone, which is what happened with the leftist policy of socialism, which was later adopted by more Progressive Liberals.

School desegregation was a very clever way that socialists worked through the black community to accomplish a cause that was not necessarily in the best interests of the black community. Consider the following. America's schools are more segregated now than ever.

---

[396] Steven Nickolas, updated May 26, 2019, "How Is a Capitalist System Different Than a Free Market System?" Retrieved August 12, 2020, https://www.investopedia.com/ask/answers/042215/what-difference-between-capitalist-system-and-free-market-system.asp.

[397] Ibid.

[398] Anne Branigin, "Black Federal Employees Disproportionately Affected as Government Shutdown Ties for Longest Ever," January 11, 2019, *The Root Magazine*, retrieved June 1, 2019, https://www.theroot.com/black-federal-employees-disproportionately-affected-as-1831672069.

[399] Ibid.

The public schools can be integrated, but to do it you would have to force the state to expand universal public institutions and redistribute wealth.[400] But what the socialists failed to explain to blacks is all of the other injustices and the nightmare scenarios that have happened under socialism in societies that have attempted to redistribute all of their wealth and expand public institutions. Socialists who are a part of the leftist movement had their own special interests with school desegregation, and it was not to provide a better standard of education for black children. If anything, they are saying or at least suggesting that black people are not capable of providing themselves with a first-class education. In order for them to get that, they need to be educated by whites because they are just incapable, inferior black people. Some skeptics will argue that black school districts are not funded enough, or that systemic racism is the problem, but if you think that is the case, YouTube has a long movie called *A National Disgrace* about the failed public school system in Detroit. It talks about an over-funded school district ran entirely by blacks that was over-funded and corrupt with overpaid administrators and with substandard test scores. This had nothing to do with past injustices; the money and resources they had just were not being managed properly by the all-black school board. Failing schools, which is what leftist socialist causes produced indirectly, especially in the black community, is producing more functional illiterates in the black community than in any other community in America, but they accomplished a major goal at the expense of the well-being of the black community.

The *Harvard Educational Review* did a study on black children who attended suburban schools. It was determined according to the

---

[400] Mike Stivers, 2018, "The Socialist Case for School Integration," *Jacobin Magazine*, Education/Race, July 2018 Issue, retrieved June 2, 2019, https://jacobinmag.com/2018/07/the-socialist-case-for-school-integration.

study, which was done on 15 school districts and over 90 schools, that white children in middle-income and upper-middle-income integrated schools outperform their black counterparts significantly. [401] The study took into account factors such as academic disengagement, explanations for black student underperformance, community forces, societal school and system factors, and policy implications and recommendations.[402] Despite all of these considerations, black children still do not generally perform academically as well as their white counterparts, even in integrated schools today.[403] Some of the terminology and the lingua franca, if you will, that is used by white instructors and in textbooks and on standardized test may be culturally biased, but if that is the case, why are black students lagging behind Asian students, some foreign-born immigrants such as East Indians and now Hispanic students across the board in general education standards? So there are some other factors involved in why black children are not performing as good generally in integrated schools. If the same amount of money, time, and teacher school mentoring and contacts were all the same as for the white children, how was having integrated schools any better?

Even today, you can suggest many ways to argue the point, but even after Jim Crow and the passage of both the Civil Rights Act and the Voting Rights Act for blacks, we still have subtle racial biases, which can result in racial oppression. The solution intended largely by socialists for inclusion on a much broader scale with full social and political participation with inclusion in school, at the

---

[401] Dorinda J. Carter, Editor's Review of John U. Ogbu's "Black American Students in an Affluent Suburb: A Study of Academic Disengagement," Winter Issue 2014, retrieved June 20, 2020, https://www.hepg.org/her-home/issues/harvard-educational-review-volume-74-issue-4/herarticle/_38.

[402] Ibid.

[403] Ibid.

voting booth, in the courts of Justice, in society everywhere as consumers, in employment, the workplace, and more was a part of a broader plan.[404] With integration and racially mixed classrooms for years up until just recently white children often scored higher on standardized tests[405], they more often were placed in higher ability groups that black children were. [406] One reason was from a system called racial tracking which started in the early 1900's. and lasted until the pandemic.[407] This separation on ability group often caused resegregation again.[408] Now according to the same article during the pandemic they planned to change the system of racial tracking with detracking,[409] but to do it they had to lower expectations.[410] That is the same way DEI is lowering academic standards to a greater or a lesser extent. According to another report from NPR not only has redlining resegregated public schools,[411] but another phenomenon also called district session has happened.[412] It is when a school secedes from a district. This often is an all-white or majority

---

[404] Mike Stivers, July 9, 2018, "The Socialist Case for School Integration: Why Integrate?" *Jacobin Magazine*, July 2018, United States Education Race, retrieved June 2, 2019, https://jacobinmag.com/2018/07/the-socialist-case-for-school-integration.

[405] Laura Meckler August 16, 2023 at 6:00 a.m. EDT What happened when an Ohio school district rushed to integrate classrooms The Washington Post Democracy Dies In The Darkness retrieved July 21, 2024 https://www.washingtonpost.com/education/2023/08/16/shaker-heights-academic-tracking-classes-racial-equity/

[406] Ibid

[407] Ibid

[408] Ibid

[409] Ibid

[410] Ibid

[411] Sequoia Carrillo, Pooja Salhotra JULY 14, 2025:13 AM ET The U.S. student population is more diverse, but schools are still highly segregated NPR Network retrieved July 21, 2024 https://www.npr.org/2022/07/14/1111060299/school-segregation-report

[412] Ibid

white school[413] which forms whiter and wealthier school districts. [414] Schools can absolutely be racially integrated, but do they have to be? School desegregation is how the Progressives indirectly supported integration but not for the best interests of blacks. They had some different motives for it.

The Socialist Party had no interest in the black communities' issues or improving them and they believed that the world had no obligation to the Negro either.[415] A Socialist Party member said in a letter to another member, "You will jeopardize the best interests of the Socialist Party if you insist on political equality of the Negro."[416] As you can see from this statement, the Socialists didn't want blacks to have political equality with whites, either, because in socialism, only a few have control over the centrally planned government and economy,[417] and it was never intended for blacks to have it. If you notice, they did not care about economic equality for the Negro because in socialism, everybody is economically at a disadvantage except for the few who are in charge of the centrally planned government and economy.[418] The socialists did not participate in the civil rights movement necessarily for the good of blacks; their primary

---

[413] Ibid

[414] Ibid

[415] Ibid.

[416] Ibid.

[417] Jim Chappelow, reviewed By Gordon Scott, updated Jan. 29, 2020, "Centrally Planned Economy," Investopedia,. retrieved July 7, 2020, https://www.investopedia.com/terms/c/centrally-planned-economy.asp#:~:text=Examples%20of%20Centrally%20Planned%20Economies,China%2C%20Vietnam%2C%20and%20Cuba.

[418] Ibid.

goal was first and far most to fundamentally change America and eventually turn it as socialist as possible, if not totally socialist.[419]

In fact, one of the National Socialist Movement's (NSM) more prominent members made a very racist comment about "Niggers, Mexicans, and Jews" on a blog post.[420] Not only that he said some very degrading things about homosexuals and he compared all of the above groups to child molesters who boldly speak their minds and rally, march, and protest for their sick causes.[421] It is very racist to suggest such a thing about these groups of people from a white man, but most people don't know what and who they are supporting when they support socialists like this. He sounds like a Klansman or a neo-Nazi himself. This interview was conducted in 2008.[422] These Socialists are not Democratic Socialists, who don't appear to be racists, at least from appearance and speech. They may be, though, if you just dig a little deeper. This type of socialism is a part of the left's progressive movement, not Conservatives.

The leftist progressive movement in America is a political one that seems to be shaping up more like the Socialist Party. They have a style of governing that more resembles those of a Socialist. Under this type of governing, the state regulates and controls almost every aspect of your life.

According to a Conservative official, the American Nazi Party is being portrayed by the news media as the ultra-right conservative,[423]

---

[419] Mike Stivers, July 9, 2018, "The Socialist Case for School Integration: Why Integrate?" *Jacobin Magazine*, July 2018, United States Education Race, retrieved June 2, 2019, https://jacobinmag.com/2018/07/the-socialist-case-for-school-integration.

[420] "National Socialist Movement,". retrieved June 5, 2019, https://www.splcenter.org/fighting-hate/extremist-files/group/national-socialist-movement.

[421] Ibid.

[422] Ibid.

[423] Ibid.

but nothing could be farther from the truth. According to him, Nazis are a part of a different movement than ultra-right Conservatives.[424] Nazis have no part in the ultra-conservative movement![425] That's not what Conservative stand for or represent.[426] Nazis believe in a white supremacist ideology.[427] Conservatives believe that we were created by God with rights granted by a creator.[428] Your rights come from the Creator and cannot be taken by government.[429] If the government can give your rights, they can take them away too.[430]

According to the ADL website the National Socialist Movement is currently the largest Neo-Nazi group in America[431]. American Socialism is a Left-Wing Movement and Neo Nazis are very racist so is it fair to say at least Neo-Nazism has ties with the left and not the right and maybe the right is not so racist after all.

The question to ask here is who are the real racists? Racism has just taken a new form from the old KKK of the former Confederate South to the more modern radical and leftist movement.

In the YouTube documentary *Afro Germany—being black and German*, a DW documentary, a biracial Afro German journalist from former West Germany interviews an activist in Germany at a rally/protest by Afro Germans to get the name of a street changed in Germany whose name has racist connotations to it that stem

---

[424] Ibid.

[425] Ibid.

[426] Ibid.

[427] Ibid.

[428] Ibid.

[429] Ibid.

[430] Ibid.

[431] ADL The National Socialist Movement https://www.adl.org/resources/profile/national-socialist-movement

from the German colonial period in Africa.[432] He also said a lot of aspects of German colonial history are not widely known.[433] He said we could not really begin to understand National Socialism without looking at the colonial antecedents because we find out there are ideological, political, but also personal continuities, linking German colonialism and National Socialism. [434]

At one time in history from just after WWII up until the fall of the Berlin Wall, West Germany remained for the most part a Federalist Republic.[435] East Germany, which ended up on the other side of the Berlin Wall, became Socialist,[436] under communist control, which resulted in a different type of educational philosophy and style of educating for its citizens as such. On the same program, before the journalist, who is also biracial, discussed some of the racial biases she has had to deal with living in former West Germany, which is a republic with an economy more like the west,[437] an interview of a biracial black and white woman who was raised in former East Germany was conducted where she discussed prejudices and negative reactions against her growing up in the east. So you can be either a socialist or a capitalist and have a bias toward

---

[432] "Afro Germany—being black and German," DW Documentary, The German Public Broadcast System, March 29, 2019, retrieved June 8, 2019, https://www.youtube.com/watch?v=pcfPVj5qR1E.

[433] Ibid.

[434] Ibid.

[435] History.com Editors, "History: 1949, May 23, Federal Republic of Germany is established," https://www.history.com/this-day-in-history/federal-republic-of-germany-is-established.

[436] "German Democratic Republic DDR Created in 1949,"Conservapedia, retrieved December 25, 2019, https://www.conservapedia.com/German_Democratic_Republic#cite_ref-2.

[437] "Afro Germany—being black and German," DW Documentary, Mar 29, 2017, retrieved June 4, 2020, https://www.youtube.com/watch?v=pcfPVj5qR1E.

a different racial group.[438] This raises another question, could you be a Democrat or a Socialist or a Democratic Socialist and have a racial bias toward another group of people?

If blacks had not fallen for the leftist progressive policy of integration (on progressive terms), with a current spending power of $600 billion to $1 trillion, depending what source you use,[439] African Americans would have really had something by now. That is the GDP of a whole country; in fact, lots of countries in the world don't have GDPs like that. This brings me to another reason why influencing blacks was good for the left. A black community with a GDP like this with America's resources and technology and a free-market economy in a constitutional republic could have done business with sub-Saharan Africa, black people, and nations of the Caribbean and Central and South America in a way that it would have lifted them out of a lot of the poverty, social problems, and racism that they are still living in today. That would undermine the white race's ability to keep political, military, and economic advantages over black people globally. But thanks to the advice of both Progressives and the left, the black community got the shaft both in America and the rest of the world.

Integration is actually something some white Liberals and Conservatives could agree and work together on, and by doing so they could have worked together to make things better for both at least for the fair monetary exchange between the two. Integration is one of the only progressive causes that could have worked out for the better of the two groups; with this one, some of the benefits could have gone beyond monetary ones. Integration would have

---

[438] Ibid.

[439] Ellen McGirt, updated Feb 28, 2018, "Race Ahead: a New Nelson Report Puts Black Buying Power at 1.2 Trillion," *Fortune* magazine, retrieved June 12 2019, http://fortune.com/2018/02/28/raceahead-nielsen-report-black-buying-power.

been fine; it would have been great if that worked for everyone and if whites had spent billions of dollars of their money at Black-owned businesses and for-profits like blacks poured all of their money into white-owned endeavors. Now we have immigrant groups that are not spending any of their money at Black-owned, for-profit organizations. If everybody spends their money at Black-owned for-profits at the rate that blacks do at non-black for-profits, then complete integration would work. If those are not the terms of integration, then it would have just been better if blacks had taken the civil rights that they got form the civil rights movement and stayed to a greater of lesser extent partially segregated, at least to an extent from the greater American community and did what the black community did in the Greenwood District of Tulsa, Oklahoma, up until it was burned down in June 30 of 1921.

When blacks tried to completely integrate with whites, all of the blacks with college degrees that spanned the range from associates, bachelor's, master's, and PhD degrees and even MDs and lawyers all went to white institutions with a wealth of knowledge to help build and develop a community, or their white community maybe I should say. Blacks with trades and even just on-the-job training, like the training required for a butcher, a carpenter, or even a locksmith that doesn't require a college degree, all left the black community for white corporations and small businesses and the government with skills that you could really use to build a community and its economy. This is why blacks never had a community with an economic safety net that could provide some of its employment and well-being over the past 50 years. Thanks to the cause of integration, invented by socialists and carried out by Progressives, some blacks stayed physically in a location with other blacks but drove miles away to white institutions to work and some physically left the black community and physically integrated with whites in some of their communities, which eventually became all black. As a result of this cause and its after effect, we now have really bad neighborhoods.

Integration could have been a great thing, and there is nothing wrong with it if everybody is on the same terms or had enough common denominators with each other as far as economics and where you spend your money is concerned, as well as politics and political issues, morals, and ethics, but everybody was not. Since whites had some advantages to begin with from the past before the civil rights movement and they continued to practice group economics, they continued to have these advantages today in general as a group, so it did not work out for blacks. If you are going to have integration, have it for the right reason, not for somebody's intent.

Again, there is nothing wrong with integration if (1) everybody can come to a consensus on what is and is not acceptable interaction with one another; (2) there is agreement on what is and is not necessary practice and what is and is not acceptable, and no contracts can be signed to make anything official between groups; and (3) nothing can be government or institutional mandated behavior for any group or all groups for that matter.

Since the beginning of integration, some places in American society have become almost completely integrated without any disunity because of race. Some other places have remained uniquely white, uniquely black, or uniquely Hispanic, all with their own uniqueness and little character. It's as if integration had no effect or only a little on some of these places, and integration only happened in places where it was necessary. Some places went from all white to all black or all white to all Latino due to white flight into the suburbs, and some places when from all black to all white due to gentrification, but does that mean that it really worked at solving racial disparities or was it for another purpose?

Blacks, whites, and Hispanics all actually have more in common than we do differences, so I'm not saying that Blacks should not interact and communicate with people of other ethnicities, but in places where the uniqueness of other ethnicities are, is where they have their unique little private-sector economies where their money exchanges hands several times in their community before leaving, and if it benefits everyone else to do so, then why don't African Americans do the same thing?

We could all even intermarry with one another, which would create another race of people or some new and different opinions about the world around us if that works for everybody.

By complete integration, I am not saying blacks should completely segregate themselves from American society; they should absolutely participate in the American experiment called a Republic with one another and everyone else in America and not isolate themselves from the greater society, but they have to be realistic about what naturally drives people to act like they do as groups and consider a new course of action if necessary.

Dr. Claude Anderson puts it in a simple, short video presentation. To take ownership of your community, the first level you start on is economics with business ownership by making your business community stronger with money that circulates (exchanges hands) throughout the community.[440] He calls it group economics. Second, you go to politics and buy your politicians,[441] and third to the court systems,[442] so you have laws changed in your favor. Fourth, you go to the media and publish your own publications with your own media

---

[440] Dr. Claud Anderson, May 11, 2016, "The Building Blocks of Group Economics," retrieved December 18, 2019, https://www.youtube.com/watch?v=o_6xU7FnHoI (36 secs.).

[441] Ibid., (1 min. 0 secs.).

[442] Ibid., (1 min. 36 sec).

outlets,[443] so they are in your favor. The last level is education.[444] During the whole time you are establishing this, you must have a code of conduct[445] that almost everyone in the community follows. Now with a setup like this, you can really acquire resources that you need to exist equally and fairly in society.

From there, in a sense, it would be fair to say as the next step, you can restructure society the way you want it. You can just blow up what is there and re-create something else different or maybe even customize it like you want it.

An example of how ownership and control of your community through economics, which is the first tier in Dr. Anderson's ladder, gives you power in a way that politics, including identity politics, which is a progressive cause is the changes made by the accusation of Twitter now "X" by Elon Musk.[446] As owner, he had the authority to make changes in Twitter[447] that the political machine could not make, and they have limited power in stopping him from making the changes. This is the kind of power blacks would have had more of if they had followed Booker T. Washington's model of having a strong business community by practicing group economics before trying to completely integrate into society rather than just integrating into society without it so someone else like the NAACP, the Democrat party, or some other philanthropic organization can make limited

---

[443] Ibid., (1 min. 55 sec).

[444] "Dr. Claude Anderson 5 levels to control," retrieved April 5, 2022, https://www.youtube.com/watch?v=YR6YYz9_Dc8.

[445] Ibid (2 mins.).

[446] Tim Newcomb, Oct. 31, 2022, "New Technology: 5 Ways Elon Musk Wants to Change Twitter," *Popular Mechanics*, retrieved November 12, 2022, https://www.popularmechanics.com/technology/a39816369/how-elon-musk-will-change-twitter/.

[447] Ibid.

changes or at least make the appearance of change for the better while advancing their cause.

When you don't have a powerful-enough business community where you practice group economics giving you all of the benefits that I mentioned above, your community, especially the really bad neighborhoods and sometimes not-so-bad ones, for years were before the migrant crisis were subject to more arrest quotas by police just because they have to make a certain number of arrests every day. According to a Baltimore city police officer who spoke out on arrest quotas of black men in its all black Sandtown neighborhood and how they are targeted for arrests, it is because the cops have a fear of them[448] and in police culture, when you have a fear of someone that you think might hurt or kill you, it gives you the right to use force on them or even take their life.[449] He said the way the laws are set up now, you could be arrested for just about anything.[450] He explains how you can be arrested for something as simple as jaywalking, throwing a cigarette butt on the ground, or carrying a spring-assisted pocket knife, but the crime is really for being black.[451] He also stated that for the same crimes, you generally can't make arrest quotas in the all-white neighborhoods of Baltimore;[452] for that, the black side of town was the place to go.[453] Lower-income people are more likely to be victims of these practices regardless of race, but black people are more likely

---

[448] Slate TV. A Former Baltimore Cop Explains Why the Department Targets Black Men. retrieved July 17, 2020 https://www.youtube.com/watch?v=4HyKlFUMBiA (6 min 19 sec)

[449] Ibid., (6 mins. 40 secs.).

[450] Ibid., (11 mins. 30 secs.).

[451] Ibid., (12 mins. 10 secs.).

[452] Ibid., (10 mins. 50 secs.).

[453] Ibid., (11 mins. 15 secs.).

to be lower income.[454] The clip was made before the push was made to defund the police. With them defunded things won't be any better in these neighborhoods and with no police the crime and murder rates will go up a lot and drugs like fentanyl will kill a lot more people all in these black communities. With a defunded police force these communities will be taken over by some really dark elements that will produce mayhem on a greater scale than we are seeing now. Defunding the police is being pushed by progressives. If it were up to conservative this would not happen.

Since the black communities' economic infrastructure has collapsed as a result of integration and the displacement of so many white-collar skilled blacks to white suburbs because some neighborhoods went from bad to really bad, the police can go forth and arrest sometimes without consequences. Sometimes people should be arrested if they violated the law, but often even people who didn't really deserved to be jailed, fined, or imprisoned got harsher-than-necessary sentences or they were sentenced when they should have never been questioned by law enforcement to begin with.

With a setup like Dr. Anderson's five-tier ladder, you can be a lot more effective at keeping your young men out of prison for selling five grams of crack cocaine because you're in a better position to demand it through the legal process. This ladder would change the ballgame and maybe even the playing field for blacks in just about every topic being discussed in this book. Integration killed that one, and it was orchestrated by the left on their terms so they could redistribute wealth and expand public institutions, which would expand government, increasing their bottom line. They don't care about the

---

[454] Tracy Oppenheimer, July 24, 2013, "Cop Fired for Speaking out Against Ticket and Arrest Quotas," Reason TV, retrieved July 17, 2020, https://reason.com/video/how-quotas-pervert-police-priorities-fir/.

black community, just their agenda. I will say again: integration was not a bad thing. It was a good thing on the right terms, and it could have worked if it were for the right reason—and it could still work today if everyone were on the same page.

If you don't like the way your history is being taught in public schools, then on a local level, you can challenge state authorities to have changes made in your favor, and you can use your media to publish music videos and TV shows that are more wholesome and that don't make your young men look like thugs and dope dealers. For you to be able to do this we will have to have the freedom of speech and freedom of the press and the republic that America is. Another reason why I fell this way is because the little public grade school that I went to in the 1970s, which was all black with all black teachers and administrators, taught us American history, but they taught us black history that I am sure the surrounding white communities did not teach to their children, socialist and/or communists philosophies, which are being pushed by the left, and Progressives would never allow this; they would only allow their state-sanctioned version of it and with hidden cameras and audio devices in places where they couldn't possibly be found by a teacher; any attempts to do so could be reported to the state resulting in arrests and jail or prison time.

If you were white, why would you integrate with someone who up until that point in history either you generally did not have their best interests at heart, or you could be downright hostile toward them? The official from the Socialist Party who indicated his disinterest in the needs of the black community is an indicator that their involvement with the black community was to advance a cause that was not for the good of the black community.

A small, vulnerable minority community needs a free-market economy with low taxation and less government so it can generate its own wealth. This is what Conservatives and people on the right stand for, and this would be a good thing for Blacks. With a setup like this, a smaller minority community can get a lot done and generate a lot more wealth and power through its for-profit institutions such as small businesses, its nonprofit ones, and with local government institutions. For examples of this, just google the business pages and scroll through it. The left and now some Progressives just have some different principles that they stand for that just have not been good for blacks.

A lot of job positions are filled by networking as a community.[455] According to *Business Insider Magazine*, over 70 percent of jobs out there are not even listed,[456] and maybe up to 85 percent in some cases are filled by networks.[457] Many of these positions are never posted online on any social media page, newspaper column, or on any TV advertisement. There are some communities that have networks to fill job positions that, in essence, are ethnic communities. Even though they are not called that, that is what they really are. Even as a person within your ethnic background, you can fill a lot of positions in your business if you network in areas where people are of your ethnic background and/or race live, work, play, and congregate, which is what all other ethnic backgrounds do to a greater or lesser extent. You can use these occasions and spaces to build your

---

[455] Apollo Technical Engineered Talent Solutions Important Networking Statistics Everyone Should Know (2022) Jan 4, 2022 retrieved April 6, 2022 https://www.apollotechnical.com/networking-statistics/#:~:text=Networking%20for%20Your%20Career,-Networking%20is%20vital&text=According%20to%20HubSpot%2C%2085%25%20of,that%20recruiters%20meet%20through%20networking.

[456] Gina Belli. Business Insider. At least 70% of jobs are not even listed—here's how to up your chances of getting a great new gig, PayScale. Apr 10, 2017, 2:52 PM retrieved July 30, 2019 https://www.businessinsider.com/at-least-70-of-jobs-are-not-even-listed-heres-how-to-up-your-chances-of-getting-a-great-new-gig-2017-4.

[457] Ibid.

business community and your staff and more or less keep it as ethnically similar as possible with people of your ethnicity.

Integration and multiculturalism and diversity, which were both leftist ideas that lots of Progressives support as well, make it more difficult to do this for everyone, but for the black community especially since now we have a lot more work to do than most other ethnic backgrounds from setbacks from so many of the left's progressive policies and causes and from historical injustices. You could use these places to discuss things in your community that no one else would ever find out about outside of it. This is another reason why black people must own their own businesses because in a network where you go out and meet people and they can talk to you see where you stand on certain issues and see what you look like, they see who to tell about certain positions and who not to. For this, you have to have a community with a business infrastructure and very good networks for referrals, inside both your infrastructure and other ones. Not only that, you need small groups of black people in the black community with similar interests networking together within the black community, for example, black people who know other black people who graduated form a particular school with a particular skill, for example, electronics, that another employer is trying to fill in your local community. The black community lost that with integration and the destabilization of the black family and community structure, and progressive policies have indirectly caused a lot of this.

A hospital in your community is potentially a big employer because to staff and maintain it takes lots of skill sets, both medical and nonmedical. The hospital must have contracts with other entities outside of the hospital, so it creates a lot of jobs throughout a community and keeps lots of money flowing and in circulation in that community. Not only that, but a hospital can be also an anchor of a community's identity and sense of accomplishment as a group. This is something else that the black community lost as a result of integration, which was a socialist and leftist policy.

Before integration, black history was taught in segregated schools in a way that your identity was solid, and various institutions such as historically black colleges and universities, black hospitals, and other black institutions gave you a sense of place, self-respect, and a desire or even a duty to contribute locally in a way that everybody benefited because there was a different type of bond in the community. There were dates, people, places, things, types of comradery; some of these things are very simple and local in nature. All of these things were the purpose behind your existence as a group or as an ethnic background. Integration killed that since the cooperation and coexistence that is fostered with it ended. Since the black experience was a unique one that no other ethnic background had experienced, we had and still have different ways of relating, communicating, and dealing with one another, the way we perceive ourselves as individuals and with other groups has shaped and molded us in a certain way whether they are good or bad.[458] Had blacks not tried to completely integrate with whites and some other groups, we could have created our own communities where we could conduct business and interact with one another in a way that works for us in ways that we can relate to and understand, even if no other group can. We should decide what the things are that are not useful to the existence of a group and stop practicing them because we don't think it is necessary. This is something else that complete integration killed in the black community more than in other communities.

---

[458] Dr. Joy Dedruy. POST TRAUMATIC SLAVE SYNDROME. retrieved April 17, 2020 https://www.joydegruy.com/post-traumatic-slave-syndrome

Rethinking Integration

Another example of how complete integration affected the black community negatively is what happened to, historic Farish Street in Jackson MS[459] which was the second most powerful black business empowerment district in the nation[460], the most successful was Harlem NYC. According to an expert on the history of Jacksom Mississippi all of the businesses closed which resulted in abandoned buildings on the current site[461]. He said they all closed starting with racial integration in the 70's.[462] The expert who calls himself Brad Como Kosi Franklin blames the disastrous results of its plight directly on racial integration.[463] This type of total integration of blacks into society with no plan for wealth production or job production like the Negro Business League that Booker T Washington pushed for blacks was acquiring both through group economics. This leaves you dependent on resources and white institutions outside of your community. There were numerous other communities with empowerment zones before integration thar were built by the black community. This type of integration was encouraged and endorsed by left leaning progressives who were often socialist and communists.

The JAMA Network did an interview with two black physicians, and the topic was "Diversifying Medical Education Conversations" with Dr. Bauchner. The goal was to discuss ways to get more Blacks in medical school so we will have more black physicians. One of the physicians was dean of a prominent school of medicine at

---

[459] Chris Must You Tube show The REAL Jackson, Mississippi They Don't Show You! retrieved March 23, 2024 https://www.youtube.com/watch?v=ezAg8TN5dcA

[460] Ibid

[461] Ibid

[462] Ibid

[463] Ibid

Morehouse College, which is an HBCU Historically Black College / University. She was asked why she thought black students thrived there.[464] She said she went to Meharry Medical College, which is an HBCU, to interview with another black female physician who was an OB/GYN. They had no OBG/YN residency program, yet they had 18 students going into OB/GYN. She felt that the relationship that they had with the faculty and staff and the confidence with which the students engaged in patient care showed her that there was a learning environment that empowered those students to believe that anything was possible. She stated that when she left the University of Kansas and came to Morehouse School of Medicine, which is another HBCU, she saw that same level of empowerment. She said it makes a difference when you go to school or work every day and race is not the primary issue.[465] That you don't necessarily have the microaggressions or the imposter syndrome that sometimes follows you around as an underrepresented minority in a majority school when you're at a majority environment.[466] She believes it is the learning environment that they were able to create in our close connection with our community.[467] The students are engaged with the community the first week of medical school, and it continues throughout the four years. She stated that everybody had the responsibility to make sure that everybody walked across that stage.

This is something the black community had before integration, and it was a good thing, and frankly I think it would help if the black

---

[464] JAMA Diversity in Medical Education Conversations with Dr. Bauchner #JAMA live with Valerie Montgomery Rice MD and Clyde W. Yancy MD retrieved October 11, 2022 https://www.ama-assn.org/education/medical-school-diversity/how-get-3000-more-black-people-physician-pipeline

[465] Ibid

[466] Ibid

[467] Ibid

community had a set up like this today, at least to an extent. This is being proposed by a group of black thinkers and professionals who know what the black community needs and who have their best interest at heart, not Progressives and/or those on the left who want equity, diversity, and inclusion. With their solution, you could get the task done without it. We need a group of black thinkers like this to come up with a plan for the black community for group economics to happen. If it is up to Conservatives who are right leaning thinks they will preserve the free-market economy and capitalism and the constitutional republic you need for a setup like this to work and to flourish. Not only that the rest of black leadership needs to be like this for the black community instead of so many of our Democrat politicians in the black community that are just ineffective leadership. The host of the show, Dr. Bauchner, brought up the point that four HBCUs, which were quite small, were producing 15 to 17 percent of all the nation's black doctors.[468] One of the guests mentioned that making medical school free (which was proposed by Progressives) doesn't educate above current capacity.[469] One of the doctors suggestion was to extend the model that HBCUs currently have with Morehouse College and Howard university and get the students practicing in their communities, and with this you have a cultural change[470] not based on equity or multiculturalism, diversity, and inclusion (progressive terminology), which is something the black community had before integration, when America was more conservative. This may be the best way to solve the shortage of black physicians that are being produced by America's colleges and universities. One of the doctors on the panel also stated that for every black man that gets an MD,

---

[468] Ibid

[469] Ibid

[470] Ibid

2.5 black women do.[471] If you do the math, that equates to five black women for every two black men, which is way worse than for all other ethnic backgrounds; this was not the case before the feminist movement, and it was not the case for any ethnic background in America before the civil rights movement.

Today in America we have a different type of segregation because it is by choice. In the pre–civil rights era, when it was legal, different racial groups were forced to live in separate places to maintain racial purity or to maintain white superiority or to keep another group disadvantaged or for whatever reason. The way it was done before the civil rights movement was wrong because no one should have the right to tell a free man if he is totally free where he can live; neither should anyone have the right to put restrictions on his conduct or where he can be, so Dr. King's fight for civil rights and his movement were the right thing to do. The segregation that we are having today is not really illegal since it is by choice, so under today's circumstances integration cannot really be forced, or maybe I should say this type of segregation will have to be opposed with a different approach besides a legal one. This could, however, say something about how we feel about people who are different from us and how we react to them even today. This is a good setup for Progressive and Socialists to introduce class struggle and other concepts that will support their agenda.

If you go online and google "Hispanic business districts in Chicago" under images, you will see what they call "The Little Village" neighborhood;[472] it is a street that is lined with Hispanic businesses with all of their symbols and logos and things written in Spanish for blocks. In Oklahoma City with the same setup the Hispanic

---

[471] Ibid

[472] Acacia Hernandez | Joanna Hernandez | September 16, 2021 9:52 pm Chicago Tonight' in Your Neighborhood: Little Village WTTW News retrieved September 28, 2022 https://news.wttw.com/2021/09/16/chicago-tonight-your-neighborhood-little-village

Rethinking Integration

Chamber of Commerce did a report of business owners who wanted a revitalization[473] effort with the goal of mirroring other areas of OKC by creating a business improvement district.[474] The article stated the Hispanic community hoped to model their plan after Oklahoma City's Asian District and Automobile Alley in Midtown.[475] So Asians are doing the same thing across America with Chinatowns, Koreatowns, and Japan towns and now others. This is the case in other cities across America. Even If you are not located in these areas, you can still have networks that include people of those ethnicities that do not physically live in those locations, but the whole community can benefit from the networks in them. The question to ask here is: Is this a form of segregation and is it purposely or is it by choice? This type of setup just encourages people of these ethnicities to shop in their own communities. Communities like this produce jobs and opportunity for its residents. Arabs have the same setup in Anaheim, California, called Little Arabia[476] and also in Dearborn Michigan. You can google black business districts, and all of the pictures under images show historic images of mostly before the civil rights movement and a few afterward, but nothing really current that is a reality today. Why doesn't the black community have a setup like this? Is it because the black community attempted to completely integrate with the rest of America? From what I have presented to you here

---

[473] Morgan Chesky Updated: 11:01 AM CDT Aug 5, 2013 Greater OKC Hispanic Chamber of Commerce: Business owners want revitalization effort KOCO News 5 ABC retrieved September 28, 2022 https://www.koco.com/article/greater-okc-hispanic-chamber-of-commerce-business-owners-want-revitalization-effort/4294499

[474] Ibid

[475] Ibid

[476] HOSAM ELATTAR Voice of OC Little Arabia: The Struggle to Get Anaheim to Recognize Its Arab American Business Community retrieved September 28, 2022 https://voiceofoc.org/2022/06/little-arabia-the-struggle-to-get-anaheim-to-recognize-its-arab-american-business-community/

it certainly doesn't seem like Hispanics and Asians and Arabs are. If that is the case, is it acceptable for blacks to make the same exception with partial integration vs. complete or total integration with a strong separate business district like everyone else in the descriptions above. Progressive policies that took effect after the civil rights movement from some that were started before the movement that I have discussed in this book have put the black community in this predicament. Now they are more dependent on the government and other entities outside of their community so the progressive movement can use them to expand government while other ethnicities have these set ups in their communities, leaving them less dependent on government as a community, and this was the whole point behind having the black community like this. The other question to ask about these setups or these little ethnic spaces is, are there some benefits to these setups for minority groups in America? If there are, then why shouldn't blacks do it like everyone else does, at least to a lesser extent.

We do not need to have total segregation of blacks from society either because if we want America to exist, there needs to be some institutions in society where everybody can contribute to the country's well-being and/or existence and growth in order for it to work, and an example of that is the military. Some other examples are federal, state, and local county or city government and other organizations like the American Red Cross and many other public and private institutions that everybody benefits from regardless of race, ethnicity, religion, etc. I can tell you about the military better than most after having been in the military both active and reserve for years; it will not work if you have different US militaries of different races and ethnicities all under a command of their race and or ethnicity with a different strategy for fighting and winning the war. Every different strategy could be counter to all the others, even though just one could work for the best outcome or to win the war. In the Army we would call an operation like this a Charlie Foxtrot.

By partial integration I mean just enough integration between all groups where we respect each other to make America work. The military is an example, and maybe some other large institutions that need cooperation form everybody, but just enough separation with group economics for a group to benefit from the understanding and appreciation of its uniqueness by like-minded people if that is still necessary. Or we can have an America that is completely integrated where race, ethnicity, color, gender, or religion make no difference; either one is fine with me, but I just want to know which one we are having.

The black community has been so devastated by leftist policies and causes that if it had to re-segregate (which is a weird phenomenon that is being pushed by some on the left now but only on college campuses for now)[477] and function as a separate entity, it would either be very hard to do so or impossible. The black community in America would have the hardest time coming together to reorganize a community. This would make them sitting ducks for destruction and/or complete elimination from the picture by the left or anyone else who wanted to do it. My best guess is it would probably be done by the left. Remember integration first started in the schools, which is the educational system, and where is re-segregation starting? In the schools. This is really very concerning to me, and I am wondering what the left has up their sleeve next, because what they have had up their sleeve up until this point has been bad for black America.

---

[477] Sky News Australia. Radical leftist staff demanding 'a return to segregation. Sky News.com.au. Feb 13, 2020. retrieved October 3, 2020 https://www.youtube.com/watch?v=gPy0DBdcNU8

The number of Black elected officials has increased dramatically over the past 40 years,[478] and it has not improved the condition of black people at all.[479] That is because politics is not the end-all for social problems; it is just one piece to the puzzle. Economics is another particularly important piece, and black people don't practice group economics. There are other factors that make a difference in lifting one's lot in society like stable marriages,[480] families, education, and hard work.[481] By now, encouraging re-segregation under the left's terms, now that black people are in the condition they are in, they will have to go to the government for more. Not only that, it will encourage the divisions along race and ethnicity for everyone to continue and maybe even become worse so that next a socialist or Marxist regime can come onto the scene with socialism as the answer to finally unite everyone and solve everybody's problems.

If this happens, black people will be sitting ducks for final elimination from the picture; it will put them in the line of fire for elimination from society, especially if the government mandates what is considered black, why black people should re-segregated, and what the terms of existence and conduct as a group are since it could be different for every group. The black community will need a purpose for being a community like the one that is a mix of what was proposed by Booker T Washington of Black Wallstreet and a plan from an entity like the Harvest Institute's think tank, not the government or any other special interest groups. If re-segregation did actually happen, it would be game over for black America because they do

---

[478] Walter E. Williams. The Daily Signal. April 11, 2018. Black Political Success Isn't the Key to Black Empowerment. retrieved October 3, 2020 https://www.dailysignal.com/2018/04/11/black-political-success-is-not-the-key-to-black-empowerment/

[479] Ibid.

[480] Ibid.

[481] Ibid.

not have the incentive or purpose as a group to independently provide an infrastructure to survive like other groups do. This would be open season for the left to finish black America off.

Identity politics along the lines of race, which is another progressive tactic, is just going to introduce more political ladders and challenges to the picture, making things more complicated and making government bigger and giving it more control. It will introduce more political offices and causes to fight for that cater to special interests, which are trivial and, in the end, may even make matters worse for black Americans. It will give more black people more of a chance to get politically active in arenas that, in the end, won't make things any better for black people.

After the Civil Rights Acts of 1964 and 1967, which ended lots of the restrictions on where you could be do and live as a black person, some wards in large cities and even entire municipalities, mostly in large metropolitan areas, went from all black to all white in about 20 years. Black people would have been better off if they had practiced group economics and used Dr. Claude Anderson's five-tier system of building a community, of course with a code of conduct instead of complete integration with whites. By now, they would have been considerably better off. Some of these places would have been good places to start communities and to buy up as many of the storefront buildings as possible to give blacks literal ownership of their communities. They could have practically tailored a society like they wanted it for them, but the Black Lives Matter movement wants you to believe that because of systemic racism, you need government intervention to solve a big problem.

Do I think group economics is a save-all cure all for the black community? No, and far from it, but I do think if it had continued across the country up until now, the outcomes from it would have been positive for the black community.

Racism has been a problem in America, especially before the civil rights movement and clearly very much so before the Civil War when you consider how slavery was allowed for years by law and by popular culture and how Jim Crow laws and sundown town laws and Black Code laws were allowed for years after slavery. The Civil Rights Acts of 1964 and 1967 amended these laws, essentially making them illegal. But you have to consider what could have happened over the past 50 years or so if black people all across America had practiced group economics and been more like the black citizens of the Greenwood District of Tulsa, Oklahoma, before it was burned to the ground. As a community, blacks could have created a setting in the black community, which in some cases, is so different from what exists now, and a lot of systemic racism could be avoided.

The left and Progressives have black America so focused on systemic racism and trying to fight it (not to say that racism doesn't exist in America because sometimes it certainly does), that it is hard to see what the black community could really have if they approached it from a different angle with a different perspective. It seems like during Booker T. Washington's days, before today's progressive movement and political correctness, at least the black community could put together a community like the one in Tulsa, Oklahoma (Little Africa), that was burned to the ground in June of 1921 by angry mobs of whites. Back then, black people did not really have civil rights like they do now. They were able to practice group economics, and some of them generated wealth.

Years ago, the black community had some more incentives to practice group economics the way it was being practiced in places like Tulsa's Greenwood District. One was because whites were convinced that black people were intellectually inferior, subhuman to an extent, and just plain incapable of conducting the affairs of a civil society without guidance or just complete dominance by white involvement, and we had to prove them wrong. Another reason was because black people at the time could be treated if not a little, very hostilely at times from just being merely present in white society among whites, since so many cultural and social norms and laws and even beliefs were hostile to the existence of black people, at least before the civil rights era. I think at least one reason why the Greenwood District was eventually destroyed is because its display of blacks actually conducting a civil society and with a great deal of success in some cases went against the grain of what whites, both liberal and conservative, had been taught, or I will even go so far as to say indoctrinated to believe about Negroes (as they called blacks back then). This time, the core of what they believed as whites was under siege, and any old excuse would do to destroy it. Tulsa was not the only example of this there were multiple examples of this very same thing throughout American history, but the list is too extensive for me to go over for the purposes of the book. With everything I have presented and will be presenting to you with this book and with all other things considered, is the incentive not there to practice group economics again today with a setup like Tulsa's former Greenwood District?

Conservatives, who are on the right, generally do not support government programs, such as Section 8 housing, and welfare like liberals and progressives do, which means that everybody would have to work. As it is now, if we have a government shutdown that lasted for a month, most of its recipients could not get basic needs for subsistence; they would starve. Without the generous government handouts that the left has created, blacks would have no choice but to create some of their own jobs and ideas that generate money, jobs, and an economic infrastructure for blacks by blacks in the black community, and this would have some more advantages for the black community.

The whole point behind the left giving out so many government benefits, and especially heavily in the black community, is it keeps a group of people from learning how to provide those resources on their own. In a sense, that cripples a group and makes them more and more dependent on government, and that is exactly what socialists wanted.

A comparison was made on the attitudes of Liberals versus Conservatives on welfare, according to the *Student Daily News*. Liberals thought we should generally support welfare, even long-term welfare,[482] because it is a safety net that provides for the needs of the poor. It is necessary to bring fairness to American economic life, and it is a device for protecting the poor.[483] Conservatives oppose long-term welfare.[484] They think that opportunities should be provided to make it possible for those in need to become self-reliant.[485] It is far kinder and more helpful to encourage people to become independent, rather than allowing them to remain dependent on the government for provisions.[486]

Socialists had a goal to expand public institutions and to redistribute wealth, and welfare is a great way to both directly and indirectly help you to accomplish both. This will be discussed later on in the book. Temporary welfare is fine as long as you can get off it completely and totally with time. People can fall upon hard times sometimes, which is totally understandable, but that does not mean be dependent on a handout that you don't have to earn for your

---

[482] Student Daily News. Liberal Verses Conservative Beliefs. https://www.studentnewsdaily.com/conservative-vs-liberal-beliefs retrieved November 20, 2019.

[483] Ibid.

[484] Ibid.

[485] Ibid.

[486] Ibid.

entire life. With just 12 percent of the US population, Blacks are 39.8 percent of welfare recipients;[487] for whites, it is roughly 62.6 percent and 38.8 percent, respectively,[488] for Hispanics it is 16.7 percent and 15.7 percent respectively,[489] and for Asians it is 2.2 percent and 5.6 percent respectively.[490] Blacks have disproportionately greater representation in the ranks of welfare recipients than any other race or ethnicity, with just 12 percent of America's population.

Socialists and the left can accomplish this goal easier and quicker per capita than they can with any other group in America. This means blacks are one of the most dependent groups in America, at least on welfare. If someone wants you dependent on them for all of your basic needs, that is not a good relationship to have with them, and it means they probably don't have your best interests at heart either. It is not like a parent-child relationship where the child starts off dependent on his parents, but the objective is to train the child to become self-sufficient and not dependent on his parents by adulthood; the parents have the child's best interests at heart, and they want the best for that child. Socialism's goal is not to eventually have you self-sufficient; if that were the case, you wouldn't need it anymore. That is not in the best interests of socialists. This is also proof that feminism is not the only reason why the black community is in the condition that is in now.

If it were going to come to this, it would just be better if the black community practiced group economics, which would allow their money to exchange hands between five and fifteen times

---

[487] Brandon Gaille Brandon Galle Small Business and Marketing Advice 15 Welfare Statistics by Race, State and Payment May 20, 2017 https://brandongaille.com/welfare-statistics-by-race-state-and-payment retrieved November 20, 2019

[488] Ibid

[489] Ibid

[490] Ibid

before it leaves the black community, which seems to be about the average for everyone else, with a code of conduct to a greater or a lesser extent and just had its own subcommunity like every other ethnic background in America is doing. Conservatives who are on the right have a better setup for this.

6.

The Prison Industrial Complex

Interestingly enough, prisons are a staple of socialist political and economic systems and always have been.[491] The black community indirectly supplied the socialists with nearly half of the 2.2 million people on average for the better part of 30 or maybe even 40 years continuously, who were incarcerated in America to justify building the prison industrial complex that is synonymous with socialist and communist regimes. Not 2.2 million new prisoners every year but the maintenance of this many from new convictions, sentencings and releases provided a constant prison population of this amount with nearly half being African American continuously. Out of a population group with only 12 percent of America's population, they got nearly half of all of the prisoners they needed to build this prison infrastructure. So with the black community, they got more participants for their cause than with any other group. Using the black community as a strategic move for a more sinister agenda was actually advantageous to the socialists, who are really a branch of the leftist movement.

Before the new Obama legislation on crack cocaine black youth in the inner cities often received a ten-year prison sentence for

---

[491] Ira Stoll. The Irony of Socialists Calling for the Abolishing of Prisons. April 23, 2018. retrieved May 22, 2019 https://reason.com/archives/2018/04/23/the-irony-of-socialists-calling-for-abol

possession of just five grams of crack cocaine.[492] After the changes from the Obama presidency legislation the penalty for crack cocaine became 28 grams for a ten-year sentence.[493] This was for the first offence in some states which was considered a felony. In some states it takes two or three offences for the ten-year prison sentence.[494] The law for arrests for regular powder cocaine for possession before and after the change was always a ten-year sentence for 100 grams.[495]

When these men get out of jail or prison and apply for a job, employers do a background check, and if they have a felony conviction, it is next to impossible to get a job.[496] The criminalization of crack cocaine, which is the cheap, watered-down street version and not powder cocaine, is criminalizing black activity. This policy that ruined the lives of so many young blacks was endorsed by liberal progressive Democrats.[497] It was one of their officials who called black youth "Super predators" and stood with the signing of the 1994 Crime Omnibus law.[498]

---

[492] By the CNN Wire Staff. August 3, 2010. CNN Politics. Obama signs bill reducing cocaine sentencing gap. http://www.cnn.com/2010/POLITICS/08/03/fair.sentencing/index.html retrieved December 6, 2019.

[493] Ibid

[494] Ibid

[495] Ibid

[496] Rebecca McCray. 5 Years Later, Here Are 5 Ways the Fair Sentencing Act Changed the War on Drugs. Aug 15, 2015. retrieved May 26, 2019 http://www.takepart.com/article/2015/08/03/fair-sentencing-act-anniversary

[497] Thomas Frank. US politics. Bill Clinton's crime bill destroyed lives, and there's no point denying it. The Guardian Opinion Section. Last modified on Wed 20 Sep 2017. retrieved May 21, 2019 https://www.theguardian.com/commentisfree/2016/apr/15/bill-clinton-crime-bill-hillary-black-lives-thomas-frank

[498] Gloria La Riva. The U.S. prison system must be completely dismantled for President. Jul 05, 2016. retrieved April 15, 2019 https://www.liberationnews.org/gloria-la-riva-eugene-puryear-u-s-prison-system-must-completely-dismantled

Years prior, "The Nixon campaign in 1968, and the Nixon White House had two enemies: the antiwar left and black people."[499]

According to an article in transcript form the Niskanen Center, Nixon was the last liberal Republican president.[500] It commented on many of his radical social policies as being very liberal in nature[501]. You could argue that for the time, they may have even been considered progressive. Another article from the *Presidential Studies Quarterly* claims his domestic policy was both liberal and bold.[502] He was really the first president to engage in talks like this with Communist China's Chairman Mao.[503]

The following was from an excerpt from a Nixon political official (both are Republicans, but I will discuss this later on in the book).

> You understand what I'm saying? We knew we couldn't make it illegal to be either against the war or blacks,[504] but by getting the public to associate the hippies with marijuana and Blacks with heroin,[505] and then criminalizing both heavily, we

---

[499] German Lopez. german.lopez@vox.com. Nixon official: real reason for the drug war was to criminalize black people and hippies. Updated Mar 23, 2016. retrieved May 7, 2019 https://www.vox.com/2016/3/22/11278760/war-on-drugs-racism-nixon

[500] John R. Price Niskanen Center October 27, 2021 The Last Liberal Republican President, with John R. Price retrieved January 16, 2023 https://www.niskanencenter.org/the-last-liberal-republican-president/

[501] Ibid

[502] John C. Whitaker Journal Article Nixon's Domestic Policy: Both Liberal and Bold in Retrospect Presidential Studies Quarterly Vol. 26, No. 1, The Nixon Presidency (Winter, 1996), pp. 131-153 (23 pages) Published By: Wiley retrieved January 16, 2023 Presidential Studies Quarterly

[503] Ibid

[504] Ibid.

[505] Ibid.

could disrupt those communities.[506] We could arrest their leaders, raid their homes, break up their meetings, and vilify them night after night on the evening news.[507] Did we know we were lying about the drugs? Of course we did.[508]

This is the kind attitude toward blacks you needed just after slavery ended, to make and enforce the loitering laws or vagrancy laws, which were other terms that were enforced on blacks for wandering around and looking for a place to be, since they had no real place in free society right after the Civil War,[509, 510] and especially in the South. They were arrested for loitering and some other crimes that they did not commit, and they were forced to do labor for free, just as they did before. Often, the labor was on a former slave plantation under the same conditions, so it is not really fair to say that slavery ended at the end of the Civil War; you could really say with some honesty it went on for some years later until after Reconstruction of the South ended, in 1877. According to the Pulitzer prize book Slavery by Another Name: The Re-Enslavement of Black Americans from the Civil War to World War II a similar practice which was often just a milder form of slavey or servitude at times forced on the individual did not really end totally until

---

[506] Ibid.

[507] Ibid.

[508] Ibid.

[509] Constitutional Rights Foundation. The Southern "Black Codes" of 1865–66. retrieved February 19, 2021 https://www.crf-usa.org/brown-v-board-50th-anniversary/southern-black-codes.html

[510] Facing History and Ourselves. The History of Slave Patrols, Black Codes, and Vagrancy Laws. retrieved February 19, 2021 https://www.facinghistory.org/educator-resources/current-events/policing-legacy-racial-injustice/history-slave-patrols-black-codes-vagrancy-laws

The Prison Industrial Complex

WWII.[511] Now they are doing the free labor in the prison industrial complex instead of on a slave plantation.[512] Like the vagrancy laws of years past, crack cocaine use and possession, which has been a drug of choice for many inner-city youth, has been labeled as black activity without really calling it that you are using this activity to criminalize more heavily and eliminate one group from society just like the vagrancy laws were used to criminalize the free black population just after the Civil War.

Black kids, especially from certain little pockets in the black community, have been criminalized for crack cocaine because the media has labeled them as more likely to be thugs from inner city gangs that shoot and kill and rob and steal,[513, 514] but when white kids in the suburbs do regular powder cocaine, which is much more potent and just as harmful to one's health, it is sometimes criminalized, but it is more likely to be medicalized and worthy

---

[511] Douglas A. Blackmon Slavery by Another Name: The Re-Enslavement of Black Americans from the Civil War to World War II retrieved December 31, 2023 https://www.pulitzer.org/winners/douglas-blackmon

[512] Gena M. Florio. Five Ways the US Prison Industrial Complex Mimics Slavery. Feb 17, 2016. retrieved April 28, 2019 https://www.bustle.com/articles/142340-5-ways-the-us-prison-industrial-complex-mimics-slavery

[513] We Are The Drug Policy Alliance Race and the Drug War. retrieved June 1, 2020 https://www.drugpolicy.org/issues/race-and-drug-war 12-09- 19

[514] Equal Justice Initiative: Racial Double Standard in Drug Laws Persists Today. retrieved June 1, 2020 https://eji.org/news/racial-double-standard-in-drug-laws-persists-today

of professional counseling or rehabilitation therapy.[515] An example of this is the difference between the cable TV shows *Cops* and *48 Hours*, which feature more Blacks per capita as criminals and illegal drug dealers and users. On the other hand, the TV show *Intervention* is more likely to feature whites as innocent victims of the meth and speed crisis and worthy of help as innocent victims. This is the equivalent to character assassination of black youth by the leftist-controlled media, which is the platform that it is done from.

Now, if the feminists want men to bash or degrade, so many black men have criminal records; they have plenty of their mugshots to feature on the evening news for murder, armed robbery, theft, and drug dealing at any given time between all of the large population centers across America not because they're black but because they are men. With these same images, the racists can now shame black people and just simply prove their false points that they have been saying along that they are backward, ignorant, and inferior, making them the brunt of jokes and that they deserve to be thrown in jails and prisons almost en masse because they are black, not because they are men. There are no policies in effect to stop this, thanks also in part to the explosion of illegal drugs, which started to hit the scene in the '60s.

In a communist country where socialism is a part of society, at the height of the power of some their most brutal dictators, you had

---

[515] Erin M. Kerrison, Ph.D. White Claims to Illness and the Race-Based Medicalization of Addiction for Drug-Involved Former Prisoners. p. 10. retrieved June 1, 2020 https://www.google.com/search?q=White+Claims+to+Illness+and+the+Race-Based+Medicalization+of+Addiction+for+Drug-Involved+Former+Prisoners&sxsrf=APq-WBsWnAGrv1ne1kHUxrwDc4Ng4U_XJw%3A1649440174631&source=hp&ei=rnVQYtjpI-7B_Qaj6LKoDw&iflsig=AHkkrS4AAAAAYlCDvmxHx1N30OukzqQqNBB626wNt2uo&ved=0ahUKEwjY-Ly9g4X3AhXuYN8KHSO0DPUQ4dUDCAk&uact=5&oq=White+Claims+to+Illness+and+the+Race-Based+-Medicalization+of+Addiction+for+Drug-Involved+Former+Prisoners&gs_lcp=Cgdnd3Mtd-2l6EANQAFgAYMgHaABwAHgAgAEAiAEAkgEAmAEAoAECoAEB&sclient=gws-wiz

lots of prisoners and lots of prisons. What has happened is the black community has provided the socialists with between 40 percent and 50 percent of the prisoners from just 13 percent of the total population who are currently serving a sentence in a county jail, state jail, or federal prison or in juvenile detention. That's a million out of 2.2 million.[516] This has happened either directly or indirectly as a result of the previous two topics discussed.

When some of these men get out of prison, they go back to a life of crime and drugs, usually in certain sections of the black community. This is often because there are not enough and in some cases no programs to provide job training for these men. This is one reason why you have these pockets in the black community with bad neighborhoods with boarded-up houses, vacant lots, burned out and condemned houses, walls with gang graffiti covering them, and houses that someone lives in but the owners cannot sell. Some of them have fences around the front and back yards, giving the appearance of little fortresses, and most of these houses have been broken into at least once; some have been broken into a number of times. This has run a lot of blacks out of these communities, along with black businesses and institutions that were the anchor of these communities. These pockets have more violent murders than most other parts of the black community. It has displaced a lot of the black community over a period of 30 or 40 years, and it has uprooted and dismantled black institutions, culture, and identity.[517]

---

[516] Mother Jones. The Race Gap in US Prisons Is Glaring, and Poverty Is Making it Worse. Crime and Justice. retrieved October 14, 2020 https://www.motherjones.com/crime-justice/2018/02/the-race-gap-in-u-s-prisons-is-glaring-and-poverty-is-making-it-worse/

[517] Marcus Gee. Another great migration is under way: Black Americans are leaving big cities for the suburbs. Chicago. Published April 29, 2018. retrieved June 5, 2019 https://www.theglobeandmail.com/world/article-another-great-migration-is-under-way-black-americans-are-leaving-big

Had it been up to Conservatives, the problem with illicit drugs would never have gotten this bad. What policies do they have now that over one million men are missing in the black community due to incarceration or homicide and various other causes? This is another reason for which feminists can celebrate because so many men have been eliminated.

Most of these one million are either on some kind of parole or probation, meaning they are being carefully monitored by the law, or they are owned by the prison industrial complex where they are doing billions of dollars of labor for multibillion-dollar corporations for practically free.[518] This is nothing more than a new form of slavery,[519] which is what was intended by the left and Progressives. Why aren't Progressives implementing some policies to get so many black men out of prison, or is this where some of them intended for them to be, like many of the racist white Southern Democrats who voted to keep slavery intact before the Civil War and Jim Crow after it was over?[520]

Now the incarceration is starting early for teenage kids in schools, who are taken to juvenile detention and straight to detainment through the school-to-prison pipeline.[521]. This is just another way that the left can keep the prison industrial complex filled with prisoners for their socialist society that they want to create. In these

---

[518] Vicky Peláez. The Prison Industry in the United States: Big Business or a New Form of Slavery? Global Research, February 24, 2019. El Diario-La Prensa, New York and Global Research. 10 March 2008. retrieved June 7, 2019 https://www.globalresearch.ca/the-prison-industry-in-the-united-states-big-business-or-a-new-form-of-slavery/8289

[519] Gina M. Florio. Bustle 5 Ways The U.S. Prison Industrial Complex Mimics Slavery. Feb 17 2016. retrieved June 8, 2019 https://www.bustle.com/articles/142340-5-ways-the-us-prison-industrial-complex-mimics-slavery

[520] Mackubin T. Owens. The Democratic Party's Legacy of Racism. Editorial December 2002. retrieved June 10, 2019 http://ashbrook.org/publications/oped-owens-02-racism

[521] Marilyn Elias. The School-to-Prison Pipeline. Teaching Tolerance Race and Ethnicity https://www.tolerance.org/magazine/spring-2013/the-school-to-prison-pipeline November 24, 2019

societies, historically lots of people who did not conform to the states' policies of what was a considered a good socialist were sent to prison, and black kids are being detained young for one of the left's causes. These kids will be in prison in the future to manufacture goods as free or very cheap labor. The United States has more of its people incarcerated than Russia or China (per capita and percentagewise),[522] and China is one of the biggest socialist regimes that still uses prison labor for manufacturing goods for sale that we buy every day.

There is a link between a person's conservatism and less illegal drug use, happiness, hard work, closer family ties, less materialism, less envy, more honesty, and stronger relationships with your children and stronger family ties.[523] Liberals are a lot more likely to smoke marijuana than Conservatives.[524] Since Liberals are more likely to be leftist and they are more likely to use illegal drugs,[525] why would they create a war on drugs that was successful at spreading drugs and the black-market they created that involves crime, prostitution, money laundering, and a lot of other illegal activities that lead to jail and prison time that have plagued the black community

---

[522] Katie Sanders. Is the U.S. prison population as big as Russia, China and North Korea combined? Punditfact https://www.politifact.com/punditfact/statements/2014/dec/16/matthew-cooke/us-prison-population-big-russia-china-and-north-ko/ retrieved November 24, 2019.

[523] Jim Meyers. Monday, 16 June 2008 12:47 PM Newsmaxx. Are Liberals Bigger Drug Users? Retrieved February 1, 2020 https://www.newsmax.com/InsideCover/Liberals-Drug-use/2008/06/16/id/324135/#

[524] Kyle Jeager. February 1, 2020. Liberal Americans Are Six Times More Likely To Smoke Marijuana Than Conservative s, Poll Finds. Marijana Movement retrieved March 1, 2020 https://www.marijuanamoment.net/liberal-americans-are-six-times-more-likely-to-smoke-marijuana-than-conservative s-poll-finds/

[525] Jim Meyers. Monday, 16 June 2008 12:47 PM NewsMaxx. Are Liberals Bigger Drug Users? https://www.newsmax.com/InsideCover/Liberals-Drug-use/2008/06/16/id/324135/ retrieved March 1, 2020

so much? With that said, it would not surprise me if the war on drugs was not the invention of the left, meant to fail and to arrest more blacks and throw them into the prison industrial complex. Plain and simple, it is a war on the poor and blacks.[526] Since the war on drugs has failed,[527] the end result has been the disproportionate arrests of a lot more black people per capita than it has of whites and really of other ethnic backgrounds. This war on drugs has created a new industry called *corrections* out of arresting and jailing or imprisoning young black males disproportionately more than white males. From this angle, it seems like the left, who are more often progressive Liberals, are more racist than the Conservatives, who are much more likely to be from the right.

The war on drugs is worse than the drugs themselves in many cases, according to a report done by the CATO Institute.[528] The report cited the militarization of the police and how minority communities are more likely to be raided by militarized SWAT teams by DEA drug enforcers.[529] It also mentions the felony convictions that are disproportionately high and a lot higher for blacks than for

---

[526] Eric Cain, contributor. The War on Drugs is a War on Minorities and the Poor. Forbes Magazine. retrieved February 8, 2020 https://www.forbes.com/sites/erikkain/2011/06/28/the-war-on-drugs-is-a-war-on-minorities-and-the-poor/#2e1925b0624c

[527] Christopher J. Coyne and Abigail R. Hall. April 12, Policy Analysis 811. Four Decades and Counting: The Continued Failure of the War on Drugs. The Cato Institute. retrieved February 1, 2020 https://www.cato.org/publications/policy-analysis/four-decades-counting-continued-failure-war-drugs

[528] Christopher J. Coyne and Abigail R. Hall. April 12, 2017. Policy Analysis No 811. Four Decades and Counting: The Continued Failure of the War on Drugs. The CATO Institute. retrieved February 25, 2020 https://www.cato.org/publications/policy-analysis/four-decades-counting-continued-failure-war-drugs?gclid=EAIaIQobChMIttLF4p3t5wIVSL7ACh01aw4WEAAYASAAEgIsRvD_BwE

[529] Ibid.

whites because of the war.[530] It comments on how felony convictions as a result of the war result in inability to get student loans, having voting rights suspended, have the right to own a firearm taken away, and a whole host of other things.[531] There are other studies from other sources that confirm this as well. Another study confirmed that per 100,000 people who are arrested for using and selling drugs, 879 are Black, and only 332 are white.[532] It has also created an environment where the media can more easily vilify black people and especially young black males as drug users who need to be criminalized for their drug use versus white suburbanite males who should be given medical support and counseling for their fate.

Illegal drugs are a factor for so many of the homicides with guns in some sectors of the black community. Now since the police are in the process of being defunded, there has been a spike in crime, and it is affecting people of color in Democrat-run cities across America with an increase again in homicides.[533] With too many senseless murders that criminals know they can get away with, the next thing to follow will be gun confiscations, which will be a violation of the Second Amendment of the Constitution. That is what the left wants, and the gang problem and all of the murders in the black community that result from it will give them a purpose to proceed toward that goal. Once guns have all been confiscated, the gun laws can be enacted to resemble those more like the USSR during the Stalin

---

[530] Ibid.

[531] Ibid.

[532] German Lopez. Updated May 8, 2016. VOX. The war on drugs, explained. retrieved https://www.vox.com/2016/5/8/18089368/war-on-drugs-marijuana-cocaine-heroin-meth

[533] Peter Nickeas, Julia Jones, Josh Campbell and Priya Krishnakumar. CNN. Updated May 25, 2021. Defund the police encounters resistance as violent crime spikes. retrieved August 2, 2021 https://www.cnn.com/2021/05/25/us/defund-police-crime-spike/index.html

and post-Stalin eras. [534] These laws will not apply to blacks only; they will apply to everyone. When this happens, the only people allowed to use guns legally will be those sanctioned and, in some cases, even ordered to do some more sinister things than all of the handgun murders that occur in America every year, added to the ones that occur in Planned Parenthood clinics every day. This is how they can use an issue that disproportionately affects blacks to accomplish one of their goals.

If the left and Progressives cared so much about the black community, why didn't they try and stop so many black boys from being murdered in gangs or being a part of the prison industrial complex? That could be done by passing a few laws, but their policies that criminalized black activity like one hundred times more severe sentencing for crack cocaine versus regular powder cocaine as one example have created the problems to begin with. Conservatives are generally against the militarization of the police, and they are more likely to be pro Second Amendment than Liberals. Keep in mind, a police force designed by a socialist state can also be racist and a lot more brutal on everyone than one whose purpose is to protect and serve.

If they defund the police, the high crime pockets in black America that can rely on the police for some protection and that can exist as a deterrent to crime that will keep some law and order will not be present anymore. When this happens, these pockets will become completely lawless in some cases and a disproportionately high number of their victims of killing, assaults, armed robbery and the like will be blacks, and the criminals will be the rule of law, not the police. The question we should be asking is which would be

---

[534] Nikolay Shevchenko. Russia. Beyond How Russians lost their own 2nd Amendment: The right to bear arms. History. Nov 28 2017. retrieved Nov 6, 2019 https://www.rbth.com/history/326865-guns-rifles-russia-revolution

better: the current law enforcement presence or the criminal's vs. unarmed citizens? When this progressive policy is enforced, more crime will spill over into other black neighborhoods, making them really bad ones or worse. This is a slippery slope because it can be a pretext to legally remove guns of all types from all American citizens to protect themselves because a few bad people have guns. This could result in the government with all of the guns to do some more sinister things to the citizens than the criminals are maybe a lot more. This is where the left is using a black issue to progress one of their agendas when they don't have their best interests at heart.

African slaves were a free source of labor to help build the infrastructure they needed to create, which was very expensive. This is what is happening today with prison labor—to help build the new infrastructure, the black community is providing nearly half of the labor from just 12 percent of the US population because of leftists' policies and causes. This is one that the Democratic Socialists want to see put in. This infrastructure and plan is expensive, but it has to be financed. This is no different than what happened that victimized black people for many years in the past. For this infrastructure plan, the left can use black labor, just like it was used for years in the North[535] for slaves to put in their infrastructure of roads, buildings, and even as commodities on Wall Street.[536] The South, with the cotton, tobacco, and sugarcane crops, had free labor to grow for exportation and sales to foreign markets and to create an economy in America.

---

[535] Christopher Klein. FEB 5, 2019 ORIGINAL: JUN 25, 2014. Deeper Roots of Northern Slavery Unearthed. retrieved March 16, 2021 https://www.history.com/news/deeper-roots-of-northern-slavery-unearthed

[536] Zoe Thomas. BBC Business reporter, New York BBC News. The hidden links between slavery and Wall Street. retrieved March 16, 2021 https://www.bbc.com/news/business-49476247

The left likes this because black people can be used for this, and indirectly and unknowingly Democratic Socialists and Progressives support this. This is probably mostly unknowingly since the left can influence the media, and the educational system is teaching them that this is the right thing to do. When black people keep spending their money everywhere but in the black community and voting for the Democratic party 90 percent of the time this makes it a lot easier to accomplish their goal. With the situation that has been created in those really bad pockets of the black community and some that are just bad, the police were encouraged to make arrest quotas, which could supply victims to build the prison industrial complex for this leftist cause.

Now that the police have been largely defunded in large cities and stores both small mom and pop stores and big box chain stores have been looted of billions of dollars in merchandise they have stopped making arrest quotas and they have focused attention on the young black and brown youth who are doing not all but a lot of the looting so they can be demonized by the left leaning media so they can be targeted for elimination from society which is a progressive left leaning thing. They can put them back in the same prison industrial complex that they are temporarily emptying a few people from. If it had been up to right leaning conservatives and a lot of classical liberals none of this would be the case.

7.

Is DEI the New Affirmative Action

Affirmative action was instituted on September 24, 1965[537], prohibiting employment discrimination based on race, color, religion, and national origin by those organizations receiving federal contracts and subcontracts[538]. Back then Americas demographics were different and Affirmative Action was just to undo some of the damage done from years of past wrongs and discrimination to mainly blacks but some other ethnic minorities and women were included[539]. This was not necessarily a bad thing for blacks when you consider what had historically happened negatively to blacks from more traditional belief about race up until that time in history. If I were to take a guess, I would say it was probably pushed by progressives. DEI is just another politically correct way to continue Affirmative Action and to now cause more division between groups which is different from what affirmative action was originally intended for. Another thing you have to take into consideration is

---

[537] Division of Equity Inclusion and Compliance. Office of Equal Opportunity and Diversity. A brief History of Affirmative Action retrieved February 29, 2024 https://www.oeod.uci.edu/policies/aa_history.php#:~:text=On%20September%2024%2C%201965%20President,receiving%20federal%20contracts%20and%20subcontracts.

[538] Ibid

[539] Ibid

back then affirmative action required that you meet certain qualifications for jobs but with DEI at times that is questionable.

These affirmative action policies were never intended to give ownership and/or control of any of America's economy, its wealth, it resources, or its businesses to its black minority, only jobs and dependency on a system that it has no control over. This leaves you at a big disadvantage in a completely or partially integrated society, and that was by design. Booker T. Washington's plan for a strong black business community, before attempting to do this in a way that guaranteed a black minority the proper amount of ownership and control with partial integration was the best to have.

Affirmative action was instituted on many small businesses,[540] large corporations,[541] and government institutions[542] all over America, but all it did was got you a position in the white institution.

At the beginning of the affirmative action error as well when blacks did not get promotions and raises like their white counterparts; when their white counterparts were invited to secret meetings on the side or little social events, they were putting their white counterparts at a clear advantage. This was done to maintain institutionalized racism, and some businesses/institutions had a worse racial climate than others. This was more so the case at the beginning of the affirmative action movement than it is now. So, to combat this, groups such as the NAACP had to come in with lawsuits to force

---

[540] Heidi Cardenas. Affirmative Action Plan for Small Business. Chron retrieved September 20, 2020. https://smallbusiness.chron.com/affirmative-action-plan-small-business-47364.html

[541] Lawrence Hurley. Reuters. Big businesses back affirmative action before U.S. Supreme Court. retrieved September 20, 2020 https://www.reuters.com/article/us-usa-court-affirmativeaction/big-businesses-back-affirmative-action-before-u-s-supreme-court-idUSKCN0SU34620151105

[542] US Department of Labor. Affirmative Action. retrieved September 20, 2020 https://www.dol.gov/general/topic/hiring/affirmativeact

businesses to comply with racial quotas.[543] This gave the government more control or at least influence over private sector organizations and society for their interests.

Some black children that have attended terrible schools that have produced a group in certain pockets in the black community that is actually less capable. Now because of multiculturalism and diversity, which is another leftist cause, institutions were in a since being forced to comply with affirmative action and now DEI. Now they will have to cater to all the other people of non-white ethnic backgrounds and women who in many cases came from much better schools than some of the terrible ones that black children did which gives them a big edge academically. With this setup, black people or at least a smaller percentage of them will need to be factored into the equation when it comes DEI positions because if they can't compete academically with everyone else, they can be factored out especially if affirmative action is abolished altogether. I will explain why I think it may be later on in the article.

The affirmative action programs that the leftist and progressive liberal policymakers invented still did not replace all of the positions lost from blacks who lost all of their jobs because of the economic collapse due to the refusal of non-blacks to patronize black businesses, with billions of dollars resulting in their failed attempt to completely integrate; neither did it make up for past pre-civil rights era injustices. All it did was remove enough whites from some of their higher-paying jobs to meet racial quotas and replace them with blacks to make them feel as if they were or given this illusion that they had arrived and just enough to keep whites angry at blacks for taking their jobs.

---

[543] More History of Affirmative Action Policies from the 1960s. retrieved September 20, 2020 https://www.aaaed.org/aaaed/History_of_Affirmative_Action.asp

In the end, a lot of whites lost their jobs that they previously had before affirmative action, and blacks still had no ownership or control over the institutions they worked in to empower themselves, not to mention all the blatant and indirectly racist practices that continued to go on at some of these institutions that blacks could do nothing about. In other words, it kept a bit of animosity toward blacks by whites, and it didn't remedy any negative feelings that blacks have had toward whites, either. What it did do was give the government another chance to enforce laws on corporations and small businesses, thus expanding government's power and influence over society with little if any regard for the betterment of the black community as far as ownership and control of their sector of the economy is concerned. DEI will be no better, I think it will in many ways be worse.

I think affirmative action was and now DEI and are just clever ways for the left to integrate society that really causes more division in a way that they can use its expected negative outcomes for blacks to advance their agenda.

Now that black kids have been disproportionately attending Common Core,[544] and No Child Left Behind schools, which were designed mostly by the left, that just don't give a good education like traditional schools did, they are not as prepared to compete with people who were educated in places with schools that have some better choices with much better educational standards. Now there are more of other groups that must be included in the leftist / progressive Liberals' pool of DEI and multiculturalism such as Hispanics, Asians, Arabs, East Indians, and others. These groups are a lot more numerous now than they were when the leftist causes of *multiculturalism* and *diversity* were

---

[544] Casey Quinlan. Liberal Indoctrination Through Common Core and Other Fears Stoked by Conservative s. Feb 10, 2016, retrieved June 13, 2019 https://thinkprogress.org/liberal-indoctrination-through-common-core-and-other-fears-stoked-by-conservative s-f814847e6355

first coined by the leftist movement sometime in the 1960s. When these terms were first coined, there weren't nearly as many Asians and Hispanics as there are now, and some other groups such as Arabs and East Indians weren't even a part of the equation because they were so rare. A lot of these people, especially certain groups of them, since they are doing better financially than a lot of blacks, can afford to put their kids in better schools that a lot of blacks, and now they must be included in affirmative action and DEI programs. Now, as a result, a lot of blacks can be excluded because they are not as prepared academically in some cases. Since some of these ethnic backgrounds, including whites, are doing so much better than blacks in business creation, and they are just running circles around black people in STEM fields, especially at the master's and PhD levels for medical doctors, scientists, and engineers,[545] they will have the following advantages. With more business creation it will make them as groups more powerful and influential to change society in their favor in a way that it benefits them and the doctors, scientists and engineers that are created by them can be used as a tool to do it which just makes the advantages more advantageous. It will give them dominance in arenas of society that blacks just will not be able to have. In some cases, blacks start these fields in colleges and universities but drop out of them before they graduate.[546]

Since blacks are a smaller percentage of non-whites, other groups will get a larger percentage of DEI positions. Also at the secret meetings

---

[545] Natalie Escobar, Contributor Report: Black Students Underrepresented in High-Paying STEM Majors, US News Feb. 9, 2016, https://www.usnews.com/news/stem-solutions/articles/2016-02-09/report-black-students-underrepresented-in-high-paying-stem-majors

[546] Kenneth I. Maton, Mariano R. Sto Domingo, Kathleen E. Stolle-McAllister, J. Lynn Zimmerman, and Freeman A. Hrabowski III. HHS Public Access Enhancing the Number of African Americans Who Pursue STEM PhDs: Meyerhoff Scholarship Program Outcomes, Processes, and Individual Predictors. J Women Minor Sci Eng. Author manuscript; available in PMC 2011 Aug 10. Retrieved June 8, 2019 https://www.ncbi.nlm.nih.gov/pmc/articles/PMC3154119/

at offsite locations, and the little conversations around the water cooler and some other forms of blatant or even just subtle racism are not necessary to exclude black people, even in a merit-based system because blacks are just not measuring up, especially academically. It makes no difference how much money you donate to the United Negro College Fund, the National Urban league, or any other organization that funds the education of black students; if too many of them are reading and doing mathematics at levels far too low to enter college. To change this, changes need to be made at grades K-12 before they have reached college, more of them need to have a father in the home and a whole host of other things. Later in the article I discuss some of the problems Detroit's public school system was having which points out some things to do and not to do if you want to improve the educational system and the quality of education for black youth in some little pockets in the black community with really bad neighborhoods. I will discuss some examples of what needs to be changed and how later in the article.

Since these demographics are much bigger now and they must begiven a bigger piece of the pie when it comes the new racial quotes under DEI the black community lost all of the empowerment district they had like Blackwall street, Harlem NYC and Frisch street in Jackson MI with some safety nets for employment and other ethnic background have some of their own economic empowerment districts in their own communities with safety nets for employment this leaves blacks with no safety nets unless the businesses in the empowerment districts are forced to comply with DEI. Both DEI and integration were progressive policies and causes.

The reason for affirmative action was to encourage unionization of workers[547] and to infuse militancy into the workforce,[548] and the people of all races and ethnicities would integrate in the public sector and would demand social services,[549] which would come from the government. This would expand government more, which is the socialist bottom line.

When union members pay their dues, the money is often used to support someone else's political agenda.[550, 551] Unions are great, but they should only be used in the interest of the worker, not for a progressive political cause that is not in the interest of the worker. Progressive policies and causes have not been kind to black Americans over the past 40 or 50 years.

If it had been up to Conservatives, this progressive/leftist cause of affirmative action would not have been proposed and pushed like it has been; complete integration would not have either, and blacks would have the business infrastructure and all of the institutions that should be black-owned and -run that were lost in their community as a result of complete integration and destabilization from the feminist movement and all the others discussed in this article, which were created by the left. I do think that integration would have still happened to an extent in society but not completely. I think it would have happened to an extent that both Liberals and Conservatives could tolerate.

---

[547] Steve Hoffman. December 2016. Affirmative action = class solidarity. Freedom Socialist Party. retrieved August 12, 2020 https://socialism.com/fs-article/affirmative-action-class-solidarity/

[548] Ibid.

[549] Ibid.

[550] UnionFact.com. retrieved December 12, 2020. https://www.unionfacts.com/article/political-money/

[551] Americans for Fair Treatment AFSCME: Where do your union dues go? 2018–19. retrieved December 12, 2020 https://www.americansforfairtreatment.org/faq/afscme-where-do-your-dues-go-2018-19/

Affirmative action required that small businesses and large corporations give jobs to minorities who were previously discriminated against and not really allowed to participate fully in the American experiment.[552] That sounds good on the outside, but what you have to understand is that affirmative action gives incentive for blacks to continue to completely integrate with whites and everyone else. If this continues, it prevents blacks from starting their own business community and the five-tier plan that Dr. Claude Anderson advocates for the black community, with group economics so they are not so dependent on white institutions and so they don't get smothered out by all of the other ethnic groups. This keeps blacks more dependent on government, and it just makes it bigger and more powerful. If this continues, the left can continue to use blacks to accomplish more of their causes to steer America toward the cause of socialism and communism and away from capitalism and a free market, which can really be utilized now by the black community for its own good.

There is nothing wrong with having a diverse workforce but the goal here should be to achieve a qualified workforce. If you are putting more importance on a diverse equitable and inclusive workforce, if your work force is less qualified it will negatively affect the quality of your product or service. If too many institutions across America have poorer quality goods and services, it will affect American greatness and exceptionalism in a negative way. The worst aspect of DEI is its application in very technical fields where the hire or the employee needs to be good at what he does because even a small error or slip up could mean for some dire consequences.

---

[552] What is Affirmative Action and Why Was it Created? GH.org Legal Recourses. retrieved September 12, 2020 https://www.hg.org/legal-articles/what-is-affirmative-action-and-why-was-it-created-31524

Some of the best ways to increase diversity aren't even designed with diversity in mind.[553] Studies have shown current DEI methods cause backlash and bias[554] and they don't really increase diversity.[555] Three common diversity interventions used by DEI actually make firms less diverse.[556] There are other ways to increase diversity that work[557] that are not really being used by a lot of progressive DEI programs that aren't control and shaming tactics[558] because they spark engagement and increase contact between groups.[559] Law suits have been filled by the firms forced to comply just as with affirmative action which get legal action involved which is government involvement to make these companies comply like a big bully. With Affirmative Action the way it was done for years before the practice was not done as much, only five groups of people were considered for compensations and job placements depending on race, ethnicity, gender, religion and disability status. DEI is different in that it adds some more groups to the previous five plus all the letters of LGBTQAI+ which adds another three, four or maybe five more groups. It could add even more than this depending on certain ethnic and religious groups that have grown and come on the scene in just the past 10 or 20 years and maybe some others to come. With more groups to compensate with job placements, with enough pressure on supervisors to comply gives

---

[553] Frank Dobbin and Alexandra Kalev Harvard Business Review Why Diversity Programs Fail and What Works Better retrieved January 11, 2024 https://hbr.org/2016/07/why-diversity-programs-fail

[554] Ibid

[555] Ibid

[556] Ibid

[557] Ibid

[558] Ibid

[559] Ibid

them more incentive to bind rules to make it happen or face legal action. According to an article from the New York Post DEI promotes division and not unity.[560]

According to an article from Trinity College DEI is An Agent of White Supremacy.[561] It claimed that Diversity Equity and Inclusion initiatives are agents of systemic white racism in that it allow whites to remain in power and uphold the illusion that through modifications of an individual's behaviors can there be a racism-free world[562]. It is an agent of the college and will at the end of the day protect and uphold those in power at this institution.[563]

According to an article from Forbes DEI is anti-black[564] because 81% of CDO (chief diversity officers) are white and they dictate the narrative for DEI programs,[565] it still does not always address pay inequalities,[566] black issues be deprioritized,[567] and non-white groups are aggregated or placed into groups that designate certain expectations.[568] of the group.

---

[560] Rikki Schlott DEI is failing because it 'promotes division instead of unity': DEI pro The New York Post Published July 31, 2023 Updated July 31, 2023, 4:11 p.m. ET retrieved January 12, 2024 https://nypost.com/2023/07/31/dei-industry-failing-promotes-division-instead-of-unity/

[561] Karolina Barrientos diversity, Equity and Inclusion An Agent of White Supremacy: Diversity, Equity and Inclusion Trinity College Digital Repository 2022 retrieved March 14, 2024 https://digitalrepository.trincoll.edu/cgi/viewcontent.cgi?article=1001&context=stdtpapers

[562] Ibid

[563] Ibid

[564] Janice Gassam Asare Senior Contributor Forbes Magazine 4 Ways Anti-Blackness Shows Up In DEI retreived March 14, 2024 https://www.forbes.com/sites/janicegassam/2023/01/25/4-ways-anti-blackness-shows-up-in-dei/?sh=7734ba5e5e8d

[565] Ibid

[566] Ibid

[567] Ibid

[568] Ibid

Is DEI the New Affirmative Action

Affirmative action may be coming to an end. The reason why I say affirmative action policies may all be eliminated everywhere in society is because of the rift that Asian Americans made about quotas on college admittance into America's most elite universities favoring blacks and Hispanics over whites and Asians[569] under the guise of multiculturalism, diversity, equity and inclusion. They claimed it was unconstitutional.[570] This could just be the beginning of its end everywhere in America. If it stays in arenas where Asians have an advantage it may be the beginning of the widening of an already existing division between Asians with blacks and Hispanics, because Asians will feel disenfranchised. If it goes and Asian still have these advantages the division between the two could still widen because blacks and Hispanics may feel disenfranchised. The whole issue of it staying for the policy and causes of DEI diversity, equity, and inclusion and not merit was an issue being pushed by left leaning progressives and here they were able to use a black disadvantage that was largely produced by some of their previously and currently existing polices and causes to possibly keep this divide going and maybe even make it worse.

Even if affirmative action is removed from laws as a legal term but it is replaced with another euphemism for it like DEI could it be used to accomplish some other progressive goals like equity? If it had been up to conservatives, I don't think DEI or affirmative action would have ever been an issue. Now there may have been sone advantages to that.

---

[569] Dan Mangun CNBC Politics   Politics Supreme Court Rejects Affirmative Action At Colleges As Unconstitutional   Published Thu, Jun 29 2023 10:08 Am Edit updated Thu, Jun 29 2023 4:22 Pm Edit retrieved July 10, 2023 https://www.cnbc.com/2023/06/29/supreme-court-rejects-affirmative-action-at-colleges-says-schools-cant-consider-race-in-admission.html

[570] Ibid

8.

The Educational System

Every since Progressives and the leftists became involved with the US educational system, the quality of our Common Core, No Child Left Behind educational system has become progressively worse. Americans who went to school during the 1960s ranked a respectable third[571] in literacy compared with the rest of the world, with only two countries more literate than US adults; by the 1970s, adults schooled in US schools ranked fifth[572] in the world with four other countries more literate than US adults. But 16-to-25-year-old adults who were wandering America's school hallways during the 1980s and 1990s, ranked 14th.[573] In short, the literacy survey records a simple, steady progression downward.[574]

Developing countries are leading in educational innovation. More standard government schools are failing many children, especially in low-income neighborhoods,[575] which are more likely to

---

[571] Paul E. Peterson. EducationNext Publication. Ticket to Nowhere. Spring 2003 / Vol. 3, No. 2. retrieved August 1, 2019 https://www.educationnext.org/tickettonowhere

[572] Ibid.

[573] Ibid.

[574] Ibid.

[575] Lawrence McQuillan. September 24, 2018. Education Articles https://catalyst.independent.org/2018/09/24/developing-countries-lead-in-education-innovation/ retrieved May 16, 2019

be black or Hispanic. America's schools are more segregated than ever. Schools can be integrated, but to do it, the state will have to expand public institutions and redistribute wealth.[576] Integration seems great to anyone who does not seem openly rebellious. There were reasons and even incentives for policies that supported school desegregation. Some are political, some are material, and some are to foster multiculturalism,[577] which has not improved the school system because it was not intended to nor was it designed to.

These schools have been feminized,[578] so the gold standard for behavior is a good little girl,[579] and boys get suspended from school more often for behavior[580] only because they have a different nature than girls. Therefore, boys are more likely to drop out of these schools in grades K through 12. These schools are just not as good at educating as schools were at one time. I read a book by Charlotte Iserbyte called *The Deliberate Dumbing Down of America*.[581] It explains how the school systems got this bad and what the motive was for driving American schools into the ground like they have

---

[576] Mike Stivers. The Socialist Case for School Integration. 07.09.2018. United States Education Race Magazine. https://jacobinmag.com/2018/07/the-socialist-case-for-school-integration retrieved July 5, 2019

[577] Mike Stivers. Jacobin Magazine. The Socialist Case for School Integration. 07.09.2018. United States Education Race. https://jacobinmag.com/2018/07/the-socialist-case-for-school-integration retrieved July 5, 2019

[578] Don Closson. The Feminization of American Schools. retrieved August 12, 2020 http://www.leaderu.com/orgs/probe/docs/fem-schools.html

[579] Ibid.

[580] Travis Riddle and Stacey Sinclair. Racial disparities in school-based disciplinary actions are associated with county-level rates of racial bias. PNA.S retrieved August 12, 2020 https://www.pnas.org/content/116/17/8255

[581] Sam Blumenfeld The Deliberate Dumbing Down of America Tuesday, 08 February 2011 retrieved July 7, 2019 https://www.thenewamerican.com/reviews/books/item/6443-the-deliberate-dumbing-down-of-america

been. The universities have more dropouts with a higher dropout rate for black men than black women.[582] Whites are more likely to have more choices than Common Core such as magnet, charter, private, religious schools, and suburban public schools with better student-to-teacher ratios.[583] Even if black kids are fortunate enough to attend one of these schools, which is often the case, their history and culture is not really taught like it was or could have been in an all-black schools, so they come out better educated but with a loss of their sense of identity.

Schools with lots of low-income students in large urban centers with high concentrations of black students don't receive instructional resources like better-equipped suburban districts.[584] Inequalities in these low-income, mostly minority districts are compounded by a system that assigns children in high-, middle-, or low-achievement curriculums based on perceived ability.[585] As a result, these schools have fewer and lower quality resources and supplies with larger class sizes and less qualified and/or experienced

---

[582] CJ Libassi. May 23, 2018,. Center for American Progress. The Neglected College Race Gap: Racial Disparities Among College Completers. retrieved March 19, 2021 https://www.americanprogress.org/issues/education-postsecondary/reports/2018/05/23/451186/neglected-college-race-gap-racial-disparities-among-college-completers/

[583] Grover J. "Russ" Whitehurst, New evidence on school choice and racially segregated schools, Brookings Institute, Thursday, December 14, 2017, https://www.brookings.edu/research/new-evidence-on-school-choice-and-racially-segregated-schools/

[584] Chris Duncombe. Unequal Opportunities: Fewer Resources, Worse Outcomes for Students in Schools with Concentrated Poverty. October 26, 2017. The Common Wealth Institute. https://www.thecommonwealthinstitute.org/2017/10/26/unequal-opportunities-fewer-resources-worse-outcomes-for-students-in-schools-with-concentrated-poverty/ Retrieved November 24, 2019.

[585] Emma García. Economic Snapshot. ..January 13, 2017. Poor black children are much more likely to attend high-poverty schools than poor white children. Economic Policy Institutes. https://www.epi.org/publication/poor-black-children-are-much-more-likely-to-attend-high-poverty-schools-than-poor-white-children/ retrieved November 24, 2019

instructors. These schools have a difficult time getting the quality curriculum they need to educate gifted children. These schools often don't offer appropriate math or science curricula to prepare students for college. The ones that do offer them have instructors who are often inadequate to teach these subjects.[586]

Common Core is a set of standards that have been pushed for a global education system, and it is being forced on America in an attempt to dumb down America because our educational standards have traditionally been much higher than a lot of the world's, and with higher educational standards,[587] it gives you clear advantages over everyone else, making it harder for everyone else to compete with you. This one was pushed by anti-American globalist leftists.[588] It will make Americans less competitive than the rest of the world on a global scale. These globalists hate America, and they want to bring America down, so they are doing it more effectively through one of America's weakest links: the black community. That is the plan by the new global school board UNESCO,[589] which is supported by both Progressives and leftists, and black people have been put in a more vulnerable spot both by leftist policies and causes that have been created in the past and for other reasons. The black community is just in a better position to work with them and globalists

---

[586] Linda Darling-Hammond. Brookings. Unequal Opportunity: Race and Education. March 1, 1998. retrieved June 15, 2019 https://www.brookings.edu/articles/unequal-opportunity-race-and-education/

[587] William Haupt III. Op-Ed: The dumbing down of America. Watchdog.org Contributing Columnist. Nov 26, 2018. retrieved Sept 18, 2019 https://www.watchdog.org/national/op-ed-the-dumbing-down-of-america/article_61f64000-f181-11e8-a22e-6bd70b62cd6c.html

[588] Ibid

[589] Ileana Johnson. The Epoch Times. The Link Between Declining National Education Quality and UN Agenda 2030 July 15, 2018. Updated: July 18, 2018. retrieved Sept 20, 2019 https://www.theepochtimes.com/the-link-between-declining-national-education-quality-and-un-agenda-2030_2592656.html

to accomplish their causes, but it doesn't mean that they care about black people or the quality of life or the standard of education they get. They are going to get what they want from the black community.

When they earn their bachelor's degrees, black college graduates owe $7,400 more on average than their white counterparts.[590] On average, they owe $23,400 versus $16,000 like their white counterparts, including non-borrowers in the averages.[591] But over the next few years, the black–white debt gap more than triples to a whopping $25,000.[592] Differences in interest accrual and graduate-school borrowing lead to black graduates holding nearly $53,000 in student loan debt four years after graduation—almost twice as much as their white counterparts.[593] So the quest for equality through education has created the need for more outside assistance and dependence on other non-black entities to relieve the debt, which leaves black people more dependent than ever. The government can create more programs for their expansion and control and dependency on them, which will still be disproportionately higher for blacks. This is one of the main bottom lines for leftists, not all but some of the very most progressive and socialists, and they can accelerate this process through the black community as a victimhood group.

Since multiculturalism and DEI are necessary even in every type of curriculum in school, black people must be represented equally across the board. African Americans are just not represented

---

[590] Judith Scott-Clayton and Jing Li. Study by The Brookings Institute. Black-white disparity in student loan debt more than triples after graduation. October 20, 2016. retrieved October 17, 2019 https://www.brookings.edu/research/black-white-disparity-in-student-loan-debt-more-than-triples-after-graduation

[591] Ibid.

[592] Ibid.

[593] Ibid.

proportionately in mathematics and sciences,[594] especially not at the PhD level and especially since the Common Core, No Child Left Behind schools that a lot of them attend just don't prepare them for these curricula at the PhD level. So to maintain diversity, some schools have recruited black people from Africa and have given them visas, to meet their DEI quotas, but they are different than African Americans who were born and raised in America, and they may change the definition of what it means to be black in America to something that African Americans don't like, thanks to multiculturalism and DEI, which is a leftist cause.

If it were up to Conservatives, who at least tend to be more right-wing thinkers, these ridiculous concepts like Africans being brought to the Americas as guest workers instead of admitting America had slavery[595] would not be taught, by left leaning progressive school board officials in grades K-12 and we would continue as a nation to know our history, not to be proud that America had slavery, but to remember that it happened and how horrible it was so it will not be repeated. Our American public schools, which now have a curriculum and a cause and an agenda, which is dominated and influenced by the left with left-leaning Progressives as its foot soldiers, claims that America invented slavery.[596] That is ridiculous; slavery existed thousands of years before America was even a concept, before the

---

[594] Betsy Ladyzhets. December 16, 2020. Science News. These 6 graphs show that Black scientists are underrepresented at every level. retrieved March 19, 2021 https://www.sciencenews.org/article/black-scientists-disparities-representation-stem-science

[595] Manny Fernandez and Christine Hauser. The New York Times. Texas Mother Teaches Textbook Company a Lesson on Accuracy. Oct. 5, 2015. retrieved July 12, 2019 https://www.nytimes.com/2015/10/06/us/publisher-promises-revisions-after-textbook-refers-to-african-slaves-as-workers.html 5

[596] Kate Hardiman. Most college students think America invented slavery, professor finds—University of Notre Dame. October 31, 2016. retrieved July 13, 2019 https://www.thecollegefix.com/college-students-think-america-invented-slavery-professor-finds/

European colonial period, which resulted in America, was even a concept in a number of empires across the world in ancient history.[597] This will mislead or miseducate black people and everyone else the wrong way about black people and the world. This is called changing the past to fit your narrative, or sanitizing history so it is not so painful to face. Leftist textbook publishers and editors are allowing this practice to continue in our textbooks. Another ridiculous topic of study that Progressives are proposing in our public schools that is not going to help the lot of black people at all is critical race theory, and it is not going to make society any less racist.[598]

We have to be very careful about critical race theory. It was deemed a necessary part of our educational curriculum in some of our public schools in America, but it was heavily influenced[599] by Marxists, who are on the left, and they are the same organization who support the teaching of evolution with atheists.[600] It is hard to find any connections anymore to evolution and the white or Caucasian race as being higher up the evolutionary chain and thus superior and just more fit that the more inferior black or Negroid race, but evolutionists believed this at one time; they believed it for

---

[597] Tom Lindsay. Aug 30, 2019, 'After All, Didn't America Invent Slavery?' Forbes. retrieved https://www.forbes.com/sites/tomlindsay/2019/08/30/after-all-didnt-america-invent-slavery/#10cb14c37ef6

[598] James Lindsay. June 12, 2020. Eight Big Reasons Critical Race Theory Is Terrible for Dealing with Racism New Discourses. retrieved https://newdiscourses.com/2020/06/reasons-critical-race-theory-terrible-dealing-racism/

[599] Ed Stetzer and Andrew MacDonald. July 3, 2020. Social Justice, Critical Race Theory, Marxism, and Biblical Ethics. retrieved January 23, 2021 https://www.christianitytoday.com/edstetzer/2020/june/reflections-from-christian-scholar-on-social-justice-critic.html

[600] Austin Anderson The Dark Side of Darwinism Philosophy for the Many Literary Theory • Fall 2019 Posted on November 16, 2016 retrieved October 29, 2019 https://sites.williams.edu/engl-209-fall16/uncategorized/the-dark-side-of-darwinism/

a long time and have just recently debunked this claim.[601] What we have to ask ourselves is: Is critical race theory being used to replace or to continue the effect that evolution has produced (like the inferiority and superiority of certain races) since the evolutionist spin on this subject has basically been debunked? Evolution is from a school of thought that is endorsed by progressives, and their claim for years by many evolutionists was that some races that are higher up the evolutionary chain than others are superior to others, especially those who are the farthest down the evolutionary chain, such as sub-Saharan African Negroids, but it is also very racist. Critical race theory is from a progressive, leftist school of thought as well. The teaching of both critical race theory and white privilege are bad concepts to be a part of American society.

The Common Core grades K through 12 public schools[602, 603] that graduate more functional illiterates[604] than ever, that black children more often have no choice but to attend, put them often at an academic disadvantage when they graduate, and their white counterparts can afford private schools, charter schools, and less

---

[601] Lisa Wade, PhD on July 12, 2012 Sociological Images Whites, Blacks, and Apes in the Great Chain of Being retrieved January 24, 2021 https://thesocietypages.org/socimages/2012/07/12/Whites-Blacks-apes-in-the-great-chain-of-being/

[602] Joachim Hagopian The Dumbing Down of America—By Design Region: USA Theme: History, Media Disinformation Global Research, January 30, 2018 First published by GR in August 2014 retrieved August 21, 2019 https://www.globalresearch.ca/the-dumbing-down-of-america-by-design/5395928

[603] Casey Quinlan Liberal Indoctrination Through Common Core And Other Fears Stoked By Conservative s Feb 10, 2016, 3:42 pm retrieved July 17, 2019 https://thinkprogress.org/liberal-indoctrination-through-common-core-and-other-fears-stoked-by-conservatives-f814847e6355

[604] Rebecca Lake Shocking Facts: 23 Statistics on Illiteracy in America By Read more about Financial Literacy Month Updated May 12, 2016 retrieved August 12, 2019 https://www.creditdonkey.com/illiteracy-in-america.html

crowded suburban[605] schools, which was more of an intention of the left. Those same schools who have been feminized and have resulted in a higher dropout rates for black boys than black girls, the universities have been feminized,[606] resulting in lower admission rates and higher dropout rates for black men than black women,[607] and this was planned by the left to dumb America down for a global agenda. For every three black women who graduate college, only two black men do, and according to another source, it is two black women for every one black man,[608] which means a lot of black women will be single without a husband after they graduate, unless they marry out of their race or marry a black man with less education, which usually means less earning power, so a lot of black women will not have their career and a husband, unless they can find a man with a business or some other endeavor that he can support her with. Some black women have even said they would marry out of their race to find a soulmate, but the problem with that is women are a lot more successful than men with higher education in all other races and ethnic backgrounds as well. Now the men of other races and ethnic backgrounds have a lot more choices for college-educated women with high earning power in their own race. Since that is the case, black women are not as likely to be a possibility for them when they have women from so many other races to choose from. This will mean a

---

[605] Sean Scott. Education, Government, Poverty Urban and Suburban Divide Creates Inequity in Education. BDJ 364.01. May 3, 2018. https://nccnews.expressions.syr.edu/2018/05/03/urban-and-suburban-divide-creates-inequity-in-education/

[606] Jon Anthony. Return of Kings How Our Feminized School System Is Crippling Young Boys. February 14, 2017. retrieved June 9, 2019 http://www.returnofkings.com/105985/how-our-feminized-school-system-is-crippling-young-boys

[607] Ibid

[608] http://www.jbhe.com/news_views/51_gendergap_universities.html Journal of Blacks in Higher Education. Copyright 2006. retrieved September 17, 2018.

lonely single life for a lot of black women who will end up married to their careers and a lot of them have children, either because they had relations that did not end in commitments or for some other reasons, and some in this demographic are older women who are single with no children. It would never have come to this point had it been up to Conservatives, who are more likely to be right-wing thinkers, or rightists may be a better term.

After the 1954 Supreme Court ruling *Brown v. Board of Ed.*,[609] the number of black teachers in America public schools went from 82,000 to 42,000[610] because many whites did not want their children to be taught by black teachers.[611] To this day only 2 percent of teachers are black men,[612] despite the fact that 50 percent of US public school students are minorities,[613] and far more than 50 percent of teachers are white.[614] This does not encourage black children, especially black boys, to stay in school and pursue higher education.[615] Black students with black teachers are less likely to experience expulsion from the classroom,[616] which decreases the likelihood

---

[609] Nyla Pollard. January 7, 2020. The Heichner Report. STUDENT VOICE: Black boys need the guidance and mentorship of black male teachers. retrieved April 23, 2021 https://hechingerreport.org/student-voice-black-boys-need-the-guidance-and-mentorship-of-black-male-teachers/

[610] Ibid.

[611] Ibid.

[612] Ibid.

[613] Ibid.

[614] Ibid.

[615] Ibid.

[616] Erica Hines and Michael Hines. August 11, 2020. Want to Support Black Students? Invest in Black Teachers. retrieved April 23, 2021 https://time.com/5876164/black-teachers/

of the prison-to-pipeline scenario.[617] This idea was pushed by socialists,[618] who are almost always progressive and far left.

I have this to say about ethnic studies. It seems to have started in universities across the nation during the 1960s as a result of social reform movements for equity and empowerment of racial minorities.[619] Ethnic studies was first proposed by the Third World Liberation Front,[620] which was made up of staff and faculty members from a university on the Greater San Francisco Bay Area,[621] whose politicians and thinkers are some of the most or maybe even the most liberal, left-leaning progressive ones in America. This is one thing I give Progressives a pat on the back for establishing, so I am not saying everything they have proposed over the years was bad for blacks.

Here is why I give progressives a pat on the back for inventing ethnic studies. Ethnic studies courses documented facts from credible researchers that proved that black people made important inventions and contributions to society both American and globally that you could only make if you were a well-rounded intellectual. Another reason I liked ethnic studies is because some of the black inventors were phenomenal; they made some inventions that revolutionized the way we live today, and little is known about them to

---

[617] Ibid.

[618] Mike Stivers. The Socialist Case for School Integration. Jacobin Magazine. Education/Race. July Issue of 2018. retrieved June 2, 2019 https://jacobinmag.com/2018/07/the-socialist-case-for-school-integration

[619] University of Northern Arizona website. Ethnic Studies is. retrieved July 3, 2021 https://nau.edu/ethnic-studies/what-is-es/

[620] San Francisco State University College of Ethnic Studies. retrieved July 24, 2021 https://ethnicstudies.sfsu.edu/history

[621] Ibid.

the rest of the world.[622] It proved that they conducted themselves in both American society and the world in a way that your world civilization history textbooks and American History textbooks written from a more traditional view did not mention. This is just one of the reasons why Progressives seemed more attractive to black leadership, so black people fell for their polices and causes, and ethnic studies was one of a number of these causes. Ethnic studies courses were a space that blacks could go to and really feel validated as people with the same dignity as the rest of humanity when it could be found nowhere else in Western society, including America. In that space, you could hear your story being told differently, and it was the truth. These courses were often sponsored by historically black colleges and universities (HBCUs) that had lots of black intellectuals, both students and college professors, who lived the black experience in America. Some of these college professors wrote the books that they were teaching out of because they did a lot of their own research. In that space as a black person, you could feel great about yourself in a space that proved that you did not have to feel ashamed of being black.

The left wants to incorporate critical race theory into the whole purpose behind ethnic studies,[623] but the term "critical race theory" didn't exist when ethnic studies first came on the scene, so one cannot be used to back the other's need for existing. Ethnic studies is now being used by the left to transform students into activists,

---

[622] Christopher McFadden. The A to Z List of Black Inventors Innovation. July 13, 2018. retrieved May 8, 2019 https://interestingengineering.com/the-a-z-list-of-black-inventors

[623] JOHN FENSTERWALD. Ed Source. A final vote, after many rewrites, for California's controversial ethnic studies curriculum Race and Equality. https://edsource.org/2021/a-final-vote-after-many-rewrites-for-californias-controversial-ethnic-studies-curriculum/651338 March 17, 2021. retrieved June 28, 2021

even as young as first grade[624] since children are so empathetic at such a young and tender age[625] to reshape them ideologically at the core.[626] The curriculum has Marxist style called "pedagogy of the oppressed"[627] incorporated in it, and it is teaching children to hate their country[628] because it is racist,[629] capitalist,[630] sexist,[631] an oppressor of the poor,[632] a colonialist oppressor,[633] and a whole lot of other things. Since no society is perfect or without flaws, these things definitely have historical truth to them. However, if you look at the bigger picture, more people of all races and color, including black people, both male and female, have been able to come to America with its capitalist economy, with its free market as a constitutional republic being less stifled with no oppressors than they were in their country of origin and become more prosperous than in any other country in the world. This is an attempt to dismantle America fundamentally at its core and usher in socialism by the Marxists, and they are using a black cause to do it with when they don't have the best interests of black people at heart.

---

[624] Christopher F. Rufo. April 13, 2021. City Journal Magazine. Education California. The Social Order. retrieved June 28, 2021 https://www.city-journal.org/california-ethnic-studies-programs-merchants-of-revolution

[625] Ibid.

[626] Ibid.

[627] Ibid.

[628] Ibid.

[629] Ibid.

[630] Ibid.

[631] Ibid.

[632] Ibid.

[633] Ibid.

The Educational System

With CRT and white privilege, you can use ethnic studies and American history by altering both curriculums; these alterations can be as simple as a mere tweaking or a downright falsification of facts in either of the two curricula. This could lead to black children and other children of color feeling more like victims and feeling that America owes them, so why care about a nation that victimized you. It could make white children feel more like mean, bad, colonialist, capitalist oppressors, and if that is the case, then why be a part of something that makes you look bad. This will help to hand America and what it stands for over to the socialist leftists, who hate it, so that they can completely dismantle it and turn it into something else that may not be good.

An example of this falsification is the lie that the North did not have slavery,[634] or if it had, it was generally not as harsh, and it ended sooner as a general rule in the North. In a sense, this story was already fabricated so that the North would not have to take blame assessed to it for its role in slavery. Like the fact that slaves were commodities on Wall Street,[635] which is in New York City in a northern state. As a result, the South has basically taken the blame for slavery. With that said, I am not sure why it was not really taught that the North had slavery, but that is what I think.

Why do I think this about American history? When I was a little kid in the 1970s, I noticed all the publishers of our history textbooks were in six or maybe seven different Northern cities and only two Southern ones, and those two were in the upper South and probably more progressive than most other Southern cities. I

---

[634] When Did Slavery Really End in the North? Blog Post RSS. January 19, 2017, Civil Disclosure Civil War Era. Retrieved August 20, 2021 http://civildiscourse-historyblog.com/blog/2017/1/3/when-did-slavery-really-end-in-the-north

[635] Zoe Thomas, BBC Business reporter, New York BBC News. The hidden links between slavery and Wall Street. retrieved March 16, 2021 https://www.bbc.com/news/business-49476247

think I once saw Richmond, Virginia, and maybe Charlotte, North Carolina. This leads me to believe that maybe there may have been some Northern bias in the rewriting of our history. It is called sanitizing history. In a since these northern publishers sanitized northern slavery out of history.

The same thing could happen with American History, African American studies, Latino or Chicano studies, Asian American studies, and Native American studies, so the left can assign blame to America for being such a horrible, mean, ugly, capitalist, colonialist, white supremacist, wealth-mongering, racist nation. With this mentality set in, no one will come to America's rescue to save what it really stands for and why it is such a great nation.

The 1619 Project again is another distortion about the history of slavery in America,[636] and it will probably be even more destructive than writing Northern slavery out of the history books. This is another example of left-leaning influence in our public school system that is convincing black children that they are the oppressed. They are taught that in a country filled with white privilege, systemic racism, and police brutality, you will always be oppressed, so why not depend on the government more to get you out of it, which is very discouraging. It just reinforces the idea that those whites are mean, evil oppressors, which is just not true, but these are some of their bottom-line ideas for education. This casts doubt on everything else being taught by this project.

Another thing to consider about the 1619 Project it is written from the perspective of a woke black progressive female historian who is rewriting the history of America in a radical way. This could give incentive to some more Progressives who are being considered

---

[636] The America Revolution Institution. . August 14, 2020. History Education Blog. The Fatal Flaw of the 1619 Project Curriculum. retrieved January 10, 2022 https://www.americanrevolutioninstitute.org/fatal-flaw-of-the-1619-project-curriculum/

members of oppressed groups such as Hispanics, Asians, Native Americans, feminists, LGBTQIA+s, and maybe some others to write their own radically different versions of the story of America's history and introduce other things that may even offend some of the other groups, even African Americans. I say this because when the final version of history is chosen after all of them are complete, it may be up to some other radical individual or a whole multicultural and multiracial DEI panel of woke historians to rearrange everything and make the final decision on what America's story should be. Some of these things out of their biases, ignorance, or maybe even disregard for some other group will probably in some cases be the truth, some will be partial truths, and some will be lies to advance someone else's cause. The 1619 Project's content that is currently being proposed might not be the final version of US history, but it could get the ball rolling to change it from several other viewpoints, and the black issue of slavery could be just what Progressives need get this ball rolling. This is the perfect example of the saying that I have heard a number of times that "History is His Story" and it depends on who is telling the story.

Let's use another analogy. You can buy a shovel from a local hardware store, which doesn't seem sinister when it is in the bag and the receipt is in the bag as you walk out, even if you went to your backyard to dig a hole, but it depends on what you do with the hole. You could use the hole to bury something ugly that you don't want anyone to see, or you could plant a tree. Black people saw ethnic studies as an opportunity to plant a tree that provides shade if watered and cared for in a brutally hot place where you couldn't change the weather, but at least you could provide some relief from the unforgiving, relentless heat, even though it was hot in the shade as well.

Ethnic studies also keeps distinctions between groups in society so they can continue to squabble with one another and voice complaints about grievances that they have against the greater society of America in general. While this goes on, the left can use this distraction to slowly but very discretely bring in socialism. Why don't we just instead reform American history so that it tells everybody the story in a way that gives everyone justice, even if it means including the pictures of the individuals responsible for the changes so that you can see what race they are. If we do this, then I think we can scrap all ethnic studies programs and just call ourselves all Americans.

9.

The Black Power Movement

The left and socialists had a lot to gain from this movement. The movement had a lot of outward displays of black identity. The movement popularized the Afro hair style and the Afro pick used to groom it. It brought at least attention as a symbol of its prominence and solidarity for the movement by the wearing and display of the kente cloth and the dashiki at least by its leaders and some of its strong sympathizers. All of these were mere flashy trinkets and symbols that have largely disappeared now. The term "Hey what's up, bruthu" was used affectionately as a welcome to a new consciousness among African Americans. I sometimes still hear the term in a shortened version by just referring to another fellow African American from one to another on a very casual basis if circumstances permit as "Bruthu" or "Sistu.'" These terms were mere sayings that have been shortened or are not used as frequently anymore. The way it is used is a space that is only for African Americans to welcome and greet one another in, so people of other races and maybe not all blacks are really welcome in that space. One of its supposed purposes for existing was to instill pride and brotherhood of unity among African Americans so they could come together and function more as a nation or maybe just as a group for a cause, since for so many years, both blacks and whites had been indoctrinated into believing the inferiority of blacks, which would kill any self-esteem. When you feel better about yourself, you will perform better in society as a person. I think Booker T. Washington's movement in Tulsa, Oklahoma, resulted in something much better for black America because if you ask me, now African Americans are no prouder to be black than they have at any other time in the history of America.

More radical members of the Black Power movement supported pan-socialist experiments.[637] Some more radical wings of the movement was influenced by Mao and the Chinese Revolution.[638] National liberation and socialism was one of the end points for that movement.[639] Among a number of new organizations to come on board with this socialist model were the Nation of Islam and the Black Panthers.[640] As a number of different rebellions, riots, and protests took place across the country, both Marxist[641] and Leninist[642] groups sprang up among leaders of these black organizations, conferences, and conventions across the country.[643] The Black Panthers had a goal of overthrowing capitalism,[644] even if it meant working with whites to do it.[645] This is just the type of revolutionary activity that the left wants to see.

---

[637] Komozi Woodard—Sarah Lawrence College African and African Diasporan Transformation in the 20th Century:
Rethinking the Black Power Movement. http://exhibitions.nypl.org/africanaage/essay-black-power.html retrieved May 14, 2021.

[638] Ibid.

[639] Ibid.

[640] Ibid.

[641] Ibid.

[642] Ibid.

[643] Ibid.

[644] Alan Maass. The Black Power Era. Socialistworker.org. October 25, 2011. retrieved May 11, 2021. https://socialistworker.org/2011/10/25/black-power-era

[645] Ibid.

The Black Power Movement

By 1975 there were roughly 10 times more liberal Democrat political office holders,[646] compared with 1969, and 30 times more, compared with 1964, who were African American,[647] and a significant number were former grassroots activists.[648] This made it easier for progressives and the Left to influence and control the black political scene in America. According to the same article, a man by the name of Ahmed Shawki wrote a book titled *Black Liberation and Socialism*[649] that went on in the 1960s and '70s in the context of the broader African American struggle.[650] As you can see just from this title, the socialists had a lot to gain from the Black Power movement.

If the Black Power movement instilled pride, then why is it that so many blacks still favor softer, finer grades of hair as good hair and lighter skin tones, while courser, drier, harder, hair and darker skin tones are still less favorable, even today in the black community. Why are so many black people, but in particular boys and young men, especially in certain pockets of the black community, being gunned down by other black men at such high rates. Why is it that even today some black girls don't like black dolls, and some black boys don't like identifying with their blackness even today?[651] If the Black Power movement's purpose was to instill racial pride, provide economic empowerment, and create political and cultural institutions that empowered the black community, it was a failure.

---

[646] Ibid.

[647] Ibid.

[648] Ibid.

[649] Ibid.

[650] Ibid.

[651] Toni Sturdivant. What I learned when I recreated the famous 'doll test' that looked at how Black kids see race February 22, 2021. Texas A&M University-Commerce. retrieved May 8, 2021. USC Rossier School of Education 2021 https://theconversation.com/what-i-learned-when-i-recreated-the-famous-doll-test-that-looked-at-how-black-kids-see-race-153780

If it was supposed to provide economic empowerment, why doesn't black money stay in the black community? Why is it in the hands of people of other races by the billions year after year, making other non-blacks wealthy and leaving the black community poor and broke? Why is it that black people are so dependent on institutions outside of their community for so many of their jobs and all kinds of goods and services? All those outward appearances and flashy trinkets of the movement didn't change any of this.

Conservatives didn't support this because they did not support the Black Power movement like Progressives did. This was largely supported and sponsored by socialists and Marxists who had something to gain from it, and they are usually left-leaning and progressive, or they are just full-blown leftists.

The black community should have just followed Booker T. Washington's previous pre–civil rights era model after the civil rights movement of creating a strong business community where your money exchanges hands with people like you as many times as possible in the free market and capitalistic economic system that America has traditionally been as a constitutional republic. By doing so, the black community could have created their own business community, their own for-profit and non-for-profit institutions that reflect black talent, distinction, creativity, excellence, exceptionalism, and the ability of the black community and the black race to conduct the affairs of a civil society. This would have been the best way or at least a better way to instill pride in a people. This display could have been in how the institutions were named and what they stood for, resulting in ownership and control over more with resultant influence over more with the ability to change more, even to the point of making blackness an acceptable standard of beauty and being.

This could have been a display to blacks and everyone else that demands respect, acknowledgment, and honor, and by doing so, what type of hair you have wouldn't make as much of a difference, so why should it to everyone else? With a setup like this, you wouldn't want to kill people like you as much. A setup like this would leave no place for so many of your children being fatherless, allowing your sons to walk around like thugs with sagging pants or to drop out of high school and join street gangs and in some rare cases become rappers and, in some cases, discourage others for aspiring for more in really bad inner-city neighborhoods. You would discourage out of wedlock pregnancies, crime, and all sorts of other inner-city ghetto behavior. This also would demand respect from both blacks and non-blacks for blacks, something the Marxist-influenced Black Power movement just didn't do.

I would like to speak on something else and elaborate some on something else that came out of or that happened as a result of the Black Power movement. The invention of the observance of Kwanzaa[652] and its concepts are ones whose inventors claim it has origins in African culture and tradition,[653] and its intent is to give African Americans a sense of identity[654] and a source of pride[655] and a reconnection back to their African roots.[656] An iconic symbol

---

[652] Samantha Grasso. Kwanzaa's Radical Roots in the Black Power Movement. December 27, 2017. https://www.ajplus.net/stories/kwanzaas-radical-roots-in-the-black-power-movement retreived November 28, 2021

[653] Nadra Kareem Nittle. Updated on November 28, 2018. What You Should Know About Kwanzaa and Why It's Celebrated. retrieved December 16, 2021. Thought.Co. https://www.thoughtco.com/what-is-kwanzaa-2834584

[654] Ibid.

[655] Ibid.

[656] Ibid.

of the observation is an eight-candled menorah,[657] originally a nine-candled one[658] that are both corruptions of the traditional Jewish seven-candled menorah.[659] Sources claim it is simply about good will[660] and that is a message to anyone, so anyone of any ethnicity can observe it as well.[661]

Its inventors have a shady past with connections to the Black Power movement of the 1960s and '70s,[662] and for one of the inventors' actions, others did prison time.[663] Since it has some similarities in its presentation with Christmas[664] and the Jewish observation of Hanukkah,[665] another source claims that some pastors have made the horrible mistake of incorporating it into their messages.[666] This totally made-up observation, which distances black people from Christmas,[667] has absolutely no place in the pulpit. The concept of Kwanzaa has slowly lost popularity over the years. Its message was supposedly about communal empowerment.[668] It is clear this rad-

---

[657] Sam Kestenbaum. December 5, 2016. The Secret Jewish History of Kwanzaa Forward Jewish Fearless since 1897. retrieved December 13, 2021 https://forward.com/news/356188/the-secret-jewish-history-of-kwanzaa/

[658] Ibid.

[659] Ibid.

[660] Nadra Kareem Nittle. Updated on November 28, 2018. What You Should Know About Kwanzaa and Why It's Celebrated. retrieved December 16, 2021. Thought.Co. https://www.thoughtco.com/what-is-kwanzaa-2834584

[661] Ibid.

[662] Ibid.

[663] Ibid.

[664] Ibid.

[665] Ibid.

[666] Ibid.

[667] Ibid.

[668] Ibid.

ical organization founded by a rival group with the Black Panthers has done no such thing.

Neither it or its ceremonies have any African counterparts,[669] and a lot of its principles are east African,[670] while the key seven principles that define it are of Swahili origin,[671] which borrows a lot of words from Arabic.[672] The African slave trade, which resulted in the ancestors of black Americans, was done mostly in West Africa on the slave coast. Now an initiative has been started to teach all of the concepts of the fake, phony celebrations and observations in classrooms to K–12 students,[673] complete with lesson plans, coloring books, worksheets, and activities, which all vary, depending on age and grade level of the students.[674]

The Project 21 Black Leadership Network's website admits that Kwanzaa is a Marxist invention,[675] but it puts another spin on it by saying it is a lesson in conservative values[676] since all of Kwanzaa values are conservative.[677] I would agree that its values are conservative, but here is another example of how Marxists can use a

---

[669] Thomas Clough. The Roots of Kwanzaa. Weird Republic. retrieved December 17, 2021 https://www.davidstuff.com/political/clough2.htm

[670] Ibid.

[671] Ibid.

[672] Ibid.

[673] Elisa Jackson. Lesson Planet Kwanzaa in the Classroom. retrieved December 17, 2021 https://www.lessonplanet.com/article/elementary-art/kwanzaa-in-the-classroom

[674] Ibid.

[675] David Almasi. Project 21 Black Leadership Network. 27 Dec 2012. Kwanzaa Reinterpreted: Turning A Marxist Celebration Into a Lesson In Conservative Values. retrieved December 18, 2021 https://nationalcenter.org/project21/2012/12/27/kwanzaa-reinterpreted-turning-a-marxist-celebration-into-a-lesson-in-conservative-values/

[676] Ibid.

[677] Ibid.

black cause as an attempt to convince the public that they support conservative causes when nothing could be farther from the truth. Marxism is a very radically different concept from what America was intended to exist as, and it doesn't have the best interests of black Americans or of America at heart, for that matter.

Kwanzaa is a supposedly a pan-African observance by people of African descent from throughout the African Diaspora[678] that exemplifies the beauty of their culture.[679] If this is the case, should people of every other diaspora on earth have their special observances that exemplifies their culture in the same way? If this is the case, then this just redefines the concept of each diasporic racial and diasporic differences, making the concept of race and ethnicity more divisive.

The concepts of the observance are unnecessary, and they still did not have any real positives for the black community. It did not get it out of the mess that it is currently in, and it is no more prideful to be black than it was before the existence of this observation. Had it been up to conservatives and lots of classical liberals the Black Power Movement would never have been a concept.

---

[678] Pheralyn Dove. December 23, 2020. Rosetta Stone: What is Kwanzaa? Here's What You Need to Know (and What to Say). retrieved December 21, 2021 https://blog.rosettastone.com/what-is-kwanzaa-heres-what-you-need-to-know-and-what-to-say/

[679] Ibid.

10.

Mass and Unchecked Illegal Migration

For this, people are going to accuse me of being anti-immigrant and a fear monger, but that is wrong. Immigrants have actually created a lot of jobs in this country with new business creation[680] and immigrants with valuable skills are good for economic growth[681] so not all immigrants are bad for America[682]. However, illegal immigrants or illegal migrants, especially a lot of the ones coming across the Southern US border with no regulations or without going through the processes that an immigrant must go through before becoming US citizens are bad for America,[683] since there is no screening process for ones who could possess threats to the countries security.[684] What is unique about this surge of immi-

---

[680] Tom Jawetz. June 26, 2019, Building a More Dynamic Economy: The Benefits of Immigration. Center for American Progress Immigration. retrieved March 20, 2021 https://www.americanprogress.org/issues/immigration/reports/2019/06/26/471497/building-dynamic-economy-benefits-immigration/

[681] Ibid

[682] Ibid

[683] GEORGE J. BORJAS. September/October 2016. Yes, Immigration Hurts American Workers. The Big Idea Politico Magazine. retrieved March 20, 2021 https://www.politico.com/magazine/story/2016/09/trump-clinton-immigration-economy-unemployment-jobs-214216/

[684] Ibid

grants is that they are coming from all over the world now not just Latin America.[685]

Some of them have some sound reasons for immigrating, but some of the illegal ones and the negative ramifications it will have for the black community is what is being discussed. This type of immigration is another leftist policy, which progressive Liberals are more likely to support, that has had lots of negatives for the black community.[686] That is because now blacks have to compete with Hispanics and other immigrants for jobs when the black community has lost that sense of community that you need to keep so that you won't be too dependent on outside entities for your employment. They need all the low-wage, low-skilled and unskilled jobs now more than ever to pay the bills and keep food on the table, and Hispanics are pushing blacks out of that market more every day. If the black community had not been convinced to completely integrate with whites, they would have had by now a lot more in their own community. Too many illegals that don't have much of a choice but to do jobs for a lot cheaper than most other American citizens drives down wages for everyone else,[687] but everyone else will do better finding a job in the infrastructure that has been created economically by their own communities than blacks.

Hispanics, as an example, like all other immigrant groups, do have more closely knit connections and more robust networks

---

[685] Ibid

[686] Steven A. Camarota. Center for Immigration Studies. Immigration and Black Americans: Assessing the Impact Testimony Before the U.S. Commission on Civil Rights. April 5, 2008. Retrieved August 5, 2019 https://cis.org/Testimony/Immigration-and-Black-Americans-Assessing-Impact

[687] Brian Stauffer and George J. Borjas, Politico Magazine, Yes Immigration Hurts American Workers Sept / Oct 2016, retrieved August 28 2019. https://www.politico.com/magazine/story/2016/09/trump-clinton-immigration-economy-unemployment-jobs-214216

Mass and Unchecked Illegal Migration

in their communities than the black community does and a better business infrastructure. This puts them in a better position to make demands and change society for their interests than blacks, and some of their changes could be awful for blacks. Conservatives would never have allowed it to get to this point with unchecked, illegal immigration.

When President Obama was in office, he wanted to give millions of Hispanic immigrants amnesty and grant them citizenship without going through proper procedures.[688] The president claimed this would not give them citizenship, but it would allow them to stay. However, it is the first step and a big one toward citizenship, and it still may not be good for America.[689] This would give them access to jobs and resources that are essential for blacks to survive, and blacks would be pushed out of them. This would have been a devastating blow to the black community. Since Hispanics are a larger group now than blacks, this gives them a clear advantage now when it comes to affirmative action and DEI programs. Problems will only get worse as Asians and Arabs become larger groups and begin to make demands that are not in the favor or blacks. Conservatives would only have allowed immigration under the proper guidelines, protocols, and procedures, and the process would happen a lot more gradually. Some immigration would not have even been allowed, which would be a lot better for blacks had it been up to conservatives.

This was all under the guise of multiculturalism and DEI, which is another left-leaning progressive cause. With people now of so many races and ethnic backgrounds immigrating to the United States that have no common ground ethnically and sometimes racially, unless

---

[688] Devin Dwyer. ABC News. President Obama Offers Legal Status to Millions of Undocumented Immigrants. Nov 20, 2014, retrieved August 14, 2019 https://abcnews.go.com/Politics/president-obama-offer-legal-status-millions-undocumented-immigrants/story?id=27063573

[689] Ibid.

there is enough of some kind of commonality established among everyone, it will result in isolation of certain groups of people in enclaves or communities that will become something that America is not. All of them together could cause America to evolve into something different, and the people who have communities with no economic infrastructure such as the black community, who are more dependent on outside sources for jobs from the government and other private sector companies outside of their communities just as an example, will suffer the most. The strongest entities, with time, will dominate society, and they may not have the black communities' best interest at heart, just like certain groups of whites historically have not always, whoever they are. Unless everybody agrees to observe certain values that made America great, it will no longer be great in a more multicultural society either.

In addition, the National Research Council study notes that several studies have found that employers may also strongly prefer to hire immigrants over inner-city blacks. (See the document titled: "Structural Shifts and Economic Capacity Possibilities for Economic Cooperation and Conflict in Urban Settings"). A later study from an article in *American Affairs* journal from 2017 revealed a very similar comparison,[690] for some very similar reasons as the past studies. This is one of the major reasons why in the very near future for their mere existence it will be absolutely necessary for African Americans to have network-rich communities and practice group economics. That is provided that we stay a free market economy and a constitutional republic.

I would like to discuss the passing of the Voting Rights Act of 2022 or the Voting Rights Bill of 2022. Some on the left are comparing it

---

[690] Amy L. Wax and Jason Richwine. American Affairs, Winter 2017 Vol. 1, Number 4. Low-Skill Immigration: A Case for Restriction. https://americanaffairsjournal.org/2017/11/low-skill-immigration-case-restriction/ retrieved December 13, 2019

with the Jim Crow Era laws[691] and voter suppression[692] when the Civil Rights Act of 1965 was passed. What is going on now has nothing to do with what was happening to blacks in 1965, which was for a different purpose[693] than regarding voting rights, and it has nothing to do with Jim Crow laws. There is a claim by some leftists that polling places were being deliberately removed from places where blacks and Latinos were overrepresented.[694] Noncitizens currently already have the right to vote in some fourteen municipalities across America,[695] but many on the left claim that opposing the voting rights act is a threat to our democracy.[696] New York City currently allows some 800,000 noncitizens to vote in most elections held in NYC.[697] This could lead to the allowance of this practice for noncitizens in cities

---

[691] Glenn Kessler The Washington Post Democracy Dies In The Dark The Senate battle over whether election laws signify a new 'Jim Crow' retrieved January 31, 2022 https://www.washingtonpost.com/politics/2022/01/11/senate-battle-over-whether-election-laws-signify-new-jim-crow/

[692] Brenda Álvarez, Senior Writer NEA Today Are Today's Voter Suppression Laws the New Jim Crow? Published: 01/16/2022 Last Updated: 01/17/2022 retrieved January 31, 2022 https://www.nea.org/advocating-for-change/new-from-nea/are-todays-voter-suppression-laws-new-jim-crow

[693] History.Com Editors up dated :Jan 11, 2022 original: Nov 9, 2009 Voting Rights Act of 1965 History retrieved January 31, 2022 https://www.history.com/topics/black-history/voting-rights-act

[694] Carl Hulse Jan. 19, 2022, 7:44 p.m. ET New York Times The Battle Over Voting Rights After a day of debate, the voting rights bill is blocked in the Senate. Retrieved January 31, 2022 https://www.nytimes.com/2022/01/19/us/politics/senate-voting-rights-filibuster.html

[695] Democracy Docket Understanding Voting Rights for Noncitizens retrieved January 31, 2022 https://www.democracydocket.com/news/understanding-voting-rights-for-non-citizens/

[696] Ibid.

[697] Sanya Mansoor December 10, 2021 11:23 Am Est New York's Move Allowing Non-Citizens to Vote Could Lead Other Cities to Follow Time Magazine retrieved January 31, 2022 https://time.com/6127409/non-citizen-voting-new-york-city/

all across America.[698] If this policy for noncitizens becomes more widespread across America in enough municipalities by the end of the Biden-Harris administration in time for the elections of 2024, we could see nearly 13 million illegals come across the border who could all mostly vote as Democrats for the left in theses municipalities across the country and give the Democrats another four years in office to implement more left-leaning progressive policies for another four years. With the ending of Title 42, which is another progressive policy to end it, we may see up to 13,000 illegal crossings a day.[699] If you do the math, that is conservatively another 7 million in addition to the 2.7 million in 2021[700] and 1.7 million in 2020[701] and a million so far for 2023[702] for a total of nearly 13 million as a conservative estimate. These immigrants will push blacks out of a lot, and some won't care. They are getting free benefits such as free food[703], free

---

[698] Ibid.

[699] Office of Texas Governor Greg Abbott May 12, 2023 | Austin, Texas | Press Release Operation Lone Star Surges Border Resources As Title 42 Ends retrieved June 11, 2023 https://gov.texas.gov/news/post/operation-lone-star-surges-border-resources-as-title-42-ends

[700] Julia Ainsley Oct. 22, 2022, 10:26 AM CDT Migrant border crossings in fiscal year 2022 topped 2.76 million, breaking previous record News Immigration retrieved June 11, 2023 https://www.nbcnews.com/politics/immigration/migrant-border-crossings-fiscal-year-2022-topped-276-million-breaking-rcna53517

[701] Ibid

[702] Committee on Homeland Security FACTSHEET: Illegal Crossings of the Southwest Border Increased in April Ahead of Title 42's End retrieved June 11, 2023 https://homeland.house.gov/factsheet-illegal-crossings-of-the-southwest-border-increased-in-april-ahead-of-title-42s-end/#:~:text=U.S.%20Customs%20and%20Border%20Protection,%E2%80%94%20up%2012%25%20from%20March.

[703] Michael Goodwin opinion January 31, 2023 11:21pm Updated The New York Post It's the land of the freebies for NYC's 'entitled' migrants retrieved June 11, 2023 https://nypost.com/2023/01/31/its-the-land-of-the-freebies-for-nycs-entitled-migrants/

cell phones[704], free transit passes[705], free school[706], and free health care[707] and more[708] that a lot of homeless who are black and just black people period are not getting. It would not surprise me if some of them became downright hostile to blacks because of how Americans progressive media has informed them or entertained them about blacks, but this will be only a very small minority of a minority who could make a difference somewhere.

That could change America fundamentally for good. This is an example of how left-leaning politics is using the Jim Crow issues of the 1960s that affected blacks during totally different circumstances form what is going on today to accomplish their agenda. They are monopolizing a past black cause to accomplish something for them. I guess it is because they are classifying all the illegals as people of color (so all of them can go under the umbrella of the oppressed) in such a racist society as America if you are on the progressive left, which means that America is the oppressor. If it were up to most conservative, noncitizens would never have the right to vote. As far as I know most other countries in the world do not allow such nonsense to go on in their country, so why should the United States allow it?

All of the illegal immigrants, regardless of ethnic background, are just being used by the left to achieve one of their agendas. With time, as a result, there will be no difference in the standard of living in America for many of them than there is in these immigrants' country of origin, and in some cases, they would be better off in

---

[704] Ibid

[705] Ibid

[706] Ibid

[707] Ibid

[708] Ibid

the country that they came from than they will be in America, all because of some of the same progressive leftist causes that lured them here to begin with.

11.

Is Equity Really Fair

According to another report from NPR, farmers of color are suing the US government for $5 billion from past injustices by the government.[709] Do I think black farmers and farmers of color should pursue justice from the past if they were discriminated against for denial of government aid on the basis of race and no other reason? Yes, absolutely! But equity is not the way to do it, and here is why.

I was listening to a podcast by the CATO Institute on equity in law. It discussed how certain minority groups in an attempt to establish equity vs. equality were being favored for loans for farms that failed during the COVID epidemic if they were minorities[710] and some were even given a 20 percent grant as free money on top of it, and their white counterparts were completely excluded from the loan process altogether. Since 95% of all farmers are white,[711]

---

[709] Harvest Public Media | By Eva Tesfaye Published October 13, 2022 at 4:46 PM CDT Black and brown farmers sue U.S. government over repealed debt relief retrieved NPR Network October 18, 2022 https://www.kcur.org/news/2022-10-13/black-and-brown-farmers-sue-u-s-government-over-repealed-debt-relief

[710] Wen Fa Pacific Legal Foundation CATO Institute Podcast Caleb O. Brown Host of the Cato Daily Podcast May 31, 2022 Equality before the Law versus Equity

[711] USA Facts Who is the American Farmer? https://usafacts.org/articles/farmer-demographics/

3.3% Hispanic,[712] and 1.7% Asian,[713] according to these figures they all add up to 100% with 0% of all farmers being black. According to an article from McKinsey & Company only about 1.4% of US farmers identify as black or mixed race compared with 14% a hundred years ago[714]. This type of equity does not compensate for the $326 billion of land[715] with a value estimated to be 11.5 million acres lost by black farmers between 1910 and 1997[716]. Keep in mind that black people owned a lot more farmland in 1910 when America was more conservative, but as America has become more progressive and progressive polices began to affect American society, blacks lost lots of their farmland, and now with a lot more progressive politics and lifestyles and norms and after years of progressive causes have changed the whole cultural, political, and social landscape and blacks own very little farmland now leaving them more dependent, which is what Progressives want. This kind of equity has the potential to put a lot of American farmers out of business, which will lead to starvation and hunger around the world (since American farms export so much grain and other food products to the rest of the world every year) and in America on a third-world level if the government or some other entity does not step in since it reduces America's ability to be able to feed its citizens and the rest

---

[712] Ibid

[713] Ibid

[714] McKinsey & Company Our insights Agriculture Black Farmers in the US: The Opportunity to Address Racial Disparities in Farming November 10, 2021 retrieved October 11, 2022 https://www.mckinsey.com/industries/agriculture/our-insights/black-farmers-in-the-us-the-opportunity-for-addressing-racial-disparities-in-farming

[715] Leah Douglas Reuters U.S. Black farmers lost $326 bln worth of land in 20th century -study May 2, 2022 12:14 PM CDT retrieved October 11, 2022 https://www.reuters.com/world/us/us-black-farmers-lost-326-bln-worth-land-20th-century-study-2022-05-02/

[716] Ibid

of the world. If this happens, blacks and Hispanics who live in inner city food deserts which lack fresh healthy produce in many cases will most likely be victimized more by the hunger it will cause. This is the whole point behind how equity by progressives government control, and this kind of equity may give them and other government entities around the world power on a global scale. They can say here that it is not fair that so many blacks are not farmers because of discriminatory practices in the past and they can use the black communities place in society to advance this agenda.

The black farmers also feel that the Inflation Reduction Act[717] proposed by this progressive administration is a nail in the coffin of their hope of saving their farms as it is a broken promise[718] for financial aid.

Most black children do not attend schools like maybe some of the ones like the DPS that I referred to in some of the really bad neighborhoods in a previous chapter during the time that this presentation refers to, some of them go to good schools and some of the ones who do are doing just as well academically as white or Asian kids and every variation in between depending on some other factors. But if you use racial equity to guarantee a certain pass rate for standardized exams or remove standardized testing, these bad schools bring the average down for black kids overall. Here is where you can use equity to level the playing field for black children without maintaining or improving academic standards. If Conservatives had had more influence in these polices, equity would never have been an issue anywhere.

---

[717] Khristopher J. Brooks AUGUST 18, 2022 / 4:43 PM / MONEYWATCH CBS News Black farmers say Inflation Reduction Act reneges on promises for debt relief retrieved October 18, 2022 https://www.cbsnews.com/news/black-farmers-usda-loan-relief-inflation-reduction-act-ira-john-boyd/

[718] Ibid

A podcast that I listened to by the CATO Institute discussed equity in education where very elite schools were required to admit students by race-based quotas in college preparatory high schools[719] that had very high and rigorous academic standards for high schools, when black and Hispanic kids don't do as good as white and Asian kids, they made adjustments that will in essence dumb down the admission requirement to get in.[720] If that is the case, the curricula will have to be dumbed down for a less academically prepared group of blacks and maybe Hispanics,[721] but the reason why the blacks are in this situation to begin with is not because they are incapable or somehow inferior intellectually or incapable of any academic feat as a white or Asian kid but because of progressive policies from the past. Here is where they can use the condition of some blacks to dumb down the educational system for the sake of equity, diversity, and inclusion or DEI in a way that is bad for everyone. This type of equity could be forced on public schools across America if it hasn't already in some cases as a gold standard for grades K through 12. With this kind of equity with time America will not be capable of making the technological advances that America has been able to for years because of its higher academic standards, and all or most its great universities well cease to be great anymore. I say this because if kids are not being prepared for very rigorous academic standards of a university curriculum anywhere or at least in some academic institutions across the board, they will either have to dumb down or lower academic standards across the board in

---

[719] Wen Fa Pacific Legal Foundation CATO Institute Podcast Caleb O. Brown Host of the Cato Daily Podcast May 31, 2022 Equality before the Law versus Equity

[720] Ibid

[721] Ibid

all American universities, and with time, America will be just like any other nation academically and not the exception to the rule it always has been.

As an example say you have schools that have high academic standards that are disproportionately white and Asian at schools that graduate middle school students who can do mathematics and reading in more than a 8th grade level in some cases maybe 11th and 12th grade in middle school. In some really bad neighborhoods that are disproportionately black and Hispanic that graduate students from middle school that read and do mathematics frequently only on a 3rd and 4th grade level and you have rather average schools that have an even distribution of students across all races and ethnicities that commonly graduate kids from middle school that score anywhere from upper 5th grade to barely 8th grade upon graduation. In this case nearly all of the kids from the school with high academic standards will be A and B students in high school, a much smaller percentage of kinds from the middle school with average academics will do well in high school and will be C and B students and the students from the schools with lower academic standards that were disproportionately black and Hispanic will most likely be D and F students in high school If your goal is to get the proportion of students through high school the same based on race you can not use academics as a determining factor. What you can do is make the curriculum a lot easier in high school and that will get more black and Hispanic students through high school from lower academic standard school districts across the country.

But since they will not be as academically prepared to graduate enough of them to meet DEI quotas for entrance into and graduation from universities you can dumb down the curriculum in High schools and universities across the country. At the same time, you can still require high scores for white and Asian students for entrance into these universities. With just two adjustments like this you can produce equity of outcomes while at the same time lowering academic standards for universities and entrance into them because this is all equity does is makes adjustments to produce equality of outcomes.

This will make American universities less able to prepare adults for feats that require advanced academic knowledge that will make you able to think independently and solve complex issues and problems. This is what could result from equity quotas.

With time now there will essentially be no difference in the learning abilities, knowledge base and critical thinking skills of children of all races and ethnic backgrounds across America thanks to common core in grades K – thru 12 and DEI quotas for colleges and universities.

With DEI a doctor who made it into medical school because they dumbed down the standards for them to get in and dumbed the standards more because they had to graduate more LGBTQIA+, black and Hispanic students from Medical School might decide not to treat a white or Asian person because they want equity of health outcomes but the same doctor could misdiagnose and mistreat a black or Hispanic person which could very well result in a sicker or dead white or Asian person because he was not treated and/ or a sicker or dead black or Hispanic person because they were misdiagnosed and mistreated from a lousy unqualified DEI physician. This is where they used the black issues of poor health outcomes and shorter life expectances in the black community and a shortage of black doctors which again were all largely created either directly or indirectly by there progressive policies of the common core no child left behind schools, the feminist movement which allowed for so many women to be able to raise children with out a father in the home (since these children are more likely to drop out of high school and college) and more which effected the black community tremendously. There are other factors besides DEI as to why fewer blacks are getting into and graduating from Medical Schools which I discussed earlier in the article.

A similar result will happen with DEI admissions into Law Schools to correct another black issue of low presents of black lawyers and attorneys. When the admissions into law school have been dumbed down and the requirements to graduate law school and become a lawyer or an attorney have been dumbed down enough, you will have lawyers and attorneys that will just not be able to read literature and books and law journals etc. and do legal writings like a qualified lawyer should be able to in order to practice Law according to US law statutes and according to its ethics. Instead you will have Lawyers who will make decisions from their opinions and their feelings which will in many cases be shaped by political agendas and their personal values and ethics and some of those decisions could be very bias and very unjust to any particular group even an ethnic group and I am not doubting one of those ethnic groups could be African Americans just depending on who the Lawyer or attorney is and yes he could also be non-white. Again, there are other factor that contribute to why not as many blacks are not graduating from Law school and becoming Lawyers.

Negative outcomes like this will almost certainly happen in every other carrier field out there from DEI policies that require any level of education from an associate degree to a PhD.

By dropping the standards for entrance you would reach your quota for black and Hispanics but to really get equity in the percentage of Doctors and Lawyers ethnically across the board in all races in practice you would have to have some more crafty and unfair standards that were unfair to whites and Asians that either kept them from getting into Law School or Medical school, kept them from completing either of the two or that kept them from applying in the first place. This would make race relations worse in America, because it would cause a black and Hispanic VS whites and Asians division on college campuses and in society.

If Conservatives had had more influence in these polices, DEI and quotes would never have been an issue anywhere.

12.

The Mainstream Media

Let's just be honest; our music and film industry is heavily influenced by a progressive liberal agenda. Much of the garbage on reality shows and sitcoms that are watched by millions of Americans every day on prime-time TV are scripted, written, produced, and endorsed by leftists, [722] and some of this material does not paint a positive image for the rest of the world to see about [723]black Americans, which enforces bad stereotypes and the reactions that blacks get from other groups, both white and non-white (like the police and law enforcement), and sometimes each other as a result, which just proves my point. [724] Again, before I get started, this does not apply to most black Americans. "Gangsta" Rap, another rebellious form of musical expression, has had such a bad impression on a small segment of black youth that it has in the past and still is to an extent influencing their actions to the point of emulating the worthless TV video lives of rappers as being something normal, which is a recipe for jail time or a prison sentence.

---

[722] Neil Gross, Why Is Hollywood So Liberal? Jan 28, 2018 Opinion. Sunday Review. retrieved June 7, 2019 https://www.nytimes.com/2018/01/27/opinion/sunday/hollywood-liberal.html

[723]

[724] Nadra Kareem Nittle. 5 Common Black Stereotypes in TV Films. Updated April 04, 2018. retrieved May 23, 2019 https://www.thoughtco.com/common-black-stereotypes-in-tv-film-2834653.

According to a Nielsen rating of prime-time TV showings from 2013, African Americans watch on average 40 percent more of it than the national average.[725] Top television shows perhaps unexpectedly included reality TV programs and the series *Scandal*.[726] TV ONE and BET had plenty of these types of shows as well. These were some of the least intellectually stimulating selections that are possible or at least partially responsible for some negative paradigm shifts for some of the black community, but most of this genre of entertainment would not be tolerated so much by Conservatives. The black community is a big one to help keep their ratings up with viewers so they can keep this type of content on TV. This is another example of where they are getting more support from the black community, a community that they really have no interest in. Since according to these ratings, black people watch more TV, which is basically mainstream media, and since it is more left leaning than other sources of media, it is easier to convince them of their causes such as all Conservatives and Republicans are racists, and all Liberals and Democrats are safe. It convinces them that systemic racism and police shootings of unarmed young black men is what is really detrimental versus Planned Parenthood's ethnic cleansing of black people from America with its abortion clinics, and so many others that were caused by leftist ideology. Now, since too many black boys haven't had decent male role models, the film and music industry have created a new type of manhood for them to be, and not only is it an embarrassing one, but it is a destructive one. One example is the image that a pants-sagging thug is a real man and a studious, nice guy is a sissy or he is acting white. This is

---

[725] Courtney Garcia, Nielsen report confirms Blacks watch more TV than any other group, September 27, 2013, retrieved May 11, 2019 https://thegrio.com/2013/09/27/nielsen-report-confirms-Blacks-watch-more-tv-than-any-other-group

[726] Ibid,

not as prominent as it was for years, but the mentality still persists to greater extent among a certain group of blacks. Now some black youth actually believe it to a greater or lesser extent, and it has some different implications for both boys and girls. This does not apply to most black youth, but it applies to too many of them.

Prime-time TV shows such as *Jerry Springer* and *The Steve Wilkos Show* and the like have exhibited a disproportionately high number of blacks with embarrassing behavior for which leftists and people of other ethnicities can look down at blacks and laugh at them.

If it were up to Conservatives, our film, TV, music, and movie industry would never have come to this, and you would not see these portrayals of black men in rap videos as thugs and gangsters and half-naked black girls, which you don't see as often now.

In fact, you would not have sitcoms that degrade the family where the dad is always wrong, or he is stupid and talked back to by his wife and kids. You wouldn't have so many acts of violence, murder, sex scenes, cursing, homosexuality, anger, rage, and all sorts of other immorality if Conservatives or the right had had more influence and control over what goes on our media, which is nothing more than something to promote a progressive agenda, which is not a good one in a lot of instances. This promotes it and gives it more support, and with the black community, they are getting more participants for their cause. Since black people watch more TV, they can use the black community to bring ratings up for more of this type of programming. That does not mean that other races and ethnic backgrounds of Americans don't watch this type of programming because they certainly do watch their share of it.

The old sitcom *Orange is the New Black* is really bad about the way it belittles black people because what it is really saying is a lot of black people are in those orange prison suits because so many of them are disproportionately a lot more likely to be there, which is where a lot of whites, both liberal and conservative, feel comfortable with them being. What it was really saying about black people is very deceptive with the setting, theme, and background of the show, and leftists used its theme to support their agenda. They could look at this and laugh, and at the same time feel a sense of superiority in society by looking at the inferior position a lot of black people are in within society as being more likely to be jailbirds, misfits, and criminals.

The currently running TV series *Chicago PD* can at times make young black males seem like heartless super predators; it almost makes them comparable with terrorists. This leads me to believe that the media is trying to paint an unrealistic picture about young black males that is mostly a stretching of the imagination.

Cable TV has in the past had too many shows of both new reality shows and running series and past series such as *Basketball Wives, Housewives of Atlanta, Black Inc Crew, Love & Hip Hop Hollywood, Love & Hip Hop Atlanta*, and others. These shows have had too many instances of black people yelling obscene language at one another, cursing at one another, and dissing one another. I've never seen this many shows of whites or even Hispanic for that matter demeaning each other like this and making one another seem shameful. Shows such as *Blackish and Mixed-ish* with an all-black crew of actors and actresses, of which half are biracial, says something about the degree of blackness you can have or be. The left uses this to paint a picture of black people that they really like seeing and that they really want everyone else to believe. In shows such as MSNBC's *Lockup Extended Stay* show too many black people as misfits, illiterates, unemployables, criminals, prostitutes, dope fiends, and more. These are some of the groups that eugenicist Margaret Sanger wanted eliminated from society for these reasons. The left, or at least a certain influential constituency of them, may have a new agenda to characterize blacks as a new "Basket of deplorables" in reference to Hilary Clinton's statement about various Trump supporters.[727] At the beginning of this book I shared the experience that a women who immigrated to America from Grenada had in her old Brooklyn, New York, neighborhood that she doesn't like anymore and she feels she has no connection to or nothing in common with anymore, especially black people who live in conditions like that and act like people in that setting. Now who would you say the real racists are, the left or the right?

To degrade the family and men more but especially black men since the cast of this BET production is all black, the progressive liberal media produced a series called *Real Husbands of Hollywood*, filmed like *Housewives of Hollywood* with an all-black cast like *The Real Housewives of Atlanta*. To me the men of this show don't really act the way a husband should really act; I think sometimes their antics can be rather childish. The producers of shows like this say it is just a comedy, but what does this type of production say to children and young people of all races and ethnicities who watch it who have not been given real enlightenment as to what a man is really supposed to be in society? If it were up to Conservatives, this kind of garbage would never have made it to TV.

In Bill Cosby's 1968 casting of the documentary *Black History: Lost, Stolen or Strayed*, he states that 33,000 feature films had been made in the past 50 years (I am assuming before 1968) and about 6,000 had parts for black actors. He stated that the parts were produced and written by whites for a white audience. These ones constantly showed black men as being a nobody or nothing. He had no

---

[727] Katie Reiley. Time Magazine Politics. Read Hilary Clintons "Basket of Deplorables" Remark About Donalds Trump Supporters. Retrieved December 30, 2019 https://time.com/4486502/hillary-clinton-basket-of-deplorables-transcript/

qualities that could be admired by any man or women. They liked looking at pictures of the happy darky.[728] The minstrel shows prior to this showed white actors who played blacks dressed in blackface. Being lazy stupid and happy the way they were as being scared of everything with chattery teeth and eyes that bulged out of his head when he was frightened and not being able to talk or run was a portray of blacks in the movies back then.[729] Black women stood as sturdy and unperturbed like solid rocks in circumstances that scared most black men.

Cosby noticed the relentless attack on the character of the black man he was casted more as a boy than a man.[730] To me some of their clownish antics in some films and productions would remind you at times of the Three Stooges. They had stupid portrayals of actors such as Stepit Fetchin. He talked about the Shirley Temple movie with the scary black men and brave little girl Shirley and the pet-like relationship she had with them as their master in a sense. He talked about Bill Bojangles Robinson as a happy tap dancing Negro.[731] Black women and girls seemed to treat Shirley like an adult women addressing her as Mrs.[732] He talked about the British attitude of the loyal Negro who would defend his white counterpart to the death in places in the world where the people were not as westernized as the West.[733]

---

[728] BFA Presents of Black America Black History: Lost, Stolen or Strayed (1968) reelblack https://www.youtube.com/watch?v=QXn-Fm6cn9s (14 min to 15 min)

[729] Ibid (15 min to 17 min)

[730] Ibid (17 min to 20 min)

[731] Ibid (21 min)

[732] Ibid (22 min to 24 min)

[733] Ibid (26 min to 27 min)

During this time in history the depictions of black people in theater were what was expected or what was endorsed by lots of Conservatives and some classical Liberals of the time who had more traditional beliefs about race as accepted cultural and social norms and / or beliefs by whites for the behavior and appearance of black men and women. During this period in history when you had Aunt Jemima's picture on the old pancake boxes or Amos and Andy on the radio every morning and Al Jolson's caricature of a black man in blackface in the 1927's film Mammy you know that those were racist caricatures of black men and women in a more conservative America. The work the Progressives have done over time rather discouraged this kind of stereotypical look and behavior of blacks in society, and it was eventually removed from sight.[734]. This was during a time period when lots of Conservatives and some classical Liberals could look at this and laugh at it and make mockery of blacks, so we can thank the progressive movement for these changes. Also, during this time in history some who were not black were making profits from these over-characterizations of blacks. This is not to say that some Progressives did not approve of some of these behaviors themselves or even make mockery of some of them for that matter. This time in history the progressive movement and Progressives had some positives for black America; however, this would not be the case later on.

Since these were actions, that whites wanted to see from black people, it made them feel better about themselves and about the way blacks were treated in America, I think, so they do not have to feel guilty about the past. But these movies that Cosby is referring to are

---

[734] Dr. Darnell Hunt NAACP MEE THE BLACK EXECUTIVE:
A Partial Solution to Psycho-Social Consequences of Media Distortions retrieved April 18, 2023 https://naacp.org/sites/default/files/documents/NAACP%20MEE%20FINAL%20MERGED%20REPORT.pdf

ones that were made anywhere from 10 to maybe a 80 years before 1968, and back then America was more of what we would call very conservative under today's standards, but back then you know those portrayals were very stereotypical and very racist when there were a lot more conservative influences and maybe even some ultra-Conservatives under today's standards because back then they were not politically correct like today progressive leftists. Today it is difficult to even decipher how the actions of blacks in the media have so many stereotypically negative connotations from progressive and leftist influences, and the program I have discussed here is reminiscent of what I am talking about. Cosby stated that Hollywood just made movies that white ticket buyers wanted to see.[735] You have to ask yourself, could some of the movies that feature black people in their totality be to create a negative image though not as negative as in years past about blacks today for the past 50 years to present because enough whites may still feel better seeing certain images about black people, or is it because a few powerful people want to present a negative image about black people in a more progressive America?

Big Rapids, Michigan, has a museum called the Jim Crow Museum,[736] which exposes the past for what happened but in a way that we can heal and reconcile from past hurts. One of its exhibits about black women is the Jezebel image.[737] It portrays the past stereotypes of black women as being sexually promiscuous, seductive, alluring, worldly, beguiling, tempting, and lewd,[738] therefore

---

[735] Ibid

[736] Jim Crow Museum (witness understand heal) The Jezebel Stereotype retrieved May 14, 2023 https://jimcrowmuseum.ferris.edu/jezebel/index.htm

[737] Ibid

[738] Ibid

deserving of the burden of having to raise white men's mulatto children out of wedlock and black slave men's children for the purpose of producing more slave labor also often out of wedlock. The slave era's Jezebel depicted black women as having an insatiable appetite for sex.[739]

The museum also presents discussions about some films and blaxploitation movies from the 70s, 80s, and 90s as an example how black women were casted as the obligatory whore, after America was changing and becoming more progressive that belittle black women sexually in theater. In conclusion, the site states music videos, especially those by gangsta rap performers, portray scantily clad, nubile black women who thrust their hips to lyrics, which often depict them as hos, skeezers, and bitches.[740] Now 30, 40, or maybe 50 years after the civil rights movement, there is a depiction of black girls as sex commodities in a more modern and progressive America. In that same more progressive America, you have lots of black women, especially in these little pockets in the black community, who are raising children by different baby daddies out of wedlock. Which is worse, the Jezebel of a more conservative era America or the one of the present-day progressive era America in pockets of our inner cities?

According to an article written about common black stereotypes in TV and film, there are five of them. They have persisted to a greater or a lesser extent from after 1968 to the present, after American media has slowly catered to a more progressive direction and a less conservative one over time. They are: (1) the magical negro,[741] often a man who tends to appear to help white characters

---

[739] Ibid

[740] Ibid

[741] Nadra Kareem Nittle Updated on March 06, 2021 Thought Co 5 Common Black Stereotypes in TV and Film retrieved May 1, 2022 https://www.thoughtco.com/common-black-stereotypes-in-tv-film-2834653

but can be problematic because he has no inner life or desires of his own, (2) the black best friend,[742] who is usually a woman who shows up to support the heroin, but she still doesn't have much going on in her life, much like the magical negro, (3) the thug,[743] usually a black man who plays a drug dealer, pimp, con artist, or a criminal, (4) the angry lack woman,[744] who often is sassy, aggressive, and pushy, with a bad attitude, and (5) the domestic[745] in the 2011 film *The Help*. A couple of questions to ask here are how much better has the stereotyping gotten, and is it leaving a bad impression behind for blacks today?

Let's discuss Bill Cosby's situation because his is a complicated one. As an actor and comedian, he was a beloved icon in the black community. He and others that were actors during his time broke color barriers for blacks, which was a form of civil rights advancement. In 1976, he earned his doctorate of education from the University of Massachusetts, Amherst.[746] His dissertation discussed the use of *Fat Albert and the Cosby Kids* as a teaching tool in elementary schools, and his cartoon series *Fat Albert* was used as teaching tool.[747] They went through a lot just being black in the entertainment field. He was well known for his role in the 1980s sitcom as father in *The Cosby Show*. Americans of all races and ethnic backgrounds loved that show as it received very high ratings. He was one

---

[742] Ibid

[743] Ibid

[744] Ibid

[745] Ibid

[746] Valerie Strauss. Bill Cosby's doctoral thesis was about using 'Fat Albert' as a teaching tool. November 24, 2014 retrieved September 29, 2019 https://www.washingtonpost.com/news/answer-sheet/wp/2014/11/24/bill-cosbys-doctoral-thesis-was-about-using-fat-albert-as-a-teaching-tool/?noredirect=on&utm_term=.02feed0695bc

[747] Ibid

of America's favorite dads, and it was transcending across racial lines. He was beloved enough in the black community to make changes just by making the right statements because from *The Cosby Show*, he was a role model of what it was like to aspire to be a good father, and his wife, played by Felisha Rashad, was a great role model for any working mother and wife with a family to aspire to be.

Even though a husband as a doctor and a wife as a lawyer were not realistic for everyone to think they would be, it was a good image to present as a black family to everyone else in America, including black Americans. He encouraged black boys to stop saggin', pull your pants up, stay in school, stop cursing, respect your parents, don't talk back to authority figures, and a whole lot of other things.

Bill Cosby at one time condemned his own black community for spending too much on flashy goods at the expense of children's education.[748] He has been roundly criticized by some and praised by others, but there hasn't been much evidence to show whether his claims are true.[749] Those who believe spending patterns vary among racial and ethnic groups typically invoke cultural differences.[750] Whether it has to do with the appearance of success, accomplishment, or social status according to a Wharton College professor, blacks do spend more on things such as jewelry, clothing, and cars that make the appearance that one is of high status in society seem more visible.[751]

When you look at the facts, it suggests Cosby and others were incorrect to presume that cultural reasons were causes for bad

---

[748] Nikolai Roussanov Conspicuous Consumption and Race: Who Spends More on What. podcast. May 14, 2008. retrieved October 10, 2019 https://knowledge.wharton.upenn.edu/article/conspicuous-consumption-and-race-who-spends-more-on-what/

[749] Ibid.

[750] Ibid.

[751] Ibid.

spending priorities and overspending on some things.[752] But this does not mean that the critics are wrong about the consequences of careless spending.[753] Money spent on things for unnecessary consumption must be taken from money spent on things that are needed or that are good investments for the future, and according to research data, blacks and Hispanics save less toward goals such as a college degree and retirement than whites do with similar incomes.[754]

Cosby was trying to promote positive changes at least from what he has observed. This is another thing I think that has fueled the mainstream media's disdain for Bill Cosby. This type of consumption is being encouraged largely by images of products and services that the mainstream media, which is influenced heavily by leftists and promotes and tries to convince people of all races and ethnic backgrounds that they need all of the stuff being promoted for happiness through mainstream TV shows and through commercial ads. Advertisements for some products and services are sometimes targeted toward an ethnic or racial group. These advertisers don't have the best interests of the group at heart; they are interested in how much profit they can make. They don't even care whether the display is realistic or not. Black people are more likely to not be able to afford a lot of these things, so Bill Cosby in a sense is just looking out for the best interest of the black community in an area where the mainstream media is not and in other areas too where the media is really not. A lot of this is pushed by special interests, which do not have the black community's best interest at heart.

This was in 1968 when Cosby hosted Black History: Lost, Stolen or Strayed. when color barriers were being broken, and black

---

[752] Ibid.

[753] Ibid.

[754] Ibid.

people were lucky just to be able to get inside of some places to perform; he was presenting some more radical things like this that would step on the toes of lots of whites that were used to black people and their achievements being presented in a certain low-key text. He had accomplished so much, and at this point in his career, he had the potential to change society for black people. He was in position to change society in ways that the left would not like to see, let alone some conservatives, so he had to be dismantled, and his reputation and character had to be destroyed. First, he had lots of accusations from women, who have come out of the woodwork, stating that he sexually assaulted them, or he raped them. Some of these women were in tears. Some of these accusations went as far back as the early 1970s against Cosby. My question is: Why have all of these women waited until just before he was sentenced in September of 2018 before a 10-year prison sentence[755] to say something? Fortunately, he was released from prison in June of 2021.[756]

If you are going to question Cosby's moral character, you could certainly question the moral character of plenty of other actors who have been in jail and have been in trouble for a whole lot of other things, but why were they after Bill Cosby, when there are lots of other rapists and pedophiles out there who are wealthy? Men have had false accusations of rape on them,[757] and especially since the #MeToo movement, which has come out of the radical feminist

---

[755] Kyle Kim, Christina Littlefield and Melissa Etehad. Bill Cosby: A 50-year chronicle of accusations and accomplishments. The Los Angeles Times. Sep 25, 2018. retrieved May 27, 2019 https://www.latimes.com/entertainment/la-et-bill-cosby-timeline-htmlstory.html

[756] MOLLI MITCHELL ON 1/30/22 AT 11:00 PM EST Newsweek Was Bill Cosby Released From Prison? Retrieved May 3, 2022 https://www.newsweek.com/why-was-bill-cosby-released-prison-sexual-assault-conviction-overturned-1673910

[757] NSVRC Overview of False Reporting. retrieved December 3, 2019 https://www.nsvrc.org/sites/default/files/Publications_NSVRC_Overview_False-Reporting.pdf

movement. Bill Cosby was targeted by feminists, and they are a part of the movement to kill the patriarchy, because he hosted one of the best primetime TV show examples of an ideal father with respect for his wife's position in the family too. You can be both a feminist and a racist, like Margaret Sanger. That doesn't mean that all feminists are racists, but maybe some of the ones who raised these accusations against Bill Cosby were manipulated to take him down. Lots of other men were victims of the MeToo movement, but their cases were not dragged out for as long as Bill Cosby's, and they did not have this many accusations against them from so many women under so many different circumstances over such a long period, as Bill Cosby did. They were accused of their wrongdoing; you heard about it a few times on TV, and then they were punished/sentenced for their crimes in a relatively short period. Not Bill Cosby; he was really put more on display and made a spectacle of for months.

Campus tribunals, which comprise a panel of people who decide whether a rape accusation is true or false, have been handing down lots of guilty verdicts on college campuses.[758] Students who are alleged victims can contradict themselves, and the evidence can be explained away by the victim's trauma, which is just an emotional response.[759] The tribunal panels are often cherry-picked without any reasonable criteria.[760] Now there are lots of lawsuits by young men who claim that they were unlawfully expelled from colleges and

---

[758] Stuart Taylor. November 09, 2017. The Washington Examiner. Why Campus Rape Tribunals Hand Down So Many 'Guilty' Verdicts. https://www.washingtonexaminer.com/weekly-standard/why-campus-rape-tribunals-hand-down-so-many-guilty-verdicts retrieved December 3, 2019.

[759] Ibid.

[760] Ibid.

universities.[761] With that said, it is questionable with the strong #MeToo movement going on in today's culture whether Cosby's case was conducted with some similarities to a college campus tribunal. Attesting to the statistic that only 2 percent to 10 percent of rape allegations are false,[762] something else to consider is since just maybe even a sexual harassment which can be verbal or physical but technically not rape since penetration is not necessary but still can be grounds for punishment.[763] Could harassment only have sometimes been the case for Cosby's punishment? Again, Bill Cosby may not be innocent of all the accusations about him; he may be guilty of some of them, but I am not going to judge Cosby for anything.

He was exonerated of his crime and released, but why was he targeted to have his reputation smeared, because for all practical purposes he has been destroyed. Since he has had his reputation smeared in the mud like this, he does not need to be blacklisted from Hollywood and he has no credibility for the most part any more to give young kids or a community for that matter any practical advice that a wise older man with a treasure trove and a rich wealth of life experience can. He has credentials that a lot of actors and actresses don't have, but this smear campaign that took place on him has rendered him of little value. I think this was by design by the left-leaning media so he could not be an agent of change for the black community. I don't know and I may be wrong, but it appears

---

[761] Cathy Young. November 22, 2018. Sex, Lies, and Campus Tribunals. https://arcdigital.media/sex-lies-and-campus-tribunals-88cc33c30262 retrieved December 3, 2019.

[762] Emily Moon. Updated :Oct 7, 2018, Original: Oct 5, 2018. False Reports of Sexual Assault Are Rare. But Why Is There So Little Reliable Data About Them? https://psmag.com/news/false-reports-of-sexual-assault-are-rare-but-why-is-there-so-little-reliable-data-about-them retrieved December 3, 2019.

[763] Emily Yoffe. September 6, 2017. The Atlantic Education. The Uncomfortable Truth About Campus Rape Policy. https://www.theatlantic.com/education/archive/2017/09/the-uncomfortable-truth-about-campus-rape-policy/538974/ Retrieved December 3, 2019.

to me that they may have even had a vendetta out after Cosby. Sadly, Cosby hasn't been the first and he may not be the last either.

In the movie *Black History: Lost, Stolen or Strayed*, which is narrated by Bill Cosby, he discusses lots of achievements by black pioneers who were not mentioned in history books. Important historical events in black history were discussed such as medical advances made by medical doctors, especially stellar performances discussed by black service members at war. Since it was made in the 1960s, it does not show more recent advances or accomplishments in black history, but nonetheless, it still had some very encouraging information in it for black kids to aspire to. It was mostly for 12-and-over audiences.[764] This is one reason why I believe good, old-fashioned racists believed that Bill Cosby had gotten too big for his britches, so he had to be taken down, especially when you consider how very impressive his career and reputation was overall.

The media's overly extensive coverage of Bill Cosby's circumstances was not necessary, but the leftist media did this to slander his character. It was not necessary for them to cover his trial for 10 months and to be on TV every day at times. This was nothing more than an effort to smear his name in the mud, and the mainstream media played a big role in this. Cosby's first trial ended in a mistrial. Cosby was found guilty of three counts of aggravated indecent assault, and five months later, he was sentenced to three-to-ten years in state prison with fines plus the cost of the prosecution totaling nearly $70,000. All of his trial could have been conducted very privately, and the media only needed to cover it a few times, maybe the first trial, one a few months later, and one last time when he was

---

[764] https://www.rottentomatoes.com/m/black_history_lost_stolen_or_strayed retrieved October 19, 2019.

sentenced. Excessive coverage just smeared his name and his character and reputation in the mud. This was by design.

I know a lot of people are thinking why is he saying that black people in media still look bad today vs. years gone by when black people today are playing much more noble roles on TV than before such as lawyers, doctors, and so forth. I will admit that many of today's portrayals of blacks in media are not as bad as years gone by, but years ago, black people brought some very impressive and different genres of music to the scene such as jazz music, which branched off into other forms including swing, doo-wop, and bebop, which were imitated and even enjoyed by lots of whites. Jazz music had and still does have a touch of class and elegance to it. This was allowed years ago when there were more of what we would refer to today as conservative influences in media by black entertainers and singers years ago as well, even though many of them had to first perform in Europe before being recognized in America vs. the images that rap videos and rap music lyrics have brought on the scene over the past 40 years that is a lot less tasteful than jazz, since influences in media have become more progressive. Years ago when people had more conservative values jazz music could have just been dismissed or disregarded as "N-------" music and kicked out of the popular music scene by whites but instead it was embraced as any American genre of music.

The reason why I think this is because Jazz is not a part of the popular music seen like it was years ago in the Roaring 20's. It is still a form of music that is listened to by some today and it is just as classy, but since today's youth and plenty of older adult's bop to some different beats, I think it was fair to make the comparison between the two. It also shows how tastes in music have changed in a more progressive culture it has become less conservative. This also says something about the way society has degraded morally and changed with today's popular music artists have gone from the invention of Jazz in the Roaring 20's to Rap 60 to 100 years later, and they are two different types of music but that is what the tastes in music of today's youth have come to. To make jazz music rather than that of the American pop and R&B artists of today requires some different interests than today's youth generally have.

In Bill Cosby's documentary, he stated, black men were casted in media roles where they had no qualities that could be admired by any man or women. Is that any better than the images that have come from rap music videos and their song lyrics and some other media of young black men as gangsters, criminals, pimps, and thugs over the past 40 years more recently in a more progressive America? He stated that black women were solid rocks and were unperturbed under circumstances that would scare a black man out of his britches (this made him look like a big sissy); how much better are today's image of the angry black women?

For that matter, what does Tyler Perry's role as Medea say about the strong black women; if you don't think this is making mockery of the strong black women, when have you ever seen a man who is six-foot-five of any other race or ethnicity dress in women's clothes in so many movies as a woman of his ethnicity to play a strong women's role of his ethnicity? In essence Medea's role is of a rock-solid unperturbed black women who can handle anything a man can that a man should be able to handle and more, and it makes mockery of the strong black women and the black community since at times and more often in the black community women have to step up and take leadership under circumstances when there is a shortage of black men. This makes mockery of the black man because the black community especially in certain small pockets in the community has a shortage of black men and because of the position it puts black women in sometimes as his replacement. It indicates that the strong black woman is less feminine and ladylike[765] than her counterparts of other races and ethnicities. Medea is not the first attempt to marginalize black manhood or womanhood; what about the women of *Housewives of Atlanta* and *Basketball Wives* as more progressive, new-age ways of marginalizing black women and minimizing black men as ineffective leaders? They are adult women who often argue and bicker like teenage girls.

Another example is the reality series South Beach Tow has a black women cast member referred to as Bernice in the show who is at times mean, loud, obnoxious, and even masculine for a women. She looks like she could take on any linebacker of any professional NFL football team. I've never seen the likes of it from a white woman or a woman of any other race or ethnic background on any other reality show.

Just asking, but why does RuPaul a six foot six-inch-tall black male transvestite in high heels, a dress and a blonde wig have to be the queen of drag? Why couldn't our progressive left leaning media have made a tall blonde, white guy the spectacle for this one or anything else but black? Just asking!

In Bill Cosby's case, if Conservatives had had more influence, feminists, or at least not this radical feminist movement, would not have bashed him like this. If they had had more influence in society since they are more likely to be Evangelical Christians, the moral and ethical behavior that causes people to want to engage in sexually immoral behavior just probably would not happen as often to begin with. Pornography that the radical left movement is allowing or even encouraging would not happen to the point that people would be so desensitized to such raw sexual content, which makes it a lot easier to desire and do it on a subconscious and conscious level and do it

---

[765] Rachel Parker | Apr 11, 2022 | Features The "Angry" Black Woman Purchase Nineteen Fifty Six Because Black Students Matter retrieved September 9, 2022 https://1956magazine.ua.edu/the-angry-black-woman/

openly.[766] Media today has too many of some other bad nontraditional reality shows that display unnecessary emotion and too many TV shows that suggest violence, murder, and death, as well as shows with images that conjure up lots of other negative emotions, thoughts, and feelings. If Conservatives who are on the right had more influence over TV viewing, there would not be nearly as much of this type of viewing.

Since African Americans sometimes can be presented by some media outlets negatively, it can connote some negative racial stereotypes and misconceptions to the public. They can also affect the assessment of a crime and the type and severity of punishment given. This is because some law enforcers who are ignorant of certain groups of people have developed biases by what they have seen on the media. Its effect has influenced the public attitudes about race. This is also dependent on the degree of exposure to certain types of media and how much of the public actually watches them. But many of these media outlets are strongly influenced by Progressives who support the leftists' agenda.

They provided a lot of the media coverage we see on TV, and this coverage has had an effect on how the police do their job in black communities. If the officers don't know any blacks or enough of them to develop good perceptions about them, they have fearful or angry perceptions, which affect the way they police. This mostly applies to the exceptions to the rule. But let me say this, most police officers are good officers, and they make fair and just decisions when they police. This does not mean that some police officers could not have some biases toward certain groups of people. Now that we are losing police from left leaning progressives defunding the police the murder,

---

[766] Fight the New Drug Publication. The Concerning Connection Between Sex Crimes and Porn. April 2, 2018. retrieved February 29, 2020 https://fightthenewdrug.org/the-disturbing-link-between-porn-and-sex-crimes/

The Mainstream Media

drug overdose, homicide, burglary and assault rates have skyrocketed which may even be having a worse effect on the black community than police brutality.

Had black people not completely integrated with whites, on progressive terms, they would still have their own movie and private media productions and theaters. They would have their own HBCUs and the think tanks that came out of some of them, with the ideas produced, but black people lost control of them from integration on progressive terms. Black people could have made wholesome, reasonable productions and plays about themselves, but now since they don't have them, they must endure all of the humiliation and insults they get from stereotypes and downright false information about them from media sources that they have no ownership or control over and that have a different agenda. Here the conservative agenda and conservatism, which usually aligns with the right, may have had more positive effects for blacks over the past 50 years or so, verses left leaning progressives and progressivism of today since both have changed and evolved over time.

The media portrays black people in a bad light as looters during Hurricane Katrina in September of 2005, but they seemed to ignore white looters who were said to only be looking for food.[767] The portrayals in some of the more recent looters of Walmart's, convenience shops and discount chains around the country, which give the appearance that a lot more of these people are black, is being displayed to everyone by our progressive media, but they are not displaying people of other races as much who should all be thrown in jail to stay for a while regardless of race or ethnicity. Correct me if I am wrong on this

---

[767] Tania Ralli. Sept. 5, 2005. Who's a Looter? In Storm's Aftermath, Pictures Kick Up a Different Kind of Tempest. *The New York Times*. Retrieved May 5, 2020 https://www.nytimes.com/2005/09/05/business/whos-a-looter-in-storms-aftermath-pictures-kick-up-a-different.html

one, but when black and Hispanic youth riot and loot like a bunch of hoodlums it seems more likely to get national coverage from our progressive left-leaning media and the whole country sees it, but when white youth do it in very progressively liberal areas it is more likely to just get local coverage and everybody doesn't see how bad the white youth are really behaving or misbehaving, whatever you want to call it. It's like they want you to see the black youth so they will have an excuse to exclude them from society. The white youth were more likely to do it in ski masks, long sleeves, and maybe some other forms of concealment, but the black youth were more likely to not use either forms of camouflage or concealment, which made it a lot easier for media to expose them for who they are, including what they are.

This is the same narrative that was pushed after the 1915 box office movie *Birth of a Nation* in a more traditional Conservative America that portrayed the mean old black man who would come after white women and rape them. The narrative still had similarities during Houston's Hurricane Harvey in 2017,[768] thanks to our racist, leftist media.

Since this progressive, left movement has taken off, not only has the black community had more shootings and killing from guns, the whole country has but especially the black community. If Conservatives had had more influence, you would not have so many violent images of killings and dead people from video games, Hollywood blockbuster movies, action-packed cable and mainstream TV series, and gangsta rap videos that were really intended to appeal to black youth with actual shootouts on them. Children who watch these shows with no parental guidance become desensitized to acts like these, and it is a lot easier for them to do it to other people in

---

[768] Colleen Shalby. Aug. 29, 2017. Los Angeles Times. What's the difference between 'looting' and 'finding'? 12 years after Katrina, Harvey sparks a new debate. World and Nation. retrieved May 5, 2020 https://www.latimes.com/nation/la-na-harvey-20170829-story.html

reality if they were not given a good moral compass from home to follow. Conservatives would not allow so much of this type of content to even be viewed in the media. We see many more acts of violence now in a more technologically advanced society than we did when TV first came out, and you saw westerns with shootouts and duels because it is easier to deliver it to the viewer now because now we have NetFlex and an endless selection of cable TV channels that you can watch at home on TV, on your laptop computer outside of home, or even your cellphone with all the gory details of injured or killed persons and the acts of violence causing them in living color than you could when society was more Conservative than it is now.

These same Progressives and leftists have done a great job of convincing black Americans that all Conservatives are racists and that all Progressives and leftists are safe. When you throw in enough bias from an often-biased leftist news media[769] and the music and film industry, it even sends a message to whites and all other ethnic backgrounds and sometimes including blacks that blacks deserve to be where they are totally because of their own choices. This is somewhat what was intended by the 1915 Hollywood movie production *Birth of a Nation*, which portrayed the emancipated slaves as heathens, as unworthy of being free, as uncivilized, and as primarily concerned with passing laws so they could marry white women and prey on them.[770]

---

[769] Ken Stern. Former NPR CEO opens up about liberal media bias. October 21, 2017. retrieved august 26, 2019 https://nypost.com/2017/10/21/the-other-half-of-america-that-the-liberal-media-doesnt-cover

[770] 100 Years Later, What's The Legacy of 'Birth of a Nation'? NPR Network Staff. February 8, 2015. retrieved July 18, 2019 https://www.npr.org/sections/codeswitch/2015/02/08/383279630/100-years-later-whats-the-legacy-of-birth-of-a-nation

Rap music was basically a black invention from NYC's inner-city DJs[771] with some of its performers and singers being both talented and creative. It can be used to express rebellion against or approval of political polices, injustices, and other cultural issues that are happening in society. It could also be used to teach history and other factual things about the world in which we live, such as maybe the way the old Schoolhouse Rook cartoons did years ago with the three Rs but are no longer politically correct in some cases or maybe a lot of cases today. Since this is the case, rap music and rappers had to be controlled by executives and directors[772] who have links to large woke multibillion dollar corporations with their own special interests[773] that are not good for black youth who are inspired by this genre of music.[774] The multibillion-dollar NBA, NFL, and NBL, in particular the NBA and NFL whose players are mostly black, have no ownership or control over those leagues. Here is where progressives are using a black invention and something where black participation has set a precedence, and they are using it to advance their cause with no control by blacks. Since rap and hip-hop music now has a label on it as a black creation and its current influences are more negative than positive, could this be used as an incentive by the left to get rid of black people as A Menace To Society (like the name that a prominent rapper gave to himself)

---

[771] Edison Edwards Rhyme Makers 12 Gripping Facts About The History Of Rap retrieved March 25, 2023 https://rhymemakers.com/history-of-rap-music/

[772] Paul Resnikoff January 20, 2014 The Music Industry: It's Still a White Boys' Club... Digital Music News retrieved March 27, 2023 https://www.digitalmusicnews.com/2014/01/20/whiteboysclub/

[773] Khafre Jay Jul 22, 2019 1 min read Jailhouse Roc: The FACTS About Hip Hop and Prison for Profit
Updated: Feb 9, 2021 Join The Fight For Our Culture retrieved March 25, 2023 https://www.hiphopforchange.org/post/jailhouseroc

[774] Ibid

like Planned Parenthood's agenda with abortion of exterminating the Negro?

According to an issue from *The New Republic Magazine*, Urban Dictionary was deemed as being horrifically racist.[775] It is a collection of slang terms from all across the world. It is rife with racist and sexist slang.[776] Its app has been downloaded over three million times,[777] it is the 25th largest site in America,[778] and in one month it got over 130 million global views.[779] This has been invented and allowed in a more progressive and supposedly more tolerant and politically correct America as it was invented just in 1999.[780] I am almost willing to bet you that Conservatives were not behind the creation of Urban Dictionary. It has racist slang about black people in general. This is a new, modern, and very deceptive way to keep racial biases and stereotypes alive and well in a more progressive and modern America as a way to replace the more blatant racial undertones of the past in a more conservative-era America, like blackface characters in minstrel shows. An article from the *MIT Technology Review* calls it a unique insight into the way our language is evolving[781] and changing but if the site has just over 2.6 million

---

[775] Clio Chang. July 5, 2017. Why Urban Dictionary Is Horrifically Racist. The New Republic. retrieved November 1, 2019. https://newrepublic.com/article/143704/urban-dictionary-horrifically-racist

[776] Ibid

[777] Ibid

[778] Ibid

[779] Ibid

[780] Emerging Technology from the arXivarchive page January 3, 2018 MIT Technical Review The Anatomy of the Urban Dictionary Computing retrieved July 21, 2022 https://www.technologyreview.com/2018/01/03/146467/the-anatomy-of-the-urban-dictionary/

[781] Ibid

definitions for just over 1.6 million words and phrases[782] and when you can very subtly and jokingly change the definitions of word and be convincing while doing it, you can change the way people think and react for the good or the bad. I will leave it up to the reader to decide which.

Another point I wanted to make here is that this type of free speech is being allowed online; why don't they just cancel this site altogether? They can use this site for something else more sinister. It may not be up to the inventor of the site what goes on it, so most or all of the racist post may not have anything to do with the inventor of the site; in fact he may really not approve of some the content on some posts, so the racist posts and the content may be a reflection on who's doing the posting or on who decides what goes on the site and what they perceive as racist or not, not the site's inventor. I just thought I would make a note of that.

I like the way an article from *Wired* magazine states the possible effects that Urban Dictionary could have on culture.[783] According to the article, it has gone from being a source tool to becoming something inhospitable.[784] With the stereotypes it perpetuates on certain individuals and groups of people it has the ability to maintain and create more biases and maybe even more divisions between groups by race with negative intentions for particular groups of people. This article from May 2018 claims the site contains over eight million slang and cultural expressions[785] and averages just over 65 million views a month. According to another source that

---

[782] Ibid

[783] Jason Parham Culture Sep 11, 2019 7:00 AM WEIRD Magazine What Happened to Urban Dictionary? Retrieved August 25, 2022 https://www.wired.com/story/urban-dictionary-20-years/

[784] Ibid

[785] Ibid

claims slang dictionaries existed in the 1700s[786] was useful in interpreting the vernacular of thieves, cheats, and criminals.[787] This was used in a positive way. The same source claims linguists are using Urban Dictionary[788] and now it is being archived by the Library of Congress.[789] Some of its language was attempted in some Internet artificial intelligence by IBM but later discontinued when it started swearing.[790] The questions we need to be asking is what are the intentions of this site for black Americans?

I wanted to discuss something else about the looting of the Walmart stores and some other chain stores such as Target, Walgreens, and gas station mini-marts, which resulted in lots of store closings. Some of the Walmart stores are in low-income areas,[791] where the people have no other access to any other stores anywhere else,[792] and if they did, they could not afford anything else, so the discount chains are their only choices.[793] If they continue to loot and riot enough discount stores and chain stores repeatedly, once too many of these discount chains close permanently, unlike the three that reopened in Chicago, and there is nowhere for these

---

[786] Christine Ro November 13, 2019 6 minutes Daily JSTOR Arts & Culture How Linguists Are Using Urban Dictionary retrieved August 25, 2022 https://daily.jstor.org/how-linguists-are-using-urban-dictionary/

[787] Ibid

[788] Ibid

[789] Ibid

[790] Ibid

[791] Analysis by Nathaniel Meyersohn, CNN Updated 4:09 PM EDT, Sat April 15, 2023 What Walmart's pullback from Chicago says about Corporate America's limits CNN Business retrieved May 5, 2023 https://www.cnn.com/2023/04/15/business/walmart-chicago-closing-corporate-america/index.html

[792] Ibid

[793] Ibid

people to shop for basic necessities in miles, they will have no choice but to do without basic necessities, to go hungry, or maybe even starve in some cases. These people will be disproportionately black. This will be the governments' chance to step in and provide for these people their basic necessities and prevent them from starving, and for that they will love the government, which is what the progressive socialist left wants. This will help them get closer to a goal of government control.

Since all of these stores have excellent surveillance both inside and outside including parking lots, which can photograph the license plates of the cars who have driven off with stolen merchandise, they have more people who will also be disproportionately black that they can arrest and throw in prison to maintain the prison industrial complex that socialist states usually always have. These who will be disproportionately affected will be in a similar proportion that Planned Parenthood's abortion clinics have eliminated from society. In some cases there were some arrests and probably some jail time but probably not enough of either, if it had been up to most conservatives the first looters would have all been arrested and jailed and the fear of being jailed by the first few hundred maybe would be discouragement for further disruptive activity such as this, which would probably stop it for the most part. This will continue to happen across the country if you defund and dismantle the police department like progressives are pushing for. If it had been up to the Conservative right the police would not have been defunded and the low-income disproportionately black neighborhoods would have more affordable places to shop for necessities. I think conservatives would have a better solution to the looting in the long run, not progressives with a sinister scheme up their sleeve.

It has been suspected that AI CHAT GPT technology which was developed in by San Francisco–based OpenAI the creator of the initial GPT series in a location with a more progressive culture[794] is or has been programmed with some negative biases toward or against blacks that have not been completely ironed out yet.[795] An example is with medical advice.[796] With hallucinations which is a default in it programming things can just be made up[797]. But can they be terribly racist? Let's hope they get all these biases ironed out or negative consequences are bound to result. With AI and ChatGPT a lot more can be automated which can justify eliminating a lot of low and no skilled waged jobs which are ones that blacks are still a lot more likely to need. This can eliminate the need for a lot of people who fall into this category. Literally!!

---

[794] Enterprise DNA Experts | 5:49 pm EDT | April 26, 2023 | AI, ChatGPT Who Owns Chat GPT: Unveiling the Company Behind the AI retrieved February 11, 2024 https://blog.enterprisedna.co/who-owns-chat-gpt/

[795] Zachary B. Wolf, CNN 13 minute read Published 9:29 AM EDT, Sat March 18, 2023 What Matters AI can be racist, sexist and creepy. What should we do about it? Retrieved February 11, 2024 https://www.cnn.com/2023/03/18/politics/ai-chatgpt-racist-what-matters/index.html

[796] CBS News Bay Area Stanford study indicates AI chatbots used by health providers are perpetuating racism Updated on: October 20, 2023 / 6:32 PM PDT / AP retrieved February 11, 2024 https://www.cbsnews.com/sanfrancisco/news/ai-chatbots-are-supposed-to-improve-healthcare-but-research-says-some-are-perpetuating-racism-2/

[797] Steven Levy Weird Magazine BUSINESSJAN 5, 2024 9:00 AM In Defense of AI Hallucinations retrieved February 11, 2024 https://www.wired.com/story/plaintext-in-defense-of-ai-hallucinations-chatgpt/

13.

Legal Immigrants and Other Non-White Groups

Some are probably going to disagree with me on some of what I am trying to say here as well, some will agree with some of what I am trying to say, and some are going to miss my point altogether. Some may even wonder what's the point.

This past year under a more progressive Biden-Harris administration, we saw a total of 1.7 million immigrants entering the US illegally.[798] If this trend continues, the total will be between 6.8 and 7.0 million by the end of their administration. The last time this happened was in 1960.[799] For the first time, much higher percentages have been allowed to stay.[800] Immigrants, whether legal or illegal and whether they make the crossing at the border illegally or not, are coming in almost unprecedented numbers at a time when African

---

[798] Eileen Sullivan and Miriam Jordan. October 21, 2021. The New York Times. Illegal Border Crossings, Driven by Pandemic and Natural Disasters, Soar to Record High. retrieved January 8, 2022 https://www.nytimes.com/2021/10/22/us/politics/border-crossings-immigration-record-high.html

[799] Ibid.

[800] John Gramlich. The Pew Research Center. Migrant encounters at U.S.-Mexico border are at a 21-year high. retrieved January 8, 2022 https://www.pewresearch.org/fact-tank/2021/08/13/migrant-encounters-at-u-s-mexico-border-are-at-a-21-year-high/

Americans as a community do not have safety nets to deal with it. That does not mean immigrants are coming for the sole purpose of doing harm to African Americans or that they will change their feelings about blacks and do harmful things to blacks because the vast majority are not and will not, but …… people are people.

Since lots of immigrant groups have immigrated to America legally, this is something that could not be stopped or avoided when you consider it has just been a part of America's fabric from its inception. Currently, America's population is 61 percent white, 12 percent black, 18 percent Hispanic, 6 percent Asian, and one percent Native American.[801] All the way up until the civil rights movement, whites have dominated the cultural, economic, political, and social landscape of America. In 1965, the Immigration and Nationality Act overhauled the American immigration system. The Act ended the national origin quotas enacted in the 1920s, which favored some racial and ethnic groups over others.[802] It seems as if, from roughly then until the present, most immigrants have been non-white and / or of non-European origin. Since then, whites have become the minority of the population in some small towns and in several major cities in America that are in America's top 100 in population. Whites are now a majority in 52 of the biggest 100 cities, down from 70 in 1990, researchers found.[803] It is interesting to note that the info on the website Population Distribution by Race/Ethnicity was compiled from 2001 data, and it is now 2019. As they have slowly become a

---

[801] US Population Distribution by Race/Ethnicity. Henry J Kaiser Family Foundation. retrieved August 2, 2019 https://www.kff.org/other/state-indicator/distribution-by-raceethnicity

[802] U.S. Immigration Timeline. Updated on May 14, 2019. retrieved August 15, 2019 https://www.history.com/topics/immigration/immigration-united-states-timeline

[803] Eric Schmitt. THE CENSUS: The Nation; Whites In Minority In Largest Cities, The Census Shows. April 30, 2001. retrieved July 9, 2019 https://www.nytimes.com/2001/04/30/us/the-census-the-nation-Whites-in-minority-in-largest-cities-the-census-shows.html

minority in many towns and cities across America, other non-white ethnic backgrounds have started their businesses and have become major influencers of small pockets of the economies of some cities locally. With time, whites will no longer be the dominant influence locally in certain places; in some places it will be some other non-white groups. An example of this today is Dearborn, Michigan, with a growing Arab population.

Since blacks integrated with whites, they did not build economies like they had during the Black Wallstreet era of Tulsa, Oklahoma, so they have no economic infrastructure or political one to go to that was created by and for them. Since this is the case, they may continue to be discriminated against by non-white groups like they were before the civil rights movement. They will continue to be more dependent on resources outside of their group than any other group, and when resources become scarce, they will be the first group to be pushed out.

Three big groups of non-whites are becoming larger and more influential than they have ever been in the history of America. America is changing demographically, and it will eventually evolve into a different America, but that does not mean that another group's causes and the way they go about acquiring them could not become a significant problem for blacks.

Hispanics are progressing out of poverty much faster than blacks,[804] and a much higher percentage of them are acquiring college degrees than blacks.[805] A much higher percentage of Hispanics earn more money than their parents did.[806]

---

[804] Tami Luhby. June 22, 2018. CNN Business. This group is getting ahead in America. retrieved October 18, 2021 https://money.cnn.com/2018/06/22/news/economy/hispanic-social-mobility/index.html

[805] Ibid.

[806] Ibid.

According to a new study, NYC's Latino population has changed, with Dominicans outnumbering Puerto Ricans in the city.[807] They own a lot of corner stores in NYC called bodegas, but they did not always own them. Puerto Ricans were the first to establish them in the Bronx after a lot of them immigrated there after World War II.[808] They have since sold a lot of them to Dominicans, according to University Professor Ramona Hernandez, Director of the Dominican Studies Institute of Hunter College CUNY.[809] She said they were leaving NYC as Dominicans were coming in.[810] The narrator of the video also said that the bodega made sense for Dominicans because they were able to provide products for themselves, and they were able to provide jobs for themselves[811] that they could not get in the greater community in many instances[812]. At the same time, it also represented independence.[813] These neighborhoods with bodegas also have lots of their restaurants and beauty salons.[814] The narrator also stated these stores were a part of the Yemeni and Egyptian community and also Puerto Ricans,[815] so this is how other ethnic backgrounds can provide for their communities.

---

[807] Leonard Greene, retrieved May 18 2019 https://nypost.com/2014/11/13/dominicans-now-outnumber-puerto-ricans-in-nyc/ Dominicans now outnumber Puerto Ricans in NYC. The New York Post. November 13, 2014. retrieved May 18 2019

[808] Ibid.

[809] Why Do Dominicans Own So Many New York Corner Stores? AJ+ Al Jazerra Network. retrieved August 15, 2019 https://www.youtube.com/watch?v=z95x3fj9ptQ (3 min and 29 sec)

[810] Ibid (3 min and 46 sec)

[811] Ibid (5min and 15 sec)

[812] Ibid (5 min and 20 sec)

[813] Ibid (5 min and 30 sec)

[814] Ibid (5 min and 45 sec)

[815] Ibid (25 secs)

The bodega is a social space where Dominicans socialize,[816] they are an area for low-income and immigrant communities, they also serve in areas with no supermarkets, and they act as a lifeline for people who are short on cash and can buy now and pay for their items later.[817] One bodega owner in NYC used his basement to house homeless immigrants for a year.[818] He did this in spite of the fact it was illegal.[819] So Dominicans are providing goods and services like these for their own communities while at the same time they are providing employment for themselves.[820] But these stores were culturally based, and that is one thing blacks lost with integration. They lost a sense of cultural identity because they lost a lot of local institutions that represented what it meant to be a black American, but this is what the left encouraged blacks to do.

Even to this day, most probably, relations between blacks and Puerto Ricans in NYC have been very good almost without problems at all, and there were even lots of intermarriages in some cases. But as Puerto Ricans moved out of NYC, they did not sell the bodegas, which have generated lots of wealth, power, and opportunity for them, to blacks. They instead sold them to other fellow Latinos, the Dominicans. Now they can pursue other wealth-acquiring interests and game-changing influence over the political, social, economic, and cultural landscape of America while leaving their culture intact. This will give them some advantages in the future to change things in their favor, and it will leave fellow Hispanic Dominicans' ownership of the plot of real estate that the

---

[816] Ibid (6 min and 50 sec)

[817] Ibid (7 min and 20 sec)

[818] Ibid (7 min and 55 sec)

[819] Ibid (8 min and 10 sec)

[820] Ibid (8 min and 25 sec)

shop was on and, in all cases, the business. Black Americans were totally left out of both.

The bodegas in NYC have an organization called the Association for Bodegas,[821] with thousands of them under the organization. They can get together and discuss where and how to buy wholesale directly from a warehouse and sell retail for a profit. They can do this because they have a community, and bodegas are very ethnic in nature. Black businesses can do the same thing if they have a strong black chamber of commerce, but we lost the sense of community necessary for it when we attempted to completely integrate with whites.

First, let's start with Hispanics and address the situation in the Dominican Republic with the treatment of Haitians. As a result of decades of political tensions and shared fears, fed by a history of wars, massacres, and other types of injustice,[822] the people of the Dominican Republic and Haiti have shared different sides of the island of Hispaniola, but they rarely ever mix between the two sides of the island.[823] In the Dominican Republic, there is a market in the town of Dajabon, where they are getting along with one another. However, tensions fueled by racial differences and fears that go beyond the scope of economic cooperation and support of a stronger business community have made matters worse.[824] When

---

[821] Kristin Toussaint. Metro New York outraged over startup that wants to replace bodegas. retrieved May 29, 2021 https://www.metro.us/new-york-outraged-over-startup-that-wants-to-replace-bodegas/

[822] Aida Alami. The New York Review of Books. Between Hate, Hope, and Help: Haitians in the Dominican Republic. retrieved June 16, 2019 https://www.nybooks.com/daily/2018/08/13/between-hope-hate-help-haitians-in-the-dominican-republic/

[823] Ibid

[824] Ibid.

they have gone through in bad politics, things have only intensified[825] between the two nations.

Haitians have long suffered mistreatments in the Dominican Republic. In recent years, many people who were documented to be of Haitian descent who were born in the Dominican Republic[826] have been pressured to leave willingly or have been deported by law enforcement.

Consider the following case study: A second-generation Haitian woman of Haitian parents who were born in the Dominican Republic but immigrated to the Dominican Republic in 1970[827] was refused an identity card by Dominican authorities in 2008 and had her birth certificate confiscated while applying[828]. This open proceeding for a landmark legal case was called "La Sentencia," where she was the plaintiff.[829] As a result of this case, the Dominican Republic's Constitutional Court, which is the highest in the land, ruled retroactively in 2013 that immigrants with irregular migrant status should not be able to document children whether they were born in the Dominican Republic or not[830]. The aftermath of this ruling left many thousands of Haitians born in or before 2007[831] plundered of their citizenship and made stateless.[832]

VOX News, an alternative media source, sent a team of journalists to Haiti to report more in-depth on the situation. It was

---

[825] Ibid.

[826] Ibid.

[827] Ibid.

[828] Ibid.

[829] Ibid.

[830] Ibid.

[831] ibid.

[832] Ibid.

titled *Divided Island: How Haiti and the DR Became Two Worlds*.[833] Haitian merchants have been taking a nighttime boat ride from the coastal village of Marigot, Haiti, to the DR to set up their booths and sell their goods.[834] The market is in the border of the Dominican Republic and Haiti, so the two can do their trading on equal footing.[835] But when the Haitians arrive, they have to wait on Dominicans to first set up their stands and get the best spots so they are more visible.[836] The border guards stop the Haitians and allow the Dominicans to do this.[837]

The Dominican Republic has always had a better infrastructure than Haiti.[838] When Haiti got their independence from France, they were left with land that was depleted by growing sugarcane, and when the colonists left, they took all of their wealth with them.[839] Since they were the first black nation, they were basically isolated from the rest of the world[840] to conduct trade and commerce, and a racist world made sure this continued.[841] This is what, in a sense, has happened economically to black America, and you can see it in some of the really bad neighborhoods in the black community. Now the Dominican Republic, according to an official in that country, is making a more serious effort to crack down on Haitians to monitor

---

[833] Ibid.

[834] VOX Borders Divided island: How Haiti and the DR became two worlds https://www.youtube.com/watch?v=4WvKeYuwifc (2 min and 35 sec)

[835] Ibid (2 min and 40 sec)

[836] Ibid (2 min and 45 Sec)

[837] Ibid (2 min and 50 sec)

[838] Ibid (5 min and 40 sec)

[839] Ibid (4 min and 20 sec)

[840] Ibid (6 min and 20 sec)

[841] Ibid (6 min and 30 sec)

and know where they are at all times and what they are doing.[842] This has been called a regularization program.[843] This program would allow the Dominican government to round up Haitian citizens and have them deported[844], which usually results in racial violence.[845] In 1929, the Dominican Republic's Constitution drafted in legislation stating that if you were born there, you were a citizen.[846] In 2013 they made another change stating that this would be further applied retroactively to anyone, including anyone born of undocumented parents to have their citizenship revoked. [847] This ruling started all sorts of rioting.[848] Now lots of Haitians will have to put their names on a foreign registry.[849] According to a Haitian citizen of the DR, they get stopped on the streets for no reason by the authorities, and when he was stopped, he was detained.[850] Another a Haitian citizen stated he left and came back, and the authorities destroyed his house and took his livestock.[851] Some even fear for their lives. [852]

---

[842] Aida Alami. The New York Review of Books. Between Hate, Hope, and Help: Haitians in the Dominican Republic. retrieved June 16, 2019 https://www.nybooks.com/daily/2018/08/13/between-hope-hate-help-haitians-in-the-dominican-republic/

[843] Ibid

[844] Ibid

[845] Ibid.

[846] Ibid.

[847] Ibid.

[848] Ibid.

[849] VOX Borders Divided island: How Haiti and the DR became two worlds https://www.youtube.com/watch?v=4WvKeYuwifc (9 min and 32 sec)

[850] Ibid (10 min and 25 sec)

[851] Ibid (10 min and 40 sec)

[852] Ibid (9 min 20 sec)

Legal Immigrants and Other Non-White Groups

At the border crossing, the guards were checking the passports of the three darkest people on a bus,[853] the passengers are often stopped at the border, and especially those who appear to be Haitian are asked for their papers.[854] This is a very racist practice, but it happens in the DR to Haitians. Haitians, when this move was made, were treated in a very racist way by DR authorities and some of its citizens, and it is not out of the question that they may still be being treated the same way today.

In this situation, the DR had an economic infrastructure with wealth, and even though they are a poor country, they are doing much better than Haiti. They were able to enforce policies such as this one on Haitians. The question you have to ask yourself is, could Hispanics in America, once they got enough local control of the economy and politics and culture, change things so that they are really not in favor of blacks in America, and as a result blacks would receive some unfavorable treatment?

What has happened to Haitians citizens in the DR could happen with complaints from a minority of the population and enough influential and powerful people in the right places to make it happen even in America. A lot of Dominicans may be very opposed to it, which is what happened with the issue of slavery for years in America, even though lots of whites grew to eventually not approve of it. You never know how the social, political, economic, and cultural climate will change in the next 25, 50, or maybe even 100-plus years. If it does, some things that are unthinkable now may happen 50 years from now, and we could have this type of racism on black people in America. I am not saying anything as bad as what is happening in the DR with Haitian citizenship will ever happen

---

[853] Ibid

[854] Ibid (11 min and 5 sec)

to blacks in America, but if immigrant groups get local ownership and control of enough of America's wealth and resources—because they practice group economics, which result in the establishment of a crude economic infrastructure—could they enact policies and customs locally that are not in the favor of African Americans or could they do it nationally on some levels as a group? Especially if they Dr. Claude Andersons 5-Tier Ladder of maintain a community.

The reason why I went into so much detail about the situation in Haiti at its border with the Dominican Republic is because Mexican Americans, at least some of them, have a more affectionate connection with the southwestern part of America since it was once a part of Mexico at one time. It even has a lot of the Spanish names and Mexican architectural influences (like the Alamo in San Antonio, Texas) as reminders that at one time, it belonged to Mexico. All of this may give at least some Mexican Americans a different sense of belonging to this part of America since they have cultural and historical ties to it from both the distant and the not-so-distant past in a way that some other ethnic backgrounds don't, and to maybe a few of them, anyone else in this part of the country is just an outsider. Again, only a very small minority of Mexican Americans at best feel this way. If enough Mexican Americans have sentiments like this, could something happen that is not really in favor of blacks in America at least in the southwestern part of the United States or could something happen to them somewhere else in America?

An example of how neighborhoods can change when demographics change is since integration, neighborhoods that black people were scared to go to in the 1950s and before for fear negative repercussions and even hostility in some cases from the local whites or police enforcement with laws to make them leave, by the year 1990 or maybe 2000, some of those same neighborhoods became all black, which was unthinkable by the whites who were there previously in the 1940s or '50s, but it happened.

A Latino gang in Los Angeles for about 15 years forcibly attempted to remove a black community from the San Gabriel Valley with violent attacks.[855] The Los Angeles police have worked with members of the black community in an attempt to curb attacks.[856] Ethnic incidences like this, according to Maxx News Independent America, happen in other cities in America.[857] Without a community, blacks will be more subject and vulnerable to these attacks, and integration, a socialist policy backed by the left, is making matters worse for blacks.

George Zimmerman's mother of the Trayvon Martin case was a Latina with Afro Peruvian ancestry.[858] From her image in the article by the Associated Press, she appeared to be more of European or Mestizo descent than African, but the point to make here is Zimmerman could have gone to trial as a Hispanic since his mother is a Latina, and if he had, there would have been increased animosities between blacks and Hispanics as a result of the ruling.

In Lima, Peru, one of its leading TV stations allowed a ridiculous and offensive character of black people to air in TV in blackface

---

[855] Armstrong Williams. Max News Independent America. Hispanic Racism Goes Unreported. 18 Nov 2014. retrieved September 11, 2019 http://www.newsmax.com/ArmstrongWilliams/Hispanic-Racism-Blacks-immigrants/2014/11/18/id/608028

[856] Ibid

[857] Ibid

[858] David Iaconangelo. Gladys Zimmerman, Mother of George Zimmerman, Says Her Family Is 'Proudly Afro-Peruvian,' But Do His Black Roots Matter in Trayvon Martin Case? Jul 15 2013. Latin Times Magazine. retrieved July 8, 2019 https://www.latintimes.com/gladys-zimmerman-mother-george-zimmerman-says-her-family-proudly-afro-peruvian-do-his-black-roots

for a while called "Negro Mama."[859] The portrayal was of a man in blackface with ugly nostrils and huge lips and ridiculously unrealistically sized Afro wig on his head.[860] The TV station was later fined.[861] Afro Peruvians still continue to be verbally abused on the street and to be discriminated against in stores and everywhere else in Peruvian life.[862] Since Peru is a Hispanic country, you have to ask yourself if Hispanics got more influence in America, could we have Latin American–style racism like that in America, or is this just an isolated case?

In a 2006 study that 10 academic researchers conducted of various racial groups' attitudes in Durham, North Carolina,[863] six times more Latino immigrants per capita said that few or no blacks were more hardworking than whites,[864] and nearly the same percent said that few or no blacks could be trusted.[865] The study concluded the racial biases came from biases already formed by them in some of their countries of origin,[866] and some were formed from media images of blacks viewed by Latinos after arriving in America.[867]

At a meeting of city residents with Chicago city councilmembers concerning the free handouts that illegal migrants are getting

---

[859] Simeon Tegel. GlobalPost. December 21, 2013. UTC Peru's blackface 'Negro Mama' Continues to Offend. retrieved January 29, 2020 https://www.pri.org/stories/2013-12-21/peru-s-blackface-negro-mama-continues-offend

[860] Ibid.

[861] Ibid.

[862] Ibid.

[863] Christina Asquith. Diverse Scholars Ask Why Latinos View Blacks Poorly. July 12, 2006. retrieved September 27, 2020 https://diverseeducation.com/article/6086/

[864] Ibid.

[865] Ibid.

[866] Ibid.

[867] Ibid.

when lots of Chicago residents are hungry and homeless an illegal migrant who is Hispanic with a "Power to the People" tee-shirt on tells a black woman "No money for you. You Lazy!!" and she tell him "Go Home!!"[868] If she is a tax paying citizen of Chicago, she has the right to be angry and he has no right to stereotype her as a lazy black woman especially if he is in the country illegally. This is an example of bias that the black community may have to deal with currently and in the future with many other groups who have communities where they practice group economics. This guy is an example of someone who is none white who could influence policy negatively for blacks in a way that it favors Hispanics if he was ever in a position to do it and he thought it should be done. This man was able to enter the country because of progressive policies and causes of and for open borders and illegal migration.

White Latinos often discriminate against Afro Latinos and Mulatto Latinos.[869] If they do this within their own ethnic background, is it not possible that they could do it against non-Hispanic African Americans once they get enough influence in certain places?

Now black people are not in position economically or politically to make changes like that since we decided to completely integrate with whites, like the left and Progressives convinced us to do, and until we are, we will just be subject to any changes any other group wants to make in the future.

The next group to discuss is Asian Americans and the impact that they could have on blacks. During the Watts Riots of 1992, a

---

[868] Phillip Scott Podcast Migrant In Chicago Has The Audacity To Tell A Black American "No Money For You" "You're Lazy" retrieved April 9, 2024 https://www.youtube.com/watch?v=zpX7E0n3Vn8

[869] Tanya K. Hernandez. Latino Inter-Ethnic Employment Discrimination and the Diversity Defense. Fordham Law School. 2007 FLASH: p. 7. retrieved September 27, 2020 https://ir.lawnet.fordham.edu/cgi/viewcontent.cgi?article=1012&context=faculty_scholarship

Korean shopkeeper shot and killed a 15-year-old African American girl who was accused of trying to steal orange juice.[870] It was later concluded that she was simply holding and fondling the money that she was going to use to pay for it.[871] The Korean shopkeeper later only received $500 fine and probation.[872] This was a light sentence for committing a murder, but this type of justice that was rendered in favor of the Korean shopkeeper is often what happens when you have ownership and control of the local economy with businesses. The Korean community had 2,000 businesses to be destroyed during the LA Riots of 1992.[873] With this many businesses, this gives the Koreans a tremendous amount of control or influence over the local economy, the justice system, the courts, the media, and the educational system. Expect more of this to happen including police shootings to a group of people that doesn't practice group economics, doesn't own and control much, and has no code of conduct that a community should have. This incident became a factor in why the riots happened.

It didn't help any that the Rodney King verdict was ruled unfairly, either.[874]

As a result of the riots, 36 black youth were arrested[875] after a Korean shopkeeper committed this injustice on a member of the black community, but this is often the type of justice that is

---

[870] Anjuli Sastry, Karen Grigsby Bates. Special Series The Los Angeles Riots, 25 Years on When LA Erupted in Anger: A Look Back at the Rodney King Riots. April 26, 2017. retrieved May 4, 2020, NPR Network https://www.npr.org/2017/04/26/524744989/when-la-erupted-in-anger-a-look-back-at-the-rodney-king-riots

[871] Ibid

[872] Ibid

[873] Ibid.

[874] Ibid.

[875] Ibid.

Legal Immigrants and Other Non-White Groups

administered to you when you have ownership and control over little or nothing: the people who own and control can get away with murder like the Korean shopkeeper did, and the ones who don't will be subject to them. This Korean shopkeeper should have been given a long prison sentence for committing this murder, but instead she got a slap on the wrist.

The reason for this incident could have been because of racial in justices practiced on the black community from the local justice system and law enforcement and jails of Los Angeles or the state of California prison system or maybe there were some prior racial tensions between the black and Korean communities before or maybe it was a combination of the two or there may have been some other factors involved and this incident was the last straw, I really could not tell you. Personally, I think it was unnecessary or even wrong for black youth to just take all of their anger out like that on all of the Korean shop keepers, but this is what happens sometimes when a group of people fell that they have had injustices thrown at them continuously throughout history and they feel hopeless like there is nothing they can do to stop them. Unfortunately, the Korean community was the object of much of this anger and even though I sympathize for those shopkeepers it just is what it is.

Chinese and Koreans already own lots of businesses in the black communities in America. The question you have to ask yourself is: Could another incident like this between an African American and an Asian or some other ethnic group result in something like this in the black community in America again? If blacks had not attempted to completely integrate with whites (and instead follow Booker T. Washington's and not W.E.B. Du Bois advice), which was a leftist cause, they would be in a better position to deal with a situation like this should it happen. If Asians have enough control locally, they could change policies so that they are not in favor of black interests also. If this happens, then blacks will be subject to whatever those changes are, and they may have some bad consequences for the black community.

Arabs are the last group to discuss in this article. Arabs had a slave trade out of Africa, which resulted in the trafficking of millions of black Africans into the Middle East and North Africa for roughly 1,200 years.[876] They now own and operate lots of businesses like gas stations and supermarkets in the black community, of course under different circumstances and for different reasons with the world being a much different place than it was during the vast majority of time this brutal slave trade existed. Consider the following from a black Instagram account owner in Detroit. She said she heard the term "*abeed*" all her life.[877] She was called that countless times until a Somali friend who spoke Arabic told her, "No, they are calling us slaves."[878] She said she had heard it from young kids.[879] It is a derogatory term used by Arabs to refer to black people who are of sub-Saharan African descent.[880] It is not only used to poke fun at them; it is used to refer to them on a professional and regular basis as a group.[881]

She stated in the interview, "This very offensive word is deeply penetrated into everyday Arabic conversations. You can hear it at the gas station, on your way to work, during family gatherings, and even on social media posts." According to her, "You'll get a long list

---

[876] Lumen, History of World Civilization II African Slave Trade. TransSaharan Slave Trade. retrieved September 12, 2020 https://courses.lumenlearning.com/atd-tcc-worldciv2/chapter/transsaharan-slave-trade/

[877] Lina Abdul-Samad. # Muslim Girl Arabs, the N-Word and the A-Word Are the Same. retrieved July 26, 2019 http://muslimgirl.com/38120/arabs-n-word-word/

[878] Ibid

[879] Ibid

[880] Ibid

[881] Ibid

of tweets on Twitter now "X" directly using this term or defending its use. Some of them raising awareness of the awful racism in this four-letter phrase." [882] She also stated in the interview, "The Arab world suffered from colorism before the vampire of colonialism slurped the Arab veins."[883] If someone uses a derogatory term to refer to you on a customary basis, it will influence how they will deal with you on a regular basis in society. This means probably, not all, but some of their dealings with blacks will probably be derogatory. Using this word, if used in the right text, is like calling a black person the N-word (at least that's the way it seems from the testimony of the Somali Instagram account holder, and why would she lie).

From a 1981 study on race relations, Arabs owned nearly one-third of all of the grocery stores in Chicago's mostly black neighborhoods. These neighborhoods are probably mostly food deserts with limited access to affordable nutritious food. In these neighborhoods, it is frustrating to blacks with not enough education or access to money to start entrepreneurial enterprises such as a grocery store, while Arab and Asian entrepreneurs have success in a black neighborhood but blacks can't. These pockets in the black community have worse health outcomes,[884] and the black community is disproportionately represented in them.[885] If this was the case in 1981 and the Arab population has gone up since then, how much worse do you think the situation is now, or do you think it is a lot better than it was then? This leaves the black community, at least in these parts

---

[882] Ibid.

[883] Ibid.

[884] Brielle Tobin and Barbara Lynn Weaver. March 4, 2017. Health and Socioeconomic Disparities of Food Deserts. Duke Green Classroom. retrieved September 24, 2020 https://sites.duke.edu/lit290s-1_02_s2017/2017/03/04/health-and-socioeconomic-disparities-of-food-deserts/

[885] Food Empowerment Project Food Deserts. retrieved September 24, 2020 https://foodispower.org/access-health/food-deserts/

of Chicago, dependent on someone who in the future may not have your best interests for food at heart, which is a basic necessity for life.

Other immigrant groups learn the sentiments and racial undertones about various races of people through the popular culture, beliefs, and customs of the dominant cultural and social influences. In the US, African Americans, despite improvements over years, still bear negative undertones.[886] The author of another article who spent much of his youth in the Arab world says she did not recall having a race consciousness until he came to the United States at the age of 13.[887] His knowledge of Arab anti-black racism comes predominantly from Arab Americans.[888] From this it seems that the intensity of anti-black sentiment in various parts of the Arab world from Arabs could also vary greatly from nonexistent or barely noticeable on one extreme to blatantly overt on the other extreme depending on the circumstances or maybe even the individual.

Nigeria's Islamic terror group Boko Haram, which has carried out some terrible atrocities in the name of the expansion of an Islamic caliphate and the conversion of the world to Islam, is not really being acknowledged by the rest of the Arab world. A US intelligence official suggests one obstacle is racism. He claims the Arab world is incredibly racist and that they don't see black Africans as equivalent to them.[889] ISIS at the time showed approval somewhat of Boko Haram's work, but they didn't really appear to be forming

---

[886] Susan Abulhawa. Egypt Confronting anti-black racism in the Arab world. 7 Jul 2013. retrieved September 2, 2019 https://www.aljazeera.com/indepth/opinion/2013/06/201362472519107286.html

[887] Ibid

[888] Ibid

[889] Will Racism Keep ISIS from Teaming Up with Boko Haram? NBC News. Feb. 18, 2015. retrieved July 19, 2019 retrieved September 22, 2019 https://www.nbcnews.com/storyline/missing-nigeria-schoolgirls/will-racism-keep-isis-teaming-boko-haram-n307786

an allegiance with them. It doesn't appear as if the two caliphates will be becoming one anytime soon, even after Boko Haram was shown in videos parading around the ISIS flag in approval of them.[890]

A racist TV series presented on an Egyptian TV comedy series over Ramadan has black Afro Egyptians portrayed by MENA (Middle Eastern and North African) Egyptians[891] in blackface with racist, derogatory images.[892] Arab cinema has derogatory images of black women portrayed as prostitutes and as being ugly and unfeminine and portrays black people as being sluggish and lazy.[893] In one of their productions, the N-word was used to refer to black people of African descent.[894] Once Arabs get more influence in America, you have to ask yourself: Could we have Arab-style racism in America against blacks, or are these just isolated cases? If Boko Haram is a Nigerian terrorist group, that is a guarantee that they are black, and just look at all of the black Africans they have murdered who did not want to accept Islam. Lots of black Africans have been murdered in the name of Islam in other sub-Saharan African nations by other black people.[895]

Subjects like this, about Arabs and Islam, some Liberals and the left turn a blind eye to because they want to accept Muslim Arabs

---

[890] Ibid.

[891] Hansi Lo Wang NPR National The U.S. census sees Middle Eastern and North African people as white. Many don't February 17, 2022 5:00 AM ET retrieved April 19, 2023 https://www.npr.org/2022/02/17/1079181478/us-census-middle-eastern-white-north-african-mena

[892] Hana Al-Khamri. 1 Jul 2018. opinion Arts and Culture. The outrageous racism that 'graced' Arab TV screens in Ramadan. https://www.aljazeera.com/opinions/2018/7/1/the-outrageous-racism-that-graced-arab-tv-screens-in-ramadan retrieved January 28, 2020

[893] Ibid.

[894] Ibid.

[895] Islamic Extremism in Sub-Saharan Africa. RIAC Reader. retrieved June 28, 2020 https://russiancouncil.ru/en/extremism-africa

under the guise of multiculturalism and diversity DEI, which is a leftist cause, because they are different. If you discuss them, it means you are racist and/or Islamophobic, but they are a real concern for blacks.

Again, I am not saying that Arabs will ever attempt to do anything as horrible as the slave trade of Africans out of Africa in the trans-Sahel trans-Saharan slave trade that lasted for 1,200 years in America to blacks or to anyone for that matter or that they will even be as horrifically racist as they have been under some circumstances in the Arab world in America as what blacks have experienced from Arabs in the Arab world, but........ people are people.

Again, you never know how the social, political, economic, and cultural climate will change in the next 25, 50, or maybe even 100-plus years, and things could take a turn for the worse with blacks-Arab relations.

What is ironic is years ago at the beginning of integration whites protested to keep blacks from moving into their neighborhoods that were all white culturally, socially and every other way now blacks in Chicago are doing the same thing about illegal immigrants that the left leaning progressive policies of progressives are pushing and with time some of their old traditional neighborhoods may not be black anymore. The question to ask here is where will they go? Will they have to depend on the government again for relocation.

If blacks had not completely integrated with whites like Progressive Liberals and the left convinced them to, they would have their own communities, with their own for-profit and nonprofit institutions, and they would not have to worry as much about this. Because the more dependent a people are on some other entity, the more subject they will be to injustices imposed on them by that entity should they decide to do so.

Legal Immigrants and Other Non-White Groups

Another non-white group that black people were subject to as slaves were Native Americans.[896] In Oklahoma Territory from the 1840s until the Civil War, the five civilized tribes of Native Americans owned black slaves.[897] Again most Native Americans in all five tribes never owned any black slaves and Native Americans from all other north American tribes to my knowledge owned none. Not only did they own slaves, but they went on hunt-and-search missions to find and kidnap black slaves and sell them back to their white slave masters.[898] For this, they received $20 a head; back then, that was a lot of money.[899] Some of those same Native Americans fought for the Confederacy during the Civil War because they wanted to keep their slaves.[900] After whites took their land from them for so many years and called them savages, they still fought with the racist white Confederates who wanted to keep their slaves. Both sides had things about each other that they hated, but both sides cooperated with one another to keep their black slaves. If it happened before by a non-white group, then could it happen again under the right circumstances by another nonwhite group or could blacks receive pressure from more than one non-black group and whites for that matter at a time for that matter? Since the left

---

[896] Barbara Krauthamer. Black Slaves, Indian Masters: Slavery, Emancipation, and Citizenship in the Native American South, 2013. retrieved September 22, 2019 https://notevenpast.org/black-slaves-indian-masters-slavery-emancipation-and-citizenship-in-the-native-american-south-by-barbara-krauthamer-2013

[897] Ibid.

[898] Ibid.

[899] Ibid.

[900] Tom Porter. The Last Confederate Troops to Surrender in the Civil War were Native Americans Here's How they Ended Up Fighting for the South. Business Insider. June 23, 2019. retrieved August 5, 2019 https://www.businessinsider.com/how-native-americans-ended-up-fighting-for-the-confederacy-2019-6

convinced black people to completely integrate with whites, blacks have lost much of the community infrastructure needed to keep from being vulnerable again.

Also as American society continues to change, different demographics of blacks are becoming part of America; an example is black Africans from all of the various sub-Saharan African countries, the Caribbean, and Latin America who are coming to America as immigrants and without so much baggage from the historic past that black Americans have had to deal with; thus, they do not see themselves as victims in an unjust system of systemic racism and prejudice. If enough of them become a part of America in large-enough numbers, they may redefine what it means to be black in America, and if traditional black Americans don't like the way they redefine it, there will be fights between more traditional black Americans and black Africans. Some of those confrontations could become nasty as well, maybe even resulting in some divisions.

The Black-White landscape of race relations could change, too, for the worse, and if it does, the black community has been too destabilized to deal with it, and whites will still be a force to be dealt with by blacks for a while to come—even after whites are not the majority of the population in America. White Americans are not the only whites in the world; there are whites from all over the world, who could very well be immigrating to America with their own biases about race, just like many people of color will who are not black. That does not mean that some other group that was not mentioned above could not become a competitive force for blacks too.

Legal Immigrants and Other Non-White Groups

As it stands now, between the 10,000[901] or more bodegas plus Mexican food restaurants, their ethnic restaurants, Asian markets and Arab grocery stores and their ethnic restaurants, the Hispanic, Asian, and Arab communities respectively can at least provide food and bottled water for themselves. Not only that, but all of these ethnic backgrounds can also do a better job of providing more of other basic necessities with their businesses and networks that the black community cannot provide for themselves. At the same time, they can provide some employment for their communities while doing it. Whites and Jews can do it for the whole country with their economic infrastructure. The black community is the only community that is this vulnerable and dependent on outside resources, since it cannot provide things like this, and it is the left who convinced blacks to integrate with everyone else and now black wealth has been redistributed everywhere to everyone else as a result. Multiculturalism and diversity, which are other progressive agendas, are not helping matters any in this arena, either. These are just two of the causes supported and enforced by the left that have been to the detriment of the black community in America.

The left's polices and causes have resulted in a black community that is more dependent on outside entities and the government than their own institutions, and it has made the black community more vulnerable to indifference from other groups with a free-market economy and capitalism. The black community is also more susceptible to elimination from the equation altogether by racist socialists, such as Margaret Sanger's Planned Parenthood. Not only that, the left and its policies and causes have left the black community in a worse position ever to be less dependent on other outside entities. I

---

[901] Lauren Paley. What Is a Bodega? And Why Do New Yorkers Love Them? One Block NYC Explained. https://streeteasy.com/blog/what-is-a-bodega/ retrieved December 18, 2019

am certainly not saying you can't be a racist capitalist; after all, slave traders and slaveholders in the Americas wanted to maximize their profits even if it meant having Negro slaves to buy and sell as commodities on Wall Street,[902] but you can be just as racist as a socialist by favoring certain racial groups for elimination from society.

The left has been supporting and encouraging globalization. All of the ethnicities and races mentioned in this book are a part of the global community outside of America as well, so unless the left can convince these people to abandon their ethnic identities, cultures, beliefs, and religions for a new global identity that the left has for them, they will probably not be changing or become any different about blacks on a global scale from what they were when they immigrated to America.

It has been confirmed that Los Angeles, a city in one of America's most progressive states, California, is reporting an increase in hate crimes, especially against African Americans,[903] who are only 9% of the population[904] but report 46% of all of the hate crimes.[905] This has also been confirmed by the Equal Justice Initiative.[906] One of its articles also confirmed that 56% of hate crimes were targeted by anti-blackness against blacks.[907] According to the article 73% of the offenders were

---

[902] Zoe Thomas. BBC Business reporter, New York. 29 August 2019. The hidden links between slavery and Wall Street. retrieved August 19, 2021 https://www.bbc.com/news/business-49476247

[903] Taylor Torregano Los Angeles Published 6:00 PM PT Dec. 14, 2022 Spectrum News 1 Los Angeles sees record breaking increase in hate crimes Public Safety retrieved December 23, 2022 https://spectrumnews1.com/ca/la-west/public-safety/2022/12/15/los-angeles-sees-record-breaking-increase-in-hate-crimes

[904] Ibid

[905] Ibid

[906] Equal Justise Initiative FBI Reports Hate Crimes at Highest Level in 12 Years 09.09.21 retreived December 23, 2022 https://eji.org/news/fbi-reports-hate-crimes-at-highest-level-in-12-years/

[907] Ibid

whites. This poses another question: Who targeted the other 27% of these hate crimes toward Blacks, non-whites? Wouldn't it be interesting just to know who some of them are? I wonder if black lives matter will organize protests and riots to stop this. If they don't, it just shows that black lives don't really matter in this new, more progressive America.

In a Canadian suburb of Vancouver British Columbia signs were posted for a "Whites Only" playground for children of European decent.[908] It was allegedly so children could play with people like them and to escape forced diversity programs implemented in Canada[909] and so they could be in places where they were not always the minority of the population.[910] This is like something out of pre-civil rights era America. A more progressive community college Evergreen College in Washington State had a "No Whites on Campus" day[911], and a white college professor said he no longer felt safe on campus[912] so with that said with current trends since whites will become less than half of Americas population with time is it not out of the realm of possibility that something similar to what has happened in Canada could happen in America. If it does later in the future and everybody complies and responds with segregated

---

[908] Mary Walrath-Holdridge Signs allegedly advertising 'whites-only' playgroup condemned as 'vile' by Canadian mayo published 10:28 Sept 28, 2018 USA Today retrieved April 12, 2024 https://www.usatoday.com/story/news/world/2023/09/27/signs-advertising-whites-only-playgroup-canada-condemned/70983397007/

[909] Ibid

[910] Ibid

[911] Jake Salo College melts down over plan for white people-free day on campus Published May 31, 2017
Updated June 6, 2017, 8:44 p.m. ET New York Post retrieved April 12, 2024 https://nypost.com/2017/05/31/college-melts-down-over-plan-for-white-people-free-day-on-campus/

[912] Ibid

communities or at least segregated institutions of their own, blacks would be finished because we are too dependent on resources outside of the black community for existence because we lost our since of community that you need to provide some of those resources independently during integration. If this happened Hispanics and Asians and most other groups would fare in some cases a lot better than blacks. This could really become bad for blacks just depending on how far they want to take it. This time it will not be the wants of traditional white Americans causing the segregation like they did before the Civil Rights Era because of safety fears and forced integration it will be because of the progressive polices and causes of the progressive left even if more right leaning conservative whites request it because they are just tired of the wokeness and being called racist and oppressors. If conservatives had had more influence over the past 50 years or so it would not have come to this and even if it had blacks would have been better prepared to provide for their community as a whole.

14.

Black Organizations and Black Leadership

The National Association for the Advancement of Colored Peoples (NAACP) is still popular to a lot of its black members and sympathizers, but it was founded by liberal whites who were the more progressive ones for their time, some of whom were socialists.[913, 914, 915] Whites were present at the beginning and were a part of the NAACP's inception. When it was founded in 1909, only seven of its sixty members were black.[916] That was not enough black influence to make a difference, in many cases, in the direction that blacks really wanted or needed. This would almost ensure that the organization did not morph into something that would solve real problems for black people that would get then completely out of the lot that they were in at the time and even today with an active

---

[913] Nation's Premier Civil Rights Organization. retrieved July 30, 2019 https://www.naacp.org/nations-premier-civil-rights-organization

[914] Naomi Schaefer Riley. How Liberals Are Killing the NAACP. June 7, 2017. retrieved May 22, 2019 https://nypost.com/2017/06/07/how-liberals-are-killing-the-naacp

[915] Melvin Johnson. Thinking Out Loud NAACP's Founders Were White Socialists. July 7, 2012. retrieved June 17, 2019 http://blogs.christianpost.com/thinkingoutloud/naacps-founders-were-white-socialists-10757

[916] Ibid.

NAACP black people as a group are still struggling more than they really should be and that was by design. It was set up that way so the white founders, at least from its inception and for a while after, could really steer the organization in the direction they wanted it to go. It was at its inception led by white Progressives,[917] and back then the progressive counterculture was good for blacks, but now the progressive counterculture, and for the past 50 years, has turned out to be devastating to black America, very destructive. It is interesting to note that eugenicist and racist Margaret Sanger for a period in her life was a member of the Socialist Party as well.[918] She and her husband William were both Marxists and atheists.[919]

W.E.B. Du Bois, who was a prominent and influential black leader for years before the civil rights era and was one of the founders of the NAACP at its inception in 1909. He was on its board of directors from 1910 until 1934,[920] and he belonged to the Socialist Party from 1910 until 1912.[921] He was an activist and scholar and strived to create global citizenship. In 1961, he joined the Communist Party of America.[922]

---

[917] History.com Editors NAACP UPDATED:MAR 13, 2019. ORIGINAL:OCT 29, 2009 https://www.history.com/topics/civil-rights-movement/naacp#:~:text=The%20NAACP's%20founding%20members%20included,Grimke%20and%20Mary%20Church%20Terrell.

[918] PERSON. Margaret Sanger Influence Watch. retrieved August 13, 2020 https://www.influencewatch.org/person/margaret-sanger/

[919] Ibid.

[920] NAACP History: W.E.B. Du Bois. retrieved Sept 8, 2019 https://www.naacp.org/naacp-history-w-e-b-dubois/.

[921] Ibid.

[922] Communist Party US. People and Planet Before Profits African American Communist: W.E.B. Du Bois (1868–1963) February 28, 2009. retrieved October 15, 2019 https://www.cpusa.org/party_info/african-american-communist-w-e-b-du-bois-1868–1963/.

It was founded in 1909 in New York City, so it is fair to say that the Liberals and probably the left were working with some people in the black community back then and probably not long after slavery, but even then, they did not have the black community's best interest at heart.[923] This is another clever way the left could use the black community as a tool or a strategy to impose government control over everyone. None of these organizations have pulled the black community out of the mess that it is in today; they have merely placed band-aids over problems to make it seem as if they are solving them, and some of these problems were created indirectly as result of some of their policies and/or causes. It seems like since these organizations have been around, things have gotten progressively worse for the black community. None of these organizations fought for an economic infrastructure for the black community like Booker T Washington did which is critical in a free market with capitalism because that would bring justice on a scale so big that it would put them out of existence. It has plenty of black sympathizers and members. Radical progressives according to a New York official have some suggestions for a new direction for the NAACP.[924] Unfortunately, they'll send the organization further down its current path toward irrelevance. This means that the left and progressives know the NAACP has served its purpose, and it wasn't to provide true equality for black people with whites either.[925]

---

[923] Eugene Cook The Ugly Truth About the NAACP 1-1-1900 Pamphlets and Broadsides University of Mississippi eGrove retrieved January 7, 2024 https://egrove.olemiss.edu/cgi/viewcontent.cgi?article=1078&context=citizens_pamph

[924] Naomi Schaefer Riley. How liberals are killing the NAACP. Opinion New York Post. June 7, 2017. retrieved September 25, 2019 https://nypost.com/2017/06/07/how-liberals-are-killing-the-naacp/

[925] Eugene Cook The Ugly Truth About the NAACP 1-1-1900 Pamphlets and Broadsides University of Mississippi eGrove retrieved January 7, 2024 https://egrove.olemiss.edu/cgi/viewcontent.cgi?article=1078&context=citizens_pamph

Any other suggestions by Progressives are probably not going to be any better for black people, as well.

The NAACP was a useful organization for the black community before the civil rights movement and the Civil Rights Act of 1964. After the Civil Rights Act of 1968 it could continue its mission to make sure the Acts were enforced. In a short period of time afterward, when everyone got the message that they would have legal action taken on them for violating these acts and stopped attempting to nearly as much, the NAACP had lost most of its practical relevance, and it didn't really have a solid cause to stand for and needed another cause to stand for to stay in existence. To stay relevant, it has become an organization that fights for progressive causes, and in the end, it doesn't always help blacks. In its inception, civil rights were definitely an issue that needed to be addressed for blacks, but for a community to exist and thrive, another very important factor is a strong business community with economic control and influence over wealth and resources. This was what Booker T. Washington believed. Economic influence still is the best way to challenge many of the black community's problems and his National Business League was a good solution. I think economic influence is still the solution. The NAACP's mission was civil rights, not developing and fostering an economic infrastructure, so the black community suffered from a lack thereof, and the NAACP could do little to stop it. This cause should take priority for black leadership, and it needs to take priority over civil rights. The NAACP fostered and supported both polices and causes of integration that were both pros and cons to that movement, and I think the causes just recently have had some terrible setbacks for the black community over the past 40 or 50 years, give or take a few.

Most politicians who have served the black community have traditionally been Democrats. From the civil rights era up until 2000, more than three-fourths of black party affiliation has been Democratic.[926] Over that same period, between nearly nine-tenths of the black vote for president was for a Democratic candidate.[927] Over the last 50 years to the present, black Americans have consistently voted overwhelmingly for the Democratic presidential candidate;[928] that goes for senator representation, state gubernatorial races, city mayors, and many other political offices as a general rule. Again, not to keep beating a dead horse, but that is who progressives and the left more commonly support.

The National Review did an article on the Congressional Black Caucus, and it discussed how many black leaders would rather break the law for their personal interests than take care of their constituents at the expense of those that they are responsible for.[929] That does not mean some others who are not black don't do the same thing, but the fact that blacks just do it too much was the point behind of the article. It went farther to discuss how *white privilege* is a constant topic of discussion and how unfair it is to black progress.[930] Instead, the conversation needs to be about how black politicians sell the very people out they are supposed to be helping.[931] Some of the most corrupt members of the Black Caucus need to be exposed, and the article went on to list about nine of them and briefly discussed their deeds.[932] All of

---

[926] Black Party Affiliation. https://blackdemographics.com/culture/black-politics/

[927] Ibid.

[928] Ibid.

[929] Michelle Malkin. Congressional Black Corruption. Politics and Policy. July 13, 2016. retrieved August 13, 2019 https://www.nationalreview.com/2016/07/congressional-black-caucus-corrupt-democrats/

[930] Ibid.

[931] Ibid.

[932] Ibid.

these caucus members were Democrats. Not only does this happen at the congressional level, but this also goes on sometimes at a local level with some city governments.[933]

A YouTuber out of Atlanta that has been living there for nearly 30 years and was involved with local politics in the black community there, which I will speak more about later on, said politicians had been arrested and put in prison for corruption, and it sounds as if a great deal of the Atlanta politicians are black, who are voted in to office year after year by the same people without holding them accountable for any of their actions. He admitted how bad the public school system was in Atlanta and how it was producing a school-to-prison pipeline. He discussed all of the senseless violence and killing that goes on in Atlanta. But then I saw a YouTube presentation in the series *Conservative Convergence* on "The Unbelievable Corruption Taking Place in Philadelphia" that confirmed a lot of what he was saying about Atlanta, except that some of their corrupt politicians who served especially the underserved black community were not black—but they were all Democrats.[934, 935] This is the same Democrat party that is serving the black community of Atlanta. So why wouldn't this be the case in numerous American cities around the country?[936] These are the type of people the progressive left needs to keep the black community in the state it is in,

---

[933] Ibid.

[934] Conservative Resurgence. Philadelphia the Unbelievable Corruption Taking Place in the City of Brotherly Love. retrieved August 19, 2020 https://www.youtube.com/watch?v=g_AsctEdyag

[935] Anna Orso and Mark Dent Aug. 25, 2015, 10:26 a.m. Billy Penn Top: Former Mayors John Street and Ed Rendell. Bottom: Former Sen. Vince Fumo and current Rep. William Keller Why at least 39 Philly politicians got investigated over the last 15 years retrieved May 14, 2022 https://billypenn.com/2015/08/25/why-at-least-39-philly-politicians-got-investigated-over-the-last-15-years

[936] Conservative Resurgence. Philadelphia the Unbelievable Corruption Taking Place in the City of Brotherly Love. retrieved August 19, 2020 https://www.youtube.com/watch?v=g_AsctEdyag

and since the black community is more dependent on them than any other community, it is easy for them to recruit from the blacks political base of Democrats that are active in politics in the black community to do it. With a setup like this it makes it easier for them to use the black community to accomplish more of their plans for America's destruction.

Political candidates are supposed to serve their communities. The communities of their congressional districts should pay their salaries, sponsor them, and tell them what they want and hold them accountable for doing it, but the black community can't do this as effectively as other communities because they don't have a powerful-enough business community that generates enough wealth, which would give more power to influence the political scene, so it is easy for someone else to step in and pay bribes to certain officials, pay certain officials off, and get what they want done. They can also do this by financing their election campaigns if they will honor the wishes of the campaign financer. With politicians like maybe some of the ones from the Black Caucus[937] and some of the ones described by the YouTuber and some of the board members on the DPS school system[938] if you have enough of them in the right places, you can really stick it to the districts they serve, in a negative way by paying them to do nothing in some cases or things that are harmful to the districts they serve. The progressive left knows this, so with leadership like this they take advantage of it. It is very

---

[937] Star Parker published 12:01 ET July 6, 2006 Updated 2:21 pm July 7, 2006 Another disappointment from the Black Caucus The Gainesville Sun retrieved December 29, 2022 https://www.gainesville.com/story/news/2006/07/06/another-disappointment-from-the-black-caucus/31488770007

[938] Dana Ford, CNN Updated 8:54 PM EDT, Tue March 29, 2016 Bribery charges against 13 Detroit principals a 'punch in the gut' retrieved December 29, 2022 https://www.cnn.com/2016/03/29/us/detroit-public-schools-bribery/index.html

possible that the left has been doing this in the black community. This is because group economics is not practiced in the black community like it is among whites, Jews, and Asians and even Hispanics to an extent. Black Wall Street was one of the best examples of it that the black community has ever had, but that has not been possible for years because of integration on progressive terms. Integration was a socialist agenda, and it started with the public schools; then it went to society as a whole, and Dr. King even fought for that. Socialists are a part of the leftist movement who only advance their own interests. They have never had the best interests of the black community at heart. To fully integrate black people into every area of society, the question to ask is: Would it be necessary to redistribute more wealth and expand more public institutions than the ones necessary just to integrate the public schools? Had it been up to Conservatives, integration would never had taken off like it has over the past 50 or 60 years, and black people would have been in a much better position to develop a strong, powerful, and influential business community that officials or maybe some others could not come into and just bribe people and get what they want if the business establishments had an allegiance to the needs of the people.

An example of how this happens with black leadership on a local level is in a movie on YouTube about Detroit's failing public school system titled *A National Disgrace*, hosted by Dan Rather. It addresses issues such as contract steering, excessive administrative staff being paid too much, theft, and more.[939] It discussed how PTA meetings lasted for hours sometimes up until two in the morning,[940] and how chaotic they were with lots of complaints and grievances with no plan

---

[939] Dan Rather Reports—A National Disgrace. Jan 14, 2012. retrieved January 8 2019 https://www.youtube.com/watch?v=4xypiZ-hqdY (56 min and 58 sec)

[940] Ibid (18 min and 20 sec)

Black Organizations and Black Leadership

or no vision on how to accomplish anything.[941] There was nepotism in hiring, and $48 million that was not budgeted for anything just disappeared.[942] They were paid more per year to rent a fancy building downtown in Detroit than it was worth to buy it.[943] One official called it "Spending like drunken sailors" as one of his friends would call it.[944] This is why the federal government is in so much dept because of spending like this without a real purpose for every dollar or for unnecessary purposes for the spending. When a new competent, experienced, qualified superintendent recommended changes that would mean downsizing staff and closing schools, she discovered that for one school that had not been attended in years, the district was still paying utilities and so much more.[945] The staff that she presided over voted her out of office.[946] She had a plan and a vision for the DPS.[947] She stated that the board had 11 committees that would have closed session meetings where they discussed items for the agenda, and then they each had open sessions for the public[948] meeting.

It wouldn't surprise me if progressive left-leaning Democrats didn't have some or a lot of influence in deciding what is pushed for the direction of the school board agenda. It wouldn't surprise me if those 11 committees were taking orders from progressives to vote this superintendent out of office or maybe even the emergency financial manager which I will discuss later on in the article or maybe the

---

[941] Ibid (37 min and 15 sec)

[942] Ibid (33 min and 33 sec)

[943] Ibid (32 min and 21 sec)

[944] Ibid (31 min and 20 sec)

[945] Ibid (26 min and 5 sec)

[946] Ibid. (30 min and 18 sec)

[947] Ibid. (27 min and 15 sec)

[948] Ibid (36 min and 40 sec)

selection process for them to be in these committees to begin with may have even had ties to progressives. I am not saying for sure that is the case for the two but it is not out of the question. In the YouTube presentation "A National Disgrace about Detroit's Public School System," a student on a high school campus was interviewed, and she said that one of the administrators stated, "We get paid whether you all learn or not."[949] Clearly this administrator didn't have the best interest of the students at heart; maybe he or she had allegiances to someone else or only cared about advancing their personal agenda, and sadly there have been other examples of this in the black community. Afterward, they brought in an emergency financial manager who was black,[950] and in less than two years, he was ousted from office, even though he had a plan and a vision for the DPS.[951] Conservative Republicans would not tolerate this type of corruption; some might get through on their watch but not on this scale.

The DPS at the time received a $1.2 billion budget,[952] and many of the kids in that school system still received a poor-quality education, so it was not about the quality of their education; it was about the redistribution of wealth. One of the officials who worked for the board said he started to call the Feds because of all of the money that disappeared magically from the budget.[953] If it were up to right-leaning Conservatives, spending would be done more conservatively and more carefully. What is happening under Democratic supervision,

---

[949] Ibid

[950] Ibid (1 Hour 39 min and 18 secs)

[951] Ibid

[952] Ibid(57 min and 54 sec)

[953] Ibid.(33 min and 45 sec)

since school boards are funded by city government,[954] would not be as likely to happen under the watch of Conservative Republicans to this extent.

The Urban League has done some good things for the black community, but if someone else is coming into your community and building or sponsoring institutions for you to work in, even if they are providing the job training like the Urban League often does, that does not help to build your community; it leaves you dependent on outside entities. Until you can produce your own employment, and even the institutions that provide it, you will still be a largely dependent group, which is what the left wants. If the Urban League is providing job training, and even if they are supported by Progressives, it is okay if you can support them just for the job training. After that, you can take the jobs back to your community and build it yourself with those skills.

Former House Oversight Chairman and Black Caucus Member Elijah Cummings made a comment in a rather adamant way on the treatment of children at the Mexican border[955] and the way President Trump handled it in an August of 2019 speech.[956] It is fine for him to have his own opinion. The question to ask here is what is the state of his mostly black congressional district in Baltimore? Should the way President Trump handled the crisis on the border have been that much of an issue to him or should it have been the state of his district and how this crisis will affect his district negatively and what he can do

---

[954] Grace Chen. Updated February 14, 2020. Public School Review: An Overview of the Funding of Public Schools. retrieved September 25, 2020 https://www.publicschoolreview.com/blog/an-overview-of-the-funding-of-public-schools

[955] Caitlin Oprysko. 07/18/2019. 'Come on man, what's that about?': Cummings assails DHS chief over border facility conditions. POLITICO. retrieved March 22, 2021 https://www.politico.com/story/2019/07/18/elijah-cummings-detention-facilities-1421963

[956] Ibid.

to circumvent it? Often, black leadership like him is appointed and/ or endorsed by both Progressive Liberals and the left, who get a lot of their cause accomplished through the Democratic Party. This keeps him and others like him with high approval ratings with the more left-leaning factions of the Democratic Party because it is a part of their agenda to get rid of America at least as we know it today. It's good job security for them, so I think by being critical of then President Trump who was a target of disdain by progressives was job security for him. Conservatives generally do not endorse this type of wasteful, ineffective, political process—at least not quite to this extent.

This progressive agenda, which really supports mass and unchecked immigration, has plenty of negatives to it for the black community, and supporting this cause will not help his district; it only helps them accomplish their agenda. This brings me to the next point.

In an article on a progressive think tank, which made reference in its title to governance[957] and public policy, the Open Society Institute[958] summed the following up pretty well. The NAACP, along with some other organizations, participate on debates with groups who range from moderate to very progressive in their nature to address ideologies.[959] If the NAACP was really about the state that black América is in, why are so many of their members attending these meetings? The Urban League, an organization that the black community looked up to for so long, has ties with the Joint Center for Economic and Political Studies.[960] They are more in line with the Brookings Institute with their ideology, which tends to be more centric

---

[957] David Dyssegaard Kallick. ddkallick@tuna.net. January 2002. Progressive Think Tanks What Exists, What's Missing? https://www.opensocietyfoundations.org/publications/progressive-think-tanks-what-exists-whats-missing retrieved March 16, 2020

[958] Ibid.

[959] Ibid.

[960] Ibid.

in nature than progressive but probably still pretty liberal in their perspective.[961] Centrists tend to be more moderate in their thinking and views. Ideologies are not where they should be concentrating on getting the black community out of the shape it is in, but that is where two of the biggest black organizations for change for black America are at, and that does no good for the black community. The Rainbow Coalition stemmed from a social justice movement started in 1966 out of a Christian Leadership Conference started by Dr. Martin Luther King Jr.,[962] which became Operation Bread Basket,[963] which sought to mix theology and social justice, and to effect progressive economic, educational, and social policy in America.[964] These seem to be more leftist in nature than of the right. This shows that Progressives and the left have a lot of influence over the black community and its leadership with their policies and causes. Sometimes it seems as if they almost have a certain allegiance to Progressives and their causes, at least some of them anyway.

The NAACP is not expressing outrage against the murder of unborn babies in the black community by the progressive Planned Parenthood organization,[965] because they are now just basically a part of the progressive movement. This is one reason why I think a lot of

---

[961] Ibid.

[962] The Rainbow PUSH Coalition. BRIEF HISTORY. retrieved July 21, 2020 https://rainbow-push.org/brief-history

[963] Ibid.

[964] Ibid.

[965] Rev. Clenard H. Childress, Jr. GUEST COMMENTARY Jul 31, 2018 Why hasn't the NAACP denounced the racist comments made by Planned Parenthood's founder? Retrieved March 11, 2023 https://www.carolinapanorama.com/opinion/editorials/why-hasn-t-the-naacp-denounced-the-racist-comments-made-by-planned-parenthood-s-founder/article_af7e3d86-9084-11e8-b480-2fde36acadf3.html

our black leadership has been influenced by Progressives to a lesser extent or a greater extent in some cases.

In the 1960s, Cafe Society in NYC's Greenwich Village was the only integrated night club outside of Harlem, and it was starting to raise money for the Communist Party,[966] which was a very left-leaning entity. It was a sort of the radical sheet or hotbed of its day.[967] It was full of showbiz people and celebrities and socialites who were also communists.[968] It was also where a lot of prominent black entertainers gathered. The daughter of entertainer Lena Horn said her mother got a political education from some of the people there.[969] So why would some or most of the other black entertainers who were regulars not have been schooled the same? These entertainers, for example Paul Robeson[970] who was an outspoken pro-Soviet and was a target for anticommunist militants,[971] would stand out and impress many other black entertainers to become activists. Nina Simone was another example who was even banned from a number of acts and venues for her militant views.[972] The communists went to the high-profile blacks who were not necessarily in leadership

---

[966] PBS American Masters How it fells to Be Free S35 Ep1 Streaming until: 4/24/2022 @ 2:59 AM EDT 7 mins and 24 secs retrieved March 26, 2022 https://www.pbs.org/wnet/americanmasters/how-it-feels-to-be-free-lena-horne-abbey-lincoln-nina-simone-diahann-carroll-cicely-tyson-and-pam-grier-documentary/16905/

[967] Ibid (7 mins and 27 sec)

[968] Ibid (7 mins and 35 sec)

[969] Ibid (7 mins and 37 sec)

[970] Ibid (9 mins and 4 secs)

[971] Educator Resources National Archives The Many Faces of Paul Robeson retrieved May 11, 2022 https://www.archives.gov/education/lessons/robeson

[972] PBS American Masters How it fells to Be Free S35 Ep1 Streaming until: 4/24/2022 @ 2:59 AM EDT 7 mins and 24 secs retrieved March 26, 2022 https://www.pbs.org/wnet/americanmasters/how-it-feels-to-be-free-lena-horne-abbey-lincoln-nina-simone-diahann-carroll-cicely-tyson-and-pam-grier-documentary/16905/

positions in the community but who were high-profile figures in the black community to gain influence for their cause. If it had been up to more conservative and maybe even some classical Liberals back, then this would not have happened.

I think that the progressive movement has appointed some of the black community's leadership for a certain outcome. An example of the rationale behind this is when Margret Sanger said, "We should hire three or four colored ministers with social service backgrounds who have engaging personalities. We don't want the word to get out that we want to exterminate the Negro." This is I think a worst-case scenario, but sadly it was true, and I think there is some truth to it for today. I think socialist W.E.B. Du Bois was appointed endorsed leadership since he was a member of the Socialist Party like Sanger. I could be wrong on this one, so don't quote me on this one, but I don't think Booker T. Washington was endorsed or appointed by Progressives, Liberals, or Conservatives, and he had the best plan for the black community. Conservative white southerners in particular along with some others in other parts of the country were the same way years ago about black leadership in the South and some other parts of the country by only approving of leaders that would comply with what they thought were nonthreatening and that wouldn't challenge local cultural and social norms and laws designed to keep black freedoms restricted. The Good Negros they were called. I challenge you to ask the question are the new Good Negros in a sense the black politician's community activist (like the leaders of the BLM movement as an example) and philanthropic supporters that Progressives have groomed or appointed for some of their causes today to use the black community for some of their agendas?

I am not blaming the misguiding of the black community totally on the left or Progressives and their cause for the past 50 years or so. I would have to place partial blame on the condition of the black community on the naivety of black leadership who trusted Progressives so much without doing any research on who they represent or what their motives are and some of it on the blacks in the community who were uncooperative with some black leaders with some really good ideas, but most of all I blame the Progressives and the left because they were misleading and dishonest about the outcomes of their causes and their intent to inflict harm on the black community. Maybe black leadership did not really realize what they were up to, so here I will have to cut black leadership some slack.

In 1870 and 1874[973] the Mississippi State Legislature sent two black senators, Hiram Revels[974] and Blanche K Bruce,[975] to Congress,[976] when Mississippi had a reputation for being one of the most racist states in America at the time if not the most racist. All these senators could do for blacks back then was petition for rights, freedom, justice, social reform, and so forth, just like the NAACP has done for blacks for years, and the black community is still doing mediocre, and in most cases, they are faring worse than most other ethnic backgrounds in America in nearly all arenas. This does not give you ownership and control like economic influence of business ownership and group economics and wealth attainment, which gives you influence on a whole other level than just politics alone, and Progressives know, even traditional Conservatives knew it, so that is why Black Wall Street had to go and the NAACP and cultural revolution and all of the other policies and causes (even

---

[973] African American Senators United State Senate retrieved November 22, 2022 https://www.senate.gov/pagelayout/history/h_multi_sections_and_teasers/Photo_Exhibit_African_American_Senators.htm

[974] Ibid

[975] Ibid

[976] Ibid

identity politics) that are being pushed by Progressives for the purpose of creating class struggle don't give you this controlling influence either.

I believe the relationship that progressives have had with the black community from the start is like an employee-employer relationship with the Progressives being the employer and the black community as employees. In this relationship the employees think highly of their employer and have a causal relationship with them, even a friendly one sometimes to the point of gullibility. The employer often responds with a friendly rapport (in both speech and action) with some friendly gestures to his friendly and sometimes gullible advances, but he only sees a goal or a vision in that employee, not a friend, and when the goal or vision is reached, he doesn't care what happens to the employer even if it is better to dismiss him with a pink slip if necessary. At this point in time the employer cannot really afford to dismiss his employee yet because he needs him for some more things, some more goals. After the employee has been fired from his job he is scratching his head in disbelief trying to make sense of what has happened and why would it happen to him by such a great group of people, and then he remembers all the other employees that were not as friendly with the company leadership that told him they were not anybody's friends and that they operated by some different beliefs than us, but at this point when he is either living in his car or in a tent on the street in the cold and snow, it is too late. His friends that knew the truth about these employers were prepared with a resume ready and other job prospects from other contacts and networks, so they are not homeless or living in their cars, and if they were, they were not for long, but the gullible employee and others like him have neither. The prospects for another job soon are not good for him either. However, in relationships like this some good things can come out of it for both employer and employee like some really great achievements or milestones of accomplishment for a business owner or employer from the employee's critical skill base and labor and a job that will provide critical income necessary to make a living for an employee with food, clothing, and shelter, who at the time may have no other choices but that job.

15.

Bad Neighborhoods and Really Bad Neighborhoods

A bad neighborhood from appearance might not really look that bad; it might even appear to be sort of good, and others appear to be in transition to the description of the really bad neighborhoods that I've described to you in this book. [977] The ones I will be making a point about in this chapter are different from those. Again, lots of other non-blacks live in bad neighborhoods too where break-ins and crimes happen but black people are just more likely to be in one of them.

Some decent black neighborhoods have some crime, burglary, car break-ins, and other reasons to make auto insurance and homeowners insurance and some other necessities and amenities of homeownership more expensive than some other neighborhoods. These neighborhoods are the ones that are seeing a different element of the black community move into them, from areas where a lot of the children have PTSD from hearing gunshots go off around them all of the time, some of the buildings have gang graffiti written all over

---

[977] Yoonji Han Feb 14, 2023, 7:15 AM Insider Magazine The 123-year history of 'Lift Every Voice and Sing,' the Black national anthem sung by Sheryl Lee Ralph at the Super Bowl retrieved February 22, 2023 https://www.insider.com/lift-every-voice-sing-black-national-anthem-super-bowl-sheryl-2023-2

them, and there are lots of boarded-up houses[978] and burned-out houses with drug dealers and gang activity and vacant lots.[979] The boarded-up and abandoned and sometimes burned-out houses foster an environment for gang cells to organize[980] and hang out, places to make, sell, and smoke crack cocaine,[981] and places for prostitution.[982] In a lot of these little pockets in the black community with the really bad neighborhoods where the Arabs own a lot of the grocery stores and the gas stations and the liquor stores and the East Indians own a lot of the cheap motels and the Koreans own a lot of the hair supply and nail shops (where young black women and black girls can buy sometimes practical but usually trending and faddish wigs and hair weave and braids for their hair) and the Chinese own all of the rice houses many of the businesses to include all of the above which are on the main streets have bars up to their windows. Some of the businesses are closed but the building they once occupied still has the bars up to it that it had when it was still opened. In these neighborhoods, you can hear the gunshots going off all night and sometimes in the day. These are pockets in the black community with no jobs for youth, no decent educational system, and in some cases even hunger.[983] Food insecurities are higher for African Americans than any other group in America.[984] In these

---

[978] Theresa Farrell. On 01/30/2019 Vacant buildings in Kensington are homes for crime, drugs, and fear. retrieved April 16, 2020 https://kensingtonvoice.com/en/vacant-buildings-in-kensington-homes-for-crime-drugs-and-fear/

[979] Ibid.

[980] Ibid.

[981] Ibid.

[982] Ibid.

[983] Move for Hunger. Hunger is a Racial Equity Issue. April 3, 2018 retrieved May 3, 2020 https://moveforhunger.org/hunger-racial-equity-issue

[984] Ibid.

pockets where there is nothing, a black-market economy has been created from the sale of drugs. Eventually, gentrification happens in some of these pockets, and all but a few get displaced from these neighborhoods[985] to go to the bad neighborhoods that are all or mostly black that never really had any crime for years. The black flight out of these neighborhoods often into surrounding suburbs will result in some of these neighborhoods becoming really bad ones. I am not saying a neighborhood cannot be mostly white or Hispanic and be a bad neighborhood because it can but for now lets discuss the black ones.

When enough of these people (which is not the majority of them) get in them from the really bad neighborhoods because there is nothing but despair and disappointment where they came from, they become bad. These people bring their destructive mentalities that they had from the really bad neighborhoods with them. Before they get too bad or before they become really bad, as many black people as possible who could afford it have moved out of them into suburban neighborhoods. It is in these suburban neighborhoods where the predatory lenders have preyed on blacks and Hispanics, where they caused billions of dollars' worth of debt to the black community, reducing its overall wealth tremendously. A lot of this can be linked directly and indirectly to the results of the left's bad policies and causes.

To make matters worse, there are these pockets in the black community where most or all of the houses are paid for, but since the neighborhoods are redlined as bad and some that are really bad have been ridden with crime, boarded-up houses, drug dealers, gang

---

[985] Jason Richardson, NCRC Bruce Mitchell PhD Juan Franco. NCRC Nation Community Reinvestment Coalition Shifting Neighborhoods: Gentrification and cultural displacement in American cities. retrieved May 26, 2020 **Error! Hyperlink reference not valid.**https://ncrc.org/gentrification/

graffiti, and vacant lots, the owners can't sell the houses because no one wants to live in them because the neighborhood is too dangerous. This is an issue that has drained a lot of wealth from the black community because all of these houses are technically real estate that you can't sell or renovate to make a profit after a sale. These houses are often in old neighborhoods, where the average house is between 50 and 100 years old with some exceptions. Had it not been for so much destabilization of the black community as a result of feminism, integration on progressive terms (which resulted in the movement of black dollars, skills, knowledge, talent, businesses, and culture needed to preserve a community to scatter and become diluted everywhere else in America), and bad or unfair drug-sentencing laws, which were largely backed or created by the left, the black community would not have these little pockets or in some cases bigger ones.

In some of the bad neighborhoods and most of the really bad ones, there are children with PTSD from being exposed to too many gunshots and too much death afterward. The mental impact it is having on some of the children is comparable to the children who experienced war zones. Now as adults, they still suffer from PTSD. The FBI reported for 2011 that 6,329 black people were murdered. The Vietnam War only saw 57,000 deaths over the course of 13 years.[986] These bad neighborhoods or pockets in the black community collectively had the effect that a Vietnam War would have had, had it gone on for 40 years. Keeping in mind this happened within the entirety of the black community, which is only 12 or 13 percent of America's total population of about 335 million people, this is a much greater effect than it would have had on

---

[986] Amy Sherman. July 17, 2013. Politofact the Poynter Institute. A look at statistics on black-on-black murders. retrieved August 6, 2020 https://www.politifact.com/factchecks/2013/jul/17/tweets/look-statistic-blacks-and-murder/

America as a whole. According to several sources, black homicides varied from just over 5,000 a year to nearly 8,000 annually over the past 30 years.[987] Between 1980 and 1995, homicides seemed to have been at an all-time high of between 14,400 and 10,800 per year in a total population of 36 million with an average of 30 to 40 out of 100,000.[988] That is between 200,000 and 350,000 over that period, depending on whose statistics you use. Now, there are adults who come from these pockets of the black community that have negative mental side effects as a result and they could probably use some therapy, even some of the kids who are growing up in these neighborhoods could.

A lot of this did not start to happen until the effects of so many progressive leftists' policies and causes hit, either directly or indirectly, since the sex, drugs, and rock and roll era, which brought the drugs and the gangs, as well as the feminist movement, which destabilized black Americans a lot more than most other societies. It left kids with no fathers and all of the bad statistics that come with kids raised in single-mother homes with no patriarchy. Integration is the other cause, that killed the business infrastructure that could have been used by the black community to produce some of its own jobs and rectify other factors such as bad public schools.

Vice News did a special on the South-Central neighborhood of Los Angeles, where children suffer from PTSD. The journalist asked a class of middle school students how many of them had experienced a shooting by someone they know or a killing of someone

---

[987] Erika Harrell, PhD August 2007. NCJ 214258. Black Victims of Violent Crime. retrieved August 6, 2020. Bureau of Justice States Special report. https://bjs.ojp.gov/

[988] Alexia Cooper and Erica L. Smith. U.S. Department of Justice. Office of Justice Programs. Bureau of Justice Statistics. November 2011, NCJ 236018. Homicide Trends in the United States, 1980–2008. retrieved August 6, 2020 https://www.bjs.gov/content/pub/pdf/htus8008.pdf

they know by a shooting, and most of the kids' hands went up.[989] Unless they get therapy, they will not recover from these experiences.[990] It is like being raised in a war zone.[991] A man was later interviewed, and he said there were six shootings in one day in the neighborhood called Death Valley.[992] The journalist conducting the interview said there were 100 shootings in this South Central LA neighborhood.[993] In this little pocket of black America, it is an epidemic that up to 40 percent of urban poor are dealing with. The children gave descriptions with all of the gory details of shootings that some of them had witnessed.

A psychotherapist saw classic symptoms of PTSD in high school students such as sleeplessness, numbness, traumatic flashbacks, and a constant feeling of animosity.[994] He stated that the children were using their reptilian brains with fight-or-flight responses.[995] These sections of the brain were operative all day long, so the kids appear to be uninterested in learning or they can have flares of violent acts.[996] They are symptoms of a deeper problem, and children are not always able to find words for what they are feeling, so they act it out or are reactionary from it.[997] The CDC stated that more kids

---

[989] Dell. June 5, 2014. PTSD and Gang Violence In South Central LA's "Death Alley" [Documentary]. retrieved July 24, 2020 http://onsmash.com/lifestyle/ptsd-and-gang-violence-in-south-central-las-death-alley-documentary/

[990] Ibid.

[991] Ibid.

[992] Ibid.

[993] Ibid.

[994] Ibid.

[995] Ibid.

[996] Ibid.

[997] Ibid.

suffer from PTSD than soldiers returning from war zones, and now it is a serious public health issue.[998] The children fear they will get shot or robbed on their way to school.

Another school psychiatrist was interviewed, and he stated that half of all the students they interviewed qualified as having PTSD. VICE News did another special on another neighborhood in Oakland, California, that has children with PTSD. It was similar to what is happening in Los Angeles.

Trauma like this affects these children's academic performance and capability negatively[999]. Some of these children, who may have been able to had they not been exposed to all of this trauma, though try as hard as they may, will now never be able to take on rigorous and very demanding academic feats like Medical School, Law School, Engineering School and PhD Science and Mathematics degree programs. Not to worry because this gives DEI committees reason to dumb down academic standards for getting into and completing all these academic feats. Not only this, it stifles and stagnates development in these pockets in the black communities, maybe even like it does some nations with warzones or some kind of conflict going on and aids in making them dependent.

If Conservatives had had more influence, you wouldn't have had the drugs from the sex, drugs, and rock and roll movement that is a factor for the shootings with the gang violence, and you would have a better business infrastructure in the black community, so the kids would have better job opportunities and more things to get involved with from for-profit and nonprofit institutions provided by the black community. However, integration on progressive terms

---

[998] Ibid.

[999] Mental Health America How Trauma Impacts School Performance retrieved May 3, 2024 https://mhanational.org/how-trauma-impacts-school-performance

resulted in the redistribution of wealth outside of these communities and eventually the collapse of the black community. As a result of the drugs part of the movement, more little black babies since the 1990s have been born addicted to crack at a disproportionately higher rate than any other racial or ethnic group in America.[1000]

If it were up to Conservatives, there would not be so many career politicians as Democrats in the black community that do nothing or very little to help these pockets. The Democratic Party is the party of Progressives and leftists versus the Republican Party, which is endorsed by Conservatives.

In another study done in Philadelphia, PTSD was just as high among youth living in inner-city neighborhoods like South Central Los Angeles. In Philadelphia, over a six-month period in 2001, just over 18,000 people were shot, and just over 3,800 were murdered. Up until that point, during the entirety of the conflict in Afghanistan, fewer US soldiers were killed than on the streets of Philadelphia, and that is just one city.[1001] Boys as young as second graders have been recruited for gangs.[1002] It should not surprise anyone that an environment like this would produce PTSD cases in youth and now adults who live in those neighborhoods or at one time lived in those neighborhoods—if they have not received any type of psychiatric counseling. There are neighborhoods like this all over the country in black America. Again, if so many leftist policies had not existed to foster their creation, they would not have happened; if Conservatives, who are more likely to be more

---

[1000] Crack Babies. Office of Inspector General. Office of Evaluations and inspections. 1990. Retrieved June 29 2019 https://oig.hhs.gov/oei/reports/oei-03-89-01540.pdf

[1001] Steve Volk. Welcome to the City of Post-Traumatic Stress Disorder. August 23, 2012. retrieved July 28, 2019 http://www.phillymag.com/articles/philadelphia-post-traumatic-stress-disorder-gun-violence/?all=1

[1002] Ibid.

right-leaning thinkers, had had more influence, this would probably not be the case.

Gentrification in American cities is a powerful force for economic change in a community that results in cultural displacement.[1003] It is what happens when the tastes, norms, and desires of a different group replace those of the original residents and can also result in loss of historically and culturally significant institutions for a community.[1004] This is another thing that has happened to some of the neighborhoods that have become bad or really bad ones. When cultural displacement occurs, it erases your identity and the whole point behind a group's existence.[1005] Over 110,000 black residents were displaced from 187 tracts of urban land in 16 large cities across America.[1006] Hispanics did not fare nearly as poorly at just over 24,000 residents from 45 tracts of urban land in 10 cities.[1007] According to an article by the NCRC in these same tracts of land, white, Asian, and sometimes Hispanic residents increased.[1008] The article only indicated gentrification that happened between 2000 and 2013.[1009] It did not discuss gentrification that has occurred over the entirety of 40 or 45 years from just after 1975, in some cases, or 1980 until the present.[1010] The article listed 28 cities total, which

---

[1003] Shifting Neighborhoods: Gentrification and cultural displacement in American cities. retrieved June 12, 2020 file:///C:/Users/Owner/Desktop/How%20Liberal%20Policies%20 and%20Causes/NCRC-Research-Gentrification-FINAL3%20(1).pdf

[1004] Ibid.

[1005] Ibid.

[1006] Ibid.

[1007] Ibid.

[1008] Ibid.

[1009] Ibid.

[1010] Ibid.

would include 11 more cities[1011] with sizable African American populations that were not included in the 16 mentioned earlier that had experienced anywhere from 11 percent to 20 percent gentrification as well.[1012]

The Housing Act of 1949 was signed into effect by Democrat Harry Truman.[1013] Its purpose was urban renewal.[1014] It was the most effective Negro removal program.[1015] It was one of the most effective removals of black business, culture, community, neighborhoods, and property of all policies.[1016] In 1949, some Conservative, right-leaning whites were still loyal to the Democrats. However, according to another source, the switch from Conservatives being supporters of the Democratic Party to the Republicans and vice versa for Liberals to the Democrats happened somewhere between the 1860s and 1936, and by 1936 the switch was complete.[1017] With that said, it may even be fair to call Urban Renewal a more progressive policy for its time, especially when you consider it is still occurring in some forms today[1018]. However, for quite some time, it has

---

[1011] Ibid.

[1012] Ibid.

[1013] LA Progressive Newsletter. Urban Renewal Meant Negro Removal. retrieved December 26, 2021 https://www.laprogressive.com/urban-renewal/

[1014] Ibid.

[1015] Ibid.

[1016] Ibid.

[1017] Natalie Wolchover(livescience.com-little-mystery)Contributions from Callum McKelvie published October 17, 2022 When did Democrats and Republicans switch platforms? Live Science retrieved May 18, 2023 https://www.livescience.com/34241-democratic-republican-parties-switch-platforms.html

[1018] Albert Fontenot 30 Inspiring Urban Renewal Projects Social Work Degree Guide retrieved May 24, 2023 https://www.socialworkdegreeguide.com/30-inspiring-urban-renewal-projects/

been the party of the progressive left, and ever since it has been the party of the Progressives, legislative changes have been made every year in the US Department of Housing and Urban Development policies since 1932.[1019] The businesses, culture, and sense of community, neighborhoods, and property have never been restored to the black community on the watch of the progressive left. Enough of those who have left have never returned to the black community that would make it a more independent entity that is less dependent on government and other non-white entities, and more than half of those displaced over the years by these policies were black.[1020] Progressive public housing advocates[1021] who worked with interest groups and policymakers[1022] whose projects would be largely government financed[1023] and would expand government's role in providing housing instead of commercial redevelopment[1024] could be achieved at the displacement of lots of black people. Only to for the same blacks to be placed in public housing again since they cannot afford the new commercial redevelopments housing. I say that because early on, some of its biggest supporters were black clergy and activists[1025] until they found out they had been duped into Negro removal by Progressives after being forced into it by a

---

[1019] U.S. Department of Housing and Urban Development. Major Legislation On Housing And Urban Development Enacted Since 1932. retrieved December 26, 2021 https://www.hud.gov/sites/documents/LEGS_CHRON_JUNE2014.PDF

[1020] LA Progressive Newsletter. Urban Renewal Meant Negro Removal. retrieved December 26, 2021 https://www.laprogressive.com/urban-renewal/

[1021] Brent Cebul. The Boston Review. Tearing Down Black America. retrieved January 5, 2022 https://bostonreview.net/articles/brent-cebul-tearing-down-black-america/

[1022] Ibid.

[1023] Ibid.

[1024] Ibid.

[1025] Ibid.

Democrat president in 1949. There is a PBS special called *Dream Land: Little Rock's West 9th Street*[1026] that chronicles what happened in the 1950s to a black business district in Little Rock, Arkansas, and it is another example of what I mean, but this time it was both a Conservative Democratic policy and a progressive combination that took that community out.

Maybe instead of trying to become completely integrated with whites, if the black community had put more effort into preventing legislation like the Housing Act of 1949 from happening so they could keep and maintain black communities, that may have been better. If this had happened instead, then it would have resulted in just partial integration into white society and may have been better.

This is something else that has happened in the black community indirectly from the end result of years of progressive policies and causes. Destabilization of society, integration, ineffective black leadership, poor quality of education, and not practicing group economics with a code of conduct are major players in why this happened, but there are other players as well. Before many of the progressive leftist policies and causes started to take place and have effect, the black community did not really have neighborhoods like this. Maybe if more Conservatives, who were more likely to be on the right, had had more influence over the past 50 years, this may not have happened because they did not generally support so many destructive causes that I mentioned above that supported its development.

Now, while we still have free market and capitalism, the black community needs leadership and guidance like that coming from the Harvest Institute, which is a nonprofit founded and led by Dr.

[1026] Arkansas PBS. Special Dream Land: Little Rock's West 9th Street. retrieved January 8, 2022 https://www.youtube.com/watch?v=RjBeT7AyjRE

Claude Anderson.[1027] As far as I know, and I could be wrong, the Harvest Institute is not associated with or involved with any special interest groups or philanthropic groups. They are only interested in the unique challenges that only the black community is having in America as a whole. They do not deal in generalities like "minority group" or "people of color" when speaking of black America as a whole. He refers to black America on his website as America's "official underclass and the most vulnerable in the Nation."[1028]

[1027] Dr. Claude Anderson. The Harvest Institute. Vision Beyond the Dream. retrieved December 7, 2020 http://www.harvestinstitute.org/index.html

[1028] Ibid.

16.

Black Wealth Has Taken a Hit

After the black community had been destabilized by the feminist movement and the redistribution of black wealth had been added to everyone else's community from the black community because of the real agenda behind integration with some more bad drug-sentencing laws for crack cocaine, it just contributed to the creation of the prison industrial complex. It doesn't help that the Common Core / No Child Left Behind schools don't give them a good education to succeed and having ineffective, and sometimes corrupt Democratic Party leadership doesn't help either. After they get out of prison, they come back to some of the same black neighborhoods in the black community with no way to get employment and repair their lives, so they go into crime in little pockets of the black community, selling drugs and doing all sorts of other illegal activities because they have no choice. After enough time, these places become really bad, with gangs everywhere, boarded-up houses, vacant lots, gang graffiti, and maybe even bullet holes in some of the walls of buildings. As a result of these really bad neighborhoods, more intermediate bad neighborhoods have evolved. Now to make matters worse, the following scenario has taken place.

  Certain progressive Liberals were a part of a scheme that forced banks to lend money to the poor high-cost subprime rates that they would probably never be able to pay back. This practice is called predatory lending.[1029] It was well organized by congressional Democrats with a hierarchy of bureaucrats which forced some other organizations to comply. A Republican constituency, which was led by former President Bush and other Republican senators pushed for reforms of these predatory methods, but Democrats responded with inappropriate outbursts and threats to challenge GOP leaders as racists.[1030] Remember, certain Progressive Liberals worked with lots of other Democrats to pull off this scheme against the black community, which could be called racist. That is who black people have traditionally voted for and look at what they and other members of their party have orchestrated here, and it is going to negatively affect black home ownership and wealth building for years to come. As a result of all of this, the black home ownership rate has dropped steadily since 2004, and now 15 years later, it is at an all-time low.[1031]

Here is another example of the same thing that happened to the black community over the past few years, along with an entire investigation into why and to possibly have something done about it because it was wrong. If it were up to Conservatives and/or Republicans, monies would not have been given away like this just to create debt, and there would be more fiscal responsibility. Here is another example of where it would have been better if Conservatives, who are more likely to be on the right, had had more control because they are more likely to be Republicans.

[1029] Business Daily. Sorry, Hillary, You And Bill—Not Tax Cuts—Caused The Financial Crisis. Editorials. retrieved June 17, 2019 *https://www.investors.com/politics/editorials/sorry-hillary-you-and-bill-not-tax-cuts-caused-the-financial-crisis Investors*

[1030] Ibid.

[1031] African American Homeownership Falls to 50-year Low. NAREB website. retrieved June 20, 2019 http://www.nareb.com/african-american-homeownership-falls-50-year-low/.

According to the executive director of the National Council of Negro Women, black wealth has been intentionally drained, which has set the black community back generations.[1032] black wealth dropped 52 percent during the housing crisis.[1033] This was the largest loss of black wealth since the Reconstruction following the Civil War, and it all happened in the few years of the recession.[1034] African Americans and Latinos were 30 percent more likely to receive these subprime loans, and they cost these families billions in assets from foreclosures over a three-year period.[1035] Over another three-year period, it was estimated it could cost them billions more.[1036] That was according to a study from May 2012 by two universities.[1037]

From a reliable data source, it was concluded that middle- to upper-income African American women in a significant number of the cities surveyed were more likely to receive a high-cost subprime loan than other groups.[1038] Wells Fargo is a major institution that purposely sold shoddy mortgages to would-be African American homeowners.[1039] This bank deliberately tricked middle-class black and

---

[1032] Barbara Reynolds. Minorities fall victim to predatory lenders. July 16, 2012. retrieved June 13, 2019 https://www.washingtonpost.com/blogs/therootdc/post/minorities-fall-victim-to-predatory-lenders/2012/07/16/gJQAraMYpW_blog.html?utm_term=.93cd784eab6a.

[1033] Ibid.

[1034] Ibid.

[1035] Ibid

[1036] Ibid

[1037] Ibid.

[1038] Ibid.

[1039] Ibid.

Hispanic families who they referred to as "Mud people" into taking out subprime ghetto loans.[1040]

This transfer and draining of its wealth was more of an injustice to the black community than anything, and it was done very discreetly and quietly in a way that nothing was noticed. The recipient of the loan as the victim is the one who takes blame, but the party who perpetrated the scam should be put up on criminal charges. Now even if the black community wanted to rebuild itself like the Greenwood District of Tulsa, Oklahoma, which they built themselves years ago just after slavery, they don't have nearly as much wealth to do it with. Conservative Republicans stand for the small government, low taxation, and putting more influence and control back in the hands of the small community. By this, the black community could use its own savings and loans and credit unions, assess the credit of the lenders on an individual level, and give loans and rebuild a community by itself. This will just cripple the black community for years to come, but black people have en masse for nearly the past 60 years supported the Democratic Party in elections. Remember progressive left-leaning Liberals are more likely to vote for and support the Democratic Party,[1041] so if you vote for them, you are really indirectly supporting their leftist policies and causes. Conservatives are more likely to vote as Republicans.[1042] So from this, who are the real racists? The money from the community savings and loans and banks and credit unions

---

[1040] Zaid Jilani. The Intercept. New Report Looks at How Obama's Housing Policies Destroyed Black Wealth December 8 2017. retrieved June 14, 2019 https://theintercept.com/2017/12/08/barack-obama-housing-policy-racial-inequality/

[1041] Lydia Saad. January 8, 2019. U.S. Still Leans Conservative , but Liberals Keep Recent Gains. retrieved March 7, 2020 https://news.gallup.com/poll/245813/leans-conservative-liberals-keep-recent-gains.aspx

[1042] Ibid.

belongs to the community; it should not be spent recklessly because of someone else's special interests.

Three-sevenths of black families have just under one-fifth of the wealth that poor white families have, so wealth in America is still not spread out over the diversity of ethnic backgrounds; it is still more or less a white monopoly.[1043] According to some other studies that measured wealth versus income as an indicator of class and mobility in society, it would take several generations for the average black family to amass the same amount of wealth as the average white family.[1044] As the masses become poorer and less educated and more dependent on outside sources for mere survival, like the government, they have less power and influence, so they matter less, and their concerns are ignored more.

In 2012, the *St. Louis American*, which is the city of St. Louis's black newspaper, and the Huffington Post both did an article titled "The Vanishing Black Middle Class" that claimed that black America had no real black middle class left.[1045] They used data from the census and the Federal Reserve to prove this.[1046] The study used wealth versus income to prove this claim.[1047] The income standard was based on the average income of a white family, which was about $81,000 annually.[1048] They essentially subtracted expenses from income, and what

---

[1043] Antonio Moore. America does not have a Real Black Middle Class. The Huffington Post. 08/30/2017. retrieved Oct2, 2019 https://www.huffpost.com/entry/america-does-not-have-a-black-middle-class_b_59a72c5de4b02498834a8e6f

[1044] Ibid.

[1045] George E. Curry. Mar 15, 2012. The Vanishing Black Middle Class. The St. Louis American. retrieved August 17, 2020 http://www.stlamerican.com/the-vanishing-black-middle-class/article_9a766590-6e34-11e1-88c2-001871e3ce6c.html

[1046] Ibid.

[1047] Ibid.

[1048] Ibid.

you have left is net worth.[1049] One big reason for this was predatory lending practices that were given to blacks and Latinos between 2000 and 2008.[1050] Again, many Democratic Party members favored this practice, and during this period, the black and brown communities were referred to by some in the banking sector that were giving the predatory loans as "Mud people," which is a racial insult. Keep in mind, the progressive left is getting a lot of their agenda accomplished through the Democratic Party.

President Joe Biden said he wants to make his priority women- and minority-owned businesses,[1051] but that is not going to help black businesses any if the black community doesn't practice group economics. If they don't and people of other races and ethnic backgrounds do not flood into the black community and spend billions of dollars at Black-owned businesses like black people do and have for years at chain stores and mom-and-pop stores that are owned by whites and Arabs and Asians, the black community cannot change the situation it is in. You can't mandate that everybody label their business by race or ethnicity and require that everybody buy a certain percentage of their goods and services from businesses across all ethnicities' ownership unless you require it and enforce it. That is not going to happen because there is no way to enforce it, or to monitor how or if it is working either. Unless that happens, President Biden's plan for minority-owned businesses will not work for the black community. If the money is in the form of

---

[1049] Antonio Moore. America does not have a Real Black Middle Class. The Huffington Post. 08/30/2017. retrieved Oct 2, 2019 https://www.huffpost.com/entry/america-does-not-have-a-black-middle-class_b_59a72c5de4b02498834a8e6f

[1050] Ibid.

[1051] Mary Rose Corkery. January 11, 2021. The Daily Signal. Biden Says His 'Priority' Will Be Minority and Women-Owned Small Businesses. retrieved January 12, 2021 https://www.dailysignal.com/2021/01/11/biden-says-his-priority-will-be-minority-and-women-owned-small-businesses/

loans, it will put the black community in more debt to the big banks, similar to the way predatory lenders did with the Savings and Loans, Fannie Mae, and Freddie Mac crisis. This will have a similar effect on black America that a debt trap[1052] has. If it comes in the form of grants, free money can come with incentives for a certain response. If it comes from the Democrats and progressive lobbyists, the incentives can be for more progressive causes such as BLM protests and riots, and once they get the effect they want to see, they can just throw the black community back under the bus again.

Now, out of political correctness and DEI and maybe a little out of multiculturalism, which were all invented by both them and the left and now is being favored by some Progressive Liberals, there was a push to put slave abolitionist Harriet Tubman's picture on the twenty-dollar bill[1053] and poet Maya Angelou's image on the quarter[1054] instead of leaving Confederate General Andrew Jackson's picture on the twenty-dollar bill and President George Washington's on the quarter. What good is it going to do black people to have these ladies' images on our money if there is no black middle class to enjoy having access to lots of both of them? They can even make Juneteenth a national holiday, but what difference does that make if you don't own and control the institutions on the street the parades will be on. I think the designation

---

[1052] What is a Debt Trap? How can we avoid it? Hero Fin Corp retrieved April 2, 2023 https://www.herofincorp.com/blog/what-is-debt-trap

[1053] Annie Linskey June 3, 2021 at 7:56 p.m. EDT POLITICS When will Harriet Tubman adorn the $20 bill? Retrieved May 22, 2022 The Washington Post https://www.washingtonpost.com/politics/harriet-tubman-20-bill/2021/06/03/62443b5c-bcd1-11eb-9c90-731aff7d9a0d_story.html

[1054] Ylan Mui CNBC Make It The new Maya Angelou quarters could help redefine 'freedom' in America: 'What a beautiful thing' Published Fri, Mar 11 2022 11:44 AM EST retrieved May 22, 2022 https://www.cnbc.com/2022/03/11/the-new-maya-angelou-quarters-could-help-redefine-freedom-in-america.html#:~:text=The%20Maya%20Angelou%20quarter%20is,the%20kickoff%20to%20the%20U.S

of Juneteenth (June 19) as a federal holiday rather than just an observance by the Democrats is just another ploy to get blacks to vote for them in the next election.

The Civil Rights Act gave blacks the right to eat, live, work, and be wherever they wanted to be legally, and as a result, the tragedy at Black Wallstreet could not happen again without legal repercussions, since now blacks have civil rights, meaning they can sue their perpetrators if any such thing happened again and have them brought to justice. But civil rights will do you no good if you cannot afford to be in these places and you have no economic infrastructure to provide any of these institutions on your own, and you can't afford to have it in someone else's community. It will leave you dependent on activists and protests, mostly left-leaning ones, for their causes.

The Civil Rights Act was signed into law by a Democrat, but the best plans are the ones by Conservative Republicans, with a setup where you have a strong business community where your money exchanges hand in your community and generates wealth with low taxation and less government regulations, and where your for-profit and nonprofit organizations in your community can produce jobs and opportunity, which generally results in less poverty and crime and bad neighborhoods and fewer of some other social problems. If Conservatives had had more influence, it is still almost a given that even they would have had their own circles around race and ethnicity where blacks would have had a tough time, but blacks could create their own businesses communities and created institutions of their own to lend them money at better interest rates a lot better with group economics.

In America, we have seen a transfer of wealth from the bottom half of society. Wages have stagnated over the past 40 years,[1055] and

---

[1055] Drew Desilver. For most U.S. workers, real wages have barely budged in decades. AUGUST 7, 2018. retrieved August 26, 2019 https://www.pewresearch.org/fact-tank/2018/08/07/for-most-us-workers-real-wages-have-barely-budged-for-decades

the prices of houses[1056] and cars[1057] have more than tripled and more than quadrupled, respectively, since then. The price of a college education has quadrupled since 1980, as well.[1058] On top of that, blacks and Latinos lost a lot of their wealth of the past 10 or 20 years from predatory lenders who referred to them as mud people. They offered them loans for houses they know that they would never be able to pay back, and it put them in a lot more debt than whites are facing. The question to ask here is how much of this wealth transfer will affect black people and who is the wealth being transferred to mostly—and is race a factor in who it is being transferred to? If race is a factor from this example, blacks will be big losers and someone else will have a lot of their wealth that they may not ever get back.

Bank of America is starting a zero down payment option for first time home buyers who are black or Hispanic or People of Color to give them a chance to own their first home.[1059] It is a new zero down payment plan.[1060] Since no prior credit history or mortgage insurance

---

[1056] Housing priced at $100,000 in 1980 → $326,409.34 in 2019 Historical Pricing for Housing in 1980. US Inflation. retrieved July 3, 2019 http://www.in2013dollars.com/Housing/price-inflation/1980

[1057] The average car now costs $25,449—how much was a car the year you were born?. April 25, 2016. Tribune Media Wire. Retrieved July 2, 2019 https://wgntv.com/2016/04/25/the-average-car-now-costs-25449-how-much-was-a-car-the-year-you-were-born/

[1058] Emmie Martin. Here's how much more expensive it is for you to go to college than it was for your parents. . Nov 29, 2017. retrieved June 30, 2019 https://www.cnbc.com/2017/11/29/how-much-college-tuition-has-increased-from-1988-to-2018.html

[1059] Lorie Konish @LORIEKONISH Published Thu, Sep 1 20222:27 Pm Edt updated Thu, Sep 1 20222:50 Pm Edt Bank of America launches zero down payment mortgages to help minorities buy their first homes — here's who can apply retrieved September 20, 2022 https://www.cnbc.com/2022/09/01/bank-of-america-to-help-minorities-buy-first-homes-with-new-mortgages.html

[1060] Ibid

is required[1061], could these loans be given to people of color with no history or flawed histories in both putting them at risk of being in the same debt traps they were in with the subprime interest fiasco that previously targeted people of color from roughly 1993 through 2012? If the terms of these loans do not mention interest rate changes that could go up higher later in the lending process, you have to ask yourself, could this happen again very deceptively like it did with some of the subprime intertest loans of 1993 to roughly 2012 that put lots of black primarily suburban home buyers in debt with debt-to-income ratios that will in some cases keep them out of the middle class? This is being done in an attempt to accomplish equity in homeownership, and equity is a progressive cause. This equity could have very negative outcomes for blacks on their credit and their ability to stay in the middle class, which will destroy another type of equality so another form of equity will have to be devised to compensate for it. This could just be another way to produce more debt in and dependency in America with race being a factor and in this case the black community was used to help produce more debt.

Now America's distribution of wealth, is at it highest point since the World War Two Era[1062] leaving Americans in the two bottom quintiles of wealth in more poverty than ever[1063] while wealth for those in the upper quintile has more than tripled.[1064] It far out passes that of all of the developed and industrialized nations.[1065] It looks

---

[1061]   Ibid

[1062]   A Guide to Economic Inequality April 2021 retrieved February 19, 2024 https://americancompass.org/economic-inequality-guide/?gad_source=1&gclid=CjwKCAiA8sauBhB3EiwAruTRJivfj2IKkjhTXOXweV2J1oKdkvk_ZKzn3yjWD9rZNXrkxL7Ie3qEpBoCHLYQAvD_BwE

[1063]   Ibid

[1064]   Ibid

[1065]   Ibid

more like that of Mexico or Costa Rica[1066] especially if you take into account debt to-income and -asset ratios,[1067] and they are two third world nations one of them is maybe a developing nation at best. Black people still lag behind whites and Asians in many categories[1068], and integration on progressive terms, which was a leftist cause, didn't work to get black people there. This is deceptive because America just has so much more wealth than Mexico and Costa Rica do so what is considered poor in America may not be in Mexico or Costa Rica. What is considered below the poverty line in those two nations is a different kind of poverty than what is considered poverty in America.

According to the Washington Center for Equitable Growth after the Civil War, during the period of Reconstruction and even in its aftermath in the late 19th century and early 20th century, the White-to-Black per capita racial wealth gap fell from 60-to-1 in the mid-1860s to 10-to-1 by 1920.[1069] From this the wealth gap seemed to be closing when America had more conservative values. According to a report from the Rand Blog objective Analysis and Effective solutions it would currently take $7.5 trillion to halve the black-white wealth gap, and $15 trillion to eliminate it.[1070] This is after America

---

[1066] Ibid

[1067] Ibid

[1068] Ibid

[1069] Kreg Steven Brown February 24, 2023 Examining the history of the U.S. racial wealth divide shows stagnating progress on closing these disparities Washington Center For Equitable Growth retrieved January 31, 2024 https://equitablegrowth.org/examining-the-history-of-the-u-s-racial-wealth-divide-shows-stagnating-progress-on-closing-these-disparities/#:~:text=The%20authors%20find%20that%20after,%2Dto%2D1%20by%20 1920.

[1070] The Rand Blog What Would It Take to Close America's Black-White Wealth Gap? May 9, 2023 retrieved January 31, 2024 https://www.rand.org/pubs/articles/2023/what-would-it-take-to-close-americas-black-white-wealth-gap.html#:~:text=The%20median%20 wealth%20gap%20in,%2415%20trillion%20to%20eliminate%20it.

has become more Progressive which is supposedly better. 1860's to 1920's was during the period when there were a number of black communities like The Greenwood District of Tulsa's Blackwall Street when the black community practice group economic and money exchanged hands in the black community and stayed in the community. The rand blogs analysis data was compiled probably after integration under progressive terms.

Since America has become more progressive, the black middle class it seems has shrank and black wealth and the black middle class has slowly shrunk or maybe in some cases it has disappeared. Black home ownership, which is a sign of wealth attainment, and which was lost during this more progressive era in America, is at an all-time low, and this section proves both of those facts.

Socialism, the feminist movement, the common core education system, integration on progressive terms and a whole lot of other things have not stopped this transfer of wealth from out of the black community.

If Conservatives, who are on the right, had had the predominant influence over the past 40 or 50 years, these things would never have happened, at least not to this extent.

17.

The Republican Party versus the Democratic Party

This is not an endorsement for either party. The Thirteenth Amendment, which freed the slaves, and the Fourteenth Amendment, which granted civil rights, were both drafted and ratified by the Republican Party.[1071, 1072] In the Fifteenth Amendment of the Constitution, which gave Blacks voting rights, the House vote was almost entirely along party lines, with no Democrats supporting the bill,[1073] and only three Republicans voting against it,[1074] some because they thought the amendment did not go far enough in its protections. So it was Republicans who largely gave black people the right to vote and made it illegal to enslave them unless they committed a crime, not Democrats, but black people over the past 50 years have consistently voted for the Democratic Party 90 percent

---

[1071] The Radicals Behind Lincoln's 13th Amendment Posted by Pete on Jan 31st 2018 Radical Tea Towel retrieved May 25, 2022 https://www.radicalteatowel.com/blog/the-radicals-behind-lincolns-13th-amendment/

[1072] Civil War | Article The Radical Republicans American Battlefield Trust retrieved May 25, 2022 https://www.battlefields.org/learn/articles/radical-republicans/

[1073] US History II The Era of Reconstruction, 1865-1877 Course Hero retrieved May 25, 2022   https://www.coursehero.com/study-guides/ushistoryii/radical-reconstruction-1867-1872/

[1074] Ibid

of the time. Even though Republicans put the exception in the Amendment for committing a crime, it still was better for blacks than the intents of the Democrats.

As a Republican, "abolition was a central aspect of Lincoln's moral compass," the Harvard historian Henry Louis Gates wrote in 2009, "racial equality was not."[1075] Abraham Lincoln, also a Republican, was not in favor of black people holding any political office,[1076] being voters or jurors, or intermarrying with whites.[1077] He believed there must be a position of inferior and superior in society and that the Negro should take the latter.[1078] He did, however, believe that they should be able to enjoy life, liberty, and the fruits of their labor, and in the end, he gave them their freedom.[1079] He held typical racial indifferences that most whites held in his time.[1080] Although not nearly as bad as in the past, not all, but still some Conservatives still have their racial preferences and indifferences today, so before supporting a Democrat a Republican candidate or Conservative cause, black people should do their research and choose their causes and candidates wisely. Abraham Lincoln, however, did believe that all men, black or white, should have the right to improve their condition in society and to enjoy the fruits of their labor.[1081]

[1075] Dan Mac Guill Published 16 August 2017 Did Abraham Lincoln Express Opposition to Racial Equality? Snoopes retrieved May 25, 2022 https://www.snopes.com/fact-check/did-lincoln-racism-equality-oppose

[1076] Ibid

[1077] Ibid

[1078] Ibid

[1079] Ibid

[1080] Ibid

[1081] Ibid

After slavery and the Civil War ended with the passing of the 13th, 14th and th15th[1082] [1083] [1084] to the constitution, the same Republican congress and President wanted to give every black family 40 acres and a mule in addition, which may have prevented so many black families from having to be sharecroppers on white owned land, but former slave owner and democrat Andrew Jackson Veto's the legislation[1085] . Democrat Lyndon B. Johnson signed the Civil Rights Act of 1964 into law. It was known by white house staffers at the time that he used the word "N*****" frequently to refer to blacks.[1086] The article stated that he was a connoisseur of the word.[1087] I think the only reason why he signed the civil rights bill was to get blacks to have an affinity for and keep voting for the democrat party for years to come, but he had no interests in helping the black community get out of the lot they were in. After all the black community is better off and worse off in many cases than they were

---

[1082] The United States Senate The Senate Passed The Thirteenth Amendment retrieved July 12, 2024 https://www.senate.gov/about/origins-foundations/senate-and-constitution/senate-passes-the-thirteenth-amendment.htm#:~:text=On%20April%208%2C%201864%2C%20the,the%20amendment%2038%20to%206

[1083] National Constitution Center On this day, Congress approved the 14th Amendment Blog Post June 13, 2024 | by NCC Staff retrieved July 12, 2024 retrieved July 12, 2024 https://constitutioncenter.org/blog/it-was-today-congress-approved-the-14th-amendment

[1084] National Archives 15th Amendment to the U.S. Constitution: Voting Rights (1870) retrieved July 12, 2024 https://www.archives.gov/milestone-documents/15th-amendment

[1085] Nadra Kareem Nittle Updated: January 3, 2024 | Original: November 9, 2022 The Short-Lived Promise of '40 Acres and a Mule https://www.history.com/news/40-acres-mule-promise

[1086] Adam Serwer, Adam Serwer MSNBC April 11, 2014, 8:21 AM CDT / Updated April 11, 2014, 12:39 PM CDT Lyndon Johnson was a civil rights hero. But also a racist. Retrieved July 12, 2024 https://www.msnbc.com/msnbc/lyndon-johnson-civil-rights-racism-msna305591

[1087] African American Registry Today's Articles People, Locations, Episodes Lyndon Johnson, Politician born retrieved July 12, 2024 https://aaregistry.org/story/lyndon-baines-johnson-born/

before the passage of the Civil Rights Act of 1964 which adds up to zero progress. Lyndon B. Johnson was a racist, but his party the democrats are now the party of the progressive movement and the left and I just question their motives for the black community today.

Republican President Donald J Trump in 2018 signed in to law The First Step Act[1088] a sweeping criminal justice reform bill designed to promote rehabilitation[1089], lower recidivism[1090], and reduce excessive sentences in the federal prison system.[1091] This was big for the African American community.

From another published study it was found that among heavy drug users, the ratio of Democrats to Republicans was much higher for Democrats than Republicans.[1092] Another survey found an undeviating and direct relationship between liberal drug users and the use of any illicit drug.[1093] It would have minimized the number of black HIV/AIDS infections tremendously if Conservatives had had more influence in America over the drug industry, both legal and illegal.

At least one new study backs up the conventional wisdom that Conservatives, who are more likely to be Republicans, give more money to charities than Liberals, who are more likely to be

---

[1088] Ashley Nellis, Ph.D. and Liz Komar August 22, 2023 The Sentencing Project The First Step Act: Ending Mass Incarceration in Federal Prisons retrieved February 23, 2024 https://www.sentencingproject.org/policy-brief/the-first-step-act-ending-mass-incarceration-in-federal-prisons/#footnote-ref-2

[1089] Ibid

[1090] Ibid

[1091] Ibid

[1092] Jim Meyers. Are Liberals Bigger Drug Users? 16 June 2008. Newsmax.com. retrieved August 27, 2019 https://www.newsmax.com/insidecover/liberals-drug-use/2008/06/16/id/324135

[1093] Ibid.

Democrats.[1094, 1095] This is not an endorsement for the Republican Party or for Conservatives, but why would you vote for Democratic leadership 80 or 90 percent of the time when they are used more often by the left for a cause that is really not in the best interest for black people as a group either? It may even be better sometimes if blacks voted as independents, or write someone else's name on the ballet who is not an either of the above as neither of the two major parties at times or independents may seem to have the best interests of black people at heart.

Many Cuban Americans and now newer arrivals from Venezuela were diehard Trump supporters, and President Trump is a Conservative Republican.[1096] The Democratic Socialists and what they are standing for is uncomfortable to them.[1097] They know what it is like to have lived in and had to flee a Socialist regime[1098] that went Communist—at least in the case of Cuba. The leftist ideology of the Democratic Party has many of those who fled these countries for America worried.[1099] The question to ask is: Do you think it is good for the black community?

[1094] John Grgurich. Who's More Generous Liberals or Conservative s? The Fiscal Times. October 17, 2014. retrieved September 10, 2019 http://www.thefiscaltimes.com/2014/10/17/Who-s-More-Generous-Liberals-or-Conservative/

[1095] Michael Sances and Michelle Margolis. Republicans give more to charity—but not because they oppose income redistribution. Democratic Audit UK. retrieved September 12, 2019 http://www.democraticaudit.com/2017/11/17/republicans-give-more-to-charity-but-not-because-they-oppose-income-redistribution

[1096] The Right-Wing Latinos of Miami: Proud Boys and Refugees. VICE. Aug 2, 2019. retrieved August 11, 2019 https://www.youtube.com/watch?v=D9Qa1f29diE

[1097] Ibid (2 min and 20 sec)

[1098] Ibid (3 min and 50 sec)

[1099] Ibid (4 min and 40 sec)

Charitable contributions may be lower in Democratic-leaning counties, but residents support the social safety net through higher taxes.[1100] Democrat-run cities and states are losing people due to higher taxes. [1101] These higher-tax municipalities don't have the best services or infrastructure,[1102] and they generally have higher tax rates too.[1103] As unemployment and tax rates go up, citizens start to move out of these places.[1104] When the unemployment rate goes up in these municipalities, crime goes up.[1105] The unemployment rates go up because a lot of the private-sector, job-producing businesses leave as a result of all of the above. In these areas, the educational system and health care are generally not as good.[1106]

Another thing I would like to point out is grocery stores operate on a low-profit margin,[1107] so if you tax them heavier in a community with a Democrat-influenced government versus a

---

[1100] Paul Sullivan. Nov. 3, 2018. Wealth Matters How Political Ideology Influences Charitable Giving. New York Times. retrieved September 14, 2020 https://www.nytimes.com/2018/11/03/your-money/republicans-democrats-charity-philanthropy.html

[1101] Steven Malanga. Winter 2019. It's not just high taxes; it's lousy services, too. The Real Problem with the Blue-State Model. City Journal. https://www.city-journal.org/democrat-states-midterms retrieved September 14, 2020

[1102] Ibid.

[1103] Ibid.

[1104] Ibid.

[1105] Pooja Gupta. February 14, 2016. Journalists Resource Research on Todays News Topics. How unemployment affects serious property crime: A national case-control study. retrieved September 14, 2020 https://journalistsresource.org/studies/government/criminal-justice/unemployment-property-crime-burglary/

[1106] Robert Puentes. January 20, 2015. Brookings OP-Ed. Why Infrastructure Matters: Rotten Roads, Bum Economy. retrieved September 14, 2020 https://www.brookings.edu/opinions/why-infrastructure-matters-rotten-roads-bum-economy/

[1107] Barbara Bean-Mellinger. Updated November 14, 2018. Small Business Finances & Taxes Gross Profit Margin Chron. retrieved November 29, 2020 .What Is the Profit Margin for a Supermarket? https://smallbusiness.chron.com/profit-margin-supermarket-22467.html

Republican-influenced one, they will leave and go somewhere else where they are not taxed so heavily. Processed, unhealthy foods sell for less money than fresh produce and nice lean healthy cuts of meat and dairy,[1108] so places with food deserts (meaning grocery stores lacking produce and other nutritious food choices) sell a lot more of it in local grocery stores. These places happen to be where the people are more likely to be black or Latino or in rural areas where the people are also more likely to be poor.[1109] This is a reason why generally these pockets in the black community that are food deserts have poorer health outcomes and lower life expectancies.[1110]

These are reasons for so many of the pockets in black America with really bad neighborhoods. Since the black community is needier, it is understandable that they would vote as Democrats for the safety net, but you have to remember there are benefits to voting Republican,[1111] and they are contrary to the above negatives of Democratic Party political influence, so you have to learn to play both sides of the court to get the benefits of both. My question to the black community is: Why keep voting a straight Democratic ticket every election? The fact that the black community has not

---

[1108] Derek Headey and Harold Alderman. July 23, 2019. The high price of healthy food ... and the low price of unhealthy food. International Comparison Program. retrieved November 29, 2020 https://blogs.worldbank.org/opendata/high-price-healthy-food-and-low-price-unhealthy-food

[1109] Whitney Sherman. John Hopkins Magazine. Nutrition Research Shows Food Deserts More Abundant In Minority Neighborhoods. retrieved November 29, 2020 https://hub.jhu.edu/magazine/2014/spring/racial-food-deserts.

[1110] Samantha Olson. Mar 30, 2015. Vitality Grocery Stores Sell Processed Foods High In Fat, Sugar, And Salt More Than Anything Else. Medical Daily. retrieved November 29, 2020 https://www.medicaldaily.com/grocery-stores-sell-processed-foods-high-fat-sugar-and-salt-more-anything-else-327580

[1111] Mark Biernat. Reasons to Vote Republican. retrieved September 15, 2020 https://political-economy.com/reasons-to-vote-republican/

been very good at it is fine with the left because it helps them to accomplish their cause.

The Republican Party has traditionally served the black community much better in the past, and I think on a lot of issues they would today.

There are a lot of talented black people who want to make a difference in the political area in their community, but they always try and do it on a Democratic platform. A Republican platform has some advantages that a Democratic one doesn't have, even for blacks. Again although I am not attempting to endorse either of the two, I think the Republican Party has more pros than the Democrat party does. Both parties have their pros and cons, but the black community still sees the Republican platform as racist and maybe even white supremist and the Democratic platform as more caring and giving. But if you do your research and dig a little deeper, you will find that is not always the case for either of the two parties.

Therefore, it may not be a good idea to recommend that black people go from voting for the Democratic Party 90 percent of the time, which has been the general consensus for the past 50 or 60 years to supporting the Republican Party 90 percent of the time. If you are black and you want to support the Republican Party and Conservative causes, you absolutely can, but do your research on each candidate and each issue. If you did some research on some more Liberal Democratic political counterparts, you might change your mind on some of them as well. Determine where their issues will have you in the next few generations or maybe in just the next few years. Find out who they have allegiance to. This is something that black people did not really do while supporting the Democratic Party for so many years, and it turned out that some of their policies were not really good either.

Progressives, Leftists, and Black America

What you have to remember is both democrats and republicans are politicians with campaigns that have to be financed and contributors that they have to support to run their campaigns so any representative from either party could take you for a ride with empty unfulfilled promises and in the end their contributors and them where who benefited not you. But the democrats just seem to have some more sinister elements among their ranks with some more sinister ways to accomplish their goals.

However, I think as a general rule some of the best leadership for the country on all levels, local, city, state and federal but of course with plenty of exceptions seems to be from the Republican party. This is not an endorsement for the republican party nor does it imply that all democrats are bad leaders. I am just telling you what I am seeing.

According to Xi Van Fleet[1112] a writer for The Daily Caller[1113] who was interviewed on the Fox Business Journal who is a senior fellow of the 1776 Project[1114] and is a survivor of Mao Zedong's communist cultural revolution[1115] that changed China where she is from but later immigrated to the United States to escape the regime said "the Democrats have already become a Communist party"[1116]. Today's democrat party at least certain elements of it have morphed into a different animal than the one our parents and for some our grandparents voted for and catered to in the 70's and 80's. Today they have some different intents, goals, and visions for American

---

[1112] Fox Business Democrats Have Already Become A Communist Party: Maoist China Survivor. Retrieved July 15, 2023 https://www.youtube.com/watch?v=ULEJJ11obM4

[1113] Ibid

[1114] Ibid

[1115] Ibid

[1116] Ibid

society, and they have some different ways of achieving these goals that are not always conventional, than the democrats of years ago. From the looks of things many of today's democrats are unrecognizable from their predecessors of years gone by.

There are a lot of democrats with conservative values, lifestyles and morals of all races and ethnicities, to include blacks.[1117] Blacks, according to an article from the UAB News rarely associate politics with lifestyle, morals, or values,[1118] while whites more frequently do[1119] and it is incorrect to assume that unlimited welfare assistance and an open lifestyle are appropriate to the black conservative[1120]. If you are a black conservative or a conservative of any other ethnicity and you still vote democrat on a lot of issues because they support affirmative action or DEI as an example and some other programs that lots of blacks have disproportionately depended on, you should consider Xi Van Fleets comment and ask yourself do you really want to live under a regime like she did in China here in America?

If it were up to most conservative republicans especially ultra conservative right leaning ones this would not be a threat to America.

My church had literature that compared what the Republican Party stood for VS what the Democrat party stood for from their websites and what the Republican Party stands for just seemed closer to biblical values that a Christian would agree with they just seemed more moral and to me some of the ones the Republican Party stood for just seemed to make a lot more sense.

[1117] Jim Bakken Many black people are conservative, but not the way most think UAB News April 5, 2013 retrieved September 4, 2023 https://www.uab.edu/news/research/item/3336-many-black-people-are-conservative-but-not-the-way-most-think

[1118] Ibid

[1119] Ibid

[1120] Ibid

18.

The Klan's Days Are Numbered

The KKK today counts between 5,000 and 8,000 members nationwide.[1121] Back in the 1920s, when cities across the South were erecting monuments to Confederate generals, the Klan had four million members.[1122] However, there has been an impressive decrease, and to top it off, the population of the US increased significantly since the 1920s. Back then, the Klan constituted about 4 percent of the entire US population,[1123] keeping in mind that there were sympathizers who are not members and still are today, probably lots of them, during both time frames. Now, KKK or Ku Klux Klan membership is at an all-time low. That would make them less than 0.003 percent of the population, even on the higher end of the US white population if you do the math.[1124] It's a very small minority of real bad people. Klansmen are usually Conservatives, but they are a very small, almost microscopic, minority of them

---

[1121] Southern Poverty Law Center. Ku Klux Klan. retrieved May 12, 2020 https://www.splcenter.org/fighting-hate/extremist-files/ideology/ku-klux-klan

[1122] Ibid.

[1123] *KKK in the 1920s* Hiram Wesley Evans, "The Klan's Fight for Americanism. https://www.americanyawp.com/reader/22-the-new-era/hiram-evans-on-the-the-klans-fight-for-americanism-1926/ retrieved May 12, 2020.

[1124] United States Census Bureau. Quick Facts United States. retrieved June 14, 2020 https://www.census.gov/quickfacts/fact/table/US/IPE120218

as you can see, with some more sympathizers, but that is about it. Neither they nor their sympathizers by far represent the vast majority of Conservatives, and it is unfair to categorize all of them as such or as white supremist unless they are Klansman and maybe some of their sympathizers. The Great Depression did not happen until 1929, and it ended in roughly 1936, although some will say 1941.[1125] During this time period, in America there were political and economic changes going on that would make people want to look for a scapegoat for their condition.[1126] They look for anything to blame and a reason to do it, like even another group of people who had nothing to do with their predicament.[1127] During this period, Klan membership stayed between two and five million.[1128]

Today with Instagram, YouTube, cell phones with recording cameras, copcam devices that you could attach on a piece of clothing, you could easily record a cross burning or a lynching from start to finish and post it on all types of social media. If that happened, you would have protests and riots all over America, depending on how it was publicized on social media and on what action was taken against the Klan. If that happened, the Klan would look bad to the whole world, and it would make America look bad because it would make a bad impression to the rest of the world about America. The Klan would have to hide in very wooded or secluded areas far away from visibility to get away with what they did years ago because even small towns have surveillance cameras on every corner and with

---

[1125] History. Great Depression History. History.com editors. retrieved June 14, 2020 https://www.history.com/topics/great-depression/great-depression-history

[1126] Ibid.

[1127] Becky Little. Updated Feb 19, 2019. Original: Jan 15, 2019. retrieved May 15, 2020. How Prohibition Fueled the Rise of the Ku Klux Klan. https://www.history.com/news/kkk-terror-during-prohibition

[1128] Ibid.

Google Images and drones with built-in cameras with the ability to gather drone footage, you could spot any place frequented by cross-burning Klansmen. Their activity could be broken up quickly. Their methods of doing things cannot be applied in today's world. They are like Blockbuster, which was forced to go out of existence when Netflix came into existence, unless they come up with some other strategy to maintain white supremacy like Planned Parenthood (endorsed by progressives), which has murdered millions of little black babies over the course of its existence. Even if they were not caught on a surveillance camera, forensic technology is so advanced you could find a scene and decipher evidence from it a lot better than you could years ago, even if it were done miles away from nowhere with Google Images and satellite technology and rescue helicopters, which would lead to convictions. Black people are different now, and they have rights, unlike the pre–civil rights era Negro. American demographics have changed. How are they going to deal with other non-white groups such as Hispanics and Asians? If they deal with them in a way that offends too many of these groups, they will be left with different and probably worse consequences than if they do them to blacks.

The left is doing more now to divide and keep animosity going among ethnicities, and black people are a lot worse off now than the Klan could have ever made them since the leftist movement began, so to sum this one up, you probably don't need the Klan anymore to finish the job they started. The Klan was probably created out of the mentality of a fifth grader, at best a high school dropout. Planned Parenthood was created by someone with a lot higher degree of intelligence and education.[1129] It was a very ingenious strategy that

---

[1129] Margaret Sanger Biography 1879—1966. UPDATED: MAR 2, 2020.ORIGINAL: APR 27, 2017. https://www.biography.com/activist/margaret-sanger

The Klan's Days Are Numbered

Margaret Sanger as a very liberal/progressive feminist implemented, an idea that was very radically leftist and was invented for the purpose of ethnic cleansing or progressively phasing black people out of existence.

The Klan was created for a different time, place, and society, most likely by ultraconservative white southerners of that time and place as a very simple and straightforward way for maintaining white supremacy. The Klan is probably not a group that most conservative whites would have even sympathized with years ago, I don't think, so I am not saying that most of them were that racist back then. Most of them (Klansmen) were Democrats and former Confederates.[1130] The Klan is something that morphed out of the concerns, fears, and ignorance of ultraconservative white southerners of the time, which ultimately became a monster that did not represent the face of conservatism nationally at the time and certainly not today.

Just 30 or maybe 40 years ago was the age of Blockbuster. In a few years afterward, we went to Netflix. Just because we have Netflix does not mean we are out of the entertainment business; to the contrary, it makes entertainment easier to access than with Blockbuster. Likewise, we are not out of the racism business or racial division business either; some left-leaning and progressive policies and causes have just made it more effective and easier to implement.

It says on the Klan's website that one of their goals was white supremacy. With the way so many progressive policies and causes have affected black America, you may not need the Klan for that.

[1130] Retro Report in The Classroom 1924 Democratic Convention: Immigrants vs the Ku Klux Klan retrieved May 29, 2022 https://www.retroreport.org/education/video/1924-democratic-convention-immigrants-vs-the-ku-klux-klan (2 min and 12 sec)

19.

Racial Biases on Both Sides and Does It Matter?

Before going into this next section, most people, regardless of race or ethnicity or whether they are Liberal, Conservative, Democrat, or Republican, left or right, and even Progressive are not racist, and they don't really have any biases that are big enough to matter or at least not openly, but some do. What is being presented to you in this chapter again does not apply to most Conservatives.

Switching political platforms does not change any biases you may have previously had about race whether they were traditional generationally held beliefs or recently acquired ones. You can carry biases with you regardless as to what platform you stand on, including political ones too. You don't have to be white to have a negative bias about another group of people that if acted on can result in some negative consequences; you can be anything, even black. Yes, blacks can and do have their racial biases toward other groups too, but that is a whole other book.

The point here is that a Conservative or a Republican or a Democrat whether Liberal or Progressive may not necessarily always have the black community's best interest at heart either, so black people will have to learn to use the political process for what they can get from it. The rest will have to come from the economic, social, and political infrastructure of the African American community and its leadership.

The podcaster who interviewed the Grenadian woman earlier in the book, who grew up in Brooklyn, New York, but later moved to the suburbs, identifies himself as a Libertarian,[1131] who certainly seems to approve of, endorse, and maybe even support the work and the cause of the Conservative movement. I was agreeing with him on a lot, but even he made some statements in some of his podcasts about blacks and the condition of black America that offended me. This is another example of where someone who leans Conservative may still always have their biases against black people, even though I agreed with a lot of what he said about the black community. Even one or two biases like this can make a big difference for better or for worse about how you deal with a group of people. In spite of it all I think the Republican Party and the Conservative movement still has a lot to offer the masses of the black community, and this one man just had I think rather one or two negative beliefs about blacks and the black community some of the things he said about the black community, but he is just one man.

It may seem as if I am being even a little critical of right-leaning Conservatives at times in the book, but I am doing it to make a comparison and a contrast to prove how much worse the progressive left policies and causes have been against the black community over the past 50 years or so, compared with most right-leaning Conservatives from the end of the Civil War to the present and also to make you think about how some progressive leftists may really feel about blacks and how much regard they have for them if some Conservatives feel this way.

[1131] Southern Poverty Law Center. Stefan Molineux. retrieved November 27, 2021. https://www.splcenter.org/fighting-hate/extremist-files/individual/stefan-molyneux

The Atlanta Blackstar did a ranking of the 10 most racist states in America, and of them, all but one were southern states. Their site seemed to be based mostly on the prevalence of hate crimes, hate organizations, and their aggressiveness with recruiting and maybe a few other factors.[1132] The World Population Review website conducted an interesting study to determine how racist an area is. It isn't something that can be measured by polls, and surveys can be used, but they aren't always accurate. Other data, such as instances of hate crimes and hate speech, can also be used to determine where racism is most prevalent, but they still may not be a very accurate determination of how racist an area is. It's difficult to measure what regions in the US are the most racist, but an apartment search website called Abodo was used to determine which parts of the country were the most racist.[1133, 1134] They used software that track millions of tweets posted over a two-year period.[1135] They filtered out tweets with racial slurs, and they kept an indicator on a map of where the slurs occurred, and the places with the most slurs were most likely the most racist.[1136] I thought that this was an interesting barometer of determining how racially biased one can be because it uses some different indicators to make the determination and these ones are ones that you have no way of knowing about. Keeping in mind

---

[1132] A Moore. Top 10 Most Racist States in America. May 14, 2014. *The Atlanta Black Star*. retrieved September 25, 2019 https://atlantablackstaratlantaBlackstar.com/2014/05/14/top-10-racist-states-america/7/

[1133] World Population Review. The Most Racist States 2019. retrieved June 16, 2019 http://worldpopulationreview.com/states/most-racist-states

[1134] Christopher Spata Complex Map Shows Which States Send the Most Racist Tweets retrieved June 3, 2022 https://www.complex.com/life/2016/03/map-of-racist-tweets-by-state

[1135] World Population Review. The Most Racist States 2019. retrieved June 16, 2019 http://worldpopulationreview.com/states/most-racist-states

[1136] Ibid.

Twitter's subscriber and user demographics may have changed since Elon Musk's takeover of Twitter naming it "X".

West Virginia was discovered to be the most racist state, followed by Maryland and Louisiana, which were also found to be some of the most racist states based on racial slurs used on then Twitter but now "X". Based on this data from Google, the study found that the most racist regions in the United States are the rural Northeast and South.[1137] Searches containing racial slurs were most prevalent in the Appalachian region from Georgia to New York and Vermont.[1138] The highest concentrations of racist searches were discovered in areas along the Gulf Coast, the Upper Peninsula region in Michigan, and the state of Ohio.[1139] The southern half of the Appalachians and the Gulf Coast are considered to be in the South, but not the northern half of the Appalachians, Ohio, Maryland, or the Upper Peninsula of Michigan.[1140] These findings aren't an official ranking of states from the least to the most racist, but they give some idea of areas in the nation where racism may occur.[1141]

Despite lots of Democratic voter support, these places still tend to get a lot of Republican support during elections and/or they tend to more often be Conservative. According to World Population Review, the states of the northern half of the Appalachians tend to either be less Conservative than average, more Liberal than average, or about average, and nearly all of those in the southern Appalachians and the Gulf Coast tend to be either Conservative

---

[1137] Ibid.

[1138] Ibid.

[1139] Ibid.

[1140] Ibid.

[1141] World Population Review. The Most Racist States 2019. retrieved June 16, 2019 http://worldpopulationreview.com/states/most-racist-states

or very Conservative.[1142] The article does not make a distinction between rural or urban areas. The South and the Midwest are generally more Conservative than the East Coast and the West Coast.[1143] Southern and midwestern Republicans tend to be the most Conservative Americans, and West Coast and New England Democrats tend to be the most Liberal Americans, with lots of exceptions to this rule of course from all over the country.[1144]

According to CityLab.com, Conservatives outnumber Liberals by 30 percent in both Ohio and Michigan.[1145] Conservatives, on the other hand, are more likely to be blue-collar workers and perform work that is not as knowledge-based or creative but of course with lots of exceptions to this rule.[1146] States and regions of the country that are less affluent, again with lots of exceptions, are more likely to be Conservative.[1147] Conservativism, again of course with lots of exceptions, tends to be correlated with regions of America that are more likely to have a higher percentage of its citizens living in a rural region.[1148] The Appalachian region has a higher percentage of people without high school diplomas or college degrees of any type

---

[1142] World Population Review. Most Conservative States 2020. retrieved April 5, 2020 https://worldpopulationreview.com/states/most-conservative-states/

[1143] Mugambi Jouet. Exceptional America: What Divides Americans from the World and from Each Other. p. 29. Pages displayed by permission of Univ of California Press. Copyright.

[1144] Richard Florida. March 29, 2011. The Atlantic Politics. The Conservative States of America. retrieved https://www.theatlantic.com/politics/archive/2011/03/the-conservative-states-of-america/71827/

[1145] Richard Florida. February 9, 2017. The (Still) Conservative States of America. CityLab. retrieved November 27, 2019 https://www.citylab.com/equity/2017/02/the-still-conservative-states-of-america/515592/

[1146] Ibid.

[1147] Ibid

[1148] Ibid.

and more blue-collar workers than the average part of the country.[1149] According to CityLab's illustrations and data, the South is in the same position as the Appalachian region of America.[1150] Maryland and Louisiana really stood out as being in that position on the same map, as well.

Another question to pose here is how many of these tweeters were Conservative, how many were Republicans, how many were Liberals, and how many were Democrats; how many are Progressives, some of those numbers may be surprising. According to a Pew Research study, most tweeters are young, and they tend to be Democrats.[1151] Most of them rarely tweet, but the ones who do, tweet often.[1152] According to another Pew Research study, about 22 percent of adult Americans use Twitter,[1153] and those who do are less likely to identify as very Conservative; this may have changed since its takeover by Musk. Another question to pose is how many of these racist tweets were from more liberal Democrats and how progressive-minded are they even in a part of the country that is predominantly Conservative or is at least Conservative leaning? And still another question to pose is what were Progressive Liberals

---

[1149] Appalachian Regional Commission. Development and Progress of the Appalachian Higher Education Network. https://www.arc.gov/publications/DevelopmentandProgressofAHENetwork.asp retrieved November 27, 2019.

[1150] Richard Florida. February 9, 2017. The (Still) Conservative States of America. CityLab. retrieved November 27, 2019 https://www.citylab.com/equity/2017/02/the-still-conservative-states-of-america/515592/

[1151] Stefan Wojcik and Adam Hughes. April 24, 2019. Sizing Up Twitter Users. The Pew Research Center Science and Technology. retrieved March 26, 2021 https://www.pewresearch.org/internet/2019/04/24/sizing-up-twitter-users/

[1152] Ibid.

[1153] Adam Hughes and Stefan Wojcik. Pew Research Center Fact Tank. 10 facts about Americans and Twitter. retrieved April 2, 2021 https://www.pewresearch.org/fact-tank/2019/08/02/10-facts-about-americans-and-twitter

saying about People of Color and in particular blacks from their tweets all across America?

Since Twitter now "X" is under new ownership and new management, they may be changing now about what you can say and who you can criticize and how you can criticize them on Twitter, but the racist tweets from former tweeters can just go to another social media platform and speak in the same manner if they are not allowed on Tweeter anymore.

20.

How Conservatives Have Changed

Here is an example of how being a Conservative has changed over the years. In 2017, statues of Confederate General Beauregard along with others were removed from New Orleans's Jackson square.[1154] This was done despite protests from probably ultra-Conservative white southerners holding confederate flags, also in opposition.[1155] In 1950, in one of the most Conservative places in America,[1156] this would never have been allowed to happen; even the authorities would not have allowed those statues to be removed. Any protester demanding the removal of Confederate heirlooms such as this the way it was done in 2017 would have been run away or arrested and jailed or maybe even lynched even a white one but especially a black one. This may not have even been allowed as late as 1990 or 2000, but by 2017, it happened even though, according to a Gallup poll from 2014, Republican views toward the Confederate flag had not really changed since 1992. This goes to show you that

---

[1154]   Richard Florida. February 9, 2017. The (Still) Conservative States of America. CityLab. retrieved November 27, 2019 https://www.citylab.com/equity/2017/02/the-still-conservative-states-of-america/515592/

[1155]   NOLA.com. Confederate monument supporters protest at statue of Confederate General P.G.T. Beauregard. Jan 17, 2016. retrieved April 22, 2020 https://www.youtube.com/watch?v=lDxBeXzookM

[1156]   Ibid.

what used to be considered Conservative in America has changed from what it was years ago. The display of Confederate flags is something I do not approve of, either, but I don't approve of a lot of other things that I have to live with. The point I am trying to make here is that they still have some interests that are not aligned with the best interests of blacks, but the ultra-Conservatives of today are different from the Conservatives of years ago.

But what difference does it make if they remove all of the Confederate flags and monuments in the South, but in the end, black people own and control nothing because they don't practice group economics and have no real power to make change? What difference does it make if poverty and inequality still continue to persist, which leaves them subject to a lot of other injustices? Some of that can be changed and some can't but could be dealt with a lot better if you had a community that could generate wealth.

You could even remove the names of all the military bases located in southern states that are named after confederate generals to people of color and women[1157] who were unsung heroes of the country's military past, but if you don't own and control anything and you are still dependent on government and other non-black institutions like the progressive left would like for blacks to be, it will be the equivalent to some of the really bad neighborhoods all over America that were in many cases at one time all white with streets previously named after whites and now having either a Martin Luther King Drive or a Barack Obama Street running through them but no opportunity or hope for economic

---

[1157] Army base renamed after Black veterans as military plans to stop honoring Confederates. Apr 27, 2023 6:30 PM EDT PBS News Hour retrieved April 30, 2023 https://www.pbs.org/newshour/show/army-base-renamed-after-black-veterans-as-military-plans-to-stop-honoring-confederates

advancement for its black citizens by its black citizens from any of the institutions on these streets.

With that said, I would like to present to you another thought. History has had both heroes and tyrants who did both wonderful things and horrible nightmarish things too and for humanity. These Confederate generals you could argue were America's tyrants, but you can learn from the tyrants in history just like you can from the heroes. If you explain who the heroes were and why they were heroes and who the tyrants were and why they were tyrants, you can learn what to do from the heroes and what not to do from the tyrants. The questions to ask here is, should we dismantle all of the Confederate heirlooms from history if we can learn from some of those tyrants who betrayed our country, because those who do not learn their history are doomed to repeat it? Again, they are indirectly using another black issue to accomplish another one of their goals of destroying American history and Western civilization.

These Progressives will not be done after they destroy the Confederacy by claiming that these generals were traitors[1158] to the Union and that they were racists and (most of them probably were), they want to destroy America and Western society, and they are doing it institution by institution and state by state, and here is where they can use another black cause to get rid of America's free market, capitalists, constitutional republic, which was built on Judeo-Christian values unlike Conservatives that blacks can now have to their advantage especially if they practice group economics once and for all until it is as communist or socialist as they can make it or totally both.

Conservatives have some other interests that are not aligned with the best interests of blacks, too, such as defending the monument

---

[1158] Ibid

Progressives, Leftists, and Black America

that was built in Houston, Texas, honoring Sam Houston and his defeat over Mexican forces in the Battle of the Alamo.[1159] Those things take time and money to build, and they should not be a priority for black Conservatives. His victory over Mexican forces did blacks no good; if anything, it was to the detriment of black people because it gave white southerners more land to grow cotton on in Texas, and for that they needed a lot more black slaves. This is, however, not a typical case scenario. The Tea Party is another example, since they have interests that now are not really priorities for blacks. Blacks have some more immediate concerns that the Tea Party is not addressing directly, even though they stand for some good things for us to take note of, maybe even as a group. White Conservatives have some more interests that may or may not be aligned with the best interests of blacks or that are not priorities for blacks. One of the Tea Party's interests is smaller government and lower taxes.[1160] Now as a small minority under a different set of circumstances, the smaller government that Conservatives are pushing for has some advantages for black people also, but only if you practice group economics. That is what blacks need to start doing first before they start working with the Tea Party. Some of their interest will be of little or no gain to the immediate concerns of blacks who are in the most dire situations.

I think it is safe to say Mississippi is a more Conservative state that has just changed the emblem on their flag from the old

---

[1159] John Tedesco. June 20, 2020. Updated: June 22, 2020. Armed activists at San Jacinto Monument vow to use force to defend Texas landmarks. retrieved September 11, 2020 https://www.houstonchronicle.com/news/houston-texas/texas/article/Armed-activists-at-San-Jacinto-Monument-vows-to-15354911.php

[1160] Kimberly Amadeo. Updated August 08, 2019. The Tea Party Movement, Its Economic Platform, and History The Balance. US Economy and News. retrieved March 22, 2020. https://www.thebalance.com/tea-party-movement-economic-platform-3305571

Confederate flag emblem to a kinder, gentler magnolia blossom.[1161] This is another sign that Conservatives either have or are changing because they have had a change of heart from the past for the better and again thanks to pressure from Progressive Liberals on shaming them on the state's racist legacy of chattel slavery.

Consider the following. In World War II in the Pacific theater of operations, the Japanese were axis forces since the bombing of Pearl Harbor, and America worked with Chinese forces[1162] at the detriment of the Japanese, even though the Chinese Communist Party, or CCP, founded in 1921[1163] but not officially taking over until 1949,[1164] taught some hateful things about the West. Even though all of them were not fans of America and the West, we had something to gain by working with them logistically to defeat the Japanese. In the European theater of operations, the Germans were axis forces, and America allied with Russia[1165] to stop Hitler from crushing them,[1166] even though they had a Communist Party that was very intolerant toward the West, like the CCP; working with the Russians as logistical allies in opposition to Hitler's forces resulted in a good outcome for America. If World War III were to

---

[1161] EMILY WAGSTER PETTUS. January 6, 2021. https://apnews.com/article/mississippi-bills-tate-reeves-afbe916946e4b38cb29469fe0ec7cdc4 New Mississippi flag without rebel symbol being put into law. retrieved January 24, 2021.

[1162] U.S.-China Cooperation During World War II. https://china.usembassy-china.org.cn/our-relationship/policy-history/io/shared-sacrifice-u-s-china-cooperation-world-war-ii/u-s-china-cooperation-world-war-ii/ retrieved July 15, 2021.

[1163] Issac Chotiner Reconsidering the History of the Chinese Communist Party The New Yorker July 23 2021 retrieved June 12, 2022 https://www.newyorker.com/news/q-and-a/reconsidering-the-history-of-the-chinese-communist-party

[1164] Ibid.

[1165] Office of the Historian. U.S.-Soviet Alliance, 1941–1945. https://history.state.gov/milestones/1937–1945/us-soviet retrieved July 15, 2021.

[1166] Ibid.

start today, Japan and Germany would almost certainly be allies, and Russia and China would be enemies, but that is because the geopolitical landscape has changed a lot since the Japanese bombed Pearl Harbor in 1941.

The cultural, social, political, and economic landscape of America has changed since then, and it has even changed since the civil rights movement. Now Conservative Republicans are making more sense, in a lot of cases, for blacks than Democrats, who are Progressives and/or left leaning especially if the support socialism or communism. It makes more since for blacks to support them now I think.

In 1898, Wilmington, North Carolina,[1167] had a similar incident happen to its black population for some similar reasons to the Greenwood District of Tulsa[1168] when it was destroyed in 1921. Back then, the insurrection against the black community was led by right-leaning Conservative white southerners[1169] who wanted to maintain white supremacy,[1170] and they were almost all Democrats.[1171] The Republican Party at the time was the left-leaning, liberal[1172] and

---

[1167] Toby Luckhurst. BBC News. Wilmington 1898: When white supremacists overthrew a US government. retrieved September 9, 2021. https://www.bbc.com/news/world-us-canada-55648011

[1168] Ibid.

[1169] Vox News YouTube Presentation. When white supremacists overthrew a US government. retrieved September 8, 2021. https://www.vox.com/2019/6/20/18693018/white-supremacists-overthrew-government-north-carolina

[1170] Toby Luckhurst. BBC News. Wilmington 1898: When white supremacists overthrew a US government. retrieved September 9, 2021. https://www.bbc.com/news/world-us-canada-55648011

[1171] Ibid.

[1172] Vox News YouTube Presentation. When white supremacists overthrew a US government. retrieved September 8, 2021. https://www.vox.com/2019/6/20/18693018/white-supremacists-overthrew-government-north-carolina

more progressive party[1173] and back then they joined with black business owners and politicians,[1174] black and white, who were always Republican to form the Populist Party[1175] so that poor or middle-income whites and blacks could enjoy prosperity.[1176] This angered Conservative white Democrats,[1177] who were right-leaning at the time,[1178] so the local white newspaper launched a smear campaign of misinformation against and about the black community.[1179] This triggered anger by the white community against the blacks, regardless of political affiliation or whether they were left- or right-leaning, resulting in the burning of the black newspapers headquarters,[1180] the winning of white fusionist back to the Democrat Party,[1181] and the domination of Wilmington by racist, right-leaning white Democrats[1182]. During this time in America, more progressive, left-leaning whites, who were from the Republican Party, were a better group for blacks to work with when you consider the circumstance the black community in America was in at the time. I think that now Conservative, right-leaning Republicans stand for

---

[1173] Ibid.

[1174] Toby Luckhurs.t BBC News. Wilmington 1898: When white supremacists overthrew a US government. retrieved September 9, 2021. https://www.bbc.com/news/world-us-canada-55648011

[1175] Ibid.

[1176] Ibid.

[1177] Ibid.

[1178] Ibid.

[1179] Ibid.

[1180] Ibid.

[1181] Ibid.

[1182] Vox News YouTube Presentation. When white supremacists overthrew a US government. retrieved September 8, 2021. https://www.vox.com/2019/6/20/18693018/white-supremacists-overthrew-government-north-carolina

some basic principles that have distinguished America as a uniquely prosperous, fortunate, more developed, and advanced nation, that is freer, with a higher standard of living than most other nations in the world for quite some time. These principles can now be used by black Americans to be more prosperous than they ever have been as a group and especially if they practice group economics like all other ethnic backgrounds do in America to a greater or lesser extent. Left-leaning Progressive Democrats are moving America in a direction away from this into something else that is not good, and it is going to turn America into something different for all Americans to something that it has never been before. The Democrats were not friends of the black community then, and they are not friends of the black community now (especially very left-leaning ones); it didn't seem to make a difference whether they were left-leaning as now or right-leaning as in the past. Today I would go with right-leaning Conservatives over left-leaning Progressive Liberals for blacks.

The white Conservative crowd historically has never had interest in black America, even though they have changed a lot since before the civil rights movement. In spite of that, they are still making a lot more sense about a lot of things that the left is not, and for that reason, I think they would be willing to work with the black community to save America from going socialist or even communist, among maybe several other things, which would be in the best interest of black Americans. Conservatives, who are now usually on the right, stand for some things that would be useful to the black community, maybe a lot of things.

A constituent or a group of conservative democrats along with some classical liberals years ago who wanted to maintain slavery and afterward wanted to maintain Jim Crow and sundown town laws and white supremacy who were particularly nasty to blacks are gone in spite of what some Progressives might think. I think today's Conservatives know this and that these days are never going to return in America, and they are fine with that. I don't think they have a problem with it. Now, today's right-leaning Conservatives and classical Liberals are trying to preserve basic things that America stands for such as First and Second Amendment rights and the free market and capitalism and the constitutional republic that made America a beacon of hope for the rest of the world to look up to.

The progressive movement and progressive countercultural Liberal activities actually had a lot of positives for the black community in the beginning and for many years later until the civil rights movement, when the results of some of its polices and causes started to turn ugly on the black community, but was this by design? Someone can be nice to you because they want something from you like the progressive movement has with blacks but not because they are your friends. Like you can go to a job that you are stuck with that you don't like every day, but you have to because you need the income from it, so you are friendly with the boss and coworkers for that reason only. Especially the boss and the management but sometimes some coworkers too.

In the case of the black community, Progressives were just a better group of whites for blacks to work with because traditional mainstream America could be so nasty to blacks, and they catered to the needs of the black community to get a certain effect even if it was destructive to America as a whole.

Also keep this in mind while reading this article. Before the Civil Rights Era but especially before the Civil War, some traditional conservatives, classical liberals, and progressives did not approve of the treatment of blacks because it was morally wrong treatment, so they took a stand with what was the most moral thing to do to stop immorality and promote justice for blacks. For this they were attacked and or/canceled from the social, cultural, religious, academic, political, and corporate circles of the day in very much the same way that pro-lifers, Trump supporters, Christians, and conservatives are today both on social media sites and all the same circles in society described above. This was usually a very small minority of whites, especially in the south and in particular before the Civil War. So not all whites were historically enemies of blacks either. Some whites probably didn't care since it didn't affect them some probably were just not really aware of the condition of blacks, some were aware and did every they could to keep it going for various immoral reasons and lies that were just not true and some didn't make an effort to stop this horrible institution until they were informed properly about it and Americans today are not being informed properly about what is happening to our nation and how it is being dismantled by the progressive left.

Years ago before integration, when some Conservative right-leaning whites and some classical Liberals who were both traditional about race relations before the civil rights movement and often identified as Democrats could at times be hostile to blacks, but you knew where to be and where not to be and where you could not to go because some Conservative right-leaning whites and classical Liberals back then, who were often Democrats, were not politically correct, they were honest about how they wanted to divide and cause bitterness and hatred and white supremacy and what would happen to you for crossing certain lines in society. Some were actual structures such as train tracks in a community. As long as you stayed on your side of the tracks, some of the traditional Conservatives back then let you know you could do whatever you wanted on your side such as having your own business community, your own for-profits, your own non-for-profits your own HBCUs, and a lot of others over there, but don't come over here mixing with us; if you do, there will be trouble. We want our children and grandchildren to be white, not a bunch of mixed-raced mulattos. These black communities experienced some entrepreneurial success stories and some other forms of success surrounded by some more traditional, more Conservative white communities, with some more sinister elements (such as Klansmen) unless you were the unfortunate victims of mob violence such as those blacks in Tulsa on June 30, 1921. They spelled it out for us, so we know what to do and what to expect in many cases, and usually nothing happened to you, so in a sense some of them were fair. With today's Progressives, who are politically correct with agendas covered in euphemisms, it is hard to see how much more destructive and racist their agenda with wokeness, critical race theory, white guilt, the 1619 History Project, the LBGTQ+ agenda, radical feminism, abortion, and a whole host of others is to society and blacks than the damage done to the black community during a time when America was more Conservative or traditional, especially over the past 50 or so years. Now right-leaning Conservatives, who used to be mean at times to blacks, and countercultural Liberals, who used to be the best whites for blacks to get behind, have now altered their purposes. They stand for some different things now and Progressives are not black people's friends now. Now it is better for black people to stand behind the Conservative Movement because I think it is a better choice for blacks now.

Southern Baptists are another example of a group who has been around since 1845 who are almost certainly bible belt conservatives because they will not change on some issues. They have a history of being terribly racist against blacks some even slaveholders[1183]. Now

---

[1183] Tom Gjetten Southern Baptist Seminary Confronts History Of Slaveholding And 'Deep Racism' DECEMBER 13, 2018 10:02 AM ET NPR retrieved June 21, 2024 https://www.npr.org/2018/12/13/676333342/southern-baptist-seminary-confronts-history-of-slaveholding-and-deep-racism

they have taken on liberal issues and dealt with them in a more progressive way which seems at least a little more tolerant and now some are calling them too progressive. If this were years ago, they would never have taken on these issues the way they are. They would never have formally apologized for slavery and their harsh treatment of blacks as they recently have. As of 2018 the SBC had about 907,000 African American members out of a total membership of 14.8 million, and roughly 3,900 predominantly Black congregations out of about 51,500.[1184] Asian American and Hispanic participation also increased, prompting Ronnie Floyd, president of the SBC's Executive Committee, to hail America's diversity as "an amazing opportunity" for future growth.[1185] Years ago none of these racial groups but in particular blacks would not have even been allowed to set foot in a southern Baptist church let a allow being a pastor of one or attending a convention. This is proof that they have made tremendous changes at least about race.

What black people need to realize is that blacks have traditionally had Conservative values such as many conservative whites had in the past and still do today, but all of the barriers that keep the two so segregated for so many years have been removed and now we should work with Conservative whites enough to help preserve the republic called America since now blacks can really benefit from it.

[1184] David Crary, Travis Loller And Peter Smith Published 1:48 PM CDT, June 11, 2021 AP News Racial tensions simmer as Southern Baptists hold key meeting retrieved June 21, 2024 https://apnews.com/article/racial-injustice-baptist-race-and-ethnicity-religion-900a3edd93c6ab0e7836a48751048c91

[1185] Ibid

21.

Marxists, Social Justice Warriors, and the Black Lives Matter Movement

During slavery and for some time afterward, black people in America were referred to as Negros; for another period in history, they were referred to as Colored, and then during the civil rights movement, they were referred to as blacks, so the terminology that was used to refer to black people became more palatable or better to digest emotionally or maybe a little less offending. Whites, on the other hand, have always been referred to as whites, which is fine, and blacks would have been fine for African Americans. Now out of political correctness, blacks are referred to as African Americans, which is a more polite term, but what has happened to black people as a result of the progressive leftist movement over the past 50 years has not been polite, and it has not been correct either.

A social justice education professor admitted social justice education (SJE) was developed in theory by Karl Marx.[1186] But this type of SJE is led by a communist in America.[1187] Now the government public schools from K–12 on through college are inserting social

---

[1186] William F. Jasper January 29, 2019 New America Social Justice Education: Creating Little SJW Marxists in the Classroom retrieved June 10, 2022 https://thenewamerican.com/social-justice-education-creating-little-sjw-marxists-in-the-classroom

[1187] Ibid.

justice education into their curriculums; even the private, Catholic, and Christian schools are doing it.[1188] It is much easier, more sensible, and safer to get your children out of these SJE schools than to try to get the curriculum and teachers out of the classrooms.[1189] This type of education will only teach black children from grades K–12 and in colleges and universities and years later into adulthood to feel that they are victims. It will encourage them to continue to demand more justice out of a feeling of victimhood. It will keep them distracted from the impact and power they could have if they practiced group economics in a free-market economy with capitalism in a constitutional republic like America and really built a community by them and for them and how much better off they would be instead of what the special interest groups are trying to create for them. Progressives plan to create more of a reason to redistribute wealth and resources to the underserved and the unjustly treated, and one way they can do it is to expand government institutions. This will in the end prevent them from developing a more independent and less vulnerable community, which will leave them in the end more dependent on other entities outside of the black community to provide for them. This in a sense leaves you in a state of helplessness, but it supports the progressive bottom line for having the social justice movement to begin with.

The Black Lives Matter movement is another cause that these social justice warriors can protest. All we would need is another Mike Brown incident or another George Floyd incident to happen and for the mainstream media, which is largely Liberal and leftist-influenced, to provide coverage of the violence, police beatings, bloodshed, emotion, drama, shootings, noise, and a whole other

---

[1188] Ibid.

[1189] Ibid.

host of bad things in a way that angers too many people all at the wrong time. After something socially happened that was really bad, with the right propaganda from the media[1190] sources, you would have a situation that was out of control. It could potentially get so bad that the president would have to activate the National Guard and between them and local, city, county, and state police forces, they could cordon off large sections of large cities and small towns all across America with concertina wire and military-style checkpoints after maybe a week or so of rioting. The Mick Brown incident in Ferguson, Missouri, had some crude similarities. Next, they would make thousands of arrests and put them on buses, cars, trains, or whatever transportation necessary to get them all in detention centers where they would be detained indefinitely. These youth now labeled as rebellious would probably be mostly white but disproportionately black, and they would all officially have criminal records after their detentions and arrests. In fact, depending on the media's spin on it, what is publicized, what is covered, and how it is covered—what is propagandized—could make the black youth and a lot more than those who were protesting, if they are black, look like criminal elements and worthy of elimination from society. What is interesting is that most of the BLM protestors now are white youth,[1191] and they could all very well be arrested en masse with all of the black youth to fill prisons in America for cheap labor as well. Another question to ask is, Will the BLM overseers come to their

---

[1190] Conservative Book Club The 3 Reasons Why Hollywood Is So Liberal August 7 2019 retrieved October 22, 2019 https://www.conservative bookclub.com/27700/featured-article/3-real-reasons-why-hollywood-is-so-liberal

[1191] Andrea Kaplan. Jun 18, 2020Ciscon PR Newswire. New Report Reveals Demographics of Black Lives Matter Protesters Shows Vast Majority Are White, Marched Within Their Own Cities. retrieved September 15, 2020. https://www.prnewswire.com/news-releases/new-report-reveals-demographics-of-black-lives-matter-protesters-shows-vast-majority-are-white-marched-within-their-own-cities-301079234.html

rescue if the cheap labor is really needed badly enough with the current or a future worse economic situation? It will be very interesting to see how the Black Lives Matter movement goes and what will happen as a result of it.

In the end, the black community will be worse off because so many more African Americans will be in prison, and when they get out, they will be permanent felons if there is no way to have their cases exonerated.

If it were up to Conservatives, the social justice education in grades K–12 that has been happening in America for a period of years that has produced all of these social justice warriors would not have happened, and they would not be in out colleges and universities—especially some of the most liberal ones, protesting about these things and starting commotion about things like this that wouldn't be an issue now.

The Black Lives Matter rioters and looters trashed large business districts, making them unfunctional, like the stores in a section of Chicago's Magnificent Mile.[1192] These small businesses bring in millions of dollars in revenue and hundreds, sometimes thousands, of jobs to a city. After all of the destruction and carnage is over, the government will have to come in with billions of dollars to restore this infrastructure, which only makes government bigger and increases society's dependence on government. This is just what they want to see. Not only that, but it will also lead to the destruction of lots of independent small businesses, even black ones. This is how the left

---

[1192] Paige Fry, Jeremy Gorner, Peter Nickeas, Gregory Pratt, Megan Crepeau, Stacy St. Clair, Claire Hao, William Lee, Dan Hinkel, Annie Sweeney, John Byrne, and Javonte Anderson. *Chicago Tribune.* Aug 10, 2020. Police shooting of Englewood man reignites political debate and looting as Mag Mile trashed, 13 cops injured, 2 people shot. retrieved Sept 4, 2020. https://www.chicagotribune.com/news/breaking/ct-chicago-downtown-looting-20200810–3zwa3b7zzrc5vdyb4qjqywrjvu-story.html

is using a black cause, which is only sometimes true with over-exaggerated publicity from a one-sided media that tugs at emotions of fear and anger to accomplish one of their causes and will, in the end, be bad for the black community. But they don't care how badly they affect the black community.

Through the BLM movement, protests and riots have been organized and established with the help of politically correct social justice warriors, in an attempt to overthrow the country. That way, the globalists can establish a global cause for which America is a big roadblock. Now they see another cause that they can use with a struggle that black people have been having that they can use to overthrow America when in reality they do not have America's best interest at heart either.

These globalists with their causes don't have the best interest of blacks at heart; neither do they have America's best interests at heart. They only have their own interest in BLM.[1193]

For a street uprising, is getting a lot of financial support in the form of pledges of millions of dollars.[1194]

A philanthropy foundation announced it will form a Black-Led-Movement fund aimed to raise millions for the Black Lives Matter coalition.[1195] In addition, millions in grants comes from a top Democratic Party donor who is a very liberal globalist through

---

[1193] Criton M. Zoakos, The Globalists Rethinking Globalism Why the World Hates America Could the root cause of soaring anti-Americanism lie in economic factors? May 20, 2003 retrieved August 16, 2019 https://www.theglobalist.com/why-the-world-hates-america/

[1194] MOVEMENT. Black Lives Matter Influence Watch. retrieved December 1, 2020. https://www.influencewatch.org/movement/black-lives-matter/

[1195] MOVEMENT. Black Lives Matter Influence Watch. retrieved December 1, 2020. https://www.influencewatch.org/movement/black-lives-matter/

his Open Society Foundations, as well as grant-making from the Center for American Progress.[1196]

Some the founders of socialism believed in the extermination of backward people.[1197] Karl Marx believed that classes too weak to master newly established changes in society by the establishment must be eradicated,[1198] as did his counterpart, Engels.[1199] Engels, a German philosopher, communist, social scientist, journalist, and businessman,[1200] believed that a people should take charge of their own evolution by good breeding or eugenics, and he was one of the masters of communism, which has lots of differences and overlaps with the policies of socialism.[1201] An interesting trend to notice is that tech businesses and companies are beginning to spring up in large cities and some smaller ones across America, and they have been around for a while in some of them. Black people tend to not be as tech savvy as people of other ethnicities, especially Whites and Asians.[1202] By this, I don't mean just mastering video games; I mean complete mastery of things, even some easier things that may

---

[1196] Valerie Richardson. Black Lives Matter Cashes in with $100 Million from Liberal Foundations. *The Washington Times*.August 16, 2016. retrieved October 13, 2019. https://www.washingtontimes.com/news/2016/aug/16/black-lives-matter-cashes-100-million-liberal-foundation

[1197] Hunt, Tristram. (2009). *The Frock-Coated Communist: The Revolutionary Life of Friedrich Engels*. Metropolitan/Henry Holt & Co. ISBN 9780805080254, OCLC 263983621.

[1198] Ibid.

[1199] Ibid.

[1200] Ibid.

[1201] Marian L. Tupy. Socialism's Obsession With Race. CAPX. 10 November 2017. Retrieved October 31, 2019. https://capx.co/socialisms-obsession-with-race/

[1202] J Slacker. Amid a Tech Revolution Black Americans are Still Being Left Behind. Blavity: News. July 20, 2018. retrieved October 10, 2019. https://blavity.com/amidst-a-tech-revolution-black-americans-are-still-being-lefbehind?category1=community-submitted

give you advantages such as advanced mastery of Microsoft Word, Excel, and PowerPoint applications and more advanced things such as knowledge and ability to apply computer languages, for example, C++ and JavaScript and their applications in computer science on both the introductory and advanced levels. This tech revolution in high-tech start-ups is another newly established change in society that is likely to accelerate,[1203] and it is one that can be used to eliminate certain groups from society. Most high-tech-savvy geniuses at least in Silicon Valley, which is the leader of all trends in the tech sector, tend to more than likely be young Liberals[1204] and supporters of the Democratic Party.[1205]

Remember the socialist movement in America is a leftist-backed one, and Margaret Sanger was a eugenicist. Two other statesmen in Europe, who were both socialists and eugenicists, believed that falling birthrates among the higher races would have to be dealt with, or a new social order would develop. The backward people of American society of today that they are referring to here could be inner-city black people labeled as thugs. A representative of the Socialist Workers Party founded the BLM movement.[1206] It will be interesting to see where they are planning to take it and what will happen as a result.

Social Darwinism has been used to justify racism, imperialism, and eugenics under the theory that certain races of people are higher

---

[1203] Julie Bort. The Business Insider. 57 startups that will boom in 2019, according to VCs. Feb 6, 2019. retrieved October 16, 2019. https://www.businessinsider.com/57-tech-startups-vc-insiders-say-will-boom-in-2019-2019-1

[1204] Farhad Manjoo. The New York Times. Silicon Valley's Politics: Liberal, with One Big Exception. Sept. 6, 2017. retrieved October 11, 2019. https://www.nytimes.com/2017/09/06/technology/silicon-valley-politics.html

[1205] Ibid.

[1206] Ibid.

up the evolutionary chain than others; therefore, the other races are not fit to govern themselves. Thus, through evolution and natural selection, some groups would have to be eliminated.[1207] In Darwin's theory, the dark-skinned races of sub-Saharan Africa are at the bottom and are the least evolved and most primitive of the human evolutionary chain.[1208] This would include black Americans. This is the atheistic theory that socialists base some of their justification for restructuring society,[1209] and it is from the left. Lots of Progressives believe in evolution. They are a lot more likely to believe in it than Conservatives, who are more likely to believe in the Creation.

If it had been up to more Conservatives, all of the college students who are politically correct and social justice warriors would not have ever gotten this far, or there would just be no such thing as SJWs or political correctness. If it were up to Conservatives, our colleges and universities and some other institutions now who are awash with them would be different.

What good is it going to do black youth if they protest and riot and loot in accordance with Black Lives Matter because of police brutality and systemic racism and some of their other causes when it is all for an entity that does not have their best interest at heart? What good is it when black people don't own and control anything, and after all of the looting and rioting is done, a lot of the businesses that employed black youth have been destroyed? Black people will

---

[1207] History.com Editors. Apr 6, 2018. Social Darwinism. retrieved October 13, 2019. https://www.history.com/topics/early-20th-century-us/social-darwinism

[1208] Phil Moore. What Your Biology Teacher Didn't Tell You About Charles Darwin. April 19, 2017. retrieved October 27, 2019. https://www.thegospelcoalition.org/article/what-your-biology-teacher-didnt-tell-you-about-charles-darwin/

[1209] Austin Anderson. The Dark Side of Darwinism Philosophy for the Many Literary Theory. Fall 2019. Posted on November 16, 2016. retrieved October 29, 2019. https://sites.williams.edu/engl-209-fall16/uncategorized/the-dark-side-of-darwinism/

have fewer jobs because their employers' operations have been dismantled. Not only that, many Black-owned businesses have been destroyed as a result of all this nonsense. When it is all over and the economic recovery is coming, blacks will have no power to put themselves back to work, and everyone that blacks depend on for jobs will be able to very discretely discriminate against them and exclude them from a lot of the new jobs and opportunities being created, so why protest and riot with BLM? That just makes it more appropriate for the government to come with their money and resources to rebuild everything the way they want it, but what you have to realize is they can be just as racist as the controllers of a free-market economy. This is just what the Marxists[1210][1211] who are affiliated with socialists[1212] on the left that are behind BLM want, and with the new racism that they will be instituting, black people will have less ability to change and no rights to protest against. The free-market economy that we still have with low taxes and small government where you can practice group economics and build a local economy with your financial institutions, your for-profit and nonprofit organizations, with the constitutional rights we have, is still the best route. With a setup like this, you can create a lot of your own employment and tailor a local society with no racism or police brutality without arrest quotas, without defunding the police and you could rid your community of a lot of other things that are

---

[1210] Tom Kertscher. July 21, 2020. Politifact. The Poytner Institute. Is Black Lives Matter a Marxist movement? Retrieved September 13, 2020. https://www.politifact.com/article/2020/jul/21/black-lives-matter-marxist-movement/

[1211] Yaron Steinbuch. June 25, 2020. Updated. *New York Post*. Black Lives Matter co-founder describes herself as 'trained Marxist.' retrieved September 13, 2020. https://nypost.com/2020/06/25/blm-co-founder-describes-herself-as-trained-marxist/

[1212] Neal Meyer. Jacobin Magazine. 04–15–2020. Why You Should Be a Socialist—and a Marxist. retrieved September 13, 2020. https://www.jacobinmag.com/2020/04/why-you-should-be-a-socialist-review-robinson

not good to have in it. At the same time, you are decreasing your dependence on government. This is what Conservatives, who are more likely to be on the right, stand for.

Another thing I wanted to discuss is social justice reform.[1213] These reforms can have incentives for blacks to continue to see themselves as a victimhood group, and if you continue to see yourself as such by the way the legalities of the reform is labeled and or worded and what it stands for, that encourages you to continue to accept support from it, be it monetary, political, or social. A certain type of reaction is expected on behalf of whoever is providing the reforms and the reaction either by the black community may be in the interest of whoever is sponsoring the reforms and not the black community's interest. An example of this is the riots and destruction that happened from all of the BLM riots and protests in cities and towns all across America. In the end, the black community could end up being steered down a dead-end street with no options but the ones that are being offered by the sponsors of BLM, which could very well leave the black community worse off in the long run than it's now or than it has ever been, in some respects. This is different from the reforms of the Civil Rights Acts of 1964 and 1967, which were negotiated by Dr. Martin Luther King with a Democratic presidential administration under President Johnson. These reforms did not support continuing to act and react as a victimhood group. They were designed to lift a lot of restrictions on blacks in America so that they could operate in society as everyone else did. For that, you cannot continue to have a victimhood mentality. By making too many of these reforms, it keeps a group too

---

[1213] TOBY WALTERS, ed. The Investopedia Team. Updated Sep 30, 2020. Social Justice. What is Social Justice? retrieved September 13, 2020. https://www.investopedia.com/terms/s/social-justice.asp

dependent on the entity that sponsored them so they can be used whenever needed to advance another agenda.

Too much preferential treatment with provisions for anything because you belong to a particular race, ethnic background, or group, and not because you are in need as an individual or because you are in a certain circumstance gives an incentive for an entire group to be dependent on the source of the rewarder of the provisions. However, it does not give incentive to empower oneself as a group. When you are no longer empowered as a group to improve your lot without outside help, you become a burden and a cause for total elimination from society. You then become the misfits, morons, and imbeciles that Margaret Sanger intended to rid from society through Planned Parenthood. This could be the plan for the remainder of the African American community.

According to an article in the WSJ, increasing minimum wage to $15 an hour would give raises to 27 million and raise 900,000 above the poverty line, but it would put 1,400,000 out of work.[1214] The question we need to be asking is: Who will it affect the most? According to another study by the Employment Policies Institute, it would affect black and Latino teens more in inner cities.[1215] It stated that it would make them vulnerable to idleness, unemployment, and unenrollment.[1216]

[1214] Ibid.

[1215] Mark Turner and Berna Demiralp. Johns Hopkins University. Higher Minimum Wages Harm Minority and Inner-City Teens. Employment Policies Institute. retrieved March 3, 2021. https://epionline.org/wpcontent/studies/turner_09-2000.pdf

[1216] Ibid.

According to another article from the American Enterprise Institute from 2013[1217] during a more progressive Obama administration, if minimum wage goes up, it would be disastrous for minorities[1218] but in particular black male youth,[1219] which at the time had an unemployment rate of 44.3%[1220] by making it even higher. At the time the white male teen unemployment rate was 18.9%,[1221] and for Hispanic teen males it was 26.4%;[1222] it did not give figures for Asian teen males. This progressive policy would push more African Americans and a disproportionate rate out of dependence on themselves for a job to some other source, and the government would be a good alternate route to take. This is another example of where blacks are being pushed out of society when they don't have the ability to employ themselves like other groups, and higher unemployment rates are a reason why. Raising minimum wage this high is another progressive policy.

I found an interesting article regarding Mubarak's legacy with Egyptian Coptic Christians.[1223] The author proves how politicians

---

[1217] Mark J. Perry AE Ideas December 11, 2013 retrieved January 10, 2023 Raising Minimum Wage Would Be Disastrous for Minorities, Especially Black Male Teens, Whose Jobless Rate Is Now 44.3% https://www.aei.org/carpe-diem/raising-minimum-wage-would-be-disastrous-for-minorities-especially-black-male-teens-whose-jobless-rate-is-now-44-3/

[1218] Ibid

[1219] Ibid

[1220] Ibid

[1221] Ibid

[1222] Ibid

[1223] Ramazan Kılınç. The Conversation. Mubarak's lasting legacy on Egypt's Coptic Christians. March 17, 2020. retrieved February 12, 2021. https://theconversation.com/mubaraks-lasting-legacy-on-egypts-coptic-christians-132835

can use marginalized minority groups for their own interests.[1224] Mubarak did this with Egyptian Coptic Christians, who have been discriminated against and marginalized in Egypt, but they received no more protections or safety measures as a result of his leadership.[1225] In 2015, the first Egyptian president to attend a Coptic Christian Mass did so, giving messages of equality to Egyptian Christians.[1226] Coptic Christians are about 10 percent of Egypt's population,[1227] but they received no more than 3 percent of senate seats under Mubarak's leadership[1228] versus none prior to this.[1229] After he was out of office, violence against Christians increased despite the increase in political seats in the Egyptian Parliament.[1230] In the end only the leaders of the Coptic Church benefited from it,[1231] and there was no more equality as a result for Coptic Christians compared with the Muslim majority afterward.[1232]

Black Lives Matter riots and protests are getting the effect they want on society, but when they are no long getting the effect that the left wants it to get, the organizers of this activity can change the narrative and stop organizing these protests and riots. If they could get a better reaction for their cause by supporting another cause, they would do it. In fact, after this, anybody could do whatever they wanted to the black community, or anything could happen to

---

[1224] Ibid.

[1225] Ibid.

[1226] Ibid.

[1227] Ibid.

[1228] Ibid.

[1229] Ibid.

[1230] Ibid.

[1231] Ibid.

[1232] Ibid.

black people, and they wouldn't care. If it were better for them to go to another group or cause just to get the reaction they want, black people would no long be of concern to them. Anything bad could happen to black people, and they wouldn't care anymore, or as the old saying goes: "Thrown under the bus," just as Egypt's Coptic Christian minority was.

22.

My Thoughts on Dr. Martin Luther King Jr.

This one is going to hit you like a deer in the headlights of a car. It did me, and it took me a while to comprehend and to digest. Get ready and hold on to your seats! Brace yourself for this one!

There is some evidence that supports the idea that Dr. Martin Luther King supported the theory of Democratic Socialism,[1233] [1234]more like Senator Bernie Sanders, who is a Democrat and a Liberal versus Conservative Republicans such as President Donald Trump. Conservatives generally did not support this theory. This may sound critical of King's legacy, but that came with some pros and cons for black Americans. One of the pros was the Civil Right Acts of 1964 and 1967, and one of the cons was complete integration with whites.

[1233] Lynn Parramore. Institute for New Economic Thinking. Was Martin Luther King a socialist? New book may surprise you. Jul 5, 2018. retrieved October 28, 2019. https://www.ineteconomics.org/perspectives/blog/was-martin-luther-king-a-socialist-new-book-may-surprise-you

[1234] Matthew Miles Goodrich January 15, 2018 The Forgotten Socialist History of Martin Luther King Jr. In These Times retrieved June 20, 2020 https://inthesetimes.com/article/martin-luther-king-jr-day-socialism-capitalism

King graduated from Morehouse College in 1948,[1235] at the age of 19[1236]. King seems to have followed in his father's footsteps by joining the ministry. He also studied theology at Crozer Theological Seminary in Pennsylvania.[1237] He was also read in the liberal theologian Reinhold Niebuhr.[1238] While in seminary, he read literature from both Mohandas Gandhi and Karl Marx.[1239] Mohandas Gandhi, though not a Christian, was a believer in non-violence as a way to make real societal changes, and so did Jesus. Karl Marx, on the other hand, was an atheist and had a different way of bringing forth societal change. His was through the socialist ideology of Marxism; the fathers of Socialism who were the same ones for Marxism and Communism, were all atheists.[1240]

The two schools, his Christian biblical theology as a pastor and maybe a form of socialism or Marxism or some of its concepts to solve the injustices that blacks in America were dealing with in his time, are two different philosophies and schools of thought for two different places in society for two different reasons. The reason why I say this is because the bible and the theology behind it is God breathed and is his absolute moral code of conduct by a perfectly righteous, sinless, loving, all-knowing and all-seeing God, who wants nothing but the best for his creation. Man. The

---

[1235] Peter Dreier, Truthout Jan. 20, 2014 Martin Luther King Was a Radical, Not a Saint New Jersey Environment Justice Alliance retrieved June 13, 2020 http://njeja.org/martin-luther-king-was-a-radical-not-a-saint

[1236] Ibid

[1237] Ibid.

[1238] Ibid.

[1239] Ibid.

[1240] Vladimir Ilyich Lenin. The Attitude of the Workers' Party to Religion. "Marxists Internet Archive." retrieved October 23, 2019. https://www.marxists.org/archive/lenin/works/1909/may/13.htm

tenets of Marxism which overlap in some ways with other schools of thought like socialism and communism were invented by the logical and sometimes illogical thought processes of men who were usually atheistic with sometimes selfish intentions. This is not to bash their inventors or the school of thought because depending on the capitalist and his motives capitalism can be just as atheistic, logical, illogical, and selfish with their endeavors too. I may be wrong on this one, but I think King tried to use both together to achieve an outcome that you cannot be led to the same conclusion by both, since there is no real connection or overlap between the two. He sort of achieved one thing, but he did not finish the job, so all of the restrictions from Jim Crow and sundown towns and Black Code laws and some of the cultural and social norms that put restrictions on blacks were mostly or in some cases completely done away with, but the communities where group economics is practiced and sustained where a group is not so dependent on the government and so many non-black institutions outside of it was not achieved.

While studying for his doctorate that he got from Boston University, he studied the writings of Reinhold Niebuhr, who was a liberal theologian.[1241] Reinhold Niebuhr was also one of President Obama's favorite theologians.[1242] He believed that ignoring people's needs while making all of the money you could as a society was wrong. It is rumored that Martin Luther King had some of his own personal interest in the civil rights movement.[1243] Karl Marx sup-

---

[1241] The Pew Research Center On Religion and Public Life. Obama's Favorite Theologian? A Short Course on Reinhold Niebuhr. May 9, 2004. retrieved October 27, 2019. https://www.pewforum.org/2009/05/04/obamas-favorite-theologian-a-short-course-on-reinhold-niebuhr/

[1242] Ibid.

[1243] Peter Dreier. Martin Luther King Was a Democratic Socialist. 01/18/2016. Updated Jan 18, 2017. retrieved November 3, 2019. https://www.huffpost.com/entry/martin-luther-king-was-a-democratic-socialist_b_9008990

ported Socialism and along with Fredrich Engels, wrote the famous Communist Manifesto.[1244]

King believed that American capitalism ultimately needs to give way on itself so that a better economic system could arise in its place.[1245] He was not a full-blown Marxist, though, because he believed that communism's materialism undermined that system, too.[1246] His worldview would be built on something different from consumption. "Communism forgets that life is individual. Capitalism forgets life is social," he said in a 1967 speech.[1247] Since communism requires a collective effort from everyone's wealth so that it can be distributed to make an entire system work for individuals, goals and ideas are not really strived for.[1248] Capitalism allows freedom of choice and thought, but since everything is not distributed equally, some have to work harder than others, and for that reason, they never have a social life from working so hard.[1249] What exactly does King mean by that?

Democrat Lyndon B. Johnson who was a proponent and active supporter of welfare stated specifically about black Americans: "I will give them enough to survive but not enough to make a difference." In other words, it was a plan to keep black America struggling

---

[1244] Karl Marx, Friedrich Engels (2004) [1848]. Manifesto of the Communist Party. Marxists Internet Archive. retrieved on 14 March 2015. Retrieved October 30, 2019 https://www.marxists.org/archive/marx/works/download/pdf/Manifesto.pdf

[1245] Douglas E. Thompson. Economic equality: Martin Luther King Jr.'s other dream. *The Washington Post* Democracy Dies in Darkness Made by History Perspective https://www.washingtonpost.com/outlook/2019/01/21/economic-equality-martin-luther-king-jrs-other-dream/?utm_term=.dd6ff95b2ab5 retrieved October 25, 2019.

[1246] Ibid.

[1247] Ibid.

[1248] Ibid.

[1249] Ibid.

and in poverty. His war on poverty has increased black dependence on government assistance benefits.[1250]

The Civil Rights Act of 1964 signed into law by President Lyndon B. Johnson basically amended all previous laws that allowed discrimination on the basis of race, color, religion, sex, or ethnic origin.[1251] This act and some other civil rights acts basically amended all of the Jim Crow laws, sundown town laws, Black Code laws, and other laws or regulations that seem to have been put in place mostly on local, state, city, and county laws to the wishes mostly at the time of their enactment by the wants of some more traditional right-leaning Conservative whites and some classical Liberals in an effort to keep things more traditional, which made it impossible for black people to congregate together or go or be wherever they wanted to be. In 1968, it was further amended to provide more protections.[1252] When this happened, I think with time it got rid of or eliminated the environment, the circumstances, or conditions that fostered or incentivized many of the cultural and social norms and beliefs that were exhibited with them. This one makes it next to impossible or very hard for a white real estate agent or landlord to deny a black person the right to rent a property or to raise the rents on black tenants to drive them out of business or a home. These Acts make it easier for blacks to conduct business and build an economic infrastructure. Blacks can have all the benefits of these amendments without the poverty of welfare if they practice group economics like

---

[1250] https://nationalcenter.org/project21/2014/01/08/lbjs-war-on-poverty-hurt-black-americans 08 Jan 2014. LBJ's "War on Poverty" Hurt Black Americans. Press Release Project 21 Black Leadership Network. retrieved November 1, 2019.

[1251] "Transcript of Civil Rights Act (1964)." https://www.senate.gov/artandhistory/history/resources/pdf/CivilRightsActOf1964.pdf

[1252] History of Fair Housing. retrieved May 15, 2020. https://www.hud.gov/program_offices/fair_housing_equal_opp/aboutfheo/history

those blacks did in Tulsa's Greenwood District, which they have not been doing.

With civil rights, this now makes it possible for the black community to create that economic infrastructure that is needed to provide some of its own employment with its own for-profit and nonprofit organizations in a system with small government and low taxation, which is what Conservatives stand for. With the power that you get from an economic infrastructure, you can create some more rights and freedom for yourself. That is what a small, oppressed minority needs that is in the middle of forces that are either cruel to them or that don't always have their best interest at heart, which again is what the Conservative right is standing for.

Martin Luther King fought for civil rights, too, which was a good thing, but he did not fight for the economic infrastructure that the black community needs. Black people have basically been sentenced to another 50 years of poverty and being second-class citizens as a result of integration, which was another cause that King fought for. It was the socialist who promoted school desegregation to redistribute wealth and to enlarge and expand universal public institutions. By integrating society as a whole, it would get them to this goal faster; it was not about making conditions better for the black community. This is what King fought for, and he took it a few steps farther with his own community by integrating blacks and whites together as part of the solution to end injustice and racism and promoting more equality, a miscalculation on his part. This was attempted without providing the wealth and resources needed to compete with whites. This was more in line with socialism, which was a Marxist philosophy, and it fits a leftist narrative.

As a pastor, you would think that King would have been more careful and more choosey over which socialist practices he would put into practice in his movement, since it is from an atheist perspective. King was probably impressed with the socialist concept because maybe he was impressed with Marx, and he decided to put it into practice in his movement. By doing this, he was taking it to a whole new level. When he accepted it as law, all other black leadership that was close to him in his inner and outer circles seemed to accept it and followed suit. Then its acceptance trickled down to lower echelons of black leadership and authority until it became acceptable as law to the whole black community as a way to operate and deal with other groups in society as well.

Leftists know this, so it made it much easier for them to work with the black community to get a big cause of changing America in their favor as much as possible. But the rest of America and all of its other ethnic backgrounds did not accept it like this, at least not to this extent to affect their wealth. The results have been unfair for the black community.

Socialism and communism had other founders, executers of their policies, and icons of their power, and most of them were atheists.[1253] Some of them probably were not, but if they were, they kept it quiet.

There were some positives that came from King's work. This was one of the largest or maybe the largest mobilization of black people in America together for a cause, called together by another black man for the purpose of the betterment of black people. This was a display of what could be done by black people if they really wanted to. In the past up until now, nothing like this was really allowed by the greater white society by the masses of Blacks for a black cause.

The bus boycotts in Birmingham were a demonstration to black people of how much influence they had through economics to

---

[1253] https://www.marxists.org/archive/lenin/works/1909/may/13.htm The Attitude of the Workers' Party to Religion. Vladimir Ilyich Lenin. "Marxists Internet Archive."

change things in their favor. It was also a demonstration to whites to change the way they had been mistreating blacks for so many years, or there could have real and maybe even dire economic consequences to pay. Just the economic impact on the public transportation system forced them to make these changes, or the entire system would have to be scaled back or shut down altogether.

Unless Democratic President Johnson had a change of heart about blacks from the statement he made above, he probably did not have the black community's best interest at heart either when he had the Civil Rights Act passed, but I think he did it anyway for fear of negative repercussions like more riots and boycotts. Too many boycotts might have negatively affected the economy and the media attention from the riots from around the world, which would not make America, supposedly the land of freedom and justice, look good. This was something else very positive that came from the King legacy because the Civil Rights Acts lifted so many restrictions that were imposed on blacks from just after the Civil War up until then.

Another reason why Martin Luther King's movement was good was because it went so big that it got global media coverage. Global coverage on TV, radio, newspapers, books, and whatever types of media that were used during that time had the same effect on America as media coverage had on South Africa during Apartheid, which resulted in international scrutiny, shaming, and condemnation of America for such traditionally racist practices on black people like Apartheid was on black South Africans.

Martin Luther King's civil rights movement did the equivalent of what Nelson Mandela's movement did for black South Africans by ending Apartheid, but it did not provide a strategy for an economic infrastructure like Booker T. Washington's Negro Business League or Dr. Claude Anderson's five tier system of acquiring power for an ethnic background. This was necessary for a group of people to be successful and competitive, and that should have been a key focus for the rest of black leadership to pick and finish where King's movement left off, which was a very good cause.

The Civil Rights Acts of 1964 and 1967 basically replaced some laws in America that made whites a privileged class with freedoms that blacks did not have.

A lot of good did happen for Blacks because of King's work and legacy! His work in and for the black community was a very good thing, but complete integration may not have been the best idea.

Martin Luther King had a dream that one day the country would live out the true meaning of its creed. That one day all men—black, white, Protestant, Catholic, Jew, and Gentile—would be judged by the content of their character, not the color of their skin. In an ideal world, yes, that is what you want, but since we don't live in an ideal world, that didn't really happen. According to one ranking, Martin Luther King was ranked the 12th most influential person of all times and in that same ranking, Jesus Christ of Nazareth was ranked the most influential.[1254] He made the list of Britannica's "The World's 100 Most Influential Leaders of All Times."[1255] He has had streets and schools and a number of other institutions named after him in his honor all across America. In spite of how much the rest of the world honored him, we still do not live in an ideal world where black people could just abandon many of its culture, business, and private sector institutions and attempt to completely integrate with whites without first establishing some common denominators that would make it possible. No leader has ever been able to usher in an ideal utopian world, so a

---

[1254] Emmy Wallin. TOP LISTS. The 25 Most Influential People of All Time. retrieved January 11, 2022. https://wealthygorilla.com/most-influential-people/

[1255] Emma McKenna, ed. *Britannica's The World's 100 Most Influential Leaders of All Times* P. 232.

person's outward appearance and other factors about them besides the content of their character still matters.

To blacks in America, Martin Luther King was the best thing that happened for them since the Emancipation Proclamation and President Lincoln. To most whites of today, Abraham Lincoln is praised for emancipating the slaves and for the role he played in preserving the Union, but outside of that, he was just like any other president. Even though Lincoln had his issues with blacks and was not for black-white equality, believing in the superiority of the white race, we can still give him credit for what he did.

King was such a dynamic figure in the black community that when he pushed for integration of all of society, all blacks just did it, without examining future consequences. And being a pastor gave him a lot of credibility in the black community; even racist eugenicist Margaret Sanger knew that, when she suggested hiring colored ministers to set the record straight to some of the black communities' more rebellious members that we don't want the word to get out that we want to exterminate them.[1256] According to a Pew Research survey, 94 percent of Blacks believe in the presence of a God as an absolute certainty or a fair certainty,[1257] whereas only 82 percent of whites,[1258] 85 percent of Hispanics,[1259] and 67 percent for Asians[1260] do, and the rest either were not sure, or they did not believe in God at all. I think the left realized

---

[1256] Kelssi Williams on July 11, 2016 Juicy Ecumenism Institute of Religion and Democracy's Blog Planned Parenthood, Margaret Sanger & Racism retrerived June 24, 2022 https://juicyecumenism.com/2016/07/11/planned-parenthood-margaret-sanger-racism

[1257] Pew Research Center on Religion and Public Life. Religious Landscape Study Racial and Ethnic Composition. retrieved January 12, 2021. https://www.pewforum.org/religious-landscape-study/racial-and-ethnic-composition/

[1258] Ibid.

[1259] Ibid.

[1260] Ibid.

this. But the rest of America did not idolize King like the black community did, so all of the concepts of integration that black people participated in and to the degree that they did were not practiced by the greater American society.

Since this was the case, black people abandoned a lot of institutions in their communities that gave them infrastructure and reliance. Next, they started patronizing the ones in the white community. An example of this is historically black hospitals that closed or were converted to something else or HBCUs of which some are now mostly white. Before, when they were mostly black, they had black think tanks with black intellectuals who could come together and put together an agenda for the greater black community.

All other communities in America did not take integrating to this level that they stopped patronizing the businesses infrastructure in their communities and started redistributing their wealth everywhere else outside of their communities. They did not buy integration to that extent because Martin Luther King was not idolized by the rest of America like he was by the black community.

He was an impressive figure to them, a well-honored and respected one by most. To get integration to work completely fairly for blacks, there would have to be terms to it laid out that you could not really force people to do. They would only do it if they had a heart to do it. For integration to work the way King wanted it to, he would have had to radically change the hearts and minds of the people that they literally had no color or ethnic preferences for people like them. His movement just did not make changes that radical. To make it work, you would have to redistribute more wealth and expand public institutions more, but the masses in America would not tolerate anything like this.

Again, the motive behind complete integration was a socialist agenda orchestrated by the left with no real intent to better the lot of black people. It was to redistribute wealth and expand public institutions, not for the betterment of black people, because integration was done on their terms, not King's. It got the left a lot closer to another cause while the black community suffered, but they didn't care what happened to the black community afterward. With time, the government could become more powerful than ever with supreme authority to take all rights from the citizenry but not necessarily becoming more just.[1261]

He pushed for reform of American capitalism because it was not working for the Negro at the time, but he was not a fan of government welfare programs[1262], and he was an advocate of working a job and living as a man's place in society[1263].

It appears as if Dr. King straddled the fence on the issue between socialism and capitalism and a free-market economy. In some sense, his attempt to accommodate both did not work in all circumstances, but it did under some. If he were around today, he may have had friends and enemies in both camps and probably on the left and the right with both Liberals and Conservatives; where he belonged in both camps might depend on the circumstances. As far as Liberals versus Conservatives, that would probably depend on the individual or, again, the circumstances. King, however, did make a lot of statements that would lead one to believe that maybe he was more of a Leftist, or if he wasn't, he certainly believed in a fair amount of their causes. Since he did express interest in Marxist literature in college,[1264] maybe it did

---

[1261] R.J. Rummel. *Death by Government*. New Brunswick, NJ: Transaction Publishers, 1994. Retrieved June 2, 2020. https://www.hawaii.edu/powerkills/NOTE1.HTM

[1262] Joel Schwartz City Journal Where Dr. King Went Wrong retrieved January 20, 2024 https://www.city-journal.org/article/where-dr-king-went-wrong

[1263] Ibid

[1264] Peter Dreier. Martin Luther King Was a Democratic Socialist. 01/18/2016. Updated Jan 18, 2017. retrieved October 23, 2019. https://www.huffpost.com/entry/martin-luther-king-was-a-democratic-socialist_b_9008990

influence his philosophical beliefs and consequently his actions and causes that he employed in his movement, but how much they influenced him we will never know.

Since King thought that American capitalism needed to be reformed, we may conclude that maybe it doesn't need to be eliminated like a socialist or a Marxist might believe, and if it is reformed enough until it works for blacks, it can exist, which would not be in the best interests of socialists or Marxists. The question to ask here is was he really a democrat socialist at all?

According to another article from History.com King claims that communism and Christianity are incompatible.[1265] Despite this belief he had lots of leftists and socialists in his circle of influencers[1266] to influence him for wealth redistribution for the poor and the rights of labor unions and full citizenship so blacks[1267] which were leftist causes. These are not all bad things, especially not full citizenship for blacks. Wealth redistribution rights of labor unions aren't either as long as the state doesn't dictate to the employer the terms of either. Whether King was a leftist or not his work in civil rights was a plus for blacks, despite the negatives which have resulted for years later now, so go figure. According to an article from the Huffington post he was a Democrat Socialist.[1268] According to a reputable source Medium a Christian publication the principles of Socialism are clearly and plainly

---

[1265] Sylvie Laurent Jacobin Magazine MLK Was an Exemplar of a Black Socialist Tradition retrieved January 20, 2024 https://jacobin.com/2023/04/martin-luther-king-jr-mlk-socialism-class-racial-justice-civil-rights-movement

[1266] Ibid

[1267] Ibid

[1268] Peter Dreier E.P. Clapp Distinguished Professor of Politics, Occidental College Huffington Post Martin Luther King Was A Democratic Socialist Jan 18, 2016, 10:56 AM EST | Updated Jan 18, 2017 https://www.huffpost.com/entry/martin-luther-king-was-a-democratic-socialist_b_9008990

condemned in Scripture[1269], while the basic principles of free-market Capitalism are affirmed[1270]. My question is as a pastor why would King allow so many unbiblical and maybe even ungodly influencers to influence him for his movement?

On the other hand, he makes some more statements in some of his letters to Coretta Scott King before they were married that would lead you to believe that he was indeed more of a socialist than capitalist.[1271] Whether this was where he stood or not, the best setup for blacks after the civil rights movement was the one that the black community had in the Greenwood district of Tulsa, Oklahoma, before the race riots, which was the inspiration of Booker T. Washington This community was burned it to the ground in June of 1921 and that has never really happened since anywhere in America. This is the form of capitalism that made black Americans back then prosperous, happy, and with limited need for government or progressive liberal philanthropic organizations of whites or their money. It seems as if King was not really a fan of this type of economic system. Right now one of the best or maybe even the best organizations in America to get the black community to some resemblance of that time is the Harvest Institute under the leadership of Dr. Claude Anderson, but for his plan to work you need the free-market economy and capitalism with the constitutional republic like America has traditionally been, not the socialist plan that the left has for America.

[1269] G.S. Muse Medium For The New Christian Intellectual The Bible VS Socialism retrieved January 20, 2024 https://medium.com/christian-intellectual/the-bible-vs-socialism de8af0c0c686#:~:text=As%20we%20will%20see%20in,free%2Dmarket%20Capitalism%20are%20affirmed.

[1270] Ibid

[1271] #MLK Global retrieved June 21, 2022 https://mlkglobal.org/2017/11/23/martin-luther-king-on-capitalism-in-his-own-words/

My Thoughts on Dr. Martin Luther King Jr.

Dr. King admitted at a meeting with the American Psychiatric Association in 1967 that even though he fought hard for integration, he still felt that he was integrating his people into a burning house because it had lost its moral vision.[1272] This gives the opinion that even King had his negative views on integration or he changed his mind at least some about it as time passes. Why was this never taken into consideration by the black community before so much integration had occurred and before it resulted in some negative consequences for them?

I know some people are probably asking: Wasn't Martin Luther King a social justice warrior—didn't he fight for justice? No, he was not a social justice warrior in the sense of what is happening today. He had a pure agenda with motives that were designed to make changes for a group of people who had historically been treated unfairly in America. As a result of his movement, a lot of those changes came about, and it changed a lot for the black community, forcing America to change to accommodate those changes. Today's social justice issues are centered on political correctness and the left's Socialist/Marxist agenda with destructive protests and riots, and they are not necessarily to make a more just and fair society—they were designed to destroy America as we know it and make America something different than it has ever been. Martin Luther King's work made it easier for black people who were not able to accomplish the American Dream before to now accomplish it. He wanted his people to be able to live in an America of reformed capitalism, one with a free market,[1273] the way it was and the way it has traditionally been so they could reap all of the

---

[1272] http://amsterdamnews.com/news/2017/jan/12/dr-martin-luther-king-jr-i-fear-i-am-integrating-m/ New York. New Amsterdam News. AUTODIDACT 17. 1/12/2017.

[1273] Dion Rabouin. MLK on economics: A brief primer. January 21, 2019. retrieved August 10, 2020. https://www.axios.com/martin-luther-king-jr-socialism-capitalism-b3c-be755-5b23-49ad-85ab-4bba84a45947.html

benefits of being first-class American citizens. He did not want full-blown socialism;[1274] it had nothing to do with political correctness or anybody else's cause. Later on in the movement, it was influenced by some other groups but never controlled by special interest groups such as the SJWs of Black Lives Matter. It involved a more grassroots approach with peaceful, nonviolent marches with no destructive looting or rioting, and there is a difference between the two.

Martin Luther King was not liked probably by a lot of traditionalists about race who were probably largely conservatives with a lot of classical liberals included. I say this because according to a Harris Poll taken the year of his assassination in 1968 his disapproval rating was at 75%.[1275] He was deemed a troublemaker[1276]. According to a gallop poll he was given an approval rating of 32%.[1277] I am saying this was probably typical of these groups before the Civil Rights Movement. Actually, Jesus was not popular either in his time he as a very controversial figure like King and in the end his death was ordered by higher authorities like King. It wasn't until after his death that he was really appreciated for what he did like King.[1278]

[1274] Ibid.

[1275] James C. Cobb When Martin Luther King Jr. was killed, he was less popular than Donald Trump is today. Published 12:05 April 4, 2018 Updated retrieved January 20, 2024 https://www.usatoday.com/story/opinion/2018/04/04/martin-luther-king-jr-50-years-assassination-donald-trump-disapproval-column/482242002/

[1276] Ibid

[1277] Micheal Harriot MLK is revered today but the real King would make white people uncomfortable Jan 20, 2022 retrieved https://www.theguardian.com/commentisfree/2022/jan/17/mlk-is-revered-today-but-the-real-king-would-make-white-people-uncomfortable

[1278] Jenn Hatfield Pew Research Center August 10. 2023 How public attitudes toward Martin Luther King Jr. have changed since the 1960s https://www.pewresearch.org/short-reads/2023/08/10/how-public-attitudes-toward-martin-luther-king-jr-have-changed-since-the-1960s/

My Thoughts on Dr. Martin Luther King Jr.

Some claimed King was a socialist[1279], some even claimed that he was a communist[1280] but say what you will about him, his work as a radical civil rights leader forced change in America for the better that I don't think would have ever happen otherwise and I give him all accolades for it.

[1279] Brandon M. Terry Plough Was Martin Luther King a Socialist? Retrieved January 27, 2024 https://www.plough.com/en/topics/justice/politics/was-martin-luther-king-a-socialist

[1280] Communism Stanford University The Martin Luther King Research and Institution Standard retrieved January 27, 2024 https://kinginstitute.stanford.edu/communism

23.

Loss of America's Moral Vision?

Despite all the traditional churchgoers of whom some historically could be very racist themselves, the church has produced countless champions for freedom and justice and civil rights champions for the black community who were both black and white like the Quakers anti-slavery society during slavery,[1281] and after slavery it produced such phenomenal civil rights leaders as Rev. Vernon Johns and Rev. Dr. Martin Luther King Jr., John Newton, William Wilberforce, Sojourner Truth, and others. It was so worth it to have that godly Christian perspective that Christianity and the Church and biblical scripture advocates for civil rights and against slavery that all men were created equal in the image of God, and they should be treated as such.

Progressive Liberals are changing the Church's agenda so that will never happen again for black Americans, at least not from the Church, thanks to liberal theology,[1282] which is sugar-coating or altering the absolute truths that the Bible presents on a number of different

---

[1281] University of York Borthwick Institute for Archives Quakers and slavery Race History retrieved November 18, 2002 https://www.york.ac.uk/borthwick/holdings/research-guides/race/quakers-and-slavery/#:~:text=The%20Society%20of%20Friends%20(known,in%20the%20Anti%2DSlavery%20Society.

[1282] Theological liberalism in America. Capital Ministries MEMBERS BIBLE STUDY. U.S. CAPITAL. September 11, 2017. https://capmin.org/theological-liberalism-in-america/

subjects and fronts that are plaguing American society today.[1283] This is what happens when communism takes a foothold in a nation.[1284]

Booker T. Washington endorsed the Christian religion,[1285] and he believed that reading the Bible as a guide to right living,[1286] leading to better health,[1287] and to be great it was a necessity.[1288] He believed that those who do important things in life read the Bible[1289] and are not ashamed to let the masses know.[1290] He believed that we should have reverence for the most high[1291] God of the Christian Bible. He believed our schools should be creating job creators and not job seekers.[1292] It should also be mentioned the he selected aspects of the Bible that were in line with his personal philosophy,[1293] so he may have

---

[1283] Ibid.

[1284] New York Times Magazine. Case Against Liberal Theology. October 21, 1984. retrieved October 25, 2021 https://www.nytimes.com/1984/10/21/magazine/the-case-against-liberation-theology.html

[1285] JONATHAN REAVIS. To See the Negro Saved: The Religious Pragmatism of Booker T. Washington. retrieved January 30, 2021. https://mospace.umsystem.edu/xmlui/bitstream/handle/10355/48993/Lucerna%202016%20Volume%2010%20-%208-Reavis.pdf?sequence=1&isAllowed=y

[1286] The American Minute with Bill Federer. retrieved January 30, 2021. Booker T. Washington "The Bible should be read as a daily guide to right living & positive Christian service." (constantcontact.com) *AmericanMinute.com*

[1287] Ibid.

[1288] Ibid.

[1289] Ibid.

[1290] Ibid.

[1291] Ibid.

[1292] Ibid.

[1293] JONATHAN REAVIS. To See the Negro Saved: The Religious Pragmatism of Booker T. Washington. retrieved January 30, 2021. https://mospace.umsystem.edu/xmlui/bitstream/handle/10355/48993/Lucerna%202016%20Volume%2010%20-%208-Reavis.pdf?sequence=1&isAllowed=y

done some picking and choosing of what Commandments to emphasize and honor and which ones not to, but at least he did recognize the Bible, the scriptures, Christianity's significance, and the divinity of Christ.

W.E.B. Du Bois, on the other hand, pointed out the similarities between the black man and Christ as being poor, despised of his fellow man, and his crucifixion was compared to lynching.[1294] He did, however, still believe the Church could transform racially, socially, and economically in a way to provide uplift because ministers could instill moral values and virtue.[1295] Du Bois seems to refer to it instead as a religious experience, but he himself had little if any religion,[1296] and he believed at least one time in his life that Jesus was a communist.[1297] He doesn't seem to endorse the divinity or the necessity of the Bible or Christianity as Washington did.

I think Washington's plan for the black community was superior to Du Bois's even though he believed the Church and the teachings of Christianity had some positive outcomes for the black community. Had Washington's philosophy been followed and resulted in Greenwood Districts or Little Africa's, as they called it back then, all across America, wherever there was a black community that practiced group economics, I think the black community would be a lot better off now. The Greenwood District of Tulsa, which was fostered by Washington, produced jobs, opportunity, interdependence, and self-productivity. Had districts like this flourished all over America for black people, this would have been the case for

---

[1294] 9 PBS special People & Ideas: W.E.B. Du Bois. Library of Congress source. retrieved January 30, 2021 https://www.pbs.org/wgbh/pages/frontline/godinamerica/people/web-du-bois.html

[1295] Ibid.

[1296] Ibid.

[1297] Ibid.

blacks. The NAACP, which is an organization joined and encouraged by Du Bois with its multiple chapters and branches across America, just could not do this for the black community. They fostered dependence on white businesses and government, which is not godly.

But the progressive left has an agenda for the Church to render it ineffective at performing its functions in society[1298] and to tailor it for its agenda.[1299] For years, the Church has been a staple or even one of the cornerstones of the black community. The most powerful force in the civil rights movement came from the church (Dr. Martin Luther King Jr.); thank God for him and his movement. He also mentioned that he believed he was leading his people into a burning house with integration because of the country's loss of moral vision. The reason why America has lost its moral compass, which is probably worse now resulting in greater moral decline than then, is because of sin.

With loss of moral vision comes sin, and you can enforce, endorse, or legislate for some of the best policies and fight for and win support for some of the best causes, but when everything is all said and done, man is still sinful. With all of his fears, negative irrational emotions and feelings, unforgiveness, bitterness and hatreds toward others, with all of his ulterior motives, hidden agendas and selfishness, he is still sinful. That is something no one has ever been able to change about man's nature and political correctness, equity of outcomes, critical race theory, moral relativism, compromised ethical values, or being woke doesn't change it either. I think maybe King realized this by the time he made the speech with the

---

[1298] R C Sproul The Liberal Agenda March 2006 retrieved July 2, 2022 https://www.ligonier.org/learn/articles/liberal-agenda

[1299] Ibid.

American Psychiatric Society of America where he refers to America as a burning house with a loss of moral vision after years of his work in the fight for civil rights and equality for his people.

According to an investigation by a Seattle entity, only 18 percent of the rioters arrested in Seattle's May 2020 riots after the death of George Floyd were black[1300]; the rest were not black, but the way they are filmed in a distorted way, especially in other towns and cities across America, it appears as if more of them across the country are black, which would justify the fears of whites more from footage that is really a lie—and only a third reported their home of record as Seattle.[1301] Other random looters around America, who do not necessarily appear to be affiliated with BLM, appear to be disproportionately black, which creates more fears of black youth in whites. It would be interesting to know the racial makeup of the out-of-town rioters. The May 2020 riots in Seattle are just another example of how the progressive lefts Marxists and Communists can use a black cause as much destruction on America as possible. And no, I don't condone and neither do I endorse the storming of the Capitol on January 6, 2021, probably by Conservatives who are just as idiotic as the BLM rioters and looters who disfigured, spray painted and dismantled statues of historic figures that defined Americas place in the world, but peaceful BLM protestors, I am OK with. I am OK maybe with some peaceful Antifa protests but some of the peaceful Antifas may need to just be dispersed but not arrested and all of the violent Antifa protestors need to all be thrown in jail like a lot of the January 6thers. However, I support

---

[1300] Chris Ingalls. October 30, 2020. INVESTIGATIONS. Many Seattle protesters arrested are white, from other cities, analysis finds. K 5 Seattle News. retrieved December 2, 2021. https://www.king5.com/article/news/investigations/analysis-of-seattle-protester-arrests/281-908cad06-29be-408a

[1301] Ibid.

the peaceful January 6th protesters only!! Not the ones that breach capitol security and dismantled things in the nation's capitol!! Even though I am prolife I support a pro-choice person right to protest peacefully in favor of abortion. You have the right to protest anything you oppose in America as long as it is peaceful!! The Church (not just the black Church but churches across America) has never rectified the moral issues mentioned above, and from liberal theology and liberal theologians, it is losing its ability to do so, as it loses its relevance in society and its ability to point out what sin is and what its consequences are. It doesn't help that pastors and priests across America minister a message to congregants that have their own moral absolutes that are different from those based on biblical scripture, which result in their own moral relativism and compromised ethical values and are sometimes politically correct or even woke congregants who do not want to be offended about their sins, but that is a whole other book.

King as a pastor really had a duty and an obligation to foster a world more like the ideal one that God would rather man have to live in, but at the end of the day, man is still sinful, and he is still man. Is this why America is what King refers to as the "burning house" that he thinks he led his people into by attempting to completely integrate them into American society? Maybe this is why complete integration did not really work. Sin with no fear of reprisal is a sign of where your moral compass really is, and it is going to affect your moral values and what you determine to be right or wrong. Is this what pastor reverend Dr. Martin Luther King Jr. was really referring to when he used the term "loss of moral vision?"

24.
My Thoughts on President Obama

Having President Obama as president did not really do a lot of good to improve the lot of black Americans. When you consider that he was a Liberal, he had to support all of their causes and those of the left. Since so many of their causes, directly and indirectly, have not been good for the existence of the black community, there was only so much that he could do for the black community. The black community could not really hold him accountable for anything because both his and First Lady Michelle's allegiance was to America as a whole and in particular to progressive, left-wing America; it was to the establishment in America and the powers that be. Even in that position as president, there was only so much he could do for the black community; he could only do in that position what the establishment allowed. Donald Trump never held a political office either when he ran, and he ran against Senator Hillary Rodham Clinton, but he beat her in the race. That is true, but America is at least no worse off after four years of being under Donald Trump than it was after eight years of President Obama's administration. How can you say that America is any worse off after another four years with President Trump in the White House?

Something else you have to remember about former President Obama that the rest of black America did not take into consideration is that he came from a different background from the rest of black America, and his great-grandparents and great-great-grandparents and

My Thoughts on President Obama

all of the prior generations before were not slaves, and his parents and grandparents did not suffer all of the post–Civil War racism that the rest of black America did, so he was raised differently than the rest of black America. He was raised in Hawaii by the parents of his single mom who was white, until he was 10 years[1302] old because she remarried and lived in Indonesia until he was ten,[1303] so he was probably not around a lot of black people. Hawaii at the time probably didn't have much of an African American community, if they had one at all. He stated in an interview with the *National Review* in 1995 that his white grandmother who raised him had a fear of strange black men.[1304] It is not out of the question especially if his grandmother had negative reactions around any strange black men that he may have had some of his own negative bias about African Americans. As a young man after all of this and after attending some very liberal and one prestigious university, Obama went to Chicago to live with the black community, and he could not relate to what they are experiencing on Chicago's Southside and Westside. The black community was excited when he got elected, but they took none of this into consideration, but the leftist media is so deceptive, and they did not say very much about this because they wanted you to believe certain things about Obama or not to realize some other things about him. The question to ask is: Who was his allegiance really to when he was a community organizer in the black community in Chicago? Was it really to the black community?

[1302] Biography. Barack Obama. APR 14, 2020. ORIGINAL:MAR 9, 2018. Who is Barack Obama. Retrieved August 2, 2020. https://www.biography.com/us-president/barack-obama

[1303] Ibid.

[1304] JIM GERAGHTY March 8, 2011, *The National Review* Obama, in 1995: 'My grandmother, while she loves me, still has a fear of strange black men.' Retrieved April 29, 2022 https://www.nationalreview.com/the-campaign-spot/obama-1995-my-grandmother-while-she-loves-me-still-has-fear-strange-black-men/

He was not an immediate leader of the black community as president like he was when he worked with a church-based organization to improve living conditions in poor neighborhoods[1305] in the black community in Chicago. He was a Democratic Senator for the state of Illinois,[1306] and as a result of his being a senator, the black community was no better off in Chicago than they were before he became senator, so what difference did it make that they had a black senator?

The median non-white family today has a net worth of $18,100, almost a fifth lower than it was when Mr. Obama took office.[1307] From 2000 to 2013, the median overall wealth for the average black household fell about 34 percent.[1308] The wealth declined as well as an additional 13.5 percent prior to this from 2007 to 2010.[1309] President Obama was a Democrat who had lots of connections with Progressives[1310] to get him into the office of president so he could support their cause.[1311] Just take a look at what happened to black wealth

---

[1305] United States Senator Barack Obama. retrieved November 26, 2019. https://www.senate.gov/artandhistory/history/common/generic/Photo_Barack_Obama.htm

[1306] Ibid.

[1307] Edward Luce. Financial Times. October 12, 2014. The Riddle of Black Americas Economic Woes under President Obama. Retrieved November 29, 2020. https://www.ft.com/content/5455efbe-4fa4–11e4-a0a4–00144feab7de

[1308] Rakesh Kochhar and Richard Fry. December 12, 2014. The Pew Research Center Fact Tank. News In the Numbers Wealth inequality has widened along racial, ethnic lines since end of Great Recession. retrieved November 29, 2020. https://www.pewresearch.org/fact-tank/2014/12/12/racial-wealth-gaps-great-recession

[1309] Business Investor Daily Editorials. The Black-White Wealth Gap Has Widened Under Obama. 12/12/2014. retrieved November 29, 2020 https://www.investors.com/politics/editorials/pew-study-finds-growing-black-white-wealth-gap-under-obama/

[1310] Tom Hayden, Barbara Ehrenreich, Bill Fletcher Jr., and Danny Glove. The Nation Magazine. ELECTION 2008. APRIL 7, 2008 ISSUE. Progressives for Obama. retrieved November 29, 2020. https://www.thenation.com/article/archive/progressives-obama/

[1311] Ibid.

over his presidency. The president had limited power to prevent something like this from happening to the masses.

According to the Pew Research Center, 95 percent of black voters voted for Obama on his first term.[1312] For his second term, he received 93 percent of the black vote.[1313] Since he is a black Democrat, it helped the left accomplish their cause of electing another president who would follow their script, thanks to black voters.

That position of power that he held, however, is one that black kids can look at and say if a black man could get that position, then it is still possible for me to achieve greatness, and that is the positive thing that can be taken from his presidency.

President Obama may have even been obligated to go along with or maybe even endorse policies that inflicted harm on blacks by the progressive left even though he may not have really wanted to. The reason not to be bitter or angry at him is because the people who he had allegiance to may have done something negative to him if he had done too many positive things for the black community that was not in their interest, even though he may have really wanted to. I say this because in the same interview with the *National Review* that I made reference to above he stated, "Integration was not really a victory on our part."[1314] Even though he was not pushing segregation,[1315] black

---

[1312] Pew Research Center. Dissecting the 2008 Electorate: Most Diverse in U.S. History. retrieved September 9, 2020. https://www.pewresearch.org/hispanic/2009/04/30/dissecting-the-2008-electorate-most-diverse-in-us-history/

[1313] Nadra Kadeem Nittle. Updated November 04, 2019. Thought.Co. How Minority Voters Helped Obama Win Reelection. retrieved September 9, 2020. https://www.thoughtco.com/how-minority-voters-helped-obama-win-reelection-2834532

[1314] JIM GERAGHTY March 8, 2011, The National Review, Obama, in 1995: 'My grandmother, while she loves me, still has a fear of strange black men.' Retrieved April 29, 2022 https://www.nationalreview.com/the-campaign-spot/obama-1995-my-grandmother-while-she-loves-me-still-has-fear-strange-black-men

[1315] Ibid

people had a lot to be thankful for in segregated communities.[1316] He stated that there were so many successful blacks including doctors and lawyers that didn't leave the community when they became successful.[1317] Here President Obama both directly and indirectly is backing my position, maybe not totally but a great deal on integration and segregation, and he seems to be a liberal and maybe even a progressive one at that, and after all, he did marry Michelle.

President Obama was the progressive left's appeal to the masses of African Americans that they were not racists. This is the same thing that happened during the inception of the NAACP when W.E.B. Du Bois was accepted as one of their key figures in the organization. This helped them win favoritism among Negros of the time, but what you don't see here is the socialists and the role they played in creating the NAACP and their intentions for the black community, which was all designed to hide their puppet strings of intent for the organization with the puppet being the NAACP.

Consider this, both India and Pakistan had women as presidents, but years after their presidencies, women still had many of the same restrictions on them that they had before, and there was nothing they could do to change societal norms that had been practiced for maybe hundreds of years in those countries that place these restrictions on women to begin with. With that said, there were also some cultural and societal norms in America that could not be changed, either, when Obama became the first black President.

The museum director of the Jim Crow Museum in Big Rapids, Michigan[1318], discussed on a YouTube presentation an entire sec-

---

[1316] Ibid

[1317] Ibid

[1318] Ferris State Jim Crow Museum traveling exhibit at Grand Rapids Public Museum Youtube 13 One Your Side retrieved January 22. 2023 https://www.youtube.com/watch?v=rRUH98aY-ZU

tion of the museum on images that defamed President Obama[1319]. This is in a more progressive America. Who produced this imagery, we will probably never know, but I am willing to bet you that they were probably a very tiny fraction of a minority of traditional white conservatives, and it wouldn't surprise me if the same conservatives, some liberals both classical and otherwise, and some progressives, again another very tiny fraction of a minority of each looked at the images and laughed as an expression of mockery. You will see what I mean if you just go to this site and look for yourself. You know what I have to say about that! Good enough for you! You deserve to feel terrible about America having a black president if that is the way you choose to express it! It is terrible that we still have people in America that thought that way about Blacks! What this shows is that we still have some good old-fashioned old-school racism left in America or at least during the Obama administration we did. Even though I don't think we have nearly as much as years ago, nonetheless we still have some. Today, it is the racism coming from progressives that is affecting the black community the most negatively.

[1319] Ibid

25.

Sex, Drugs, Rock and Roll, and the LBGTQ Agenda

The left was largely responsible for the sexual revolution and drugs and Rock and Roll movement that started in the '60s, and more progressive and far-left-leaning Liberals[1320] supported it. Now blacks have the highest HIV/AIDS rate from heterosexual and homosexual sex transmissions and IV drug use. Blacks are only 12 percent of the US total population, but according to the CDC, they are 44 percent of those who are living with full-blown AIDS and/or those who are HIV positive.[1321] The open or closet homosexuality and promiscuity among heterosexuals is promoting the sex part.

Since the mass migration of blacks to the Atlanta Metro area has begun to the present, it has now become home to more African Americans than the Chicago Metro area.[1322] It has an impressive

---

[1320] S. Wayne Carter Jr. Carrol County Times. August 19, 2018. Carter: Counterculture, consumerism and politics. The Baltimore Sun Times, Opinion. retrieved April 21, 2020. https://www.baltimoresun.com/maryland/carroll/opinion/cc-op-carter-20180818-story.html

[1321] US Department of Health and Human Services Office of Minority Health. retrieved October 30, 2019. https://minorityhealth.hhs.gov/omh/browse.aspx?lvl=4&lvlid=21

[1322] U.S. Metropolitan areas with the largest African American populations as of 2015. December 8, 2016. retrieved October 15, 2019. https://dilemma-x.net/2016/12/09/u-s-metropolitan-areas-with-the-largest-african-american-populations-as-of-2015/

hip-hop music scene, and it is producing a lot of young artists.[1323] Since Tyler Perry's studios are headquartered there, it is also host to lots of black film productions.[1324] These are just lures for lots of aspiring young black youth who wish to attain success in this industry.

A YouTuber out of Atlanta, who has lived there for 30 years, summed up the scene in Atlanta well. Then he goes on to discuss some more things that you can only know about a city unless you've lived there for a while. As a gay man himself, he claims that STD rates are sky-high and especially in the black community of Atlanta[1325] because so many of the men have sex with one another, and they never use condoms. He discusses all of the sex parties that gay men and straight people attend but especially gay men have without using condoms. Many of the gay men are bisexual, and they have sex with women who have totally heterosexual sexual sex habits, and still they are not using condoms.[1326] He discusses how many of the single women have baby after baby by bisexual and straight men.[1327] He discusses how the lure of meth and crack is very attractive since Atlanta is a party town, and black people are more likely to contract HIV/AIDS through IV drug use.[1328] So you

---

[1323]   Max Monahan. The 10 Biggest Hip-Hop Cities in America. Apr 15, 2016. retrieved October 29, 2019. http://blog.sonicbids.com/the-10-biggest-hip-hop-cities-in-america

[1324]   Greg Braxton. Oct. 2, 2019. *Los Angeles Times*. Tyler Perry Studios, the house 'Madea' built, becomes a landmark for black Hollywood. retrieved April 25, 2020. https://www.latimes.com/entertainment-arts/tv/story/2019-10-02/tyler-perry-studios-atlanta-dedication

[1325]   Why the South still has such high HIV rates. June 13, 2017. The Conversation. retrieved April 9, 2020. https://theconversation.com/why-the-south-still-has-such-high-hiv-rates-76386

[1326]   Centers for Disease Control and Prevention. HIV and African Americans The Numbers. retrieved April 21, 2020. https://www.cdc.gov/hiv/group/racialethnic/africanamericans/index.html

[1327]   Ibid.

[1328]   Ibid.

have the spread of AIDS among the gay and straight black population of Atlanta. Gay black men still have a one in two chance of getting HIV/AIDS during their life versus one in eleven for gay white men.[1329]

Now a more recent offshoot of the sex, drugs, and rock and roll movement, the more recent transgender movement has resulted in an HIV prevalence of one in five for black trans-people vs. only 2.5 percent for trans-people of all other races.[1330] Suicide rate and suicide attempts for this group are much higher for blacks than for anyone else.[1331] This is not because of systemic racism or white privilege or from hate directed at trans people from MAGA Conservatives or most other things the progressive movement would like for us to believe it is from. It is just another way for them to advance the transgender cause and movement. Now transgenders along with homosexuals want to equate their issues and struggles in society with the struggles and injustices of blacks. This is wrong if you had gender rearrangement surgery, which is the case for the vast majority of transgendered individuals. If you had gender rearrangement surgery, or you dress yourself up as a drag queen, then you choose a trans identity, but black people who went through all of their historical injustices did not choose to be black. They do this through organizations such as the National Black Justice Coalition (NBJC) and the National Center for Transgender Equality (NCTE), which work together as a supplement to the groundbreaking national study and

---

[1329] James Myhre and Dennis Sifris, MD. Very Well Health. The High Risk of Gay Black Men Getting HIV. Updated on February 12 2020. retrieved April 21, 2020. https://www.verywellhealth.com/why-50-of-gay-black-men-will-get-hiv-3896687

[1330] New Analysis Shows Startling Levels Of Discrimination Against Black Transgender People retrieved May 27, 2023 https://www.thetaskforce.org/new-analysis-shows-startling-levels-of-discrimination-against-black-transgender-people/

[1331] Ibid

refer to it as Injustice at Every Turn.[1332] This is wrong, and it should offend black people!!

The same YouTuber who reports out of Atlanta, Georgia, was interviewed along with a panel of others who were on the forefront of the battle to combat HIV/ AIDS in the black community by the British *The Guardian* on the HIV/AIDS crisis in the gay black community in America.[1333] He has been living in the Atlanta Metro area now for just over 30 years. Since living there for a few months in 1987, I have made several visits there to visit relatives there, and we kept in touch by discussing things that are going on here and there. The man has been discussing on his program some things that you cannot really find out about a city or a metro area unless you just live there for a while.

That it was also deemed as a mecca for gay black men[1334] did not seem relevant to me until he brought it up in his program. I was not aware of this when I lived there.

In 1987 and for a several years before, when some of my relatives first got there, you could drive up and down some of the major busy streets, and the "help wanted" signs were everywhere, which was a lure for people of all races and colors. The want ads section of the *Atlanta Constitution* had lots of want ads in it also.

[1332] Ibid

[1333] The Guardian May 29, 2018 Gay, black and HIV positive: America's hidden epidemic Atlanta retrieved February 16, 2020 https://www.youtube.com/watch?v=uwxx1AUZ3v8

[1334] Associated Press updated 8/15/2005 3:07:49 PM ET NBC News Atlanta has become a Magnet for Black Gays retrieved April 9, 2020 http://www.nbcnews.com/id/8961196/ns/us_news-life/t/atlanta-has-become-magnet-black-gays/#.Xo89jW5Fw2w

The poverty rate there for black children is roughly 80 percent[1335] in Atlanta. The Atlanta Metro's population is roughly six million[1336]; it is 34 percent Black[1337] and nearly 11 percent Hispanic.[1338] The state of Georgia's population is just over 10.6 million, with roughly 80 percent of black children growing up in poverty in the Atlanta Metro[1339] and 65 percent of black children nationally growing up in single-parent homes;[1340] this all is a recipe for lots of voters that have traditionally voted as Democrats. If this trend continues, it could change Georgia from a primarily Conservative Republican state to a swing state and eventually maybe even a winner for Democrats. This would be a critical victory for the left, largely because of the black population.

Between 1955 and 1965 there were a lot of teen pregnancies in America, but that was because of the birth of the baby boom generation after so many men had returned from World War II.[1341]

[1335] In This City, 80 percent of African-American Children Live in High-Poverty Neighborhoods! Low Income Housing Authority Website. October 19, 2018. retrieved November 5, 2019 https://www.lowincome.org/2018/10/atlanta-georgia-80-percent-african-american-children-live-high-poverty.html

[1336] Atlanta Metro Chamber of Commerce. retrieved April 12, 2021. https://www.metroatlantachamber.com/resources/reports-and-information/executive-profile

[1337] Ibid.

[1338] Ibid.

[1339] In This City, 80 percent of African-American Children Live in High-Poverty Neighborhoods! Low Income Housing Authority Website. October 19, 2018. retrieved November 5, 2019. https://www.lowincome.org/2018/10/atlanta-georgia-80-percent-african-american-children-live-high-poverty.html

[1340] Kay S. Hymowitz. The Black Family: 40 Years of Lies Rejecting the Moynihan report caused untold, needless misery. Summer 2005. retrieved May 9, 2019. https://www.city-journal.org/html/black-family-40-years-lies-12872.html

[1341] The History of Teenage Childbearing as a Social Problem, Chapter 1. retrieved September 22, 2020. p. 5. https://www.russellsage.org/sites/default/files/Furstenberg_chap1_1.pdf

Back then, before the sex, drugs, and rock and roll era, America was more traditional and Conservative, so a lot more of the teen pregnancies were within a marriage bond.[1342] After America became less Conservative in its moral values after the free sex, drugs, and rock and roll era, out-of-wedlock pregnancies rates began to fall,[1343] but the ones that continued were more likely to be out of wedlock.[1344] In 2017 Hispanic women had a slightly higher teen pregnancy rate at 29 out of 1,000 births[1345] than non-Hispanic black women at 28 out of 1,000[1346] versus 13 out of 1,000 for white women[1347] and 6 out of 1,000 for Asian women.[1348] The fact reality shows such as *My Teen Is Pregnant and So Am I* are on TV is proof that America has a different attitude about the immorality of teenage pregnancy, at least that is what the leftist-influenced media would like for us to believe. As you can see, the black community is still plagued by these problems more than most other communities, and it is dealing with

---

[1342] Ibid.

[1343] Gretchen Livingston and Deja Thomas. The Pew Research Center. Why is the teen birth rate falling? August 2, 2019. retrieved September 22, 2020 https://www.pewresearch.org/fact-tank/2019/08/02/why-is-the-teen-birth-rate-falling/

[1344] The History of Teenage Childbearing as a Social Problem, Chapter 1. retrieved September 22, 2020. p. 12. https://www.russellsage.org/sites/default/files/Furstenberg_chap1_1.pdf

[1345] Child Trends. Teen Births. May 24, 2019. https://www.childtrends.org/indicators/teen-births

[1346] Ibid.

[1347] Ibid.

[1348] Teresa Wiltz. Racial and Ethnic Disparities Persist in Teen Pregnancy Rates. PEW Research Center. retrieved September 22, 2020. https://www.pewtrusts.org/en/research-and-analysis/blogs/stateline/2015/3/03/racial-and-ethnic-disparities-persist-in-teen-pregnancy-.

more of the problems that it brings than any other racial group.[1349,] [1350] I think if it had been up to Conservatives, who are more likely to be more traditional and on the right, it would never have come to this versus what the sex, drug, and rock and roll mentality caused, largely lead by Progressives and the left.[1351]

Now LGBTQIA+s are claiming that they should be compensated for past injustices as a separate group.[1352] This is wrong for them to think this way because you could be a gay man or a lesbian woman and as long as no one knew it, you could blend in with other men or women, respectively, and you could just accomplish whatever in the world you wanted to, but not if you were black. If you were black, from appearance, everyone could tell, and that is something that keeps you from just blending in with the general crowd, so LGBTQIA+s want recognition for something that was possible to hide, but your race cannot be hidden. It is wrong for LGBTQIA+s to compare themselves with blacks in this respect, and it is unfair to blacks because it minimizes black issues more and makes them less relevant! Even the Black Lives Matter movement is standing in solidarity with LBGTQIAs, which creates a stage

---

[1349] 11 Facts About Teenage Pregnancy. retrieved September 22, 2020. https://www.dosomething.org/us/facts/11-facts-about-teen-pregnancy

[1350] 11 Facts About Teenage Dads. retrieved September 22, 2020. https://www.dosomething.org/us/facts/11-facts-about-teen-dads

[1351] Alex Berezow and Hank Campbell. 30 January 2013. Lefty nonsense: When progressives wage war on reason .New Scientists. retrieved September 22, 2022. https://www.newscientist.com/article/mg21729026-200-lefty-nonsense-when-progressives-wage-war-on-reason/#ixzz6YmwySG8N

[1352] Brad Polumbo. June 17, 2019. *The Washington Examiner*. 'Case for gay reparation' is incredibly weak. retrieved September 16, 2020. https://www.washingtonexaminer.com/opinion/nyt-writers-case-for-gay-reparation-is-incredibly-weak

to make a case for LGBTQIA issues.[1353] Why do you need a stage this big to address these issues? Why not just give them justice as people in general and not as LGBTQIAs? The LGBTQIA movement, which is a leftist cause, has not been kind to blacks. Some, who are on the right, may have supported this movement to an extent, but they would never have supported this movement to the extent that the left has.

The way the Respect for Marriage Act H R 8404[1354] is being used by Progressives equates homosexuality with race. The reason why I say this is because it states that its provision is to provide statutory authority for same-sex and interracial marriages.[1355] Why do we need to provide authority for interracial marriages? The issues on them being illegal was already addresses years ago in civil rights legislation[1356] and by changing the constitutional laws of some states[1357] making them now perfectly legal unions. Most people do not have a problem with interracial marriages today, so why make them an issue in any legislation? This is another example where progressives want to equate the struggles of homosexual identity in America with being black and the injustices that were dealt to blacks for hundreds

---

[1353] Jennifer Houston External Affairs. LGBTQ Organizations Stand in Solidarity with Black Lives Matter. Neighborhood Funders Group. retrieved September 16, 2020. https://www.nfg.org/news/lgbtq-organizations-stand-solidarity-black-lives-matter

[1354] Congress.gov Summary: H.R.8404 — 117th Congress (2021-2022) Rep. Nadler, Jerrold [D-NY-10] (Introduced 07/18/2022) House Judiciary retrieved November 29, 2022 https://www.congress.gov/bill/117th-congress/house-bill/8404/text

[1355] Ibid.

[1356] Tom Head Updated on June 11, 2021 Interracial Marriage Laws History and Timeline Thought Co. retrieved November 29, 2022 https://www.thoughtco.com/interracial-marriage-laws-721611

[1357] Ibid

of years to justify having this nonsense legalized. I think it's just wrong to do this!

From the beginning of the crack cocaine crisis in maybe the early and more progressive 1980s vs. a more conservative time in America before the civil rights era and for another 20 or may 30 years later crack cocaine sentencing of 10 years in prison for five grams of crack just devastated the lives of so many black youth in the inner cities while white youth were not penalized nearly as much for a lot more regular power cocaine. According to the Pew Research Center, from 2015 until 2020, overdose death rates from fentanyl tripled[1358] and 2021's death rates for black men from the crisis were higher than for any other group of men.[1359] According to the Pew Research Center, from 2015 until 2020, overdose death rates from fentanyl tripled[1360] and 2021's death rates for black men from the crisis were higher than for any other group of men.[1361] A more progressive presidential administration and laxed enforcement policies on seizures of drugs[1362] coming across the border have not made matters any better.

[1358] John Gramlich Pew Research Center January 19, 2022 Recent surge in U.S. drug overdose deaths has hit Black men the hardest Retrieved May 8, 2022 https://www.pewresearch.org/fact-tank/2022/01/19/recent-surge-in-u-s-drug-overdose-deaths-has-hit-black-men-the-hardest/

[1359] Ibid.

[1360] John Gramlich Pew Research Center January 19, 2022 Recent surge in U.S. drug overdose deaths has hit Black men the hardest Retrieved May 8, 2022 https://www.pewresearch.org/fact-tank/2022/01/19/recent-surge-in-u-s-drug-overdose-deaths-has-hit-black-men-the-hardest/

[1361] Ibid.

[1362] Joseph Simonson • November 17, 2021 5:00 am The Washington Free Beacon Biden Administration Surge in Fentanyl Seizures Show Cartels Taking Advantage of Lax Border Policies, DHS Officials Say retrieved September 2, 2022 https://freebeacon.com/biden-administration/surge-in-fentanyl-seizures-show-cartels-taking-advantage-of-lax-border-policies-dhs-officials-say/

In a more progressive left-leaning America, blacks are almost four times more likely to be arrested for marijuana position.[1363]

There is a proposal from the CDC to have menthol cigarettes banned,[1364] which could happen. According to the CDC also African Americans chose menthol cigarettes more than seventy percent over non-menthol brands,[1365] but the menthol in them makes them more addictive than non-menthol brands.[1366] The reason for banning menthols is since blacks prefer menthols more than any other brands, if you could get blacks to quit, it would promote or even advance health equity.[1367] Equity of outcomes is a more progressive cause. The question we need to be asking is, Since menthol cigarettes are more addictive, once they are banned, could this policy result in criminal black-market activity for the very additive brand, which would criminalize the victims who are more likely to be black, which could further criminalize a large section of the black community disproportionally, resulting in more jail or prison too, like crack cocaine did for so many years? Equity is not a part of conservatives' rhetoric, and it would be better off on a lot of cases if we just didn't have it.

[1363] Kade Crockford, Director, ACLU of Massachusetts Technology for Liberty Project June 16, 2020 ACLU News & Commentary How is Face Recognition Surveillance Technology Racist? Retrieved July 23, 2022 https://www.aclu.org/news/privacy-technology/how-is-face-recognition-surveillance-technology-racist

[1364] Michael O'Riordan NEWS Daily News FDA Proposes Ban on Menthol Cigarettes and Flavored Cigars retrieved May 10, 2022 https://www.tctmd.com/news/scai-led-position-statement-clti-spotlights-multispeciality-involvement

[1365] Centers or Disease Control and Prevention African Americans and Tobacco Use retrieved May 10, 2022 https://www.cdc.gov/tobacco/disparities/african-americans/index.htm

[1366] Ibid

[1367] Michael O'Riordan NEWS Daily News FDA Proposes Ban on Menthol Cigarettes and Flavored Cigars retrieved May 10, 2022 https://www.tctmd.com/news/scai-led-position-statement-clti-spotlights-multispeciality-involvement

26.

Think about This for a While

Progressive liberals are more likely to be atheists.[1368] They are more likely to be anti–straight white male. They are generally anti–Second Amendment and anti-First Amendment.

The next facts being discussed in this chapter of the book are from certain times and circumstances that can change. Most of these things happened between 2015 and 2019.

Government is a good thing; sometimes it is essential, but the black community, especially certain pockets in the black community, is too dependent on its handouts. For example, welfare benefits are basically federally funded, administered by states, with some added funding by states, [1369]and California, the most populous US state, is currently $1.3 trillion in debt, that is, total state and local debt.[1370] According to US Debt Clock.org, on July 21, 2018, Illinois was in nearly $150 billion in debt with billions more in unfunded

---

[1368] Paul Bedard. October 09, 2012. Washington Secrets. Washington Examiner. Majority of atheists are liberal. retrieved February 1, 2020. https://www.washingtonexaminer.com/majority-of-atheists-are-liberal

[1369] Kimberly Amadeo .Updated November 09, 2019. The Balance U.S. Welfare Programs, the Myths Versus the Facts. retrieved November 11, 2019. https://www.thebalance.com/welfare-programs-definition-and-list-3305759

[1370] Bill Fletcher and Marc Joffe. January 10, 2017. California Policy Center. California's Total State and Local Debt Totals $1.3 Trillion. retrieved October 16, 2019. https://california-policycenter.org/californias-total-state-local-debt-totals-1-3-trillion

liabilities. New York's current total state debt was second only to California's, which is at $87 billion. All of these states have been governed largely by Democrats who are probably mostly progressive Liberals or sympathizers with the cause. These three states are the nation's first, sixth, and third most populated states, respectively. In the San Francisco Bay area of California, which is a very liberal part of a liberal state, in 2019 black people were only 5 percent of the total population but 37 percent of the homeless.[1371] Also in 2019, in Los Angeles, blacks were only 9 percent of the population but were 40 percent of Skid Row's homeless population.[1372] In Oakland, California, in October of 2019, blacks were only 20 percent of the population but 70 percent of the homeless, and the homeless encampments are being criminalized more every day.[1373] Again California tends to lean Liberal on most issues as a state. Since black people are more likely to be homeless everywhere,[1374] it is fair to say that they are more likely to be criminalized for it anywhere. Project participants in a study of the homelessness in San Francisco reported frequent reports of race- and gender-based discrimination

---

[1371] Justin Phillips. Aug. 29, 2019. *San Francisco Chronicle*. 37 percent of SF's homeless population is black. This is a heartbreaking problem. https://www.sfchronicle.com/entertainment/article/37-of-SF-s-homeless-population-is-black-This-14399638.php retrieved November 14, 2019.

[1372] Wholesale District-Skid Row population breakdown by race. https://www.areavibes.com/los+angeles-ca/wholesale+district-skid+row/demographics/

[1373] Democracy Now. "State of Emergency": Special Report on California's Criminalization of Growing Homeless Encampments. https://www.youtube.com/watch?v=c-9MEEzMCmbk retrieved January 4, 2020.

[1374] Teresa Wiltz. Stateline Article. March 29, 2019. PEW Charitable Trusts 'A Pileup of Inequities': Why People of Color Are Hit Hardest by Homelessness. https://www.pewtrusts.org/en/research-and-analysis/blogs/stateline/2019/03/29/a-pileup-of-inequities-why-people-of-color-are-hit-hardest-by-homelessness retrieved January 4, 2020.

by law enforcement.[1375] The overwhelming majority of black participants were approached by police 81 percent of the time, searched 62 percent, forced to move 67 percent, cited 76 percent, and arrested and incarcerated 74 percent of the time.[1376]

The total state debt owned by all 50 states at 2017 year's end was $1.15 trillion.[1377] This would put the total per capita debt assessed to each of its citizens at $3,582.[1378] Had Conservatives been running these states, it probably would not have come to this. If their government assistance systems collapse because they have no more funds to put into them, they cannot go to the federal government as a safety net because the federal government is currently about $33 trillion in debt.[1379] If this happens, the black community will be hit disproportionately harder than any other community. This is why the black community needs to start and maintain its own economic infrastructure with its own mom-and-pop stores and its own for-profit and nonprofit organizations, banks, hospitals, and so on and put itself to work if that is still possible now. That is how you assert your economic prowess and have real freedom. Boycotts only work for so long until you have no choice but to go back to the same people that you are boycotting for life necessities because

---

[1375] Chris Herring. The San Francisco Study of the Criminalization of Homelessness. retrieved September 20, 2020. https://chrisherring.org/campaign-4

[1376] Ibid.

[1377] Financial State of the States an Annual Report by Truth in Accounting. September 2018. retrieved September 20, 2020. p. 4 https://www.truthinaccounting.org/library/doclib/2017-FSOS-Booklet-.pdf

[1378] Ibid.

[1379] Peter G. Peterson Foundatio.n What Is the National Debt Today? Retrieved September 20, 2020. https://www.pgpf.org/national-debt-clock#:~:text=The%20%2426%20 trillion%20(and%20growing,to%20measure%20our%20national%20debt.

you lack ownership or control over enough. They only really work if you can do without the product or service for good.

Leftists, who are more likely vote as Democrats,[1380] have essentially gotten what they wanted from the black community after marching with us for civil rights and enforcing quotas and affirmative action and welfare and some other programs. Now they have thrown the black community under the bus, since they have no real solutions to any of the other problems that were created as a result of following their causes, and they knew it would come to this. When they want something else from the black community, they will march with them again, and when they are through with blacks, they will throw blacks under the bus again. Progressives and the left are backing policies and causes that are not respectful of the black experience today. Now, Progressives have come in disguised as considerate Democrats, pretending to be allies with black América in a political culture that appears as if it is rejecting them. This makes siding with the left a more attractive option at the voting booth, despite the fact they have an agenda with outcomes that will not be good for African Americans. Black Americans have not been benefited wholly as a group from the efforts of and the beliefs of the left in years. They put a lot of their own issues first, and they use black concerns as strategic moves to accomplish what they want, but African Americans continue to vote en masse for the Democratic Party.[1381]

[1380] Samantha Smith. September 7, 2017. Democratic voters are increasingly likely to call their views liberal. PEW Research Center. retrieved October 24, 2019. http://www.pewresearch.org/fact-tank/2017/09/07/democratic-voters-are-increasingly-likely-to-call-their-views-liberal/

[1381] Shermichael Singleton. THE HILL. Progressive politics have done nothing to help black America. retrieved November 8, 2019. https://thehill.com/opinion/civil-rights/396322-progressive-politics-have-done-nothing-to-help-black-america

Progressives have not really worked in favor of what is best for blacks in years, either. Blacks need to scrutinize the intentions of both parties, while at the same time exercising their political power and maintaining the course of their own interests through voting. Progressives and the leftists, in my opinion, both have some different interests than African Americans, and therefore, they should return more to their Conservative roots.[1382]

One day, I had a conversation with a woman who was very pro-Democratic in her political beliefs. She seemed like the type who would support liberal policies, so she was right on one thing about taxation. Because to fund all of their socialist programs, you need a government with lots of money. The very wealthy with money-making entities for lots of money for their government-sponsored programs are the biggest sources of money for them, so it makes since if it were up to them they would not allow tax write-offs for the wealthy or any other loopholes to get around taxes. It is just downright criminal if a multimillionaire or a billionaire never pays his taxes because they can write them all off if he or she has a money-making venture versus your average middle-income American who typically makes between $30,000 and $300,000 a year, and they pay anywhere from 20 percent to 40 percent of their income in taxes and deductions.[1383] Black people are more likely to be in one of the lower-income brackets so they can't just write their taxes off.

What I don't approve of is an aggressively progressive tax where the wealthy pay a lot more than the middle income and the poor.[1384]

[1382]   Ibid.

[1383]   Robert Bellafiore. New Report Shows the Burdens of Payroll and Income Taxes. March 26, 2019. Tax Foundation. retrieved April 13, 2021. https://taxfoundation.org/payroll-income-tax-burden/

[1384]   Julia Kagan. Progressive Tax. Investopedia. retrieved September 17, 2020. https://www.investopedia.com/terms/p/progressivetax.asp

This punishes the wealthy, upper class, and even the middle class unfairly.[1385] This is why you need a fairly flat rate that doesn't drain the poor out of existence either. This gets rid of lots of freebees from the government while not disincentivizing hard work among the poor. I can see the very ultra-wealthy pay maybe a little more but only about another 2 or 4 percent of the income more while everyone else should pay the same flat rate and maybe the poor pay just 5% less.

Some things that Progressives support are things we can live with and that I am for, like a less-polluted environment by using electric cars as long as the environment is not destroyed to mine for lithium[1386] and other minerals you need to make batteries,[1387] for solar panels and windmills when it is cloudy and no wind is blowing, but not a carbon tax for those who chose to use cars run by gas. Making all plastics that eventually end up in landfill biodegradable, which is something that Liberals seem to be pushing more than Conservatives, but a biodegradable car is going a little too far, although more of their ideas are good ones too. Alternative sources of energy are a great way to keep America from being so dependent on foreign oil and gas, which seems to be pushed more by progressive Liberals, and fracking, which uses pressurized water and poisonous chemicals[1388] to extract methane from miles under-

---

[1385]   Ibid

[1386]   Lithium Mining and Environmental Impact. retrieved March 11, 2021. http://www.lithiummine.com/lithium-mining-and-environmental-impact

[1387]   RICK LEBLAN.C Updated June 25, 2019. The Balance Small Business. The Importance of Battery Storage for Sustainable Energy. retrieved March 11, 2021. https://www.thebalancesmb.com/importance-of-battery-storage-for-sustainable-energy-4163010

[1388]   Melissa Horton. Updated May 8, 2019. Investopedia. What Are the Effects of Fracking on the Environment? retrieved February 7, 2020. https://www.investopedia.com/ask/answers/011915/what-are-effects-fracking-environment.asp

neath the earth's surface, is dangerous and bad for the air quality,[1389] the water quality,[1390] and one of the long-term effects of it is that it causes earthquakes.[1391] Fracking needs to be stopped; this is something that Liberals support that is a great thing.

The same woman, again in a casual conversation, who would be more likely to vote as a Democrat and vote for liberal causes, made a good point about why black youth were struggling so hard. She said when the factories moved overseas because labor was cheaper, it eliminated a lot of jobs that they depended on for employment. The same thing happened to other ethnic backgrounds, but other ethnicities have been better able to reinvent themselves and provide some safety nets for their community. Part of the reason why they have been able to do it was because they did not fall for integration to the extent that the black community did, so since their wealth does not get distributed to everyone else's community, they have more of it to work with to set up institutions that generate income and wealth in their own communities, and black people don't.

Apparently, white Liberals, who don't think they need to be or appear as competent, were speaking to a black audience. A new university study concluded that white Liberals actually make themselves appear less competent when interacting with African Americans.[1392] In one part of this study, researchers analyzed years of speeches delivered by white presidential candidates to mostly

---

[1389] Ibid.

[1390] Ibid.

[1391] Food and Water Watch Fracking and Earthquakes Issue. May 2015. foodandwaterwatch.org. retrieved February 8 2020. https://www.foodandwaterwatch.org/sites/default/files/Fracking%20and%20Earthquakes%20IB%20May%202015.pdf

[1392] Ray Hardman. Dec 3, 2018. White Liberals Rely on Old Stereotypes When Interacting with Black People. retrieved October 22, 2019. https://www.wnpr.org/post/study-white-liberals-rely-old-stereotypes-when-interacting-black-people

black audiences and next to predominantly white audiences.[1393] The study showed that when talking to African Americans, they were more likely to use words that made them seem linguistically less competent.[1394]

A group of white Democrats with African kente cloths around their shoulders and necks kneeled in a moment of silence at the Capitol Building Emancipation Hall with a group of black Democrats to show their solidarity with the black community for the Black Lives Matter movement and the death of George Floyd.[1395] The kente cloth was traditionally worn by a wealthy class of Africans who were slave traders themselves.[1396] These slave traders were directly and indirectly responsible for the export of millions of Africans to the Americas for over 400 years of the European slave trade to the Americas,[1397] but the left would never tell you that.

The kente cloth is West African in origin, and it was something that was adopted and attached to black American culture that came out of the Black Power Movement of the 1960s, but it has nothing to do with the black experience in America. For their agenda, the

---

[1393] Ibid.

[1394] Ibid.

[1395] Vox News. Pelosi Kneels with Other Democrats in 'Moment of Silence.' retrieved July 4, 2020. https://www.youtube.com/watch?v=pZgVBFYM2qk

[1396] Devon Link. USA Today. June 16 2020. Updated June 18 2020. Yes, Kente cloths were historically worn by empire involved in West African slave trade. retrieved July 4, 2020. https://www.usatoday.com/story/news/factcheck/2020/06/16/fact-check-kente-cloths-have-ties-west-african-slave-trade/5345941002/ n

[1397] Adaobi Tricia Nwaubani. *The New Yorker* My Great-Grandfather, the Nigerian Slave-Trader. https://www.newyorker.com/culture/personal-history/my-great-grandfather-the-nigerian-slave-trader

left can put on this show and further convince the black community that they are really on their side when really, they have other interests.

With political correctness, which is a leftist concept, there are certain things that you can't say that might offend anyone, and some things are reworded to soften a blow of one's opinion or to sugar-coat something and make it easier to deal with. Years ago, when Klansmen were hanging and lynching black people in the South, there was no such thing as political correctness. They had a goal to get rid of so many black people, but so does Planned Parenthood in the name of family planning and women's health or women reproductive rights. It is just a more polite or coded term for ethnic cleansing of the black race. Now it is harder to tell who the real racists are, but at least you knew the Klansmen were racists years ago before political correctness.

There has been talk by some Holocaust survivors that Donald Trump's America has some looming similarities to Germany before the Nazis took power.[1398] That may be the case, even from a Conservative who is from the right, like Donald Trump; hopefully he is not leading America down that road. But even if it is, you cannot deny all of the policies and causes that the left has supported that have been bad for black America, and Trump at least superficially was starting to turn things around in a different way than some of his predecessors. But that's no guarantee that America is in the clear. Donald Trump is probably not going to be another Hitler because before Hitler came to power, he had to convince enough people in the popular voting constituency and the masses that he

---

[1398] Clark Mindock. 9 April 2018. The Independent. Holocaust survivor says Trump's America 'feels like 1929 or 1930 Berlin. https://www.independent.co.uk/news/world/americas/us-politics/donald-trump-us-holocaust-survivor-nazi-germany-berlin-stephen-jacobs-a8296956.html retrieved December 7, 2019.

could deliver on a grand scheme with no realistic or practical solutions to Germany's problems and needs, so he had to more or less invent something that sounded great. One of the ways he did this is with the invention and building of the autobahn.[1399] At a time when Germany had one of the lowest rates of car ownership,[1400] he convinced the German people that it was a necessity.

President Trump has gained the popularity of the masses by convincing the public that he can govern a nation and solve some of its problems. This is despite the fact that he had some projects that the masses of American just don't approve of, such as the wall that he was having built along the US-Mexico border.[1401] However, he still addressed some more realistic problems that the nation was having with some more realistic and practical solutions, a lot differently than Adolf Hitler did in Nazi Germany. If anyone was going to come on the scene like Hitler did, it would be more likely to be a Democratic Socialist. If this were to happen in America, it seems to me that it would be more likely to be from a Democratic Socialist who promises lots of free stuff such as free health care, free college, free a lot of other things, or things that would be really cheap if everyone just pays a little more in taxes, but they aren't really convincing enough yet to the masses. If they do convince the public to approve of any of these plans, they will be from the same left that convinced the black community that they needed to be completely

---

[1399] Hans-Joachim Voth, Nico Voigtländer. 22 May 2014. Nazi pork and popularity: How Hitler's roads won German hearts and minds. VOX CEPR Policy Portal. https://voxeu.org/article/nazi-pork-and-popularity-how-hitler-s-roads-won-german-hearts-and-minds retrieved December 7, 2019.

[1400] Ibid.

[1401] Steve Kull. *The Washington Post.* Americans don't want Trump's border wall. This is what they want instead. Jan. 11, 2019. https://www.washingtonpost.com/news/monkey-cage/wp/2019/01/11/americans-dont-want-trumps-border-wall-heres-what-they-think-should-happen-instead/

integrated with whites to improve the quality of their lives, and so far, that has not happened. Since it doesn't appear that the left has the best interest of black America at heart, it just may be better for black America that Donald Trump gets reelected to a second term instead of electing a Democratic Socialist to the office of president.

In a democracy, since everybody can vote, then whoever the majority is can get what they want.[1402] In a republic, the majority cannot deny rights to a minority;[1403] therefore, since Blacks are a minority, it would be better if they lived in a republic[1404] rather than democracy. The republic is the very thing that the left is trying to destroy with democratic socialism. A democratic socialist could also be very racist too. The private sector economy that a minority group would need to have to empower themselves would be replaced by more government regulations and control.

Time magazine did an article that addressed climate change[1405] and how it was related to environmental racism.[1406] The article commented on an oil refinery that was built in the early 1900s[1407] and on how it was polluting the air of a mostly black South Philadelphia neighborhood[1408] and on how its black residents are more likely to have respiratory conditions as a result.[1409] It discussed how black,

---

[1402] DIffen. Democracy vs Republic. retrieved January 13, 2021. https://www.diffen.com/difference/Democracy_vs_Republic

[1403] Ibid.

[1404] Ibid.

[1405] Justin Worland. July 9, 2020. *Time Magazine* Why the Larger Climate Movement Is Finally Embracing the Fight Against Environmental Racism. retrieved July 25, 2021. https://time.com/5864704/environmental-racism-climate-change

[1406] Ibid.

[1407] Ibid.

[1408] Ibid.

[1409] Ibid.

Think about This for a While

Latino, Native American, and Asian kids were more likely than white children to be in houses next to a toxic waste dump that pollutes the air they breathe. All of this is probably true. A few months later, a group of black voters from across Philadelphia[1410] held a meeting to discuss climate change,[1411] organized by Third Way.[1412] Third way is a center-left Washington, DC, policy think tank.[1413] But you have to remember all of this was discussed at an environmental climate change meeting, and the purpose for meetings like this is to eliminate the use of fossil fuels without considering their benefits[1414] and to promote the use of solar, wind, and alternative energy sources, not necessarily to make the environment a nicer cleaner place for people of color because the left has a whole laundry list of things they have done to the detriment of the black community. This is another way the left is using another black issue of equity and injustice to achieve one of their agendas. The Green New Deal is another way that they can address economic, social, and equity implications[1415] of climate change. The Green New Deal will

---

[1410]   Ibid

[1411]   Ibid

[1412]   Ibid

[1413]   Ibid

[1414]   Marlo Lewis, Jr. • 07/11/2018 Climate Change, Fossil Fuels, and Human Well Being The Competitive Enterprise Institution retrieved July 29, 2021 https://cei.org/blog/climate-change-fossil-fuels-and-human-well-being/?gclid=EAIaIQobChMI3rWt2q-I8gIVT-3tvBB25tQtJEAAYASAAEgKp3fD_BwE

[1415]   Ceres New 'Green New Deal' resolution turns Congress' attention to climate change February 7, 2019 retrieved July 25, 2021 https://www.ceres.org/news-center/press-releases/new-green-new-deal-resolution-turns-congress-attention-climate-change?gclid=Cj0KCQjwl_SHBhCQARIsAFIFRVVOkae2VaKazmGijwN4KKwGUR1Bxd8htb0tLriYOhaQKlESgi TadOQaAk6uEALw_wcB

cost anywhere from $10 trillion to $100 trillion to implement,[1416] and that is what the left wants—not to help people of color.

I was listening to an episode of the *Bill O'Reilly Show*, and he mentioned the playing of the Black National Anthem at the Super Bowl. He said there was no such thing as a Black National Anthem. Well, an unofficial version of it actually does exist. It was adopted years ago and has never really honored anywhere else but in the black American community, but I think the Super Bowl was a very inappropriate time to play the Black National Anthem. The Black National Anthem was written by the civil rights leader James Weldon Johnson in 1900, who eventually became the national field secretary for the NAACP. This was during a different time in history when there weren't nearly as many Hispanics, Asians, and other ethnic backgrounds in comparison with blacks, so the country's demographics were different, and black people were having some different struggles back then than now, and the oppression was so much worse back then, and slavery was still fresh in the minds of many blacks who had actually experienced it back then, so you had some different mindsets from that experience.

Just 53 years before the creation of the Black National Anthem in 1900, in 1847, the African Colony of Liberia[1417] was created for slaves by the American Colonization Society[1418] and was ruled

---

[1416] Janet Nguyen October 8, 2020 Marketplace Why it's hard to put a price tag on plans like the Green New Deal retrieved July 25, 2021 https://www.marketplace.org/2020/10/08/why-its-hard-to-put-a-price-tag-on-plans-like-the-green-new-deal/

[1417] Relief Inc. History of Liberia retrieved April 2, 2023
https://www.reliefinc.org/history-of-liberia.html?gclid=Cj0KCQjwz6ShBhCMARIsAH-9A0qWB_omBQHeuX9I-_tmmIVnaJH3ZU1jF4bnn36aOQUhG6BLWRk7RGcUaAj-0gEALw_wcB

[1418] Ibid

Think about This for a While

by some of their descendants until 1980,[1419] which was known as Americo-Liberian Rule until it was violently overthrown in 2006.[1420] The "Marcus Garvey Back to Africa" movement lasted well into the 1920s,[1421] when he was deported back to his native Jamaica in 1927,[1422] so back then for these two reasons I could maybe see justification for a Black National Anthem and a National Black-flag especially if you were planning to live in the country of Liberia on the continent of Africa, and maybe it could be used for that country. During this time in America from 1847 until 1927 some black people were in a lot in society that was probably not any better than being black anywhere else in the world so by leaving America, they had nothing to lose by giving life a shot somewhere else so here I could maybe justify maybe having a flag and National anthem for blacks. It is 100 years later, and I don't think we need to have a Black National Anthem now, since times have changed. I think now we need to drop the Black National Anthem and move on. The Black National Anthem has lost its popularity among African Americans rather like the observation of Kwanzaa did, but both are still being encouraged on the black community by the left and woke Progressives, which will only make the divisions between everybody worse.

Another thing to consider is if African Americans insist on a Black National Anthem and if it is played at Super Bowls and

---

[1419] Republic of Liberia retrieved April 2 https://www.liberiaforward.org/history-of-liberia?gclid=Cj0KCQjwz6ShBhCMARIsAH9A0qVeO9y47SipokFip2ul3Oeto6axlu9hAwuoO-qSVst0aQU4Q4PIWnkEaAnx3EALw_wcB

[1420] Ibid

[1421] David Van Leeuwen Marcus Garvey and the Universal Negro Improvement Association National Humanities Center retrieved April 2, 2023 http://nationalhumanitiescenter.org/tserve/twenty/tkeyinfo/garvey.htm

[1422] Ibid

other major events in the country, then should we have a Hispanic American, Asian American, Native American, and a white American National anthem? If this is the case, should we have LGBTQIA+ and Feminist National Anthems? What about Arab Americans, since they are a growing minority, can we have an anthem for them? The answer to this is no and no. I think this would be a great time for progressive socialists to introduce the concept of class struggle and maybe others from another black cause. I think it is time we drop the Black National Anthem and call ourselves Americans and go with the American National Anthem; it's a great song and very patriotic. This is just another attempt I think by the left and Progressives to divide us by race and ethnic background.

Since the crisis at the border has increased under a more progressive Biden-Harris administration, sex trafficking of black women and girls has increased dramatically.[1423] In the past two years 40 percent of sex trafficking victims were black women[1424] when blacks are only 13 percent of the country's population. According to the same source, when asked, traffickers admitted that trafficking of black women and girls would land them less time in jail[1425] if caught vs. white women and girls.[1426] Fifty seven percent of arrests from juvenile prostitution now are of black children.[1427]

I overheard a conversation from a man who would more than likely vote as a Democrat who approves of the ban on assault

---

[1423] Samantha Davey Snapshot on the State of Young Black Women and Girls Sex Trafficking in the USA The Congressional Black Caucus Foundation retrieved February 6, 2023 https://www.cbcfinc.org/wp-content/uploads/2020/05/SexTraffickingReport3.pdf

[1424] Ibid

[1425] Ibid

[1426] Ibid

[1427] Ibid

weapons that is being enforced by Governor J.B. Pritzker of Illinois. This same law a lot of the state's law enforcers in Illinois say they will not support or enforce. Even the NRA is on the side of law enforcers who do not want to enforce these laws. The man also stated that the NRA and the whites who are not enforcing it are planning to use those weapons in a race war to go on a rampage and kill all of the black people. This sounds like he is referring to a constituent of Conservative white Republicans to him they may even be considered MAGA white nationalists who would more than likely be Klansmen or their sympathizers who are very small minority of them, or maybe he is saying that a lot more whites than Klan sympathizers would join in on this effort. I say Planned Parenthood's progressive policies on abortion and now the new policy, which will make it easier for you to go to a local drugstore and buy an abortion pill to end your baby's life, has murdered and will in the future murder more little black children than assault weapons ever will by these conservative MAGA republicans that he is referring to. If it is advertised in a way that appeals to an Afrocentric or Latino audience, it will really make it easier to just ethnically annihilate the black and brown races in America through abortions and termination of pregnancies. It will intensify Margaret Sanger's ploy for ethnic cleansing of the black and brown races from America, which stem from progressive policies and causes. It's hard to say how many this would kill the most, the white nationalists NRA gun owners (as they are called) or the murder of so many black youths on our streets in urban centers from the fentanyl crisis and gun violence because of defunding the police, which again are being allowed and caused by progressive policies and causes.

If you want to eliminate a group from the picture, what better way to do it than fostering an environment of hatred toward them? According to an ATTN:COM publication, Southern California is a hotbed of hate groups.[1428] It is second only to Texas in its number of hate groups according to the site.[1429] The majority of these hate groups are concentrated in Liberal cities along the coast.[1430] If these more progressive Liberal bastions of America claim to be more tolerant than their more Conservative counterparts, then why is it that California, maybe America's most progressive state, is the home to so many hate groups and hate crimes? If it is any better than Texas, which leans Conservative, it certainly seems to be beating it in propagation of hate. According to Statista.com, California in 2020 reported 1553[1431] hate crimes leading the pack compared with Texas at 467[1432]. With just 30 percent more people, it had more than three times the hate crimes. New York State, which tends to lean Liberal and Democrat like California with just two-third of Texas population, had 466 hate crimes,[1433] tied with Texas.[1434] Florida, which leans Conservative, was not even in the top fifteen on Statista's site,[1435] but the NAACP issued a traveler's advisory for

---

[1428] Kyle Jaejer Why Southern California is a Hotbed for Hate Groups FEBRUARY 18TH 2017 Why Southern California is a Hotbed for Hate Groups retrieved May 20, 2023 https://archive.attn.com/stories/15067/why-southern-california-hotbed-hate-groups

[1429] Ibid

[1430] Ibid

[1431] Statista Society Crime and Law enforcement Number of Hate Crime Offenses in the United States in 2020 by state retrieved May 20, 2023 https://www.statista.com/statistics/737930/number-of-hate-crimes-in-the-us-by-motivation

[1432] Ibid

[1433] Ibid

[1434] Ibid

[1435] Ibid

African American drivers in the state.[1436] My question here is how is New York faring in hate crime toward African Americans than, say, Florida? Well, according the New York State report on hate crimes, bias against race/ethnicity/national origin was the most common bias type in crimes against persons,[1437] and black individuals were the most commonly targeted group[1438]. Blacks were targeted more for property crimes than any other group as well.[1439] It seem here that progressive Liberal left-leaning environments may be more hostile to Blacks than right-leaning Conservative ones. The progressive left would have you believe police brutality is a bigger problem for Blacks, so we must defund the police, but they are the very ones that will respond in your defense in the event of a hate crime.

Reverend Vernon Johns, who blazed a trail for Dr. Martin Luther King,[1440] grew and sold vegetables to his black community[1441] and rather encouraged a form of economic independence to a lesser extent from the more racially biased and indifferent white southern attitude of Blacks at the time in Alabama, at least, with his incentive to not buy vegetables at their stores if you can grow your own. This is similar to Booker T. Washington's "cast your bucket where

---

[1436] Jesus Jimenez Published May 21, 2023 Updated May 22, 2023 The New York Times N.A.A.C.P. Issues Florida Travel Advisory, Joining Latino and L.G.B.T.Q. Groups retrieved May 23, 2023 https://www.nytimes.com/2023/05/21/us/naacp-florida-travel-advisory-desantis.html#:~:text=The%20National%20Association%20for%20the,color%20and%20L.G.B.T.Q.%2B%20individuals.%E2%80%9D

[1437] Hate Crime in New York State 2020 Annual Report Criminal Justice Research Report New York State Division of Criminal Justice Services

[1438] Ibid

[1439] Ibid

[1440] Michael Kilian and Tribune staff writer Chicago Tribune Jan 16, 1994 at 12:00 am Vernon Johns: A New Hero For America The Chicago Tribune retrieved May 27, 2023 https://www.chicagotribune.com/news/ct-xpm-1994-01-16-9401160435-story.html

[1441] Ibid

you are" philosophy and "produce a strong business community of your own." At about the same time Revered Adam Clayton Powel Jr. encouraged boycotts of NYC 125th Street Harlem grocery store,[1442] the latter inspired Dr. King to have the Birmingham bus boycotts.[1443] I think it is very interesting to note three of these four men were pastors, and the other, though not a pastor, certainly seemed to endorse the pastors' book of instruction and the following of its teachings, and all four addressed the problems of the black community through economics. Then maybe it is not wrong to address it from this angle, or maybe it's the right thing to do.

Chicago's South Shore neighborhood, which is mostly African American, is seeing an influx of illegal immigrants flooding into their neighborhood.[1444] This is being allowed under a more progressive Biden-Harris administration through the polices of a former mayor Harold Washington (Democrat) in 1985.[1445] Their attorney claims they want them to come but not to all be concentrated in one community.[1446] They are not currently at the beginning of the migrant surge being flooded in to the Pilsen, Belmont Cragin, Logan Square, Little Village, South Chicago, South Deering, or Hegewisch[1447] communities, which have a supportive cultural infrastructure. I think this is the case because they don't want all of

---

[1442] Ibid

[1443] Ibid

[1444] CBS Chicago 2 Chicago residents fear migrants being housed in former South Shore school retrieved May 28, 2023 https://www.youtube.com/watch?v=faZVg2BNTD4

[1445] Erica Gunderson January 14, 2023, 5:30 pm Latino Voices Politics Welcome to Chicago: Exploring What It Means to Be a Sanctuary City retrieved May 30, 2023 https://news.wttw.com/2023/01/14/welcome-chicago-exploring-what-it-means-be-sanctuary-city

[1446] CBS Chicago 2 Chicago residents fear migrants being housed in former South Shore school retrieved May 28, 2023 https://www.youtube.com/watch?v=faZVg2BNTD4

[1447] Ibid

these illegal immigrants in their neighborhoods. These are not black neighborhoods, but blacks haven't been practicing group economics like some of the other ethnic backgrounds often do in some of the other examples I just listed above. Now all of these mostly non-white immigrants can walk the black communities streets, not the other ethnic communities, potentially putting African Americans at risk. A young boy was interviewed in the meeting, and he asked the panel members why all of these migrants weren't put in the Hispanic community.[1448] That is simple because they don't want them, and they practice group economics so they can make more demands that are in favor of the wants of the people in their community. This meeting seemed as if most of the participants and concerned residents asking questions were women, very few were men[1449], but this is typical in really bad neighborhoods in the black community.

[1448] African Diaspora News Channel Podcast Black Chicago Residents Say No To More Migrants Being Housed In Their Neighborhood. Retrieved May 28, 2023 https://www.youtube.com/watch?v=kTuWPS4CxjI

[1449] Ibid

27.

The Right Versus the Left for Blacks

Small government, low taxes, and a free-market economy where you can use your for-profit institutions, local financial institutions, small businesses, and nonprofit institutions to create a lot of your own jobs is a good thing to have in a society where you will have to compete with a lot of other minority groups for resources. This is what Conservatives and the right would like to see happen. With this, you can get a lot done for your community on a local level where you are not so dependent and subject to whatever changes another group incurs on you. With this setup, you would not be so subject to the indifferences and discrimination that other groups could impose on you. With this model, you could use Dr. Claude Anderson's five-tier strategy to insulate you from a lot of oppression and injustice dominating in these areas locally: (1) economics, (2) with politicians, (3) law enforcement, (4) media, and (5) education, in that order. For this to work as a group, blacks must practice group economics! That is imperative, or it won't work! Conservatives and the right have a much better way to operate to set up something like this.

For years in America, these things like a free-market economy, capitalism, the benefits of living in a constitutional republic and the five-tier system didn't benefit blacks like they do a people who are really free, so if you still have the same mentality about these things as past blacks did you will react to them as you have in the past. Actually, the rest of America used these benefits in a way that resulted in injustice to blacks. They used their economic power and the five-tier system that I mentioned above to do it. You could use this system to institute local forms of government influence such as Jim Crow, which was statewide in all Southern states, sundown towns, which were local city or county, and Black Code and zoning code laws for housing and some other things that were used in northern industrial cities, now blacks can use it to their advantage locally if they practice group economics. Other ethnic backgrounds such as Arabs with their grocery stores, Koreans with black hair care products, Chinese with their rice houses, and some other groups could come into the black community and move into some of the same vacant buildings and become very successful. These people did not have the same mentality as blacks. Since they did not have this type of mentality, they could see all that a country like America has to offer, including the five-tier system with the code of conduct, but first, you need others like you who don't have a different mentality. The right has a better vision for this type of success in America versus the left and this is what an ethnic minority needs if it is to thrive as a group.

This may be a much better setup for Blacks because if the left and Liberals, at least far-left-leaning progressive Liberals, get their way, we will have socialism, and that will put our fate in the hands of the leftists who got the black community to this point into all of the mayhem discussed in this book to this point because the consequences of not doing it could mean something worse. Supporting Conservatives would be a very good thing for blacks. Blacks can now actually benefit more now from some Conservative causes since the Civil Right Bills of 1964 and 1967 have passed because we now have less restraints on us and more basic rights. When Black

Wallstreet of the Greenwood District of Tulsa, Oklahoma, was burned by an angry mob of whites, they didn't have basic civil rights that we have now from the Civil Rights Acts, and now that could not happen without some legal ramifications and serious lawsuits. Tulsa was not the only place in America where the black community was destroyed like this.[1450] It happened in several other towns across America before the civil rights movement, but the Tulsa was one of the best examples of black group economics in action and independence from so many outside entities.

Since some of the founders of socialism believed in the extermination of backward people and the eradication of those who could not master newly established changes in society; it may be better if black people supported Conservatives on eradicating socialism—if this is the plan for black people by them who are largely supported by the left and some of their liberal counterparts who unknowingly think they are backing a utopian plan for equality. Right now, blacks are the most vulnerable of all of the largest ethnic groups in America.

The left wants to change America radically so that the free-market economy and the American Dream of home ownership, business ownership, and everything else that comes with the American Dream will be gone. But the right doesn't want to see this happen. On top of that, they want to maintain traditional constitutional rights that America has always had with natural sovereignty, and now blacks can benefit a lot from this. If the left gets full-blown socialism, it will be worse for everyone whether it does or doesn't slowly progress to communism. Since the Civil Rights Act of 1964 passed, giving blacks rights, they can now enjoy a country like America with all of the bounties it has to offer. If the left gets their

---

[1450] Michael Harriot. The Other Black Wallstreets. The Root Black News Opinions Politics and Culture. 02/15/18. https://www.theroot.com/the-other-black-wall-streets-1823010812 retrieved January 9, 2020.

way, this will never happen. In a setup like socialism, you would have one central governing authority that decides what groups of people are served and which groups are eliminated from society, and those governing authoritarians can make these decisions with racial, ethnic, or religious biases in mind.[1451] This concerns the more Conservative right, and it is probably better for blacks that this doesn't happen.

Some will argue that if Conservatives had had more influence in America, they would have overturned the Civil Rights Act of 1964 and 1967. This would have made it easier for them to proceed in making America the way it was before the civil rights era. Well, consider this, so many southern Democrats at that time did not approve of the legislation that it took a coalition that was 38 percent Republican and the rest Democrats to finally approve of the Civil Rights Act.[1452] Since it requires two thirds of the Senate to vote in favor of a bill to become a law,[1453] I think there would always be enough Liberals voting on an issue most of the times that had to do with turning the clock back that it would make it hard for them to do this. For this reason, I don't think the laws they would need to change things enough would happen, like the 38 percent of Republicans that made it possible to approve of the Civil Rights Act even while more than half of Democrats did not. The world is a different place now than it was years ago. You also have to consider that America would receive pressure from the international community if too many Conservatives chose to remain traditional.

[1451] Kiernan Ben. September 1990. Cultural Survival Quarterly Magazine. The Survival of Cambodia's Ethnic Minorities. retrieved April 9, 2020. https://www.culturalsurvival.org/publications/cultural-survival-quarterly/survival-cambodias-ethnic-minorities

[1452] Landmark Legislation: The Civil Rights Act of 1964. retrieved June 6, 2020. https://www.senate.gov/artandhistory/history/common/generic/CivilRightsAct1964.htm

[1453] Ibid.

With social media it would be easy to post injustices for display across the world that would result if they did decide to turn the clock back. International pressure was a big reason why South Africa was forced to change their polices on Apartheid.[1454] Therefore, I think the Thirteenth, Fourteenth, and Fifteenth Amendments of the Constitution and the Civil Rights Acts of 1964 and 1967 would all be safe from change, even if it were up to most Conservatives.

[1454] Catherine Barnes. Incentives, sanctions and conditionality. *Accord* ISSUE 19. February 2008. retrieved June 6, 2020. https://www.c-r.org/accord/incentives-sanctions-and-conditionality/international-isolation-and-pressure-change-south

28.

What If Black America Were a Nation?

Atlantic Magazine did an article that compared Black América to other nations if it were a nation.[1455] It came up with the fact that Black America had socioeconomic disparities and structural subjugation that undermined the United States' greatest contribution to humanity which, in a sense, is life, liberty, and the pursuit of happiness,[1456] despite the fact that it has a strong manpower and purchasing power.[1457] According to the article, which was written in 2014 based on 2010 statistics, the median wealth per adult for blacks was just below that of Brazil's and about the same as it is for the average Palestinian adult.[1458] It was considerably below that for the average adult in China and Mexico.[1459] It was about half that of Mexico's, and it stacked up only a little better against

---

[1455] Theodore R. Johnson. Oct 14, 2014. What If Black America Were a Country? retrieved October 30, 2019. https://www.theatlantic.com/international/archive/2014/10/what-if-black-america-were-a-country/380953/

[1456] Ibid.

[1457] Ibid.

[1458] Ibid.

[1459] Ibid.

China[1460] because China's economy has been experiencing explosive growth since 2010. Therefore, black America probably stacks up worse against China now than it did then. It put the human development index for blacks, which factors in health, education, financial security, life expectancy, and income, at 30th in the world versus five for America as a whole.[1461] In GPD per capita, it placed Black America at 46th among all nations in the world.[1462] Again since Black America, and now sometimes Hispanic America, lags so much further behind whites, it skews the average for America, so whites are probably doing a lot better than average, and they may actually be in fourth or maybe even third place on the global human development index, and that is for most categories. As for as employment is concerned, black America would be one of the worst 30 nations, and that ranking is globally.[1463]

Another article compared high school graduation rates for white Americans with those of people in the UK and Finland, and black Americans with those of Chile, South America, and Poland.[1464] As far as wealth is concerned, it ranked black America with Portugal and post-communist Lithuania.[1465] Infant mortality rates for whites

---

[1460] Ibid.

[1461] Ibid.

[1462] Ibid.

[1463] Theodore R. Johnson. Oct 14, 2014. What If Black America Were a Country? retrieved October 30, 2019. https://www.theatlantic.com/international/archive/2014/10/what-if-black-america-were-a-country/380953/

[1464] Ian Bremmer. June 29, 1915. Time Magazine World/Racism. These 5 Facts Explain America's Enduring Racial Divide. retrieved May 3, 2020. https://time.com/3931216/these-5-facts-explain-americas-enduring-racial-divide/

[1465] Ibid.

were comparable with those of Japan and Switzerland, and black America was more comparable to countries such as Thailand and Mexico, which are both third world, and at best, developing countries.[1466] The article put incarceration rates for black Americans as the third worst in the world,[1467] and black men at the time the article was written were the most incarcerated group of men on earth, and the homicide rate for black America is just above Burma's at 15 percent and just below Nigeria's at 20 percent.[1468]

Food insecurity among black Americans is about 22 percent.[1469] According to the USDA Department of Agriculture website, food insecurities as a global average are about 26 percent,[1470] which puts Black America somewhat comparable with the global average. The percentage for North America, meaning basically the US and Canada, was about 12 percent,[1471] and since blacks and Hispanics typically fare worse in statistics like this, whites probably fare considerably better than 12 percent. Food insecurities early in life affect a child's ability to succeed academically, to function emotionally, and to contribute as a productive citizen throughout adulthood.[1472]

[1466]   Ibid.

[1467]   Ibid.

[1468]   Ibid.

[1469]   Move for Hunger. Hunger Is a Racial Equity Issue. April 3, 2018. retrieved May 3, 2020 https://moveforhunger.org/hunger-racial-equity-issue

[1470]   Michael D. Smith and Birgit Meade. Amber Waves. United States Department of Agriculture Economic Research Service. retrieved June 10, 2020. https://www.ers.usda.gov/amber-waves/2019/june/who-are-the-world-s-food-insecure-identifying-the-risk-factors-of-food-insecurity-around-the-world/

[1471]   Ibid

[1472]   American Youth Policy Form. Aug 24, 2015. Blog. Food for Thought: How Food Insecurity Affects a Child's Education. retrieved June 10, 2020. https://www.aypf.org/blog/food-for-thought-how-food-insecurity-affects-a-childs-education/

In 1976, the Soviet Union had 2.6 million criminal convictions, of which 1.67 million were minor crimes and nearly one million were serious crimes or felonies out of a total of roughly 147 million.[1473] The black community in America has 36 million African Americans with an incarceration rate of about twice what the USSR's was during the years of its communist regime nearly 15 years before the fall of the Iron Curtain, if you do the math. When Joseph Stalin's forced labor system reached its peak in 1947, it had about 15 million prisoners.[1474] Out of a population of 147 million total, that is a little over one in ten people.

Living and working conditions in US prisons are not nearly as inhuman as they were in the Soviet Gulag,[1475] but they are nothing to be taken lightly either, and they are used for a similar purpose in America as very cheap labor.[1476] Blacks are more likely to be in one of them than anyone else in America. Before just recently arrest quotas, which unfairly arrested and jailed or imprisoned blacks,[1477] have been done a lot more frequently in black neighborhoods[1478] and often for offenses that don't deserve a prison or jail term.[1479] During the Soviet Communist Era in the former USSR, arrest quotas were done by the

---

[1473] Central Intelligence Agency (Unclassified) Directorate of Intelligence. The Soviet Forced Labor System. https://www.cia.gov/library/readingroom/docs/CIA-RDP83M00914R001200120005-5.pdf

[1474] Ibid.

[1475] Ibid.

[1476] Ibid.

[1477] Selim Algar and Josh Saul Metro. NYPD set arrest quotas for minority cops in their own communities: suit. September 1, 2015. *The New York Post*. retrieved September 24, 2020. https://nypost.com/2015/09/01/cop-suing-over-minority-arrest-quotas-says-he-faced-retaliation/

[1478] Ibid.

[1479] Ibid.

NKVD and the KGB to maintain a supply of labor for the Soviet prison system known as the Gulag.[1480, 1481] This has basically happened in America disproportionately more with blacks.

According to the Pew Research Center, from a 2020 article incarceration rates have dropped 34% for black Americans since 2006, even though it was still currently at 1,501 out of every 100,000[1482] who were incarcerated, or one in sixty-six, if you do the math, which is still way too high! If it included those currently serving a sentence, it did not include those who were previously incarcerated. That is still higher than any nation on earth, which is terrible! According to a source from 1997, 16.2 percent[1483] of all blacks will spend time either in jail or prison, and just over one in four[1484] African American males will spend some time in either jail or prison. This number is lower now but it was and may still be comparable with at least a quasi-totalitarian regime. From the 2018 US census, out of a total population of 43 million African Americans,[1485] with a countrywide average of 1 in 26

[1480]   Mass Violence And Resistance - Research Network The Nkvd Mass Secret Operation N°00447 (August 1937 - November 1938) 24 May, 2010 Werth Nicolas retrieved February 8, 2022 https://www.sciencespo.fr/mass-violence-war-massacre-resistance/en/document/nkvd-mass-secret-operation-n-00447-august-1937-november-1938.html

[1481]   The "Rational" Mass Violence of Stalin's Secret Police Reviewed by Andrew Janco (University of Chicago) Published on H-Human-Rights (March, 2009) Commissioned by Rebecca K. Root (Ramapo College of New Jersey) retrieved February 8, 2022 https://www.h-net.org/reviews/showrev.php?id=23648

[1482]   John Gramlich. Pew Research Center. retrieved December 25, 2021. https://www.pewresearch.org/staff/john-gramlich/

[1483]   Thomas P. Bonczar and Allen J. Beck, PhD. BJS Statisticians. Lifetime Likelihood of Going to State or Federal Prison. Bureau of Justice Statistics Special Report. retrieved December 21, 2021. https://bjs.ojp.gov/content/pub/pdf/Llgsfp.pdf

[1484]   Ibid.

[1485]   Black Demographics: The African American population. retrieved May 24, 2020. https://www.census.gov/quickfacts/fact/table/US/PST045219

being incarcerated,[1486] if you do the math, that equates to roughly 1.6 million people; that is more than in any nation on earth. As you can see, though it has improved significantly, this has been going on for quite some time, and incarceration rates are still way too high for blacks. If you average the last 30 years, you would get similar ones with the USSR of one in ten from 1976.

The question to ask here is, did black America fare better off before the liberal movement in America than they do now after years of its aftereffects? I think in Tulsa, Oklahoma's, Greenwood District, which is where Black Wall Street or Little Africa existed, they practiced group economics versus integration, which was a socialist idea. In just 30 or maybe 40 years, some of them amassed enough wealth to put large portions of the black community to work. And they did it without a lot of outside help from the government. The single-mother epidemic had not exploded, resulting in all the bad statistics you get when kids are raised in a single-mother household. The black community was able to create more choices for kids and youth in the black community for employment, and they would not be so dependent on outside sources for it. Incarceration rates would probably not be this high if the black community had more economic control/influence. Things that have been affected negatively as reflected on the human index assessment of nations such as education, the hit that black wealth has taken as a result of the housing crisis and predatory lending, the destabilization of the black community through the feminist movement, and integration are other factors that black America was compared to. However, the other countries are not affected as much by the liberal programs because black America has to be the only place in the world or one

---

[1486] Ashley Nellis, PhD. The Color of Justice: Racial and Ethnic Disparity in State Prisons. June 14, 2016. The Sentencing Project. retrieved May 24, 2020. https://www.sentencingproject.org/publications/color-of-justice-racial-and-ethnic-disparity-in-state-prisons/

of the only places where 65 percent of the children are being raised by single mothers. If Conservatives had had more influence over the past 50 or 60 years, I don't think these things would be nearly as bad for the black community.

The City of St. Louis, Missouri, is more than half African American. The northern half of the city is all African American, and part of the southern half of the city is African American as well. An international institute placed some families from Syria in the north end of the city.[1487] Some of their complaints were gunshots going off overnight, and apartments with too many mice and bugs and even some with rats.[1488] They are afraid to go places alone in the neighborhood that they were placed in, so they go everywhere in groups.[1489] The refugees complained of being afraid of going to the store to buy groceries.[1490] One Syrian woman stated that it was so bad, she has warned other Syrians by phone from refugee camps in Syria not to come to St. Louis.[1491] Some of the Syrian refugees have been relocated to the north St. Louis area of Hodimont and Page according to the article,[1492] which is practically all African American; some say it is worse than the refugee camps they came from in Syria[1493]. This is an example of the really bad neighborhoods

---

[1487] Kevin Killeen. October 24, 2016. Syrian Refugees Afraid of North St. Louis. retrieved October 29, 2019. https://www.thecoli.com/threads/syrian-refugee-families-in-st-louis-hood.477953/

[1488] Ibid.

[1489] Ibid.

[1490] Ibid.

[1491] Ibid.

[1492] Rob Fox TMF Archives Syrian Refugees Think North St. Louis Is Worse Than A Refugee Camp retrieved September 11, 2022 https://archive.totalfratmove.com/syrian-refugees-think-north-st-louis-is-worse-than-a-refugee-camp/

[1493] Ibid

that were referred to earlier in the book, which became like this directly and indirectly because of leftist progressive policies. This article was written in 2016, and very little if any has changed in St. Louis since then. If black America were a nation, this is also an indicator of where it would be in some cases and its ability to maintain order as a nation.

From earlier in the article: between 1980 and 1995 homicides seemed to have been at an all-time high of between 14,400 and 10,800 per year in a total population of 36 million, with an average of 30 to 40 out of 100,000. Over a fifteen-year period, that is just over a staggering 190,000 murders.[1494] When you take into account that all of the maybe tens of thousands of African Americans a year (that figure would be on the low end of the scale) who fled some really bad neighborhoods that were not really bad when they were all white for something better over the past 40 or 50 years, it is maybe the equivalent of that many people being displaced from a second- or maybe a third-world country due to warfare, bad political policy, corrupt leadership, lack of jobs, bad schools (some with metal detectors at the entrance door), and a whole host of other problems where the people have limited power to make changes and in some cases no power.

In 1989 the streets of Los Angeles provided a war zone like scenario with escalating gang violence creating a great opportunity for the Army to train their surgeons[1495] for casualty volumes and types of injuries that you will only see in a real combat zone at King

---

[1494] Erika Harrell, PhD. August 2007. NCJ 214258. Black Victims of Violent Crime. retrieved August 6, 2020. Bureau of Justice States Special report. Retrieved February 11, 2022 https://bjs.ojp.gov/content/pub/pdf/bvvc.pdf

[1495] Kenneth J. Garcia Times Staff writer Nov. 7, 1989 12 AM PT War & Nation Army Surgeons Training for War--at King Hospital retrieved May 3, 2024 https://www.latimes.com/archives/la-xpm-1989-11-07-mn-884-story.html

Hospital[1496] in Los Angeles. The article stated at the time hospitals in Detroit, New York, Miami and Washington[1497] provided similar combat zone scenarios[1498] but not like King in Los Angeles[1499] and that King 1988 treated almost 3,500 trauma victims[1500], with over 100 gunshot wounds and dozens of stabbing a month[1501]. If the police are completely defunded, which is a progressive left leaning cause and really almost a policy it is not out of the realm of possibility that scenarios like this could happen again in some more of our urban settings where the residents are mostly people of color. This has all got to be somewhat comparable with a country with guerrilla war going on in some nations on earth!

A lot of these problems would never have occurred had it not been for all of the leftist policies I have explained to you throughout this book.

Affirmative action and school desegregation, at least the leftist agenda of those who masterminded them, were clever ways to make it seem like they really cared about the black communities' concerns and issues when they really didn't, and Black Lives Matter is no different. Because when you look at the big picture of what has happened to the black community over the past 50 years of both of these programs and many others, you have to ask yourself: Is black America any better off 50 or 60 years later?

[1496] Ibid

[1497] Ibid

[1498] Ibid

[1499] Ibid

[1500] Ibid

[1501] Ibid

According to a report from the Kenner Commission, that answer is no.[1502] The study to prove it goes over a number of areas to make its points, which are too extensive for me to go into in this book.

From a BBC news report, researchers say the levels of PTSD in US inner cities are comparable with to those of refuge populations around the world.[1503] But here it goes unrecognized, leaving the individual to cope alone.[1504] The same report claims PTSD rates are 46% for those living in the inner cities[1505] vs. 11% to 20% for veterans returning from war in Iraq[1506]. Veterans who return from war are out of these war zones usually for good, but children in these pockets in US cities have been there all their lives.[1507]

The black men to female ratio being approximately 88 men to every 100 Black women (Governing, 2019).[1508] Comparing this to the ratio of white men to white women of 97 to 100[1509] there is a clear disparity. In certain neighborhoods there were only a median

---

[1502] Tonja Renée Stidhum. February 26, 2018. Blavity News. New Study: African Americans Are No Better Off Than They Were 50 Years Ago. retrieved October 2, 2020. https://blavity.com/new-study-african-americans-are-no-better-off-than-they-were-50-years-ago?category1=news&category2=trending

[1503] Aleem Maqbool US inner-city children suffer 'war zone' trauma - BBC News retrieved May 22 2021 https://www.youtube.com/watch?v=xfKLfBbFiLo

[1504] Ibid

[1505] Ibid

[1506] Ibid

[1507] Ibd

[1508] Keenon Glover/Southern Digest Sep 25, 2019 Updated Sep 25, 2019 Numbers Don't Lie: Gender Disparities in the Black Male Community retrieved February 18, 2024 https://www.southerndigest.com/culture/article_306ac4c6-dfd7-11e9-928c-f3ec25dfe75c.html

[1509] Ibid

of 81 black men for every 100 black women.[1510] According to Statistics Times as of 2023 Russia and Ukraine who have been ravaged by war for a few years now had male to female ratios of 86.725 to 100[1511] and 83.83 to 100[1512] more comparable with black Americas than the rest of America.

[1510] Mike Maciag Governing January 22, 2019 Where Have All the Black Men Gone? https://www.governing.com/archive/gov-black-men-gender-imbalance-population.html#:~:text=Nationally%2C%20the%20Census%20Bureau%20counts,they%20totaled%20at%20least%202%2C000.

[1511] List of Countries by Sex ratio retrieved February 18, 2024 https://statisticstimes.com/demographics/countries-by-sex-ratio.php

[1512] Ibid

29.

Is This Progress Or Is It Progressive?

Racial violence and race riots have happened throughout American History. One website titled Black Past[1513] has a timeline of the events from 1526 to the present. The article lists uprisings from various times in history including: "Revolts of the Enslaved" (1526–1842) of which there were 14[1514], "Antebellum Urban Violence" (1829–1851) of which there were five in four different cities[1515], "Civil War Reconstruction and post-Reconstruction era violence" (1863–1899) of which there were eighteen [1516], "race riots" (1900–1960) of which there were 23[1517], "urban uprisings" (1960–2000), which include thirty one[1518], "campus violence" (1961–1972), which included six, and "21st century racial violence," which included seven riots that all happened from 2000 until the present. On the same website from a link titled "Lynchings in the United States Since

---

[1513] Black Past Racial Violence In The United States Since 1526 retrieved May 13, 2022 https://www.blackpast.org/special-features/racial-violence-united-states-1660/

[1514] Ibid
[1515] Ibid
[1516] Ibid
[1517] Ibid
[1518] Ibid

1865," one ad claimed that 3,436 people were lynched in America from 1889 to 1921, so from 1865 to 1888 and from after 1921 until they basically stopped happening, there may have been thousands more. Some of the ones in the ad may include ones that occurred in any one of the above riots that occurred most probably before 1960. When you consider all of the riots and the utter destruction, they caused in the black community that occurred before about 1970 all the way back until the urban Antebellum riots which start around 1829, when America was more conservative, you see utter devastation caused in US cities around the country because of them.

Now to the point I am trying to make here. If you go into the really bad neighborhoods of America in large cities and small towns all across the America and see the utter devastation caused by the left's policies and causes without causing any violence or firing any shots from a weapon, you can see what I mean. These policies and causes have affected the African American community in just about every major city in America, large and small, that has sizeable African American population. They have affected and devastated more black urban areas and on a greater scale in just the past 50 years since American politics and culture have become more progressive than all of the other years from before 1970 all the way back to the Civil War and Reconstruction era and Antebellum urban violence years, when America was more conservative.

During the period that included Antebellum violence, which started in American cities as early as 1829, through the end of the civil rights era the destruction in the black community was often caused by violent acts by angry white mobs who physically went into black neighborhoods and burned large sections of them down and lynched black people and sometimes angry black mobs who in a sense were venting frustration over unfair treatment so they burned down parts of their own communities that had institutions or even structures sometimes that represented white repression, oppression, racism, or privilege even if those institutions were essential for the existence of the black community. Again what has happened to the black community in the later, more progressive years has been a lot more devastating that what happened before the civil rights era if you do a careful analysis.

Which was worst, the mass exodus of blacks out of the South because they were ran off their property and land by the Klan in a more conservative America or the mass exodus to the suburbs or back to the South or just other neighborhoods over the past 40 or 50 years because the neighborhoods just got bad from drugs, gangs, bad Common Core or No Child Left Behind schools, employers leaving from Democrat-ran gerrymandered districts and from the aftereffects of some other progressive causes after progressive causes start to effect the black community negatively.

Another question to ask here is which was more devastating, what has happened as a result of a more politically correct America of second- and third-wave feminism, the millions of abortions conducted at Planned Parenthood clinics, political correctness, Common Core and No Child Left Behind educational standards, mass incarceration, the school-to-prison pipeline, Black Lives Matter protests, the promotion of LGBTQIA, and really bad neighborhoods (only) with senseless murders, boarded-up and burnt down houses, vacant lots, gang graffiti everywhere and no opportunity for betterment in a post–civil rights era America of a more progressive America, or the lynchings, bombings, and burning of black people out of their houses and off their land by ruthless mobs of Klansmen and their sympathizers to a greater or lesser extent, the restrictions put on basic freedoms of blacks, vagrancy laws that were enforced just after the Civil War used to arrest black people and put them to work in a mild form of slavery to rebuild the South and sometimes just for profit, to Jim

Is This Progress Or Is It Progressive?

Crow laws, sundown towns, zoning codes in Northern cities (which put restrictions on where black people could live, work, and even be), and mob violence that happened to blacks personally, their businesses, and their property in urban areas across America before 1960 clear back to the Antebellum period in America by mobs of angry whites from race riots of a more conservative America? To really answer this question, you must take into consideration where black America has come from, what it is today, and what it could have become.

Which propaganda did the most harm to blacks, movies from the past, such as *Gone with the Wind* and old movies that portrayed black men as someone who would cheat at voting polls, push white women off the street, and the negative portrayals in the film *Black History: Lost Stolen or Strayed* before 1968 in a more conservative America, or a more progressive American media propaganda of today that would lead you to believe that Black Lives Matters and progressive liberal Democrats really cares about black people?

Which divides the lines between race more, the more conservative old-school ways that were more obvious such as Jim Crow, sundown towns, and zoning codes, which made an integrated society illegal, or the more progressive tactics that are more deceptive such as critical race theory, which forces whites to admit their privilege and that they are oppressors and apologize for it and to admit that you are oppressed if you are black or Hispanic?

The genocide or ethnic cleansing, whichever you want to call it, that has happened to the black community since abortion, which was a radically left-leaning progressive cause, is comparable maybe with the millions of dead African slaves that did not survive the trip across the Atlantic during the Atlantic slave trade to America, so their dead bodies were thrown overboard and eaten by sharks leaving trails of blood behind them. According to several sources about 12.5 million

Africans[1519] were transported across the Atlantic in the Middle Passage during the entirety of the Atlantic slave trade of which about 10.7 million[1520] survived to journey. Of the 10.7 million,[1521] less than a half million[1522] were brought to what is now the United States. A lot more black babies have been murdered in Planned Parenthood clinics than the 1.8 million who did not survive the trip over from Africa and all of this happened since abortion was legal since Roe VS Wade from 1973 to present which was a more progressive cause.

How about the messages and the destruction of black peoples image communicated about blacks through the exhibits in the Museum is Racist Memorabilia which were all constructed during a more conservative time in America's past with more conservative values from today when it was just confined to America VS some of the messages from Urban Dictionary which is online and now the whole world can see it on the World Wide Web with a global appeal so people can just spew racial, ethnic and religious hate at each other from everywhere all over the world to include blacks which comes from a time where more progressive values are being forced on them. How much better are the two for society, the destruction that happened in more past conservative America or present more progressive America.

This is not progress!!

[1519] Slavery and Remembrance The Trans Atlantis Slave Trade United Nations Educational Scientific and Cultural Organization retrieved May 23, 2022 https://slaveryandremembrance.org/articles/article/?id=A0002

[1520] Ibid

[1521] Ibid

[1522] Henry Louis Gates, Jr. | Originally posted on The Root The African Americans Many Rivers To Cross 100 Amazing Facts About the Negro How Many Slaves Landed in the U.S.? PBS Nine retrieved May 23, 2022 https://www.pbs.org/wnet/african-americans-many-rivers-to-cross/history/how-many-slaves-landed-in-the-us/

30.

Rethinking Reparations from Slavery

If you go online and do a Google search on reparations from slavery for Blacks, the search engine must include about 15 or so pages of documents on the who, why, where to start, and how to proceed with the process with countless different ways to do it, and who's to say any one way is right or wrong. Some of the reparations for blacks included wrongs from police brutality,[1523] mob violence from angry white mobs that destroyed black communities years ago (e.g., Black Wall Street),[1524] victims of forced sterilization,[1525] etc.

Reparations from slavery for black Americans is not an unreasonable request if you consider that some other groups have received some compensation for their pain and suffering. Some examples are Japanese Americans who were held in internment camps during WWII and German Jews for the pain and suffering they endured during Jewish Holocaust in Hitler's extermination camps. In the case of Japanese and Jews, it was easy to assess who would pay since

---

[1523] Alexis Karteron Parent Category: Slavery to Reparations Category: Reparations Published: 07 February 2022
Vernellia R. Randall Founder and Editor Professor Emerita of Law The University of Dayton School of Law Reparations for Police Violence retrieved October https://socialchangenyu.com/wp-content/uploads/2021/12/Karteron_45.3_Reparations-for-Police-Violence.pdf

[1524] Ibid

[1525] Ibid

only one or two entities were involved, and the events that caused it were a lot more recent and many of the institutions and/or people responsible were still around when reparations were requested and paid out. In the case of reparations from slavery for blacks there are a lot of entities and nations involved over a much longer time period than what some other groups endured.

The Atlantic slave trade, which was almost totally responsible for the transporting of the ancestors of African Americans to what is now called the United States, goes back several hundred years. From the beginning of the British colonial period, beginning in 1619 British slave traders who already had colonies in Africa and had African slaves brought to what is now the United States[1526] to the Jamestown Colony of present-day Virginia[1527] from then until the Revolutionary War, which ended in 1776, the British had a lot of Africans transported to what was then 12 of America's 13 original colonies.[1528] If you are African American, the chances are you can probably trace your ancestry back to at least one of the slaves brought to the Americas by British involvement in the slave trade. After the Revolutionary War ended and the colonists from former England declared their independence from England and declared themselves Americans and citizens of the United States, some of them continued with buying and selling of slaves from Africa as Americans. This practice was not deemed illegal in America until 1808;[1529] however, the last slave ship from Africa, the Clotilda,

---

[1526] Crystal Ponti Updated: AUG 26, 2019 ORIGINAL: AUG 14, 2019 History Channel retrieved September 30, 2022 https://www.history.com/news/american-slavery-before-jamestown-1619

[1527] Ibid

[1528] Ibid

[1529] The Clotilda The Last American Slave Ship Visit Mobile Alabama retrieved June 3, 2023 https://www.mobile.org/things-to-do/history/african-american/clotilda/

docked illegally in a Mobile, Alabama, seaport in 1860.[1530] If you are a black American, there is a good chance that you could be a descendant of slaves brought to the Americas by these American slave traders. The French empire in America, which at one time included former Louisiana Territory, which was all west of the Mississippi River, was carved up into what is now 15 US states.[1531] It also included at one time all of the states that border the Mississippi River east of the river[1532] and most or all states that currently boarder the Ohio River[1533] and the Great Lakes.[1534] The French had slaves brought to these territories and lands to help develop them.[1535] If you are African American and you have roots in any of these parts of America that go back enough generations, you just may be able to trace your ancestry back some of the slaves or at least one brought to these places by French slave owners and slave traders. Since Louisiana Territory and the state of Florida were Spanish possessions, if you are African American, you just may be a descendant of the small handful of slaves brought to what is now the United States by Spaniards.[1536] The Dutch settlers, many of whom founded

---

[1530]   Ibid

[1531]   Joel K. Bourne, Jr Published May 22, 2019 Culture Race In America Last American slave ship is discovered in Alabama National Geographic retrieved October 29, 2022 https://www.nationalgeographic.com/culture/article/clotilda-the-last-american-slave-ship-found-in-alabama

[1532]   Slavery in Colonial British North America retrieved October 9, 2022 https://teachinghistory.org/history-content/ask-a-historian/25577

[1533]   Ibid

[1534]   Ibid

[1535]   JOHN C. RODRIGUE Slavery in French Colonial Louisiana 64 Parishes reterived October 9, 2022 https://64parishes.org/entry/slavery-in-french-colonial-louisiana

[1536]   American Latino Heritage Fort Mose Site Florida https://www.nps.gov/nr/travel/american_latino_heritage/fort_mose.html#:~:text=Enslaved%20Africans%20first%20set%20foot,free%20and%20enslaved%20black%20colonists.

the former New Amsterdam colony, which is now New York City, and a few other small Dutch settlements in primarily New England, brought slaves to the Americas,[1537] so if you are African American, maybe you can trace your roots back to one of the slaves that were brought over by the Dutch. If you are African American you may be a decedent of the slaves that were owned by the five so called civilized tribes of Native Americans. This opens up a whole other can of worms. That is never discussed about American slavery, but it is the truth.[1538] Had it not been for the help of other Africans selling their own into slavery to Europeans there is no way that Europeans could have single-handedly been that successful on their own at pulling of the trans-Atlantic slave trade.[1539] Since living and mere survival conditions in Africa were so harsh for European settlers and with all of the logistical challenges of navigation of such a harsh interior of the continent, it would never have been possible for Europeans to pull off on their own. This poses a very important question. Should all of the above nations (to include the African Nations) be held accountable for paying reparations to each African American who can properly trace their ancestry back to possession by one of these entities during these times in history?

The world was different during the colonial period, and it continued to evolve and change through that period until today. The

---

[1537] Life in New Amsterdam Educator Resource Guide Museum of the City of New York Fredrick Andrea C. Mosterman Slavery In New Amsterdam retrieved October 9, 2022 https://mcny.org/sites/default/files/2016-11/MCNY_Educator_Resource_Guide_Lesson4_0.pdf

[1538] Adaobi Tricia Nwaubani Updated Sept. 20, 2019 11:06 am ET The Wallstreet Journal THE SATURDAY ESSAY
When the Slave Traders Were African

[1539] Kevin Sieff The Washington Post Democracy Dies in the Dark An African country reckons with its history of selling slaves January 29, 2018 at 3:24 p.m. EST retrieved October 9, 2022 https://www.washingtonpost.com/world/africa/an-african-country-reckons-with-its-history-of-selling-slaves/2018/01/29/5234f5aa-ff9a-11e7-86b9-8908743c79dd_story.html

world was a different place then with some whole different value systems, different cultural and social norms in society, and so forth. Now, many of the entities in all of the above countries and nations that were involved in the slave trade or slavery probably don't even exist anymore, and even if they did, they are probably so much different from what they were then, you would probably not recognize very many if any of them from what they were and what they stood for then. This makes it very hard, if not impossible, to assess blame to the exact entities or nations or just certain organizations in those nations or maybe even just certain individuals for slavery. Therefore, reparations would probably be demanded and paid unfairly by some groups, nations, and their entities since there would be different assessments of the who, what, how, and why on how disbursements and payments should be dispersed fairly would be different for everyone, and it could vary depending on who is doing the assessing and some other factors. Any entity could argue for or against any reparations by proving that someone else experience was worse that someone else's, and anyone could have very valid points for or against payment.

How much would each of the European nations mentioned owe each African American? How much would each of the African Nations or ethnic backgrounds in Africa involved in the slave trade owe African Americans? How much would the five tribes of Native Americans owe African Americans? Last but not least how much would América owe African Americans? How much would each nation owe and how would they pay it? If African Americans, ask for their reparations then what about blacks from all the other Caribbean and Latin America countries who had ancestors brought over from Africa as slaves? Could they and or should they ask for reparations from former colonial powers and fron the countries they currently live in that were built on the backs of their ancestors labor?

Any amount given for reparations under current and/or future rates of inflation and price increases, which come with inflation (and we have seen an example of that under the more progressive Biden-Harris administration), has the potential to render the value of the money a lot less valuable if adjustments for the two are not made accordingly.

Reparations from slavery for blacks has been discussed during the 2020 Democratic Primary.[1540] No amount for every African American or plan to return entitlements or way of proceeding with reparation has been agreed upon, and it is not for certain if it will happen at all. If you give reparations to black people from slavery and from all injustices, whether they be economic, political, social, and so forth, no party will really agree on what the amount would be and how it would be given back. No one really knows where to start by assessing wealth or wages that were never given for work done or for pain and suffering. Let's just say, for example, enough entities agree to a figure of $300,000 to $500,000 on average, and some would get more and some less, depending on a formula used to make the determination of who gets what.

Until the black community develops a crude free-market economy within their community to put this wealth in and to utilize it properly for them—and they have a code of conduct as to how they will function as a society—here is what would happen if you allowed reparations. Since black people own no banks, they would put the money until it was spent into a bank owned by some one of another race or ethnic background, which would benefit the other ethnic background, with more wealth and opportunities to loan it

---

[1540] P.R. Lockhart. Updated Jun 19, 2019. /Vox. The 2020 Democratic primary debate over reparations, explained. retrieved November 10, 2019. https://www.vox.com/policy-and-politics/2019/3/11/18246741/reparations-democrats-2020-inequality-warren-harris-castro

out and generate more wealth for them. Some of the money would be spent on real estate, houses, cars, expensive clothes and jewelry, lavish trips and cruises, and some other things that people just enjoy having or engaging in, which black people don't make or produce. That goes for lumber yards, land with forests to make boards, sand, gravel and rock pits for concrete, bricks and cement for houses, and a whole host of other industries that make products that go into the construction of houses as an example. It would make the people who own these entities wealthy with black reparations money. All of the money spent on these things would go from black people into the hands of people of other races and ethnic backgrounds who make and produce these things and make them a lot wealthier, so it would be a big transfer of wealth to those people, a big money maker for them, which is what has been happening to the black community since integration. It would be one of the greatest transfers of wealth ever from one segment of society to another. Some blacks would invest a lot of their money in stocks and bonds and build big IRAs and 401(k)s and CDs and all sorts of other investments, but if a stock market crash happened, it could mostly or all be gone in a few weeks or days. Even without a stock market crash, black people don't take most of these investment opportunities, so they would not make most of the money or wealth off them; someone else would, and they would be investments into their endeavors.

Right now, black people don't have an economic infrastructure in their own community to put this wealth into or to circulate it so it stays in the black community and generates more wealth and is in the control of other black people because we don't practice group economics. For stockholders of other races and ethnic backgrounds, this would be another opportunity to make more money. After all of the physical assets that black people bought were all used up and the investments all dried up, if black people were still being disadvantaged for being black, you could say no one owes you anything now, so everything that is happening to you now is your fault because you were paid back everything that was due to you. Reparations could really be used to redistribute wealth back to the wealthy and to banks that don't deserve it, if the black community does not have a setup to use it to generate more wealth for itself.

This will not restore any unique national character or identity because so much of it has been lost from integration and some more of the left's progressive causes, and you don't need money to restore culture or heritage.[1541] There have been in the past and still are lots of groups who are very poor, and they have been able to maintain a distinct identity and a rich cultural history without a lot of wealth.

It is interesting to note that former President Barack Obama did not support reparations for Blacks from slavery, neither did he endorse any such programs, but neither did former presidential candidate Senator Hillary Clinton or Senator Bernie Sanders.[1542]

One of the reasons for reparations was to end mass incarceration, but you don't need reparations for that.[1543] To change a lot of that if you change the black community by reversing what destabilized it to begin with and putting an economic infrastructure in it that is largely controlled and owned and run by blacks you would have much lower incarceration rates. That is what should have probably happened to begin with instead of complete integration, and by reversing some other things that have been caused by the left over a period of years, you can change a lot for the black community without reparations. Another point behind it was to invest more in

---

[1541]   Ibid.
[1542]   Ibid.
[1543]   Ibid.

historically black colleges and universities,[1544] but that is not going do black people any good if too many of the degree programs are liberal arts degrees that don't educate the mind to be able to build and maintain a community by and for blacks. Most of these liberal arts degrees support the progressive left's agenda and one of their end results.

It would not help the black small business community to grow their businesses;[1545] it would help them start more businesses, but if you have no market because your money does not exchange hands in your community and you spend your dollars outside of your community, it would just result in more failed black businesses if other races and ethnic backgrounds don't spend more of their money to the tune of billions of dollars like black people do with other businesses from people of non-black ethnicities. This is just a recipe for a lot more debt. If we practiced group economics, it would not result in so much debt, and maybe then reparations would work.

Even if the reparations are in the form of land as in the "Forty acres and a mule" saying, if it is taxed, and you can't afford the tax, then the government can take the land from you. Even if it is not taxed and if it is just sitting and not producing any income because you don't have a market to sell its produce, it is useless to you. If you try to farm it or mine a mineral resource from it, such as oil, coal, or iron ore, if you have no market to sell your produce and no entities to sell your mineral wealth to because everyone else buys from people of their own ethnic background and race, it really does no good for you to produce with it if you can't make any money off it. The same would go for real estate or any other operation since black money doesn't circulate in the black community as it does for

---

[1544] Ibid.
[1545] Ibid.

everyone else, and black people's enterprises would be more likely to fail. You can build your own house on free land, but that doesn't generate any income; it only provides you with a place to live, and unless they have historical significance or some unique architecture or they have a unique quality about them as in a prime location for people to move to and live, with time, houses usually depreciate in value. Other ethnic backgrounds would have a better setup to generate wealth because more of their income circulates in the communities.

You don't need reparations to end redlining and segregation.[1546] To end redlining, just get rid of the laws and policies that indirectly encourage it. Integration has not made black people any better off, but one of the end results of reparations is supposedly to end segregation. If you end segregation but black people are no better off, it won't make a difference.

To come up with the proposed $800 billion[1547] that the state of California and the US government does not have for reparations for black people in the state of California with 1.3 million black residents,[1548] the government would have to print up almost another trillion dollars'[1549] worth of paper money. With a current national deposit of well over $30 trillion, if reparations were suggested for black people across the country and they used California's model to do it, the US mints would have to print up trillions of dollars of worthless paper money that it does not have. This would drive the country into hyperinflation, which would threaten its existence.

[1546] Ibid.

[1547] JANIE HAR March 29, 2023 AP News California reparations amount, if any, left to politicians retrieved April 27, 2023 https://apnews.com/article/california-black-reparations-racism-e7377631044ef6325b042ea56456d81b

[1548] Ibid

[1549] Ibid

America can't even afford to pay black people reparations of this amount. Any attempt would bankrupt the country, but that is the whole strategy that the progressive left is doing behind the scenes with reparations to get rid of America by using a black cause to do it. If the country goes bankrupt, it would be all over for the blacks; we would have nowhere else to go like America, and the reparations money wouldn't be worth nearly as much as it is now if its worth anything.

Reparations is just another strategy from the left to redistribute more wealth into the hands of the wealthy, and they are working through the Democratic Party—the one they usually always work through to push reparations. If you ask me, I think it is just another policy or even another cause to get black support for the Democrat party for the 2024 election, along with all of the illegals that will have come across the board by the millions by then to lock in a guaranteed winner for a Democrat president. From this Progressives don't have the black community's best interest at heart.

31.

Conclusion

The belief that America could not end up just as socialist or communist as the former USSR or present-day communist China because the likes of it have never happened throughout its existence is from a normalcy bias. Normalcy biases happen when people become too comfortable with the reality of life that they are used to because they have never experienced anything else. I think we should all as Americans put all of our differences aside regardless of race, ethnic background, gender, or religious belief, or whether we are liberal or conservative, left or right, or Democrat or Republican, and come together and try and save this great republic we call America. We have something that is really unique that no other country or place on earth has and no one else has really ever been able to duplicate. Some have with some of our institutions to a greater of lesser extent, depending which nation you are referring to and what thing it is about America to which you are referring. If we act now, we still have time before this precious window of time closes and it is too late. I think it is too late for black America, thanks to progressive policies and causes.

Many leftists will claim that since blacks were slaves, the policies that they either support, endorse, or enforce such as integration, affirmative action, equity, and reparation from slavery are necessary to repay previous injustices from the past. I will agree with them

Conclusion

that injustices from the past certainly were detrimental to and are a part of the reason for the condition of the black community today. I will also say that what has happened to the black community as a result of all of the left's policies and causes have put blacks in a more unequal and unfair position, or they have not improved the lot of blacks. Many of their policies and causes have made matters worse for the black community, but the left is saying they must be done in the name of equality and for equity. What has happened to the black community over the years because of their policies and causes has not resulted in equality, but many leftists will argue that they have or that they have gotten the black community closer to it.

Progressives and the left seem to want to change America so much from what it initially stood for, but maybe some things about America don't need to be changed. Some things need to stay the same. It seems as if the left is implementing strategies to make America more equal with the rest of the world. Maybe the opposite needs to happen. Maybe they should be implementing a strategy to make the rest of the world more like America, with policies and causes that made America such a great nation. They don't want to because they don't have anyone else's best interest at heart either.

The black community's problems cannot be solved by blaming all its woes on white supremacy, systemic racism, and police brutality; and teaching critical race theory and wokeness and equity is not going to turn everything around all of a sudden, either.

It appears as if the progressive left is on the black community's side with BLM, white privilege, and wokeness, but they could very easily flip their script on black people and become ugly, just as they did with health care workers who were considered heroes for treating and caring for the sick who were infected with and dying of COVID until they were forced and/or mandated to take a vaccine against it and then vilified for not taking it by being fired from their jobs.

Progressive policies and causes in some respects have set black people back years, maybe over 100 in some respects. As black people, would it have been strategically better under some circumstances at least to support more rightist-thinking Conservatives and classical Liberals at least for the past 50 or so years in America and the Republican Party? Because strategically, the left's Progressives and Democrats are not working with blacks to the advantage of blacks; they are doing it to their advantage. Black people are just a strategic move for them, but in the end, this has had terrible consequences for blacks. That could change in the next 50 or 100 years if there are any African Americans left. Progressives may have some better plans for blacks to follow, but for the foreseeable future, it doesn't look as though that is going to happen.

I say the agenda for black people is the same as it always has been, but we have a different puppet on stage, performing the show. The stage looks a little different today with some different lighting and different props; and the theme and plots may even seem a little different today than yesterday, but the puppet master is still the same, so the end game hasn't changed: keeping black people dependent, powerless, and second-class citizens.

The legacy that black American trailblazers have left for America is one that America can be proud of, but I don't think there will ever be a recovery for black Americans, thanks to progressive leftist policies and causes. The forces that black people are coming up against are not good. Some of the most prolific fights for freedom for black people were slave abolitionists, both black and white and many of whom were bible believing Christians. Black people have been affected so profoundly that they almost need to have a new consciousness movement. Where that movement will start, I don't know. It may even be over with for the black community in America; the damage done may be beyond repair, too great to salvage it, as a community. Thanks to progressive leftists, no band of ruthless, racist, hateful, bloodthirsty conservative Ku Klux Klansmen could have done a better job of it.

As a result of so many years of the progressive leftists policies and causes, the black community has been steered down some dead-end roads, with not a lot of choices or sometimes without any good options.

I am not saying that Conservatives would not have thrown some roadblocks in the way of black progress, some of them probably would have, with some even to the detriment of that progress. With that said, however, I think the black community would be better off now had traditional Conservatives and classical liberals had more influence over the past maybe 50 or so years. I just think a lot of outcomes would have been better for blacks had they had more influence.

Not everything that the progressive left has done historically has been a bad thing for black Americans especially when you consider how harsh and unjustly blacks in America had been treated by the greater American society during slavery, up until the establishment of the NAACP and for some years afterwards up until just before the civil rights movement; some things that they did were good for black America during a time when probably the majority right-leaning conservative whites who were often Democrats and some of the classical liberals were not always nice to blacks, since they went against norms in society at a time when so many of them and laws were just not in favor of blacks. What progressives proposed for blacks during this time period was not really a bad deal.

Since what is conservative and what is considered liberal and what has been considered progressive and left or right has changed over the years, I think the conservative and right-leaning movement and what it has become vs. what it has traditionally been has some very good things that it supports that would be of benefit to Black America vs. the way so many of the progressive left's policies and causes have just wreaked havoc with a trail of devastation that is probably permanent on the black community over the past 40 of maybe 50 years. The progressive left has gone too far now, and if changes are not made, it will take the black community out of existence. We need a different balance in America of left and right that will restore a sense of consideration and respect and decency for one's differences and views while keeping in mind that it is still America, so we have to continue some of its traditions and practices whether they are political, economic, social, or cultural that made it great.

I have presented to you in this book plenty of reasons why I think some right-leaning Conservatives have historically been racist against blacks, but what left-leaning Progressives have proposed for Blacks over the past 50 or so years has been much more devastating on the black community than any conservative, right-leaning whites have over any period since the end of the Civil War or maybe you could argue before the Civil War, depending on how you look at it.

For years from after the Revolutionary War all the way up until just before the civil rights movement too many classical liberals and Conservative right-leaning whites, often Democrats, or sometimes whites that were just more traditional about race is the way I should state this, could be very nasty and racist at times to blacks while more progressive liberal Republicans were much nicer and kinder to blacks. Because of this they were able to talk to black leadership and tell them their lies about how they would make America this utopia of equality, equity and fairness for blacks when they had no one's best interest. I would wager to say they hated whites liberal and

Conclusion

conservative, and they were just as racist and mean against blacks as the rest of America. Unfortunately, they were able to get a lot done in the advancement of their causes through the black community because of bad race relations. This is something that may be hard to swallow for some, but it is probably true, partially because of bitterness that blacks harbored and still have by some today from past cruel treatment.

During this period in history most Conservatives were more likely to be Democrats, and back then political correctness was not really a concept. With political correctness you can use certain words or euphemisms is probably a better term that are less offending and that promotes or seem tolerant[1550] but behind the scenes you could be doing some very devastating things to a group you speak tolerantly or kindly of. Back then it was OK to say things that were intolerant and that offended minority and disadvantaged groups, so a white person could just call you a "N*****" blatantly with no guilt or shame in some circles or circumstances, and it was perfectly acceptable even though the terms "Negro" or "Colored," which were used on a more professional level, were more acceptable or less offensive, so you knew who the racists were. Today the progressive left are almost always Democrats and since they are politically correct, it is hard to determine how racist and mean they are to blacks today and what they may have planned for blacks in the future, and how much damage their policies and causes have caused on black America, but with a certain element of right-leaning Conservatives of the past, since they were not politically correct, it was easy to tell who the real racists were.

I think the reason why progressives have been able to get so far with the black community is because so many whites who were

---

[1550] The Free Dictionary (adj) By Farlax.

traditional about race in America were so nasty to blacks for so many years but now that they have changed about blacks, the legacy of past treatment still hurts, so blacks are still usable for progressives. That may change in the future, but by then it may be too late to save the republic, which I would like to see happen.

Allow me to use another analogy. Before the Civil Rights Movement but especially before the Civil War black people were that odd kid that nobody picked to play on their team, and he got laughed at and talked about by the other kids and he got beat up and chased home by lots of bullies every day after school. Sometimes it was scary just showing up for school, he just wanted to play with all the other kids. But another kid 'the progressive' talked to him nicely even complementing him at times and let him play on his team unlike all the other kids who were traditional conservatives and classical liberals about race, but the progressive was a racist too and he didn't like the black kid either and he hated all the other kids who used to pick on the black kid too. He had another vision for all the kids, the school, the playground, the teachers and everyone else to take the school and this little black kid was just one of his puppets out of several others that he could mold into what he needed through his past emotional traumas of rejection to get what he wanted. Once he got what he wanted he could change everything in a way that was bad for all the kids for America, by making it a Socialist / Communist country.

Now traditional conservative and classical liberal whites really stand for something that will benefit blacks so now we should stand with them and work with them to preserve the constitutional republic with a free-market economy and capitalism especially if we practice group economics and build strong black communities like Booker T Washington encouraged blacks to do like Tulsa Greenwood District known as Little Africa. For these reasons I think blacks should support them even though they are more likely to be right leaning and conservative (along with a lot of you classical liberals), republican and evangelical Christians. I don't trust what the left has up their sleeve for blacks next.

The progressive left has flipped their script on black America from the days when they were kinder to the causes of black Americans or at least they seemed to be even though they didn't really have the black communities' best interests in their kinder days. Today they are a different animal from years ago, and what they have done to black America over the past 50 years or so has been ugly, mean, bad, and cruel. The progressive left has become anti-Black. They are no longer our friends anymore; I don't think they were ever our friends to begin with or anyone else's for that matter. Infact they hate this country so that qualifies them as anti-American.

What has happened to black America as a result of all of these progressive policies and causes has been equivalent to sabotage. Dictionary.com describes "sabotage" as any undermining of a cause. One of the Cambridge dictionary definitions for "sabotage" is to intentionally prevent the success of a plan or action. Some thesaurus.com synonyms, which were softer in nature, for *sabotage* are to suppress, to impair, and to wreck. The dictionary's definition states to damage or destroy equipment, weapons, or buildings in order to prevent the success of an enemy or competitor or to intentionally prevent the success of a plan or action. It also gives the definition of war as a state of armed conflict between different nations or states or different groups within a nation or state. The question to ask here is: Has the progressive left declared war on Black America? Because black America has not declared war on America or the progressive left. In a sense, black America has had the equivalent of a similar destruction by bad policies and causes. After all, consider the description of black America in comparison with white

America in the section of the article "What If black America Were a Nation." Now ask yourself if that does not seem like a nation that has been ravaged by war or that has at least had its effort to exist as a group thwarted.

The slave trade, slavery itself, and the brutal acts of the Ku Klux Klan after slavery were acts of forceful and more blatant sabotage. However, it does not have to happen forcefully or violently as in an act of war; it can be, but it can be subtle and gradual with planned steps,[1551, 1552] the way Progressives have done it.

Now racial demographics and race relations are different, the distribution of wealth is different and now politics, politicking and the political landscape are all different than they were before the Civil Rights Movement, we just have some different societal forces coming up against the existence of America and some of them are very dark and very evil and they are spiritual in nature and it all only seems to keep changing for the worse so I think we should support conservative and classical liberal whites and everyone else from all of the others of other ethnic groups that want to if we want to save the country.

I think we need to go back to American pre-1950's moral values and embrace our Judeo-Christian biblical values and do a lot of praying and a lot of repenting, if we do it might save our country, if not as a nation America will have some very dark days ahead if we survive it intact as a nation. I think we can keep our free-market economy and capitalism and just make reforms to it. I think we should honor our Constitution as a constitutional republic. I think

---

[1551] Deep Patel. 8 Ways to Stop Self-Sabotaging Your Success. retrieved September 11, 2020. https://www.entrepreneur.com/article/324900

[1552] Stefan Thomke. September 04, 2019. How to (Inadvertently) Sabotage Your Organization. retrieved September 11, 2020. https://sloanreview.mit.edu/article/how-to-inadvertently-sabotage-your-organization/

we need to continue to improve race relations. I think if we just do this as Americans across the board not just as blacks but as a nation, if we cooperate on this across all boundaries, we can get out of this as a nation and possibly save our nation if that's still possible. If we don't, we will lose our nation and the present and the historical treatment of blacks, among plenty of other reasons that are all related to sin which are historical and currently taking place will be a factor in its final demise, whether it be all of a sudden or progressively and in the case of our country it seems that so far it is being done progressively.

What do you think?

Milton Keynes UK
Ingram Content Group UK Ltd.
UKHW020139260924
448838UK00011BB/487